LETTING GO

An Ordinary Woman's Extraordinary Journey
of Healing & Transformation

LETTING GO

*An Ordinary Woman's Extraordinary Journey
of Healing & Transformation*

Nancy A. Kaiser

Aronya Publishing

Letting Go
An Ordinary Woman's Extraordinary Journey of Healing & Transformation
Second Edition
©2015 by Nancy A. Kaiser

Front Cover Photography by Nancy A. Kaiser

Cover and text design by Janet Aiossa/Adam Hill Design

Published by:
Aronya Publishing
P.O. Box 51
Todd, NC 28684
828-265-4220
nancy@nancykaiser.com
www.NancyKaiserAnimalCommunicator.com

From "Til You Give It Away" © 1990 David Roth/Maythelight Music (ASCAP)
Used by permission ~ www.davidrothmusic.com

From "Looking In For Number One" © 1988 David Roth/Maythelight Music (ASCAP)
Used by permission ~ www.davidrothmusic.com

From "For Good" and "Defying Gravity," from the Broadway musical *Wicked*
Music and Lyrics by Stephen Schwartz
Copyright ©) 2003 Stephen Schwartz
International Copyright Secured. All rights reserved.
Used by permission of Grey Dog Music (ASCAP).

ISBN-13: 978-162776161-1
ISBN-10: 1-62776-161-6

Printed in the United States of America

LETTING GO

*An Ordinary Woman's Extraordinary Journey
of Healing & Transformation*

*To those with the courage
to seek answers.*

May my journey hasten your own journey!

CONTENTS

Chapter 1

The Dream

"*I never wanted this house. I never wanted to be here. This is all your dream and I feel like I'm just along for the ride.*"

My heart froze as these startling words rolled from my husband, Bob's, lips. They would change my life in ways that I could never have imagined. I felt like I'd been hit in the stomach with a bat. I was speechless, very uncharacteristic for me. I stammered, "It didn't occur to you to say something in the last four years?" He said he was confused.

I needed time to process what just happened. It was surreal. It was as though I'd just crossed over into a different dimension. Had the past three and a half years of my life been based on a lie? No, we'd made every decision together. What about his secret dream to own the top of a mountain and his happiness and excitement at the party before we moved? What the hell was going on?

The next morning, I told him that I really didn't know if I could continue to live with him. How would I ever know if we were doing what he wanted? He offered no answers, nodded, and walked away.

Later, I asked him to explain what had changed, what he wanted. He didn't have a plan. He seemed to know what he didn't want. Finally he mentioned several things he wanted, none of which seemed to involve me. In the middle of our discussion, he went outside leaving me in utter amazement.

I took off my wedding band, placed it on his side of the dinette, and cried. He came back in and asked if I wanted to talk about "it." Apparently "something" was upsetting me. Ya think? I didn't know how anyone could be so disconnected from the reality of what was occurring. I felt like a complete and utter failure.

Over the next week, I suggested going to counseling to understand what was happening. After no response from Bob, I made an appointment with a local psychologist. He reluctantly agreed to go, but the day before the appointment he backed out. He declared, "There was no point," since he'd always be the person who stole my dream house. I told him he hadn't been listening to a thing I'd said. I was crying over a relationship that was dying not a house! Our official separation began that day when he moved from our camper. I will never be able to fully express the utter sense of disbelief, hurt, and failure that consumed me.

My dream-turned-nightmare began ten years earlier while vacationing in the North Carolina mountains. Bob wanted to retire in the New York mountains. To avoid longer winters, I asked if he could be happy in the Carolina mountains. He thought so.

We returned to our farm in New Jersey and spoke with my parents, who owned the farm with us. They agreed to move, but it was too much for them at their ages. In deference to them, our plans were shelved for the time being.

As much as I loved our farm and equine hospital, I was experiencing too many aches and pains from the physical demands of the farm. I was anxious to *let go* of all of my responsibilities. When the move got delayed, it was hard to accept.

I realized I needed to let go of the expectation of moving. I kept telling myself that wherever we were supposed to be wouldn't be available until we were ready. By surrendering to this belief, I moved out of my preoccupation with the future and went back to living in the Now: the only place we truly live in. I had to accept that everything happens for a reason and have the faith that all was in perfection, which isn't always easy to do.

Both my parents died of cancer in 2000. Their close proximity on the farm had made care-giving a thousand times easier. It was clear that postponing the move had been in everyone's best interest. *Everything does happen for a reason....*

After their passing, I began searching the Internet for property in the Carolina mountains. We wanted land, so we could build our dream retirement home. My search began as a diversion from all my grief and sadness. I had been blessed with terrific parents, and coping with their absence was tremendously difficult.

We went to North Carolina with a list of prospective properties. The realtor showed us photos of a property that had just come on the market a week earlier. Well, the little light bulb in my head flickered. Was this my special spot that wouldn't be available until we were ready?

I knew a short time after walking onto the land that my soul was home. Bob said he felt the same way. We spent the rest of our week hiking and enjoying the area that was to be our new home. The property included the top of the mountain and 40 percent of it was bordered by state game land; simply perfect. Bob shared with me a secret dream he had to own a mountaintop. (Not that we ever own anything in Nature.) "Wow, he does love it as much as I do," I thought.

Feeling as though my soul had found its home was something I'd never experienced before, although I've lived in several beautiful places. In my 50s, I was moving into a home of my own choosing for the very first time.

Over the next three years, we prepared the land for our new home. Although I still had all of the responsibilities of running the farm, hospital, and veterinary office, I spent untold hours getting educated about all aspects of house building. To my surprise, I felt such joy when I was working on the house and property.

As the move got closer, I had to focus on the downside of relocating – like leaving the farm that I'd loved and worked for the past 27 years. It was a very special spot that held the graves of a number of my cherished animals, not to mention the ashes of my parents. It was the place where I'd learned so many lessons.

Having a farm is a lifestyle choice you make, a 24/7 job. My lifestyle centered on Bob, the only man I've ever loved. I gave up my pharmacy career to concentrate on what I truly loved: Bob, our farm/hospital, and the animals. We were blessed to truly love what we did every day. The poet, Rumi, wrote, "Let what you do, be what you love." These very wise words offer an enjoyable life, if you follow them. We had done just that.

The farm allowed me to experience the thrill of birth. Each time a mare foals, it's as miraculous as the first time. The farm allowed me the privilege of assisting individuals at their time of transition back to spirit too. Nature is always about balance. Hopefully, you enjoy the highs, and remember what the lows have come to teach you.

The farm, my animals, and some of our patients taught me the most powerful lessons. They uncovered my animal communication and healing abilities. The farm facilitated my opening to my soul's true purpose. Without my husband's practice and the farm, I might never have discovered my true calling. Now, I was making a choice to let go of my home for 27 rewarding years, which had taught me my purpose for this lifetime.

For 53 years I had lived within an hour of where I was born in New Jersey. I'd been blessed with so many wonderful, close friends. My move would take me 600 miles away from everything I was familiar with. I knew I'd be leaving everyone, but it didn't really hit home until the day arrived.

Our town bought the farm to reincorporate it into township acreage that surrounded it. We felt the farm deserved to be protected and not developed. The farm had given us a great life, so in return, we sold it for preservation. The closing was in late December 2003, with an agreement for us to remain until the following May 1, our 27th anniversary.

We made many trips to the mountain moving everything we could pack onto or into our trailers. We moved *everything*. It was exciting, but extremely stressful. We loaded the trailers in between veterinary, farm, and office work, drove down, unloaded everything, and drove back the next day. It seemed never-ending.

We moved old tractors, a new tractor, a sailboat, thousands of tools, veterinary equipment, an operating table, not to mention all of the treasures from our home. I moved all of our art and fragile things in my car and horse trailer. Many were my mother's and contained memories of her and my childhood.

It finally came time to move the horses. I had two brothers remaining, Randy and Stormy, who were the last of a line I'd begun in the early '80s. They were both very big horses with very little experience trailering. I hired a friend from North Carolina – who would keep them for me initially – to ship them in her large trailer. We followed with a trailer full of stuff for her farm. The trip took 12 hours.

The horses arrived in great shape, but I didn't. I was responsible for their safety and well being, and until they were put into their new stalls, I'd been on edge. The next morning they both looked wonderful, but I was ill-prepared for the trip back. I had been so focused on getting the horses to their new home safely, I hadn't thought about the fact that I was leaving them so far away. In 40 years, my horses had never been more than an hour away. For the last 27 years, they had lived with me. I hadn't considered that my relationship with my horses would be altered in ways I didn't yet comprehend until it happened.

Bob and I argued about the best way to drive back. He suggested a route that I knew was way out of the way. When I expressed this, he snapped at me. Maybe he was emotional about leaving the horses as well. I was having enough trouble leaving the horses; I didn't need his attitude. I didn't utter another word.

Separation anxiety struck, and it struck hard as I went in and out of tears. It was killing me to walk away from several things in their stalls that looked potentially harmful without correcting them. My emotions overwhelmed me for the rest of the day.

I couldn't let go of worrying about my horses. I really couldn't let go of them. What did I expect? Of course, I had to *let go*. I'd never considered how moving would change my relationship with my horses, so I was grieving an unforeseen loss.

Bob took the route he wanted, which added a couple of extra hours to the trip, and he knew it. He was angry with himself, but directed it towards me. All of a sudden, he pulled over. He had run out of gas. I didn't say a thing. The tension in the truck was unbearable. We had to be towed in after a part broke while trying to start the diesel with too little gas.

After the repair was completed, Bob needed to fill up with gas. I thought he turned the wrong way, but didn't say a word. I'd learned my lesson hours earlier. When he realized what he'd done, he turned around and still missed the road.

I mentioned that I'd been afraid to open my mouth. He was glad I was. "It was about time!" I was stunned, deeply hurt, and bewildered. What was going on? Who was this person? How dare he speak to me like that? Doesn't he know the pain and hurt I'm feeling? Doesn't he care? I kept my mouth shut, but came so close to saying we better rethink our plans. I decided to give him the benefit of the doubt. After all, this was the person I loved and who loved me, or was it? I let it go.

I never said another word that day or the following. I spent the time bouncing back and forth between the loss I was feeling over the horses, and the utter confusion about what was going on with my husband. I truly didn't understand where all of this anger was coming from. What had I done? He certainly didn't want to talk about anything.

We got back to the farm and went back to business as usual. Nothing more was said about the trip. Later, I would realize this was probably the biggest mistake of my life. My spirit was weary for the first time ever.

A few weeks later, we held an auction. My parents left 80-plus years worth of things, beautiful things, but things I couldn't use in a mountain house. Again, I was totally unprepared. I thought people would value my folks' amazing furniture, crystal, dishes, glassware, and linens, but instead they stole them. I was appalled as I watched all of the familiar things of my childhood be bid on by strangers. It was the hardest day of my life. I felt my parents, whose ashes were spread around trees not far from where this whole fiasco was occurring, were being disrespected.

There were some happy moments when friends would tell me about something they'd bought to remember us by. This was the only thing that saved the day for me, plus the fact that most everything was gone. I was utterly exhausted by day's end.

One powerful lesson was that things are just things. I'd always heard the cliché: one man's trash is another man's treasure. Well, in this instance, it was the exact opposite. My family's treasures had been treated like trash, or at least that was how I felt.

I learned the real value lies in the memories stored in the treasures. In losing my parents, I had learned that all you really have are your memories, so you better make good ones. This was definitely not a good one. It took a long time to let go of the pain of that day.

After three years of planning and preparation, it was time. I walked around the farm, in tears, making a video and saying thanks and goodbye to everything that was so dear to me. My heart was ready to move. I knew I couldn't keep up the pace I had for the past 40 years of caring for horses.

I kept reminding myself, while shedding tears of gratitude, that "To everything there is a season and a time to every purpose... ." My time in this special place was over. I was moving on to the next chapter in my life; whatever that was to be. I let go of the place I had identified with for more than half of my life. I said goodbye and it hurt, but my heart knew it was right for me.

I've returned to my friends and the farm numerous times since moving. I harbor only fond memories of life on Fair Chance Farm, which proves my choice was the *right* one. The farm was my slice of Heaven; my life of peace and serenity amidst hard work. It holds the memories of joys and sorrows, births and deaths, but then, aren't these what life is about? I *was* the farm, but now I had to let go completely. My soul was ready to move on.

Upon arriving at our new mountain location, I felt the joy of what the future held for us. I didn't really know exactly what that was, but I knew I was where I was meant to be. My mission was building our home for the rest of our lives.

Bob returned to New Jersey the day after we arrived, which confused and upset me. He'd made dental and medical appointments for the week after our move. He was planning to speak with people from the Christian Veterinary Mission, which was meeting in New Jersey. He was planning mission work with them. My eyes got huge and I said, "But we're building a house!" He assured me that his mission work was in the future. I just shook my head and walked away. He drove out, as the moving truck arrived, leaving me the frustrating job of setting up our new base alone.

I called Bob with some problem and heard a lot of background noise. I asked where he was. He said at lunch. Where? He was at the Christian Veterinary Mission meeting. In a very angry tone I said, *"You're at a meeting!"* I never said another thing after that and never initiated another call. Obviously, this meeting was more important than building our home. The thought of that was too painful, so I ignored it. I felt lied to by the person I trusted most in this life. I didn't have time to deal with this, so I let it go. I was building a house.

I have two close friends with the same name, but spelled differently. Michelle, dubbed little Michelle, introduced me to Michele, dubbed Master Michele, because she's a Master Gardener. Since they will be mentioned a lot in my writing, I wanted to clarify this.

I'd spoken with Master Michele before my discovery about the meeting. I thought Bob was staying with her, but she hadn't heard from him. I was surprised and wondered where he was staying. Since this was Bob, who I trusted implicitly, I figured he must have gotten a motel room in town. Well, he did, just not in our town.

Bob called a couple of times. I answered his questions without engaging in any conversation. I was hurt and confused. He returned and I said nothing about his trip. My friends were crazed that I would let this go. I assured them that I wouldn't. I wanted it to be a constructive discussion, which would take proper timing.

A couple of weeks later, while out to breakfast, it felt like the proper time. I began calmly, but it escalated into a very emotional scene. I accused him of lying. He said he didn't lie. I said he lied by omission. Eventually, I walked out of the restaurant in tears. The hurt was intense. My lover, best friend, and life partner had deceived me. My emotions were raw, so no matter when I'd have chosen to talk about this, the result would have been the same.

The house parts were delivered the day after Bob's return. Because of the access to the house site, we had to unload everything onto our trailers to move them up. It never occurred to me how much material is involved in building a house. I felt a great sense of accomplishment when everything arrived safely. We had hired a field expert, whose job was putting together Deltec houses, which are round. He made the process flow perfectly.

Over the next two weeks, our expert guided the group of contractors in erecting our home. Bob's youngest son, a house framer who lived in Florida, came to help build for the first month. I knew this was time my husband would cherish. To be able to build a home with his son was something not a lot of men could experience.

Watching something you've put so much of yourself into begin to take shape is an amazingly satisfying experience. I had never done anything quite like it before. It wasn't without its frustrations, but they always seemed to be followed quickly by solutions. What was becoming stressful was the skyrocketing cost involved. I'd worry about how much we were spending, and then feel the joy of seeing our dream come to life. My mind led me down the path of stress, worry, and fear. My heart told me this was the right thing to do.

A few weeks into construction, Bob informed me that he was flying to New Mexico. He had plans to donate his operating room table to a Native American group that trained veterinary technicians. This gift had been arranged through the Christian Veterinary Mission several years earlier. I was stunned that he would consider a trip while we were building our home. I started to express my feelings about the timing of the trip as he handed me his flight schedule. I was speechless. A man, who'd hardly made a flight reservation in almost 30 years, already had his. Obviously, my input was of no importance to him.

While Bob was gone, one of our cats went missing. Lucky was always around and came when called. I used my telepathic communication skills to ask him to show himself. The next morning, he was lying in the steel building. I simply said "thank you" and went on my way. A little while later, I found him lying in the rain by the camper. I froze. He was limp. I felt so guilty that I hadn't paid more attention to him earlier. I was 600 miles away from the small animal vet that I had confidence in; one of those dear friends I'd left behind.

I rushed Lucky to the vet's office. He was admitted to their hospital and died the next day. Poison was the diagnosis. The vet guessed antifreeze. I'd worried about my animals confronting the wild ones on the mountain, but it was an inorganic predator that took Lucky. We did have the construction crew's cars and trucks around. I watched my remaining three cats and two dogs very closely.

After my parents lost their last dog, Lucky had become my mother's companion and comforted her following my father's death. After my mother's passing, I found him numerous times sitting under the tree we planted for her on top of her ashes. I was in awe of this. He had been such a support to her, and now he was gone. I was having a hard time letting go of him. I had no one to share my grief with.

None of my other animals got into whatever Lucky had. Over time, I realized that he was ready to go. The person he had come to help in this life didn't need his love anymore. His job was done and done well. When Bob got back, we tried to bury him. Our rocky mountain wouldn't let us dig a grave. Bob was determined and got his tractor stuck. Later, I realized that he really wasn't doing it for Lucky or me. He was doing it to assuage the guilt he felt about the lie he was living; the lie that I was still in the dark about. Lucky didn't want to be on the mountain, which I really didn't understand at the time, but would in the not too distant future.

After Bob returned, I headed to see my horses that lived 125 miles away. He could deal with the responsibilities of house construction for a change. My horses had lived outside my door for the past 27 years, so this scenario was a tremendous challenge for me. As I got in my car, Bob said he was depressed about how much the house was costing. I told him that we were too deep into it now to stop. If we had to put it on the market later, so be it. The value was there. It would have been a perfect opportunity to get into a discussion about what was going on with him, but I needed to see my horses.

So, I drove two hours to the barn thinking of nothing but his comment. I left a message the next day saying we needed to talk. This was just a house. What was more important was our relationship. When I got back, my husband was genuinely pleased to see me. I hadn't felt that kind of energy from him in years, which made his astonishing words, the next evening, even more inconceivable. *"I never wanted this house. I never wanted to be here. This is all your dream and I feel like I'm just along for the ride."*

After Bob's "confession," I was an emotional, crying wreck one minute, and then the next someone focused on getting the house finished enough to be protected from the weather. My fantastic dream had now turned into my worst nightmare. The depth of that nightmare I wouldn't really know for some time to come.

I just couldn't understand why he let us start the house, and neither could anyone else. We were a mere six weeks into construction. I was in a place I had never been to before in my life, and I was there alone. As far as I was concerned, my best friend and lifelong companion had just died. He looked and sounded like Bob, but he wasn't him.

I was 600 miles from my home, my friends, and my support. I was devastated and *very* afraid. I was exhausted – physically, mentally, emotionally and especially, spiritually. I felt isolated, abandoned, and betrayed. My life was out of control. I was one sad and confused soul. I felt so alone. I wanted to simply stay in bed and cry, but I couldn't. I had animals that needed me and business to deal with.

Several days later, I was getting ready to meet with realtors about listing my dream. It was hard enough to think about that concept, but to actually do it was unbearably painful. I wanted to give the listing to the realtor that we had bought the land through, but Bob felt we should interview several agencies. I would leave in the middle of the meetings, because I was so overcome with emotions. I couldn't stand to hear all of the raves about the house design and the views. One realtor kept calling it a "World Class Home." Just before running out in tears I said, "It's just a house. It's not a home."

We chose the realtor I wanted from the start making my torture completely unnecessary. I will *never* forget signing the listing agreement. The realtor brought another new realtor along to learn the process. We reviewed marketing strategy, pricing, whatever. I felt like I was in the other dimension now. My business mind allowed me to get the paperwork done without any outbursts.

As I described the best way to market the property, my tears fell. To me, the property was about the views and the energy on the mountain. You had to be on it to *feel* it. When I tried to talk about the view, I couldn't get the words out. Reality struck hard. The poor young realtor was fighting her own tears, and she didn't even know me.

Bob seemed devoid of emotion and oblivious to my agony. Never once during any of my outbursts of raw emotion did he try to comfort me. To this day, I think that was the hardest thing for me to accept. He didn't care about me. Where had my husband gone? What had I ever done to deserve this treatment?

After the realtors left, Bob asked if I wanted to go out for lunch. I looked at him in disbelief. We ate lunch hardly speaking a word. So, what was that about? One minute we were dissolving our life together, then we're not, but we are. I just couldn't keep up with it all. It was an emotional roller coaster, and I was falling off.

After lunch, Bob called his father. Later, when I called my father-in-law, Vince, he was really confused and concerned. I explained what was happening, my shock, and utter confusion. I was trying to be sensitive, since I was speaking about his stepson. I told him that I feared we were heading to divorce, but I wasn't sure yet. He fell silent. I knew I had just stunned him with that fact.

Bob had told him the house had gotten too expensive, so we just listed it and would build a smaller house on the property. Hello, what just happened;

slipped into that other dimension did we? I assured Vince that we were not building another house. Talk about denial and deception.

Several days later, I called and told Vince my worst fears had become reality. We were separated and filing for divorce. I could feel his sadness and disappointment. Vince was quick to tell me that I would *always* be his daughter-in-law, no matter what. His words affected me deeply. I missed my own father terribly, especially now. My father-in-law has filled that void for me as well as anyone might. My father had really big shoes to fill. I couldn't have withstood another loss, and I wasn't going to have to. I was so pleased and greatly relieved.

So there it was: my marriage was over. I thought I'd been a good wife, and we'd lived a wonderful life together. I assumed our relationship was forever. The mountain, which was my spiritual home and where I expected to die, was up for sale. The magnificent house would never be my home. My best friend had disappeared. My future was uncertain. My identity was gone. I was afraid, devastated, and alone. Who was I? Where would I go? What would happen to me? Oh, my God, I don't have anywhere to live! I can't stay in a camper on the side of a mountain in winter. What a shocking realization to wake up to one morning. I was lost.

I handled the construction issues and any office chores in my usual, efficient way. Then, I'd transform into an emotional, blubbering idiot in the camper. My dogs didn't understand what was happening. They were so worried about me. I knew from my animal communication practice the damage that could be done to the animal members of a family undergoing the stresses of divorce. I explained to everyone that they didn't have to take on my negative energy. I was capable of dealing with it myself. My animals knew better than I what a joke that was. I needed them to stay healthy.

Without them, I might not be writing this. There were times when it seemed easier to simply leave this life and try again at another time. What always loomed before me was my responsibility to my animal friends. Who would take care of them? They became my salvation. As I look back, I was more concerned about my animals than myself; an unhealthy pattern of mine. This was a lesson I was trying to teach myself, although my trauma wasn't allowing me to see it.

The day after "those" words were uttered, I was on the phone to my dearest friends. I needed help, support, and sympathy/empathy. I needed to hear that I wasn't losing my mind. I needed to talk to someone I could trust. I needed to be loved. I got all of that, and so much more. I am blessed with many wonderful friends. I called on them all, and they responded regardless of the difficulties of their own lives. Being so far from everyone I knew and loved was devastating. I was so needy, which was something I'd never felt before. I was usually the one trying to be there for the other person. Now, I was experiencing the opposite role.

I felt so much better after my conversations, but soon after I felt alone, isolated, and abandoned again. How could that be? I was still on my mountain that had been so healing, so special, and so powerful. How had I gotten into this mess? I never saw it coming. I'd lost all confidence in myself. Until this happened, I felt I was pretty in tune to what was happening in my life. I was normally very intuitive. This shook me to the core.

I split time between fear and grief. Fear of the future, fear of the unknown, fear of the Now – fear, fear, fear. Where would I go? What would I do? How will I survive? Why did this happen? Grief over the loss of my husband and best friend, the person I most trusted, took control of me. I grieved the loss of the life we had planned together. It was overpowering, debilitating, and all consuming. My heart was broken. It felt like stone.

Bob told the folks we'd bought the land from that it was for sale. I assumed he'd told them the truth. Bad assumption, I found out later. It took a month until I could get through a discussion without getting emotional. I didn't want to appear uncaring or rude, so I stopped by to apologize to Fred and Eunice. I felt so guilty.

I rambled on about my disbelief over our separation and eventual divorce. They just looked at me stunned. Fred got very quiet and went outside to putter, while I continued to talk to Eunice. She shared her disbelief about my news. Apparently, my husband told them the same thing he had told his father. I couldn't believe it.

Fred died later that fall. I felt so bad for Eunice, since I knew how painful it was to lose a husband. We became better friends simply because we shared a common tragedy. After Fred's death, Eunice told me Fred went outside that day because of his shock over our pending divorce. He was upset and didn't want me to see it. Eunice and I continue to visit when I check on the property. I always plan for a quick hello, but I never leave before an hour.

My business mind sent me to the bookstore for resources on divorce. I would study it just like anything else I'd done in my life. I came back with a book, *The Unofficial Guide to Divorce*, by Sharon Naylor. It was set up like a tour guide. I highly recommend it. It satisfied my mental needs. Divorce was my new project.

The other book fed my spiritual side. It was *Spiritual Divorce* by Debbie

Ford. It was just what the soul doctor ordered. Debbie shares her own experience with divorce and the possibilities for the life that follows. It was inspiring and hopeful. Normally, I'm a voracious reader. After I finished these two books, I was unable to read for nine months.

Reading was something I always loved, but I simply couldn't concentrate. I couldn't stop my conscious mind from creating negative images of my future, or painful memories of my past married life and expectations never to be realized. I was a prisoner of my thoughts. My ego wouldn't allow me to live in the present. I seemed to have no control over the negative thoughts in my mind. Distraction was my solution. TV was the answer to my incessant, destructive thoughts. As luck would have it, the Olympics were on that summer. Whatever it takes to get you through, just do it.

I remember watching the drama of the death of President Ronald Reagan. I spent the entire time crying and utterly distraught. I was unable to stop watching coverage. Why was I so upset over the loss of this man? I was sad when John Kennedy was killed, but I didn't fall apart. Now, I was falling apart. I was grieving lost love, not of the Reagans', but my own.

Bob and I had been so in love in the beginning. Our love was everything a girl hopes for. Time and life stole it from us, and we let it. Why? I couldn't answer that. I marveled at the Reagans' accomplishment, and Nancy's strength and self-control. I felt a deep sense of loss, which overwhelmed me, but I kept watching. When she finally gave in to her emotions and laid her head down on his casket, I became despondent. Tears poured from me. I finally surrendered to my deep sense of lost love.

Desperation was an unfamiliar emotion for me, and I didn't like it. It's not a place you want to make major decisions from. All I heard from everyone was, "Don't make any big decisions." In an ideal world that might work, but I was a long way from the ideal. I wasn't given a choice. I had to find a house. As easy as it was to find the mountain property, it was proving to be the exact opposite to find another place.

Because of the animals, I knew I couldn't rent, which would have been the ideal solution. How could I be expected to do this all over again? No one cares, so, "Just do it," like the ad says. My time was divided between ending an old life and beginning a new one. I didn't want a new one. Who decided I needed a new one? It certainly wasn't me. I was trying to manage the chaos that arose from one person's decision to change his mind.

To this day, I'm still not sure which is harder; ending or beginning. I will never forget splitting our assets and liabilities for the property settlement. My business mind was making things equitable, while my emotional/spiritual side was struggling with ending our relationship. Things on paper – 29 years of a life shared with someone – was so much more than *things*. Yet, there it was a list on a page. After it was completed, I went into the camper and just cried. I still couldn't believe this was happening. Our 29-year relationship distilled down to stuff on a page.

I seemed to be losing everything, or at least many of the things, that mattered to me. Why? The time I spent in the camper seemed like ten times as long as it was. I was used to being busy. I never had enough time in the day to get it all done. Now, I had nothing but time, and I hated it. I was so unhappy, which was another powerful and unfamiliar emotion. I was lost and despondent.

Thanks to my ego, I spent time either grieving over my Past or fearing for my Future. I was a human *doer*, not a human *being*. I couldn't live like this. I kept questioning everything I had done. What could I have done better or differently? Was I a bad person? I was honest, and did the best I could. I treated others well. There was a nonstop dialog in my head, as I questioned everything about me. Who was I? I certainly wasn't the vet's wife anymore. I played that role for 27 years. It was my identity and it changed in a heartbeat, but not by my choice.

I felt like a failure and struggled every waking minute with the unwanted changes happening all around me. My turmoil was the result of another's choice to live his life without me. My confidence and self-esteem plummeted. If it weren't for my friends, I would have fallen into an even deeper depression. The grief over my losses was overwhelming. I had fallen into a darkness of spirit, which I nicknamed the *Abyss*. It was frightening and lonely in the Abyss.

Chapter 2

The Abyss

I emerged from the Abyss to search for a house for my animal family and me. I wasn't having much luck, because my heart wasn't in it. My heart was on this mountain. To me it was nothing short of a cruel, sick joke. It's like someone handing you your dream, and then pulling it away. I looked at hundreds of listings. I couldn't have a house with stairs into it, because of my old dogs. I needed a house that wasn't close to traffic for my outdoor cats.

My biggest problem was I hadn't let go of the expectations I had when I moved here. I was supposed to be living on a spectacular property, which made my soul sing, with my husband "until death us do part." No wonder nothing was working. I had found my perfect spot, but it had been snatched out from under me.

My heart was shattered into millions of pieces. Throughout my life, my heart has always led me in the *right* direction. Follow Your Heart was my last foal's registered name. Whenever I struggled with decisions, following my heart was the answer. The most important life decisions I'd made taught me that you didn't want to make those choices with your mind.

My mind's decisions might have seemed right at the time, but usually I'd been led astray. Decisions made from my heart *always* stood the test of time. For me, the ideal was to let my mind assimilate the information, and then make the choice with my heart. No wonder I was having trouble finding a new location. My heart was home on the mountain.

The guiding force of my life was out of order. I felt abandoned, not just by my husband, but by me. This disconnected feeling fed into my increasing lack of self-confidence. How could I ever make a decision that I would be sure of? Winter would be here before I knew it! So, I spent my days wandering about the mountain trying to keep myself out of the Abyss, while looking for a house to live in. At night, in spite of my friend the TV, I tumbled back into the Abyss.

While I fought the Abyss, Bob was away for almost three weeks driving his operating table to New Mexico. It was easier without him around. The tension when he was there was horrible, although he seemed unaffected, which made me sad and angry

During his trip, my Yellow Labrador and dearest friend, Shadow, became very ill. Having run a vet hospital for so many years, I'm usually not an alarmist. I'd been treating Shadow for a diarrhea problem for a few days, which appeared to be resolving. Early one morning, he started throwing up blood. Fear gripped me, and I panicked. I wouldn't survive another loss, and especially not Shadow.

I rushed Shadow to the vet and they took him from me. I was overcome with emotions, because I didn't realize I'd have to leave him. When I got teary, they immediately took me to him. I couldn't have another soul taken from me, even just for a few hours. I regrouped and communicated to him that he had to stay. Luckily, the vet felt he'd be fine after a round of antibiotics. He had picked up digestive bacteria that were prevalent in the area. I was only without him for a few hours; that I could handle.

I was riddled with guilt. I knew that on a spiritual level my animals were absorbing my negative energy. I accepted full blame, whether true or not. I had dealt with this type of problem in my animal healing practice many times. Our animals are continually trying to help us deal with our challenges.

While working with one family and their animal's health challenges, I was given an explanation about companion animals. I was "told" that companion animals come to answer cries for help from human souls on earth. We are in need of their love and support. I knew in my heart that this was truth. I experience their help constantly.

I knew I'd be relying heavily on them in my current crisis, my most difficult yet. I had another long discussion with my animal family about not taking on my negative energy. I assured them I could handle it myself, but they knew better how incapable I was of dealing with my negative emotions. This was also about learning that I could handle life on my own. I kept telling the Universe, "I got it. You can stop now." I'm afraid I was telling the wrong player. I needed to be telling my Self. The challenges continued until I started to grasp the lessons.

My mission for now was to get out of the Abyss. My help came from my friends and my animals. They were my rocks, my angels, and my salvation. You really find out who your true friends are when you fall into the Abyss. They helped me, regardless of their own troubles, climb from the Abyss and enter the Tunnel. At least with a tunnel you have something to aim toward: a way out.

Years ago, I was told by a clairvoyant counselor that I would go through a tunnel and emerge from the other side a different person. I would need to do this in order to come into the full power of my abilities in this life. I didn't know what the heck she was talking about. Her interpretation of the tunnel sounded like an awful thing. My life was great, so I just smiled and let it go. It was one of those significant bits of information, which at the time seemed so innocuous. A decade and a half later, I was thrilled to be in the Tunnel. Anything was better than the *Abyss*!

Just prior to Bob's confession, I'd taken my three-year-old horse, Randy, to a lameness specialist in Charlottesville, Virginia. He'd developed a progressive hind-end lameness early in his yearling year. With digital x-ray equipment, we were finally able to see the damage in both of his stifle joints. The stifle is the knee joint of the hind leg. It is unique in that the horse can lock his stifle joint, allowing him to relax all of his muscles and sleep standing up – a tremendous advantage in the wild. To have this much damage in a horse that had never been ridden was devastating.

As each new x-ray appeared, my heart broke further. From what I saw, I knew I would never have a sound horse. I started to cry, but the vet said he didn't think it was hopeless. He felt Randy was young enough to remodel the joints given time. I had lots of time. He injected his stifles with a combination of agents to quiet inflammation and promote healing.

My heart told me it wasn't going to make any difference. Nothing that we'd done over the past two years had helped, including my spiritual healing techniques, which were successful for many animals. When we hadn't gotten positive results from our medical and spiritual treatments, I knew Randy's soul didn't want its physical form to be healed. I just kept ignoring what my heart knew. Talk about denial and avoidance. I just couldn't *let go* of him, not Randy. I was happy to try anything that might relieve his discomfort and delay the inevitable.

It's amazing what animals are willing to go through to teach us. They stay so we can learn how to say good-bye and let go. I was faced with it repeatedly in my practice. I've witnessed animals endure almost no quality of life for years, until their person was ready to accept their fate and release them. I have vowed to my animals that I will *never* allow them to suffer for me.

My expertise doesn't make it any easier or hurt any less. My experiences allow me to recognize it sooner and hopefully save my friends from unnecessary suffering. I've always felt euthanasia is the last great gift you can give your animal friend(s). It's something that you never take lightly, you hate to have to do, and it is *always* difficult, regardless of whose animal it is.

Many times animals have expressed their confusion during euthanasia consultations. They simply didn't understand the intense sadness within their person regarding their impending transition. Animals understand reincarnation. They perceive death as a beginning rather than an ending. To them it is the start of a new, and inevitable, cycle of spirit. Their teaching has dissolved my fear of death and shown me the continuity of our spirits.

I was trying to embrace this lesson with dear Randy without much success. To me, it has always appeared a conundrum. Our animals hold on in order to teach us. We have to let go in order to learn. The more we can't let go, the harder they hold on. When we finally let go they let go, and hopefully, the lessons are embraced.

It was very hard to have Randy so far from me. I'd spent 27 years providing nursing care and intense observation for our clients' horses. Now, I couldn't do that for a horse that meant the world to me. As I drove out of the farm, I prayed my feelings about this treatment would be wrong.

I came back in a few days, and then as often as I could over the next two months. What I found was really no improvement. In fact he was worse. Based on my own shoulder injections and my pharmaceutical education, I knew I should see improvement quickly. It just wasn't meant to be. I was supposed to call the vet in a month or so. It ended up being twice that. I kept trying to give him more time, because the alternative was unacceptable to me. I was still unable to let go and terrified of what another huge loss might do to me.

Days turned into weeks, weeks into months. My stone cold heart was making finding a house impossible. I knew the closing process would take time, so I couldn't wait too much longer. I knew I'd never find anything that could even approach the sense of home that this mountain gave to my soul. I needed somewhere that would allow me to undergo the immense healing process that was inevitable.

Before I moved, I'd bought a ticket to see Josh Groban near Philadelphia in late July. This young man's voice touches my soul just like my mountain property. Leaving in May, I knew I'd be seeing my gal pals at the end of July. The trip back to New Jersey was a gift, one of those coincidences. I met with the divorce lawyer for about an hour, which sealed the deal. There was no going back now: counsel had been retained. Besides this meeting, my trip distracted me from my trauma in North Carolina.

I visited with my in-laws, Vince and Gloria, while I was in the area. I wasn't sure how they would handle the situation. I didn't want either of them to be uncomfortable. They were very caring and supportive. I could sense how concerned they were for me. Nothing had changed between us, which encouraged me.

I had such a great time with my friends, and Josh Groban didn't disappoint. My soul was touched, and my broken heart even started to stir, which was hopeful. The time I shared with my gal pals was healing. They actually had me laughing uncontrollably. Laughter had been absent from my life for the past month.

One of my most treasured qualities is my sense of humor. Without humor, life is dreary. I'd totally lost the ability to smile or laugh. My friends gave that back to me while we were together, which was a gift I treasured immensely. I will never be able to thank them for giving me the strength to go back and face what I had to. Exemplifying the old cliché, "timing is everything," the timing of this concert trip was perfect.

I had dinners with four of my oldest and dearest friends. I'd known Amy since we showed horses as kids. Her husband, Peter, was our lawyer. They'd known us for years and were as bewildered as I was. Peter was the first call I made after Bob's confession. He had the ideal one-word description of Bob's behavior, which was, "incomprehensible." One word that reflected what I'd felt from the start.

The other couple consisted of Kit, who showed with Amy and me, and Gary, who worked for my husband before specializing in small animals. He was my small animal vet until I moved. I had introduced Kit and Gary forever ago. Their concern and support meant the world to me.

I hated to leave, because I felt so much stronger and almost happy in New Jersey. I couldn't stay, because I had animals that needed me as much as I needed them. One of which was Randy. I had to talk with the vet about Randy's lack of improvement. The vet was very sorry, but he didn't have any other ideas. He'd thought it was worth a shot, but with no positive change more injections wouldn't help, which I already knew.

This was the end of the line for Randy. I began to cry, knowing what I had to do. Why this dear soul? Why did this happen to me? Like I was the one getting ready to leave. I was devastated all over again, but I had to make the best decision for Randy. I've had to decide for all of my animal friends, but normally at the end of a full life. Randy was only three years old. I thought we'd have many years together. I had to stop making this about *me*. It was about Randy and what his soul wanted. I had to keep my promise. I had to let go.

After talking with the vet, I communicated with Randy, and he assured me that he wanted to go. He was happy to have helped his mother, Squiggles, achieve her soul's purpose (another story for another book), but it was time for him to leave. My soul was raw from all the pain of my broken marriage and now this. I *had* to let go, because he was ready. I had no right to keep him here.

In my work as an animal communicator, I've learned from the animals that reincarnation happens. It happens for us all. After I discovered my spiritual skills, I began asking if I had known the animals that came to be with me. I have one of my deepest love-bonds with Randy's soul. He was my Labrador, Gentle Ben, who came just after I was married and stayed more than 13 years. He returned as my tiger cat, Rainbow. He stayed about eight years, and then disappeared. I felt I had let him down. You can imagine my delight, just after Randy's birth, when I heard his soul was Ben/Rainbow.

This decision of Randy's also cost me my friend, who was boarding the horses. I value my friends above all else. I have great friends, and I think I am a great friend. A true friend should be understanding, forgiving, and supportive. My friend sat in total judgment of me and my decision to euthanize Randy. I didn't share the history I had with Randy's soul or our conversation. I knew she wouldn't accept the reality of it.

She had to know how hard this was for me, but she was unyielding. She didn't want to hear what I was saying. If I didn't agree with a friend's decision about something, I would voice my dissent, but be there to support my friend regardless. I knew that Randy would return again. Our bond is that strong. I miss him dearly and look forward to the day when I hear that my new friend is really an old friend. Mark my words, it will happen.

When you make the final decision to send someone Home, you need to do it yesterday. Knowing what awaits is excruciatingly painful. Bob was away again, so I asked my friend to make an appointment with her vet. It had to be the following week, which was agonizing for me.

While I waited, Bob reappeared. I told him about the conversation with the

Virginia vet, and my appointment to have Randy put down. He just listened and nodded. I was stunned. I fully expected him to tell me he would take care of it. Again, I was confronted with the realization that he didn't care at all about me.

I drove to the farm to meet a stranger to do the most difficult thing any animal loving person will ever do. A stranger! I waited half an hour for the vet, which gave me time to say goodbye to Randy, and explain to his younger brother, Stormy, what was happening. I expected my friend to be there, but she never showed. I have never felt so *alone* in all my life. I tried as hard as I could to send Randy off willingly, but I broke down into torrents of tears as the vet injected the poison. It didn't matter to me that he wanted to go. I didn't want him to. I couldn't *let go.*

His soul was out in a flash. He was free of the physical body that was so impressive, yet gave him so much trouble. I thanked the vet and drove my broken heart back to the mountain in floods of tears. Bob never made one comment when I returned. He really doesn't care! When am I going to get it?

I know it's not the spiritually evolved thing to say, but I don't think I will ever be able to forgive Bob for my ordeal that day. He did teach me a huge lesson. I was on my own, and I'd better start to accept it. This was when I finally did get the lesson, but it took extraordinary pain in order for me to learn. I desperately needed to change my method of learning, if I was to survive this life experience.

Compounding my pain, I received some outrageous news that Bob had been to the local court asking about divorce before he'd ever said a word to me. I'll never forget my shock when I first heard this. How could he let me go through that agonizing week trying to get him to talk and attend counseling, when he wanted a divorce all along?

Confused... Didn't have a plan... I don't think so. Who was this person? How dishonest and cruel. This was not the man I fell in love with and married so many years earlier. Accepting what *was* allowed me to change my focus towards my future. However, I couldn't focus too far into the future, or I'd tumble back into the Abyss.

After Randy's death, I returned to my house hunting. I made arrangements to look at a few properties. These were new log houses with lovely long-range views. I thought to myself, I could heal looking out there. When we met with the builder to discuss his houses, he seemed disinterested, so we left.

I stopped at an open house for lunch at a house I'd seen before and liked, except the driveway was too steep. I really had no intention of doing anything but eat. This was the nicest house I'd seen. The rooms were large with a stacked stone fireplace similar to what I had imagined in my Deltec. The more we talked, the more I started to consider the possibility of this house. The builder was agreeable to changing all of the master bath and half bath fixtures to mine. He was agreeable to anything, so I decided to buy it.

There were things about the place that weren't ideal. Besides the steep driveway, the house was in a forest, which made me claustrophobic, and there was no view. But, other important things were present. It was new, so I wouldn't have things to repair. There weren't stairs into the house for my old dogs. The house was up a gravel road, so my cats wouldn't be near the main road. There was another house near me for security, in case I needed help. I was concerned about the gravel road's accessibility in winter, but my realtor assured me it wouldn't be a problem. There were more pluses than minuses.

My ultimate motivation was one of concession. I was tired of looking, tired of worrying, tired of being disappointed, and tired of everything in my life going *wrong*. I gave up my hopes for something better and settled. I think Randy's loss sapped what little strength I had left. The grief over losing my dear friend wore me down. I felt so defeated.

I really didn't care where I lived, just that I had a house before winter. I just couldn't fight whomever I was fighting any longer. What I wouldn't realize for a long time was that I was fighting my Self, my soul, *me*! I had no more resiliencies, no more reserve. I accepted my fate for the time being. What other choice did I have? I just gave in. Let go, you ask? No, it was more *give up*.

I still couldn't, and wouldn't for a very long time to come, let go of the life I anticipated living down here. I couldn't let go of the mountain property. I couldn't let go of the Deltec house. I couldn't let go of the dream. I really couldn't let go of the grief over the loss of Bob and my marriage. Is anyone seeing a pattern here?

It was interesting, because I was able to let go of the physical person that had been my husband. His choice to live apart from me required that I release him. There's not much one can do when that happens. I accepted it on the physical level. I still was trying to understand and accept it on the emotional and spiritual levels.

I did learn that you don't have to understand something in order to accept it. Acceptance led me to a less volatile place where I could look at what I'd accepted, and then find the understanding. If I didn't understand and learn from it, I would simply recreate another similar scenario to teach me. Eventually, I did accept that Bob preferred to live without me. I kept trying to understand why. I have accepted that it *is*, and that's all that really matters.

My inner voice reminded me of a significant lesson Nature taught me while Bob and I vacationed in one of my favorite spots in the entire world, Saba. Saba is an island in the Lesser Antilles near St. Maarten. Saba is a place where people and Nature live in complete harmony, thus creating a tremendously healing energy. Saba has a mountain covered by rainforest, which we climbed. The trail is actually a set of stairs, and is a fairly strenuous climb.

On one of our hikes, I was getting anxious to get to the top. I kept looking far into the distance. Each time I did, I felt overwhelmed. *I'll never make it.* I'd have to shift my attention back in front of me to keep from slipping and falling. Each time I focused in front of me, I felt much better. Then, I'd look ahead and become exhausted again. Eventually, I saw what Mother Nature was teaching. Don't look too far ahead; just focus on what's in front of you, and you'll be fine. These were powerful lessons, which I would need to truly embrace if I were going to survive this dark night of my soul.

My life on the farm had been so jam-packed with responsibilities that I spent my days fully in the moment. Working around animals, especially horses, teaches you to stay present. You can get hurt if your attention isn't on the horse. It's a lesson that can be taught very quickly and powerfully. The Now was where I spent most of my time, although I really wasn't aware of it.

Once the proverbial rug got snatched out from under me, I hardly ever stayed in the Now. I split my time between past and future, but mostly my uncertain Future. For my whole life, I always knew what I was doing and what I wanted. My conscious mind was holding me prisoner with the unending barrage of thoughts concerning my fearful future.

I didn't even recognize what my mind was doing. It was debilitating and exhausting. My spirit was weary. I was handling the Tunnel better than the Abyss, since I wasn't paralyzed by my emotions anymore. I'd found a house to live in, which gave my immediate future a tad less uncertainty. I had to pull my focus back into the present moment, as I got ready to move all of *me* off my mountain. Moving would distract me from my pain.

I was somewhat excited about the fact that I'd found a house to live in. It showed me I could function on my own. My mind was busy with all the things necessary to purchase the house. Luckily, thanks to my family inheritance, I could qualify for a mortgage and meet my living expenses. I didn't have an income-producing job, and I wasn't getting any support from Bob.

Our divorce would net half of whatever we'd accumulated during our 27-

year marriage plus the money from my family inheritance that was invested in the mountain dream. I could take care of my animal family and myself, which was crucial to me. A friend sent me an email with something his grandmother used to say. "If someone turns away your love, they didn't deserve it to begin with." It really gave me pause. Bob didn't deserve my love or me anymore.

Many of my friends felt I should go after so much more, but I didn't. They didn't agree or understand, but they accepted my choice. It was interesting that my friends held so much anger towards Bob. I hadn't gotten to anger yet. I was hurt and grieving. Anger would come later. It made me realize how much they cared about me.

I spent countless hours trying to reflect on what I could have done better, or differently, over the past 29 years. I know that it takes two to make a relationship and two to lose one. I searched our past trying to learn from what might be my mistakes, my opportunities for learning. The only way I could keep from repeating those was if I learned from them. I couldn't really learn from them if I didn't recognize them.

It was a long and painful process. I don't know if I'll ever truly finish it. My mistake was that I assumed too much of the blame. I was left with such a feeling of defeat that I felt a failure. This was another feeling that was completely foreign to me.

I'd always been successful at whatever I'd done. I had a successful show career with my horses. I had been voted most likely to succeed in high school. I graduated third in my class, with highest honors, from Rutgers College of Pharmacy. I found a wonderful man to marry and managed our farm/hospital/veterinary practice with him until he retired. I accomplished everything I'd chosen to do in life. I had been blessed.

I didn't understand failure. To have failed at the thing that was most important to me seemed ludicrous. I spent my time focused on what I had or hadn't done. You know: shoulda, woulda, coulda. The only thing I knew about failure was if it happened, you'd done something wrong. I lived my life trying to do only right. It was imperative that I figure this out for my future sanity.

For years, I shouldered all the blame for our intimacy problems, since they centered on pain in my lower back and right pelvic joint due to congenital birth anomalies. It was so agonizing to think about that I chose not to. My avoidance ultimately resulted in my attaching all sorts of negativity to the issue. Bob didn't need to blame me, I did that all by myself, whether I admitted it or not.

Being raised in a family that kept their feelings hidden made it difficult for me to even think about my intimacy issues, no less talk about them. It was neither *right* nor *wrong*; it was simply how I *was*. As long as Bob didn't press it, I could avoid the agonizing topic.

It never occurred to me, until recently, that he really wasn't concerned about my pain. He wouldn't even remember that pain was the reason behind our inactivity. It never occurred to me that if he truly loved me he ought to be concerned about me, ought to be supportive and sympathetic.

I did exactly what he did. I made it all my fault, my inadequacy, and he let me. It wasn't just about me. It was about us. I didn't deserve my guilt or my anguish. I had suffered for the wrong reasons for a person who truly hadn't cared. He had no idea the deep suffering I experienced. It was in my subconscious always ready to rush to my conscious mind whenever anything reminded me of it.

Once I realized this, I could *let go* of it all. Now, it was finally gone, and all it took was recognition, acceptance, and release. What took me years, and great suffering to uncover left so effortlessly, which was another valuable lesson for my future survival.

My days became consumed with the new house. I'd waver between the excitement of having a house of my own, and the disappointment over my lost dream. The house I'd just purchased was the antithesis of everything I wanted in a house, which was one floor, low maintenance, a stunning view, and round.

I have childhood memories of sleeping in a round room in my grandparents' house that I always loved. I didn't understand why, but I've remembered it my entire life. When I saw the ad for the Deltec Company, I thought an entire round house would be fabulous. The mountain property was the perfect location with its spectacular views. So, I end up with a high maintenance log house, all wood interiors, stairs to a second floor, and no view. But, it was mine.

Months later, when working with a trance channel/spiritual counselor, he told me something that he hears often in the work he does: "We don't always get what we want, but we *always* get what we *need*." This house was the epitome of that Truth. It wasn't what I wanted, but I had to accept that it was what I needed. Of course that acceptance wouldn't happen for a very long time, and not without a tremendous amount of personal self-evaluation. My acceptance, and eventual surrender, would lead to understanding, change, growth, and ultimately, spiritual evolution.

For now, though, I had a house to get ready to move into. As luck would have it, the log house was about 16 miles from the mountain property. I wasn't aware of it when I purchased it, but it made moving fairly convenient. Although it was only 16 miles, it took me 30 minutes to drive from one to the other. Welcome to winding, two-lane mountain driving!

The builder worked on the renovations that we'd agreed to. I hoped using parts of my dream house would make it a little easier to move into the log house. I wouldn't feel like I'd lost everything. These were things I'd spent a great deal of time choosing. I hoped they'd help alleviate the feeling of having totally wasted the time spent planning the Deltec.

So, I moved stuff, and the builder made the log house take on some of the elegance of the Deltec. The master bath was transformed into a more rustic version of my dream master bath, but still quite lovely. It gave me a great sense of pleasure and accomplishment to see that the fixtures I'd chosen looked so pretty. I felt a tiny glimmer of success.

It was a time of mixed emotions for me. I was relieved that my animal family and I had a house to live in before winter. New seemed like a smart thing to buy. While I somewhat enjoyed getting things for the house, I didn't like the amount of money I was spending on a house that meant nothing to me. I didn't know where I wanted to live other than my mountain property, but the dream of ever living there was gone. This house was transitional. I took things one day at a time, and still do. Anything other than that gets me into big trouble.

As the renovations moved along, I started bringing carloads of things over. We hadn't unpacked anything, so I simply had to load it in my car. Every time I moved a little more of me off the mountain, the reality that I'd never live on this special, powerful mountain began to sink in. I had known this for months, but I tried not to focus on the inevitable.

I tried to make the most of the time I had left on the mountain. I just couldn't get past the grief I was still experiencing over the loss of my marriage. It tainted everything in my life. I no longer felt the same wonderful feelings I had on the mountain. I couldn't see the beauty in the gorgeous long-range views that used to make my heart sing. All my heart did was ache. The energy of the mountain hadn't changed nor had the views. I changed, and I didn't know how to change back. I was powerless.

I walked the dogs around the property many times a day just to give us exercise. They still loved it. They didn't know anything had changed. I tried to learn from them to appreciate it for as long as I lived on it. I needed to stay in the Now with them. No lost expectations, no depression, no pain, just happy in the moment. I simply couldn't do it. I couldn't imagine ever being happy again, or ever laughing again. The Tunnel was a definite step up from the Abyss, but I had a tremendous journey ahead to return to the person I used to be, and *needed* to be again.

I arranged for Bob to take care of the dogs and cats while I returned to New Jersey to see my dear friends. Once I moved, I'd be staying put, since I was solely responsible for the two dogs and three cats. It is restrictive to have dogs and cats, but I wouldn't have traded them for anything. Without my animals, I would have never survived.

As I pulled off the mountain with the last of my belongings, I burst into tears and cried all the way to the log house. There was no going back. It was real. I no longer lived on my mountain. Bob didn't come running after me saying it had all been a terrible mistake. Please don't go! To this day, he has never even said he was sorry. The only thing he said was that it was sad. Ya, think? I guess I kept hoping he'd realize he'd made a terrible mistake, and decide he wanted this house, this mountain, and most especially, me. But, that never happened.

Chapter 3

The Log House

I followed the movers to my new log house. When they finished, I headed for New Jersey. The thought of staying in *that* house without my animals terrified me. I stayed at a motel in Virginia, which taught me what alone really feels like: absolutely dreadful. My animal friends never allowed me to feel alone. They are consummate companions, especially my dogs. I was on my own, and the empty motel room gave me a huge dose of *alone*. It was the first time that I got a real sense of just how alone I was going to be.

The realization of what I had done that day was overpowering me. I tried to distract myself with TV without success. My aloneness consumed me with destructive thoughts about my uncertain Future. It was a long night, but I survived. For some reason I didn't feel so alone in the car. Driving forced my mind out of the pattern of disparaging thoughts that it seemed so comfortable in. I headed off repeating, "Today is the first day of the rest of my life."

I drove towards my old home, my dear friends and in-laws, and away from all the pain that North Carolina held for me. Once again, my friends and in-laws renewed me. I was kept busy the entire time meeting everyone around meals. I felt so much better in New Jersey, so much stronger, less alone, almost happy. My mind stayed out of the dastardly past and future and focused only on the present. I felt once again supported and loved, which was something that I needed terribly and meant the world to me, then and now.

My dear friends, Michele, David, and Michele's mother, Marie, who made their home my home, were dealing with a tragedy of their own with Logan, a wonderful four-year-old Golden Retriever. Logan lived life to the fullest every waking minute. You couldn't help but be happy in his presence. Logan was diagnosed with stage four cancer, which was devastating.

Michele and David committed themselves to doing whatever was necessary to help him, while still retaining quality of life for whatever time he had left. I was shocked at the diagnosis in a dog so young. Logan taught me that the Golden Retriever breed is fraught with cancer.

So, my friends began the fight that little Michelle's husband, Mike, had been engaged in for quite some time. Mike had been diagnosed with melanoma cancer before we moved. None of their support for me ever wavered despite the crises that they were experiencing. Given my medical background and my experiences with my folks' cancer, I was able to provide help and support to them. I was thrilled to return some of the strength they'd provided me since my separation. What they were dealing with helped put my own drama in perspective. My trauma, although painful, wasn't fatal. Friends helping friends is what life is about.

I drove to the shore, which I'd wanted to do before I moved. It was something important that would have fulfilled a need in me, but I let other responsibilities interfere with it. At the time, I wasn't even aware I put everyone else's needs ahead of mine. It would take time and great pain to even begin to recognize this unhealthy pattern of my life, this negation of Self.

As a young child, I'd spent my summers in a house next to my grandparents' home. I lived those summers on the beach and in the waters of the Atlantic Ocean and the Shrewsbury River. In high school, I learned about the right of eminent domain. The state took our family's shore property to build a road into a nearby park. My parents bought a spectacular home across the river from our *stolen* one.

I will never forget the beauty of the full moon creating zillions of twinkling lights on the river and ocean. I never took that view for granted, *ever*. Each month, when the heavenly miracle appeared, I ran around the house making sure everyone saw it. It touched my soul deeply.

Bob and I used to walk the dogs at that same park. We spent many wonderful hours on that beach, which afforded a fabulous view of Manhattan and the Verrazano Bridge. The area held so many special memories for me:

happy memories of the wonderful life I had been privileged to lead until we moved. I wanted to wander around my home turf and bathe myself in happy memories of the wonderful times I'd spent there.

I drove past my old house, my high school, and then out to the park. We always walked the dogs at the far end, because it was less crowded and provided the best view of the "Big Apple." I pulled into one of the closer parking areas and walked toward the water. Once again, I was totally unprepared for my response.

When I gazed out at the ocean, sadness consumed me and tears flowed. The emotions ignited were not the ones I'd hoped for and needed to feel. The happiness of my time spent there was buried too deep beneath the pain of my lost husband, expectations, and dream. Instead of feeling the emotions I experienced on the beaches and in the water of my happy childhood, I felt overwhelming sadness, grief, and abject pain. I didn't stay long. I couldn't.

I walked back to the car and just cried until I had no more tears. I thought my wonderful memories would provide a route back to the happiness of my Past. Was I ever wrong. I know; there isn't any right or wrong, only what is. It was hard to accept that concept, while I sat absolutely distraught and alone in my car. This had been a huge mistake. Hello! Remember, there are no mistakes, no accidents? There are only opportunities for learning. Bah!

I always tried to keep my emotions in check while visiting friends. I didn't want to become some whiny, clingy so and so, that drained my friends of their energy. In retrospect, the barrage of childhood memories that had flowed from the far reaches of my brain served to heighten the sense of loss my heart and soul felt.

I was hopeful there'd be a time when I'd remember those happy times at the Jersey shore and feel the joy of my wonderful childhood. It just wasn't that time yet. As with my last visit, it was over before I knew it. However, this time what loomed ahead was horrifying: the log house and my fearful future.

The overnight in the motel was better, but still difficult. I was feeling nauseous when I got to the mountain. I figured I was having a panic attack over being in the log house alone. I didn't encounter any resistance from Bob as I piled the dogs into the car. He knew he'd be in for a big battle if he tried to separate them. I told him I'd be back the next day to pick up the cats. I didn't have room for everyone in the car.

Once again, I drove off the mountain an emotional disaster. I arrived at the log house distraught and in a panic. I was afraid of being alone, of the uncertainty of my Future, of everything. I tried so hard not to cry, because I knew how much it upset my dogs. The boys were confused enough. I didn't need them worrying about me and getting sick themselves. I had to be strong for them. Could I really be creating this nausea with my mind? I knew I could.

A little radio I'd bought helped drown out the dreaded silence. In the silence, my conscious mind had a field day bombarding me with grievous thoughts about my Past, and fearful thoughts of my uncertain Future. The music saved me from the cruelty of my ego. I made it through the first night with my dogs by my side.

The next day, my TV man erected a temporary dish for me. I'd been concerned that he might have trouble finding a signal, because of all the trees around the house. He found one, but only with the dish on a tree. I *had* to have TV to combat my ego.

Before my trip, a young man, who was installing Corian® surfacing in two bathrooms and on the kitchen island, asked if I had my horse in the area. I told him about the perfect farm that wasn't taking boarders. He'd been past that farm recently, and thought they were. I tried not to get my hopes up, but I needed something positive to happen.

When I returned, he'd left a message saying the perfect farm was accepting boarders. Thank you! My dead heart stirred. Could I be this lucky? I called and asked the barn manager, Kim, if she remembered me. She did! They had a stall for Stormy. I almost cried, but this time tears of joy. My equine salvation would be in the mountains soon. What perfect timing. *Everything happens for a reason....* .

I wanted to rush right over for Stormy, but I was inundated with new house responsibilities. I had all manner of contractors: electricians, plumbers, cabinetmakers, landscapers, and of course, the builder to deal with. It became a nuisance and very frustrating. It was so different from my experience with the Deltec.

I loved the Deltec: it was my dream and creation. Everything flowed with it. Nothing flowed with the log house. Things got accomplished but nothing flowed. In my heart, I didn't really want it. I liked the house itself, but I absolutely abhorred the location. I felt closed in by all the trees. I had no view. I felt no connection to the acre it sat upon. For me, it was nothing more than a place to survive the winter.

The differences between the two properties were stunning – opposite ends of the poles, so to speak. I was naïve about a new house. Based on my experience, I would never buy a new house again. Building a house of your own is a completely different thing. It is your intention to build. You expect to have challenges and frustrations, but you are ready to accept those in order to manifest your dream.

A new house is someone else's creation. This presented a big challenge for me. I had to work within the parameters of the house itself. I did have some of my Deltec things incorporated into this house, but they were just things, which didn't restore my lost happiness.

Once I moved in, I soon realized another stark contrast to my perfect mountain property: the communications. I had to have dial-up with the connection speed of ten years ago. It was a constant frustration for me and another thing that fueled my anger at where I was living. Due to the dial-up, I couldn't receive incoming calls while on the Internet. I was so desperate for contact with my support staff that the thought of missing any calls was paralyzing to me. I'd have to drive two miles to a cresting hill to find a cell signal. In my fragile emotional state, my ego created fear about being unable to reach someone in an emergency.

Shortly after I moved in, the phone went down. I truly panicked! I'd lost my lifeline to everyone. I couldn't believe my reaction. I'd been an independent, capable woman. Now, I sat in a panic. In hindsight, I recognize that my disconnection with the physical world was simply reflecting my deeper fears of feeling disconnected from Self, my soul, universal knowing, God, Source, All That Is, whatever you want to call it. My response arose from deep within my wounded Self. It would take me many, many months before I'd recognize this.

My fear and angst disappeared the second I heard a dial tone back in the log house. I couldn't believe the level of fear that had overwhelmed me, how fast it came, and how fast it left. My inefficient communications in the log house was an outward reflection of what was going on within me: unrest, constant turmoil, frustration, fighting. These were things I wasn't used to experiencing. They would fester, causing a constant state of stress and anxiety for some time to come.

The most challenging time was at night. Even my TV wasn't getting the job done. I fell into a terrible depression filled with unhappiness and loneliness. My mind created a constant flow of negative thoughts of both past and future. Initially, I wasn't even aware that my ego was in control. I got so caught up in the destructive thoughts and how to cope with them that I didn't understand what was happening.

Years ago, I worried constantly. It had been a way of life for me. About 15 years ago, when I started along my spiritual path, I let go of worry. The more I learned, the less I worried. It was a slow process that occurred as I learned spiritual truths and embraced them within my life. My lifestyle, working with and caring for animals, kept me present. What luck.

When you're dealing with critically ill horses, you have to be in the moment. It was an added bonus for living the life I loved. As a result, the time I spent worrying about the future disappeared. When my husband changed the rules and decided to abandon me, my time spent in the Now came to a crashing halt.

Moving afforded me some relief from my relentless ego. I learned it takes far longer to unpack than it did to pack. All the decisions, choices, memories slow the process down incredibly. Many were items from my childhood, my mother's treasures, and my father's things. I didn't know when I made the decision to bring these treasures with me what a significant role they would play in North Carolina. They afforded me a look back into my *happy* Past, not the *sad* Past that I had found myself in lately. It was a wonderful reprieve that I truly needed.

As more and more of my prized possessions were positioned around the log house, it started to feel like it was really mine. I felt like I was still being taken care of by my dad, because my sole source of income was my family inheritance. At 54, I still felt like daddy's little girl. As I was unpacking my office boxes, I found the pocket protector my dad used in our family drugstore. You know, one of those silly plastic things that probably cost less than a dollar. To me, it was priceless. It still has the pens, pencils, and grease pencil that I watched him use all my life. While packing up the office in Jersey, I just couldn't bring myself to throw it out. It had been a part of him for as long as I could remember.

The rush of emotions I experienced when I unpacked it in the log house was overpowering. The floodgates opened and the tears poured out. I missed my dad so much. I could have really used his guidance and support at this most difficult time in my life. It was a powerful release of a great deal of still repressed grief, sadness, and pain involving the loss of my father four years earlier, and my husband only recently.

I've recognized my father's influence in my decisions many times during these terribly challenging times. He taught me well throughout his life. He was a marvel in dealing with people, which was something I aspired to learn. People that knew us both tell me how much I'm like him. It is the highest compliment anyone could give me. I am proud to be his daughter.

A week before my father died, he told me that he thought everyone would be okay. I had to fight back the tears. I saw in that simple statement what his whole life had been about. To him, he was our provider, our caretaker, and our protector. He was here to make sure his family was safe and secure. It was so shockingly simple, yet profound, to learn what he felt his purpose in life was.

I assured him we would be all right. It was okay for him to go. That evening, with those words, my heart *let go* of him. Eight days later he died; I hope satisfied that he had achieved his purpose. Because of his disclosure, I have an image of his spirit smiling that special smile of his knowing that he is still providing for and taking care of his little girl.

Yes, Daddy, you will always be taking care of me. The mark that you left on my soul is permanent. I am grateful for you and your contribution to my growth. It is the strength of character that you displayed throughout my life that will form the basis from which I will heal from my dark night of the soul. I am forever in your debt. I couldn't have chosen a better father.

The tears that flowed, as I unpacked his penholder, which contained all of these emotions, insights, and memories, were positive and *good*. What a wise decision to move that little gem to the mountains. Was it a coincidence? Not on your life.

Hanging the artwork and photos was the last of my moving-in chores. Each held a happy memory, but given the circumstances of my current life, they also inflamed my sense of loss and grief. Seeing the many treasures from our married life was challenging for me. I just couldn't let go of the disappointment I harbored over my lost marriage and mountain home. I envisioned myself hanging them in the Deltec.

The artwork went up first and then the photos. I unpacked "my life" in black and white and color. The memories these pictures held were powerful. Many were of my various show horses and held wonderful memories. Countless pictures were of the farm and my animal family, which ignited special memories of my "children." My soul called them to me over the years. I'd been their provider, caretaker, and protector while they shared their teaching, their lives, and their love with me. I was a conglomerate of the knowledge they shared during the short time they stayed.

It is only a relatively short time that we get to share with our animal friends. We know it when we enter into a relationship with animals, and we're still willing. The unconditional love that we receive from them is well worth the cost. To me, unconditional love is companion animals' greatest lesson to humanity. A lesson we're missing, and I include myself in the collective "we."

Each of the pictures took me back to the specific show, horse, and experience. Especially wonderful times that reminded me of how truly fortunate I was. Each was reflecting my happy and fulfilling life. They were helping me heal, which I hadn't anticipated at all. How could I not be grateful?

All of a sudden, I realized most of the animals in the photos were dead, but still teaching me a valuable and necessary lesson for my survival, my healing, and my growth. They helped me believe that I could return to the once happy, joyful, successful, and satisfied woman they knew and loved.

I am grateful for two particular photos of me. One was taken by a professional photographer when I was about two years old. It's always been a favorite of mine. I have a big smile, Shirley Temple ringlets, and a mischievous twinkle in my eye. It just gives me a lift every time I see it. I feel the light, joyful energy of that child. The other photo was a candid shot taken at a Cornell reunion. Once again, I have this great smile. It radiates happiness and contentment. Both sit on my dresser and remind me of the person I have been all my life. They challenge me to become that woman, to release the little two-year old within, to have fun, and to love living again.

My greatest gift from the pictures that now surrounded me was the gift of *seeing*. I began to see how lucky I'd been. I was trying to be grateful for what I had, since it was more than many had. I had good health, a wonderful family and animal family, and fabulous friends. I could meet my monthly expenses, had a reliable car, and a new log house. I worked hard trying to embrace gratitude, but it was work, and it shouldn't be. It should be a place of being.

The recent events of my life blocked my ability to feel grateful. Instead, I felt abandoned, alone, and isolated. I was cranky. The most important person in my life had deceived, lied to, and betrayed me. You got it. I felt sorry for myself. As much as I tried, my ego would send me there in a moment's notice. Wham, there I'd be.

When I first saw the lesson, I felt guilty. How could I feel sorry for myself? Shame on me: I'd lived a spectacular life for 53 years. How dare I complain? I felt ashamed. So, I had a bad year and a half. With all my memories in view, the log house was starting to look more like a home, though I was a long way from ever considering it one.

Although my familiar things were scattered around, there was still something missing: house plants. I was so busy unpacking and trying to find a place for everything (and everything in its place). I can't tell you how many times I heard my grandmother say that to me. I hadn't even thought about plants. I just knew something wasn't right yet. I didn't have enough of the plant nation in the log house.

Wal-Mart was having a sale and I came home with six huge, beautiful hanging baskets. Their presence changed the energy in the house immediately. The house felt warmer, happier, more balanced, and harmonious. Now, thanks to my new plant friends, the log house felt warm and inviting. If I could only get that sense of harmony within my spirit, I could be happy again.

In addition to the demands of moving, I was also concerned that the separation agreement still wasn't finished. The lawyer was taking forever. Bob was to teach in the fall at the Indian reservation in New Mexico. I feared he'd be leaving soon, since it was October.

We finally got the paperwork to review and sign. There were some areas that Bob didn't understand, so I told him to call Peter for someone to help him. I didn't want anything coming back at me. His new lawyer was trying to make it much more complicated than necessary.

Eventually, Bob told me when he anticipated leaving. I was worried that he'd leave before the settlement was signed. It had been hard enough trying to get things accomplished when we were in the same area. I was also *very* concerned that someone would convince him that he shouldn't return my family's inheritance. If he had been the man I married, I wouldn't have given it a second thought, but that man was gone.

Bob asked to visit Licorice and arrived with a pile of mail to discuss including papers from Ford Credit. My car had been registered in his name for tax reasons. I'd been trying to get my name on the loan, and then eventually register the car in my name. Ford required that Bob remain as co-signer. Bob wasn't happy, but oh well! It had taken me three months to get to this point. I was so glad they had come before he left, since they had to be signed and notarized.

Next, Bob handed me a four-page letter from his lawyer. I'd known something was up. I didn't get too far into it, before all of the anger I had been suppressing erupted. The, proverbial, s___ hit the fan! This lawyer was telling Bob that the property settlement was totally inequitable, and he should sue *me* for alimony. I went ballistic! Apparently, he hadn't explained about my management of the veterinary office, hospital, and horse farm. She questioned my integrity and my honesty.

I tried to calm myself down in order to have a constructive conversation. The minute I started to ask him about how he felt about what she said, I felt abject rage overtake me. I'd been attacked and became very defensive. How dare she question my motives and me? Who the hell does she think she is? Did he agree with what she wrote? Did he think I was being unfair? I could hardly get the questions out. I was seething, and he knew exactly what I was thinking. If looks could kill, he would have been dead.

Bob didn't think he should get alimony, but he felt he'd worked really hard and should end up with more to show for it. I looked at him in utter disbelief and shock. After I'd spent so much time trying to make everything fair, equitable, and understandable for him, he was questioning it. I began to explain how incompetent his lawyer was to miss a large component of our assets.

Bob's response totally floored me. He'd forgotten about our annuity and felt better considering his equal share in it. How can someone forget about such an important thing? How fortunate that he married such an honest woman. Obviously, I could have made off with a vast sum of money without his even realizing it. Lucky man!

We drove to the bank to sign and notarize the Ford papers. What happened at the bank was another shocker: another piece to the puzzle that would come together eventually. Bob pulled out his New Jersey license for identification. I just couldn't believe he still had a Jersey license. I told him I'd be by later to get the car insurance papers I needed for Ford Credit.

All I did was obsess over the lawyer's attacks against my integrity. Why did he still have a Jersey license? The only reason was that he never planned to stay in North Carolina. I found that inconceivable. I was concerned that he agreed with his lawyer, was considering fighting in court, and/or reneging on returning my inheritance. I flew in and out of anger and rage. While I was in rage, I really couldn't function. What she wrote was disrespectful and attacked every part of my being.

After discussing this with friends, each one pointed out that it was her job. She was representing Bob, and the only information she had was what he told her. I did agree with that, but it didn't make me feel any less violated. I planned, very carefully, what I would say to him. I was mounting my counter attack as though my life depended on it.

Bob was waiting for a call from his lawyer when I arrived. I told him that I was still furious. I wanted him to know the facts as they would appear in court. I reminded him that the only thing coming to me that was not being split equally was my inheritance money. If we had finished the house and lived in it, then I'd feel differently. I told him this lawyer wanted us to fight in court to create more billable hours.

Since he'd forgotten about the annuity, I couldn't be sure what else he forgot about. I assured him that everything from our 27-year marriage was being split equally. I reminded him that I'd given up going to veterinary college to begin our relationship, and I'd also left my pharmacy career to run his business. I didn't need to tell him how this would appear in a divorce case. Angrily, I told him that if it hadn't been for my folks and me, he would have never had his vet hospital and breeding farm. He listened without any comment.

I expected him to tell his lawyer the entire truth about me, and my extraordinary contribution to our marriage and his business. I spoke my piece, got the papers I needed, and the dogs and I left the mountain. I felt better as I drove away. I had defended myself. I was proud of the person I was. I had no regrets.

When I got to the log house, I was spent. The emotional toll of the day was enormous. From Bob's lack of response, I wasn't sure what to expect. The last thing I told him was that I wanted the papers signed before he left. Early the next morning, the phone rang. Bob wanted to sign the papers, so we agreed to meet at our bank. I felt such a tremendous sense of relief. I would get my family's money back. I had succeeded in convincing him how big a mistake it would be to end up in court. The next step would be the divorce hearing in the New Jersey courts. Bob left the next day. So be it!

Chapter 4

Reunited

I was totally drained from the past day. The anger and rage I had experienced was unlike anything I had felt at any time in my life. I needed my horse back in my life, and I needed him now! After Randy was euthanized, my friend kept saying Stormy should be in training. I didn't agree, but I just didn't have the strength to fight, so I let her start him. Starting him was something that I wanted to do, but I just gave in. This decision forced me to let go of another significant expectation. I wanted to get on him for the first time at a place where he'd feel safe and behave himself. I made arrangements to go ride him and meet my friend's mother for lunch.

I hadn't told them yet about finding the new farm for Stormy. I wanted to tell them in person. It was important to me that they understood my reasons. I thought it had always been understood that their farm was temporary, since it was 126 miles from my house. There was no point having Stormy if I couldn't ride him.

I never anticipated what happened. I was so tired of being surprised by people and their reactions to my decisions. This was another of those emotional events for me. It had taken three years of my life and many hours of hard work to get to this moment in time. I'd been with Stormy every day from the instant he appeared from his mother's womb, until I left him at my friend's farm seven months earlier.

How would he behave? How would he feel? What would my friend say when I told her I was moving him? Stormy was wonderful. He behaved and was very comfortable. I hadn't ridden in a while, so my focus was totally on him. I'd expected my friend to help with him, but I didn't wait. I was too anxious to finally achieve what I'd been waiting three years to do.

Out of the corner of my eye, I saw my friend drive her truck to the barn. The next thing I saw was her driving out. I didn't understand, but I didn't care. I was busy on my baby. I was hoping she'd return, so I could tell her my news. She did return, so I spoke with her before lunch. Mrs. B., who I considered my second mother, had trained me 30 years earlier. I rented her garage apartment while I was in college and became more than a boarder to her. I knew it was special for Mrs. B. to see me once again in her ring.

I was the closest thing to happy since June. I'd just ridden my horse for the first time, and I'd found a gorgeous farm half an hour from my house. What more could I ask for? I was *very* apprehensive about my impending conversation. Horse people are a strange group. I'd learned that through the 40 years I spent dealing with them. I was one, so I felt qualified to make that assessment.

I knew our relationship had changed because of Randy, but I didn't realize how much. She seemed cold, almost angry, which I didn't understand. I shared my good news. I kept telling her it didn't have anything to do with her or her care. I was thrilled that I'd found a wonderful place for him. I knew Stormy was going to be a tremendous aid to my healing.

Something about her attitude just kept me trying to get her to understand. She was very distant. At one point, I reached for her shoulder trying to comfort her, since she seemed so hurt. Why was this all of a sudden about her? Angrily, she snatched her shoulder away from me. Well, that was it. I felt anger surging up in me, so I didn't say another word.

She asked when I would move him. I said in a few of days if that was convenient, since I was anxious to have him closer. She said she usually got 30 days notice. My anger swelled. I told her if she needed an extra month's board fine, but I'd be back for him in three days. I'd been involved with horses for over 40 years and had never heard of such a thing. I followed Mrs. B. to lunch and shared my news with her. She accepted it better, but I could see how disappointed she was. I knew she imagined her daughter and her adopted daughter riding into the sunset together, so to speak. I tried to get Mrs. B. to understand how hard it was to live so far from Stormy, that I needed something positive to focus on, and I couldn't have found a better farm.

I am blessed with an amazingly beautiful, young horse. At the time of his conception, I could never have known the significant player he would be in my healing. What I truly enjoyed was working with youngsters. I didn't know or care if he ever went to a horse show. His sole purpose was to make me happy, and he couldn't accomplish that living so far away. Mrs. B tried to understand, but at 93, with her life focused on showing horses, it was very difficult for her to let go of what a fabulous show prospect he was.

A month earlier, I'd come to give Stormy some vaccinations. When I called the night before to tell my friend I was coming, she told me she had dewormed him. I was quite confused, since we'd agreed that I'd be responsible for the horses' routine work. Apparently, once my husband was out of the picture, she started treating my horses without my knowledge. I needed to know what my horses were being given and when. I was livid!

The next morning, I arrived at the farm with the vaccines drawn up in syringes. I told my friend what vaccinations I was about to give him, and she screamed at me that the vet gave him shots the other day. Confused, I asked what specific shots. She just said whatever he needed. Why didn't she say this last night? I'd just driven 126 miles for nothing, and the vaccines would have to be thrown out. I was seething.

I had a short visit with Stormy and started to walk out of the barn. My friend asked, "You're leaving?" I had plans to meet Mrs. B for breakfast and then get back to my other obligations. My visit to vaccinate happened a few weeks after I'd put Randy down. Did she expect me to want to spend time with someone that had left me to do that alone? I thought to myself, she's in the same dimension with my husband. I walked angrily out of the barn and never looked back.

I hadn't gotten a bill yet for those shots, so I called her vet's office to find out what I owed them. The secretary couldn't find any record of Stormy having any vaccinations in September. Then, she said the vet was due there that morning. I told her to tell the vet not to give Stormy anything. I was moving him in two days and didn't want him stressed with shots.

I knew my friend was angry at me about my decision with Randy, but I never thought she would do anything to jeopardize my horse no matter what she thought of me. Well, I was wrong. She allowed my horse to be unprotected from several deadly diseases. She lied to my face, while her right hand gal looked me right in the eye and never said a word.

Now, I was about to do what I'd advised our clients to *never* do. I had to move my horse to a new environment knowing he was unprotected for these diseases. I was willing to assume the risk. I had to get him away from her and back under my care.

I called my friend to remind her I was coming for Stormy. I arrived at the farm to find all of my stuff piled out in front of Stormy's stall, and only a worker present. My bridle and two spare halters were missing. When we went for the keys to unlock the tack rooms, the keys were gone. I was stunned and deeply hurt, since my integrity and honesty were being attacked again. I loaded Stormy in the trailer and told her worker that I'd be back the next day for my missing equipment. Another 250-mile trip! Once more, I felt disrespected by someone I considered a friend. First I was hurt, but then I flew into rage.

Stormy shipped wonderfully to his new home. This was the first time he'd been on the trailer alone. I spent the long trip obsessing over what I'd just been subjected to. I went in and out of hurt, anger, and tears. Why was all of this happening to me? Why was everyone treating me so badly? Well, everyone wasn't. It just felt like everyone.

Eventually, after much soul-searching, I came to realize it wasn't just about me. I was a player in their dramas as well as they in mine. They each had their own issues, but that realization would take time for me to see. I arrived at the farm exhausted from worrying about Stormy's inexperience on the trailer and the insulting way I had been treated.

Later that day, an email alerted me that my bridle was in the mail. She'd forgotten my halters, which she mailed a few days later. I probably should have expected her behavior regarding Randy and moving Stormy, but I'd never forgive her for putting my horse's health and well-being at risk. For me that was the final blow. She had lost a good friend.

The fact that she owed me money from another horse would force me to have to keep her in my awareness for a long time into the future. If it weren't for that, she'd have been eliminated completely from my life. Mrs. B was still a good friend. She was trying to understand and be supportive.

The next day, I went to see my dear Stormy. It was so wonderful to arrive in half an hour rather than two. He was out in his own huge, grassy pasture. I called him. He answered and galloped over. He was genuinely happy to see me. I started to cry, because someone cared for me, and I so needed that. I missed being with my horses so much. They are a part of me and always will be.

Now, I had my last one back in my daily life. My salvation had arrived. This was the first positive thing that had happened to me in four months, except for buying a house. But, this was so much more important to my healing, my recovery, and my sanity. He was my angel with four legs, who would give my life some sense of purpose again.

Two months after Stormy arrived in the mountains, an old friend in New Jersey emailed this poem that embodies the significance of Stormy to my life.

"In The Heart of A Horse"
When your day seems out of balance and so many things go wrong
When people fight around you and the day drags on so long
When parents act like children, in-laws make you think "Divorce"
Go out into your pasture
and wrap your arms around your horse.
His gentle breath enfolds you, and he watches with those eyes
He may not have a PhD, but he is, oh so wise!
His head rests on your shoulder
You embrace him oh so tight
He puts your world in balance, and makes it seem all right.
Your tears they soon stop flowing
The tension is now eased
The garbage has been lifted, and you're quiet and at peace.
So when you need the balance from circumstances in your day
The best therapy that you can seek
is out there eating hay!

The unknown author had obviously spent time with horses. I just burst into tears, when I read the poem. It was truly synchronistic. It spoke the truth about how much all of my horses have meant to me over the years, and how much they've enriched me.

The farm was simply beautiful and absolutely perfect. Kim, his daily caregiver, was very capable. She was a younger version of me. I couldn't have asked for anything better. I had absolutely no concerns for his well-being. I'd be a mere half hour away if anything serious came up.

The downside of having horses in the mountains is the lack of veterinary service. For me, it wasn't too much of a concern. I had all those years of experience. What I didn't have was a veterinary license. For all of the worrying and stressing that I did in all other areas of my life, I did none regarding Stormy. I knew I could handle anything that might come along. If not, he'd ship to wherever to deal with whatever. I wouldn't let negative thoughts create an unhealthy reality for Stormy.

It was interesting because my thoughts were still out of control in the rest of my life. With Stormy it was different. I found it intriguing that I had all the confidence in the world with him, but absolutely none with my Self. I had spent my life caring for and loving horses. It had been my true joy. I was very good at what I did, and it showed in my self-confidence and knowing around them.

I needed to get to that same level of self-confidence about the care and well-being of my Self. I was terribly inept at caring for *me*. Through my experience with Stormy, it became painfully apparent that I had spent a life focused totally away from me. I had been completely unaware of it until that moment in time. This would prove to be one of my biggest lessons as I clawed my way out of the Abyss, into the Tunnel, and eventually, out of the Tunnel.

I trained Stormy about four days a week. He was only two, and didn't need too much exercise. He was wonderful and seemed to enjoy the attention. I felt like I had purpose to my life again. I have a wonderful rapport with horses, which is rooted in my deep respect and love for them. Working with Stormy boosted my deflated self-esteem, which had taken a severe beating over the past six months.

When I was at the farm, I was fully in the moment. In that intense state of presence, I felt the joy I used to. There is something so serene and peaceful about anywhere horses are. To look out over the pristine pastures and see them grazing in these huge, grassy fields touched my heart. My heart was stirring with life again, albeit slowly. Being at the farm bathed in the energy that I'd spent so much of my life in was nourishing to my soul.

One of *the* most spiritual times for me was at night in my old barn, when I'd just listen to the sounds in total darkness. I'd hear the horses munching hay, moving around the stalls, snorting hay dust out of their nostrils, breathing. Those sounds and the stillness bought me as close to Being, to Presence, to my Essence, as anything. They were magical, healing, mystical times that touched my heart deeply. With the arrival of Stormy, I hoped to recover some of that. It was imperative I reawaken those feelings in order to heal my heart, and ultimately, my soul.

The rest of my days were spent in frustration dealing with house related things. It seemed unending. At night, if I didn't keep my ego occupied with mindless TV, it would launch a barrage of negative thoughts and emotions regarding my Past and Future. I still found myself unable to concentrate enough to read.

I felt alone, isolated, abandoned, and so unhappy. My dogs and cats were my sole companions. Without them I would never have been able to deal with the nights. I owe my life and my sanity to them. They worried about me and showered me with unconditional love.

After a month in the log house, Shadow came down with a urinary infection, which I recognized from a past bout. I called my dear vet friend, Gary, to verify my diagnosis and treatment plan. He agreed. On Monday, I brought Shadow to the local vet to confirm the diagnosis. She dispensed another antibiotic, and he recovered without complication. "Okay, I handled it. I can do this. You don't have to keep creating things to teach me that I can handle life on my own." My trouble was still thinking it was something or someone other than me that was creating. I was just not getting it.

Living alone for the first time in my life was the hardest thing I'd ever done. I wasn't very good at it. It was my life now, and I'd better figure out how to deal with it and soon. I checked on the mountain property fairly often. It was agonizing for me, and I'd drive away either utterly depressed, in tears, or both. My heart was broken. I just couldn't *let go* of the lost dream of living in that spectacular spot with my husband. I couldn't accept what had happened. I judged it as bad, which made it hurtful. So much of my energy had been put into its manifestation.

All of these feelings took over while I was up there, leaving me in a terrible emotional state when I left. It just kept the wound raw. Healing was never going to happen until I could truly accept what had happened. I needed to embrace my belief that *everything happens for a reason* and apply it to my dream, which seemed my "mission impossible."

Acceptance was quite a long way away for me. I returned to this glorious spot many more times and left it a beaten mass of negativity with a heart that ached and a wounded soul unable to heal. My fantastic dream morphed into a hideous nightmare. I truly couldn't understand how something that had seemed so meant to be, flowed so easily, been so joyful, and made my heart sing could have ended so disastrously.

My belief that *our thoughts create our reality*, therefore we create our reality, was being deeply challenged. I would *never* have created this. Why would I? I just wouldn't, or couldn't, believe that I had any responsibility for creating the trauma in my current life. I did accept my share of the blame for the loss of our relationship. However, I felt this was his creation, not mine. I couldn't accept responsibility for creating so much hurt and pain for my Self.

LETTING GO

The work on the log house was moving along, but I began to have doubts about the integrity of the builders. I had a hard time getting information from them regarding the outside contractors in case of any future issues. Once they finished the work agreed to, I paid the remainder of the purchase price. Did our relationship change after that!

The real estate agent claimed there was a one-year warranty on all new house construction in North Carolina. I had some things that needed repairs, but my calls were ignored by the builders. People, who appeared so nice and helpful in the beginning, now wouldn't respond at all. The real estate agent wasn't much help either. My mistake had been considering him a friend. I was getting increasingly frustrated with everything involving the log house. No one was being accountable for their actions.

After a couple of months, I decided I needed legal counsel. My realtor referred me to a local attorney. Our meeting lasted for over two hours. Bottom line was I didn't have enough claims against them to make it worth the cost of his legal fees. I felt so defeated. Honesty had lost another battle to disreputable people. I didn't have the financial resources to be able to fight on principle. To this day, I have not met one person who had a good thing to say about these builders.

I walked around with a tremendous weight on my shoulders. My realtor saw how beaten and unhappy I was. I admitted that living in North Carolina with no friends, feeling so alone and abandoned, depressed me. He said that I should list the log house and go back to New Jersey where I belonged. "What if the log house sells first?" I couldn't abandon the mountain property like my husband had. He said I could dictate when I would sell.

My depression was growing. All the trouble with the builders, plus all the frustrations getting things done in the house made me want to run from it. After giving it some thought, I told the realtor to list it. I'd been struggling with the concept of staying in North Carolina for months. It was draining me physically, mentally, emotionally, and most importantly, spiritually. I told anyone who suggested I simply move back home that I couldn't afford to move back to Jersey. I knew my income would cover my expenses in Carolina, which did bring me some peace of mind.

While I couldn't afford to move back to Jersey financially, I couldn't afford to stay in Carolina emotionally. I was a wreck, and I wasn't getting any better. I needed my friends first hand, not just on the phone. It got to the point that I felt leaving this life might be the best option. What brought me back from that thought were my animals. Who would take care of them? What would happen to them? It wouldn't be fair to them.

Many months later, I looked at my reasons for choosing life and noticed that none of them had anything to do with me. The reason I stayed was for others. This was one of the lessons I was trying to teach myself, but still wasn't recognizing. My animals saved me from making a terrible mistake.

The decision to move back to New Jersey was finally about me. I thought it was best for me on all levels. Once I made the decision, my spirit lightened somewhat. The door to the prison that I'd been living in had been unlocked. It wasn't open yet, but unlocked was encouraging.

I was distraught over the lack of accountability I seemed to encounter everywhere along my path. I continually felt disrespected, which had always been a real hot button for me. Once more, another of those spiritual lessons my soul was trying to teach was being completely overlooked. I was too busy looking outside rather than within. I'd always been accountable for my actions. I respected people and animals. Lack of accountability and lack of respect certainly weren't *my* issues.

Many times I'd heard about our shadow self, but I really didn't understand the concept. I felt I was a good person, who lived the right way. My shadow self must be insignificant. It would take me a long time to acknowledge that I did indeed have a shadow self. It can be our greatest teacher, once we recognize and accept its existence. We shouldn't feel guilty about having one, because it's not right or wrong, it simply is.

For now, I'd simply keep ranting and raving about the lack of accountability and respect in my little world and the world in general. I was living within my own blindness. It's all about timing. Eventually, the student would be ready.

Bob and I talked on the phone regarding the property. Every time, he had the same two questions; how is Licorice, and have you heard anything from your lawyer? Apparently, he had no interest in Shadow or me. I really didn't care how he was either, so his disinterest didn't carry any hurt with it. Every time Bob asked about the lawyer, it was like he plunged the knife a little deeper into my heart and twisted. He fanned the embers of my pain each and every time with that question.

Hearing his voice over the phone was bad enough, but then to have him so impatient to be rid of our marriage hurt all the more. Whatever progress I may have made was instantly sent flying backwards with that question. I'd spent many hours trying to figure out what had really happened to us. It still seemed surreal. I felt thrown away.

It just seemed that all I meant to him was someone to run his veterinary business and farm. Once Bob retired and the farm was sold, my usefulness came to an end. I really felt used and abused. I just couldn't believe I hadn't seen or felt this coming. The reality was I hadn't. I had completely missed it. My lack of awareness led to the complete collapse of my self-confidence, which was now almost nonexistent. My self-esteem followed in a downward spiral.

I had worked so hard for 27 years managing the vet office and the horse farm. The motivation behind all of my efforts was always love – love for my husband, and my love for the animals and the land. My job was seven days a week, no holidays off. When you're responsible for animals, and especially other peoples' very valuable animals, you must have competent help. Competent help was hard to obtain, so most of the time I did it myself.

My father always taught me, if you want something done right, do it yourself. I was a good student. It was my choice, and at times it did get old, but I did it. I was *always* accountable for the obligations of my lifestyle choice.

When we took vacations, they were fabulous ones. I was blessed with four *dreams come true*. Dream one was watching the Royal Lipizzaner Stallions perform at the Spanish Riding School in Vienna. Dream two was a two-week safari in Kenya. Dream three was a horse pack trip in Banff, Alberta, Canada. Dream four was swimming with wild dolphins off Oahu, HI. All four realized dreams were profound for me. Each experience left a different and lasting mark on my soul. Each dream was enhanced, because they were experienced with the man I'd chosen to spend my life with. Reliving these dreams made it even harder to accept the reality of my impending divorce.

Of course, my first ever dream come true happened 41 years ago, when I got my first horse at the age of 13. This dream would chart the course of the rest of my life. Until recently, it was a happy and rewarding life, due in large part to the horses' presence in it. You can see why I expect to live the dreams that I dream. I learned as a teenager that miracles do happen, and they happen to me.

After one of Bob's phone calls, I couldn't help questioning the choices I'd made throughout my adult life. It was a life consumed with him: working with, caring for, and loving him. When I made my choices, they were good ones. How could one regret a life that afforded me such wonderful memories?

All the heavy farm work netted me a very bad back, injured left knee, and a left shoulder with more calcium than the sports medicine doctor had ever seen. I accepted the physical consequences of the choices I made. Doing most of the chores myself allowed us the luxury of traveling to exotic destinations, and having some horses of my own. My horses were some of my grandest teachers.

Many times over the recent months, I found myself telling friends that all one can do is make the best choice with the information available at the time. I don't think you can ask anymore of yourself. I still do believe this to be truth. However dissatisfied I was with the recent events of my life, I knew I was doing the best I could with the situation I'd been left with. I was trying to "make lemonade from the lemons of my life." I was trying!

I constantly relived our life together trying to comprehend why Bob preferred to end it. Was our marriage so bad? Was he so unhappy that he'd rather live apart and alone? Apparently he was, and I hadn't noticed. I felt bad about that. We'd been planning the house and property together. We *had* been happy. He *had* been happy.

What happened? When did it change? I couldn't answer the what, but I finally started to piece together enough of the puzzle that I could answer the when. After the farm sold, he started acting strangely, so I imagine whatever happened did so then.

I had so many emotions I was trying to deal with each day: all the ponderings about my failed marriage, the troubles with the builders that weren't accountable, other contractors that were less than competent, and I was having doubts about my realtor friend.

My emotional reactions to anything negative were so exaggerated. I felt a failure and lived in a state of defeat most of the time. I didn't know what I was going to do. My depression was fed with each obstacle that blocked my way. Even though they were relatively small obstacles, they seemed enormous to me.

I challenged myself to find something positive in each day: just one thing. Most days, it was Stormy and the beautiful farm I'd found. Eventually, winter arrived and his training stopped. I was devastated. Now, what would I do? With Stormy in work, I felt productive and purposeful. Without his training, I slid into a deeper depression traveling backwards in the Tunnel.

I discovered the Tunnel wasn't one-way, which was not good. I did manage to stay out of the Abyss thanks to my friends and animals. I struggled to find things to occupy my time each day. I didn't get up nearly as early as on the farm, simply because it made the day that much longer.

Many times on the farm I complained about not having enough time to get all the work done. I looked forward to days when I could get everything done in a day. Now, I sat in the log house longing for those action packed days on the farm. I would trade in an instant. My life had been consumed with *doing* for the first 53 years. I didn't know how to just *be*. It was agony, and the hardest thing I'd ever attempted.

At night, I sat terrified of the next day. I tried to stay busy just to keep my mind from dragging me down the road of nonstop, negative thinking. Each morning, I told the dogs that we were going to have a good day today. I smiled and spoke to them in an upbeat, positive tone, but my heart was just the opposite. I knew they picked up the true energy from my heart, but I tried. I hadn't had a good day since June 21, 2004, and that was the simple truth.

At the end of the day, I felt like I'd done nothing worthwhile, and my life was being wasted. I knew I would never get the time back. I felt so unfulfilled and useless. My entire life had been filled with purpose until recently. I remembered how excited I'd been to discover my communication and healing skills, which I believed was my life's purpose. I recalled how little time I could devote to them in New Jersey.

My obligations seemed unending, and my days on the farm flew by. There always seemed to be something or someone that required my time. I was exhausted from the weight of all the obligations I carried on my shoulders. Now, I had very few responsibilities, but I still felt weighed down. The obligations I had were reduced to those of my animal family and me. One would think I should feel no pressure or weight on my shoulders. It would take me a very long time to recognize that the weight was caused by my reluctance to accept my responsibility to Self.

I hadn't been aware of it until now, but I had put Self behind all else. I'd been totally unaware of me and my needs. I didn't know how to just *be*. It was uncomfortable for me and downright terrifying. *Being* is a state of consciousness. It's something that should come naturally. It simply *is*. In order to *be*, you must stay in the present moment, which was a place I didn't frequent these days. I had strayed so far from my true Self that this natural state was foreign to me.

Being caused me great anxiety, so I worked very hard at finding things to *do*. I was a creature of habit and doing was something I had perfected. What I wouldn't understand, until much later, was that all my doing wasn't going to help me heal from my "dark night of the soul," or emerge from the Tunnel. My doing was not going to teach me the lessons my soul was fighting so hard to get me to see.

My "mission impossible" was to learn to focus on me and be comfortable simply being me. Learning to be with Self would ultimately allow me to fully let go of all that was causing so much pain and hurt. It would prove to be the most difficult of jobs for me.

On our last trip to Hawaii, Bob and I had purchased a timeshare on Maui, which became mine after our divorce. Our first use of it was scheduled for the last half of February. Everything was already paid for, so if I didn't go the money would be lost. Master Michele's mother, Marie, agreed to join me. Maui gave me something to look forward to, but with some apprehension. I'd be in the most romantic place on the face of the earth experiencing my first vacation as a divorcée.

My best friend, Linda, lived in Honolulu, so we'd stay the night with her before flying to Maui. I couldn't wait to see Lin. We'd spent hours on the phone since all my marital troubles began. Linda knew me better than anyone, except for Bob, who was dead to me. We were forever friends from the early 60s. I just had faith that I was supposed to go, I needed to go, I deserved to go, and therefore someone to care of my animal family would appear. I had faith!

Chapter 5

Holiday Heartache

*T*he holidays were fast approaching, which really caused my depression to deepen. My dear friends in New Jersey wanted me home for Thanksgiving and Christmas/New Year's. Their wish was heartwarming, but I couldn't because of my animals. Their love, support, and concern for me during that first holiday alone meant the world to me. I'd been waiting to hear about the date of the divorce hearing. I began to inquire as the end of the year drew closer. It was just another thing that I had no control over that fed my deepening depression.

My Carolina friends, Barbara and Ernie, invited me for Thanksgiving. To get to their home, I had to drive close to the mountain property, which was extraordinarily difficult. Our target date for moving into the Deltec had been Thanksgiving. So, I found myself driving past the mountain heading to someone else's home for it instead.

As I drove past the road that led to the property, I simply burst into tears. Being so close to the place where I should have been spending Thanksgiving ignited the pain of my loss all over again. Not only didn't I have parents for the holidays anymore, I didn't have a husband either. My broken heart ached.

I regrouped before I got to my friends' home, and enjoyed a wonderful time with their family. I really hadn't felt like I'd celebrated a holiday since my folks had died four years earlier. I had hoped the move to our new dream home would allow me to start new holiday traditions. So much for best laid plans.

I drove home utterly depressed from the realization that I would *never* celebrate anything in my gorgeous creation with the heavenly view! How was I ever going to let go of this grief, hurt, loss, pain? How? The answers to those questions continued to elude me.

A week or so later, my brother, Ejay, arrived and got to see the mountain house and property. We had a nice, albeit short, visit. We talked about being alone and having no friends, since he lives the same type of life in Florida. He said it took him a couple of years to acquire some friends in the area. The thought of a couple of years was more than I could deal with in my fragile emotional state.

I told him that I was going to put the house on the market and go back to New Jersey. As he was leaving, he told me I wouldn't have any trouble selling, since this was a really nice house, which gave me a spark of confidence that I had done something *right*.

Shortly after Ejay headed to Florida, the lawyer's secretary called and asked about the best court date for me. I didn't understand why that mattered, since neither of us had to appear. "Aren't you filing for your maiden name?" Yes. "Well, you have to appear to get your name back." I totally lost it. All the anger that was buried deep within found its way to the surface in a heartbeat. It was *my* name, why did I have to appear? Why hadn't the lawyer told me four months ago? She knew I wanted my name back.

I had five animals and no one to stay with them. Her best advice was that I didn't have to appear if I didn't want my name back. I told her in no uncertain terms I wanted my name back! I wasn't going through life with the constant reminder of someone who tossed me aside like a piece of worthless garbage. My married name was something I had no trouble letting go of. I was frantic. I needed someone to take care of my animals, because I *had* to have my name back.

I called Bob to discuss the lawyer's information. Shockingly, he said that he'd take care of everyone if I couldn't find help. I never expected him to offer. I felt a sense of relief tempered by apprehension about his staying in my house.

One of the girls who rode at the farm said she could stay for me. What a blessing. Kelli had taken care of the horses when Kim went on vacation, so I knew she was very reliable. The simple fact that I knew Kelli was reassuring. I contacted my husband and told him that I'd found someone. I kept trying to find out when I had to be in court, so I could coordinate with Kelli. For some reason, life had gotten so hard for me.

LETTING GO

It became apparent that this hearing wasn't happening in 2004, which made me even angrier, since I'd have to organize tax information for someone who had disrespected me so. Finally, they called with a date of January 11, so I could coordinate my trip. I'd be seeing my friends again, which in itself picked up my declining spirits.

The realization that Christmas was just around the corner fueled my already high stress level. Plus, I was coming down with a head cold. I was amazed I hadn't been sick sooner, given the time I spent bathed in my self-created negativity. I was having a hard time finding any holiday spirit. The contrast between the Christmas holidays of the first 53 years of my life and the one approaching was staggering.

I began writing my Christmas Letter, which was an exceptionally emotional task. I wanted to just forget about it, but I couldn't. It wouldn't be fair to all my friends, who always looked forward to it. I knew they'd all be waiting to hear how our new adventure was going. I cried and cried as I wrote about my news. I worked very hard to not sound too morose. I didn't want to elicit pity. I just wanted to inform them of my situation and give them my new contact information.

The response to my letter was astonishing and unexpected. I received calls and heartfelt notes expressing concern, support, love, and best wishes for my future. I will never forget them. They meant the world to me. It was awesome and heartwarming.

As Christmas drew closer, I began to receive gifts from my dear friends. With each one that arrived, I was filled with a sense of being cared for and not forgotten. Each gift made me feel less isolated and alone at a time of year that is renowned for having that affect on single people. They eased my depression, which was invaluable to me.

One of my biggest surprises occurred when a good friend, Alice, asked if I'd like a visitor. I was thrilled at the thought of company, so she got flights for between Christmas and New Years. I had a very special gift to look forward to.

I did enjoy finding gifts for my dear friends, who'd been so instrumental to my survival. While shopping at Hallmark, I found a little plate that read, "Sometimes on the way to a dream, you get lost, and find a better one!" I so needed to believe it to be true. It sits on my dining table, and I read it everyday. I'm starting to be able to believe it might be true, but that *better one* is nowhere in my sights yet. Once I can truly embrace it as Truth, then the better one will appear in no time. For now, I read it and have faith.

Holiday Heartache

I decided to put up a few Christmas decorations. I was trying not to let my depression win. I was in no emotional state to put up my tree. I have a fabulous ornament collection that was started by my mother in the early 70s. I've added to it while vacationing around the world. Each ornament holds a memory for me, and my emotions were too raw to withstand unpacking my collection. They would have to wait till I was much stronger.

After living in the house for a few months, I began to question my water source. The spring on the mountain property needed no filter. The log house did and after changing it every three weeks, I knew something wasn't kosher. It was a community spring shared with three other log houses. I called my neighbors and told them I thought we had a problem.

I called Jerry, who'd installed the Creston spring. He came over, assessed our situation, and gave me the bad news. We shouldn't even be using this as a source of water. Great, I thought; the builder from Hell strikes again. Jerry recommended a well shared by two houses. I showed my neighbor, Mitchell, what Jerry found and that he could improve the water quality with some work on it. Mitchell contacted the other two homeowners with the information. It was inconceivable that this spring could have passed inspection for a CO – certificate of occupancy. I was right about that. Apparently, there wasn't a requirement to test the water, which was another very expensive assumption by me.

I also needed to fence an area for the dogs. While we weren't close to the main road, their old age had robbed them of their hearing. Shadow was almost totally deaf and his brother Licorice's hearing was suspect. When it was dark, it was impossible to see the black one, and I didn't want it to be a concern for whoever was caring for them in my absence.

I'm not a big fan of fences and cages, but I found myself in a situation that really necessitated a fence. I researched the Internet and found a fence that appeared to be just what I needed. It would install easily and not be too noticeable. I ordered a kit to ship right away. It was expensive, but it was safe. I needed to feel that my dogs would be secure.

Kelli called. She couldn't take care of my family. Does no one do what he or she says they will? Is no one responsible? I tried to sound understanding on the phone, which was very hard, since I flew into fear as we spoke. It was so intense that I felt nauseous.

As soon as I hung up, I broke into hysterical tears. I was sobbing uncontrollably with my worried dogs at my side. Well, I had no control over my reaction. I couldn't stop crying. I had to be in court. It couldn't be changed. I had to get my name back. I *had* to. I couldn't breathe. All of a sudden, some part of me took control. I stopped my crying, took a deep breath, and started up the stairs to deal with my crisis.

The phone rang and it was little Michelle. It was uncanny how many times we've called each other at critical moments. Michelle had been dealing with her husband's cancer since before we moved. She'd been a rock for me ever since my tragic story began. How does she always know? Was it coincidence – hardly; synchronicity – definitely; telepathy – absolutely.

I burst into tears when I heard Michelle's voice, and was unable to say anything understandable. The whole incident brought my sense of isolation and loneliness to the forefront. I was so far from everyone. I was all alone. I had to deal with everything alone. I hated it. I didn't choose this. Get over it. Deal with it.

All I kept hearing Michelle say was calm down. Calm down! What's wrong? I slowly gained some semblance of control and began to tell her my problem. After we talked for a while, I was in a much less emotional state. My panic had lessened, so I was able to cope, to think, and to act.

I emailed Bob that I'd need him to stay with the dogs and cats. I was totally unprepared for his answer. He wouldn't be able to come back, because of back and neck pain. His message ended with – good luck. I was enraged. Back and neck pain – is he kidding? I'd dealt with pain daily for the past 30 years. I simply couldn't believe the lack of accountability.

My panic returned along with anger at my soon to be ex-husband. His response just screamed, "I don't care about you!" I really thought I'd gotten this idea by now, but I obviously hadn't. I wasn't able to fully let go of the identity of being his wife. Perhaps, it would be easier to let go once the divorce was final. Our relationship ended long before our court date, so I'd felt divorced for almost six months already.

His indifferent reply to my request for help did send the message home. I'd never again confuse this man with the one I'd spent more than half my life with. I may be slow, but I did get it that day. I finally *let go* of him. I had to find a way to get my name back. I wouldn't be branded for life with his name. No way! I'd let go of the name *and* the man – mentally, emotionally, and spiritually. Now, I just needed to go through the process of letting go legally.

I was at the bank visiting with my friend, Carolyn. I was telling her about my recent dilemma, and she thought she knew a young gal that might be interested. She knew her from her church and felt her to be quite reliable. Carolyn's friend, Jodi, called me and sounded interested, so we arranged to meet at my house. I wanted to see how she'd be with my dogs.

I liked her immediately as did my dogs. They were always a good judge of character. I explained that I'd be installing some fencing off the side of the house, so she wouldn't have any trouble when she let them out. Jodi liked the sound of that.

Jodi would go to her regular job during the week. At lunchtime, she'd come home to let the dogs out and stay with them a little. It wasn't an ideal situation, but I felt they would be fine. I would make it to the divorce hearing. I was supposed to have my name back.

My prayers had been answered and in the most unlikely way. I was trying to learn to let go of having to figure out everything myself. Since I wasn't having much success anyway, why not let go and let some other power work things out? I had embraced the belief of a higher power, years earlier, through my healing work with the animals. I didn't question that anymore, but I felt I'd lost its influence in my life, for what reason I didn't know. I had lost faith in it and in myself.

I was trying to embrace that faith, and let something far greater and wiser than I bring my life back to a place of harmony and balance. With Jodi's appearance, I began to rekindle my sense of faith that *everything happens for a reason* and *for our highest good*. These Truths would prove to be the keys to my healing, my transformation, and my emergence from the Tunnel.

On Christmas day, I didn't want to sit home alone feeling sorry for myself, so I went to the movies. This was something entirely new for me on Christmas. My Christmases had been spent with my family. My mother loved the holidays and decorated our home beautifully each Yule season. It was always a proverbial winter wonderland. Each holiday centered on a wonderful meal, which they worked so hard to prepare.

My mind is jam-packed with fabulous holiday memories. My critters were all that was left of my family now. I was working at getting through the day, and the holiday season, as best I could. For two hours that day, I forgot about all my problems and was treated to a gift from my Self. Then, the season was over and I had survived.

New Year's had never been a big deal for me, so I really didn't look forward to it with any apprehension. When you have a farm full of horses, who don't know Thanksgiving from Christmas from the New Year, you celebrate in a different manner than the rest of the world. A week and a half after New Year's Day, I'd be in New Jersey with my dear friends and in-laws with the hope that this New Year would be a much better one for all of us.

LETTING GO

My landscaping jobs were getting done in fits and starts, as my mother would've said. I still hadn't received the fencing for the dogs, so I called. The company couldn't find the order. Are you kidding? Luckily, I'd printed a copy of it. I explained my dilemma that I had to leave in two weeks for a divorce hearing. I *had* to have it installed before I left.

The gal placed the order again and assured me it would arrive in plenty of time. I tried to understand why these things kept happening to me. I'd never experienced so many screw-ups in my entire life. What was going on? I was still looking in the wrong place to find the answer. I was still looking outside Self.

I was looking forward to Alice's visit – my first official guest. I'd met her and her husband Roger on a four-day whale-watching trip in Maine. We discovered that we lived about three miles apart, but it took a common passion for whales to meet. We actually saw thousands of whales of many different species, while surviving a night in gale force winds. It had been quite a memorable adventure. Out of those shared memories, a friendship was forged.

Alice's visit meant the world to me. She'd already experienced the deep sense of grief and loss I felt. Twelve years earlier, Roger died of cancer in his mid 40s. It had been a tremendously difficult time for her. When we went to dinner a year after his death, Alice shared that of the hundreds of people at his memorial service, we were amongst a handful that had kept in touch. I sat there stunned when I heard this. I think the fact that I showed concern and support years earlier was coming back to me now. It's funny how everything's connected throughout time. *What goes around comes around... .*

Since Alice had known us both for so long, her feelings about my situation held great weight for me. The thing I was most surprised at was her anger towards Bob. Alice felt betrayed and hurt as well. She knew Roger would have been appalled by the situation. Roger was one of the most wonderful people I've ever met. The more I got to know him, the more I recognized that Roger was an "old soul." Roger set a wonderful example of how to live one's life. I felt blessed that I had the opportunity to know him and spend time with him before he died.

Alice and I spent a lot of time talking about loss, grief, etc. While Roger had died in the physical, my husband had died – for me – emotionally and spiritually, but it was a loss no less traumatic for me. Knowing her story, I listened to Alice's thoughts and ideas with keen interest. She recalled Bob's enthusiasm for the house and property at our farewell party.

I brought Alice to the Deltec and my mountain. I wanted her to experience this extraordinary spot. I was happy to share something with her that had meant so much to me. Being on the mountain and feeling the serenity of the place made it easier for Alice to understand my deep sense of lost expectations. I was so appreciative of her caring support.

I drove Alice to the airport on New Year's Eve a much stronger woman than I was when I picked her up. I will be forever grateful to Alice for dropping her life to console a friend in need. One of my favorite quotes is, "A true friend is someone who reaches for your hand, and touches your heart!" I had just dropped a True Friend off at the airport. Alice had touched my stone cold heart with her generosity of spirit. She will never know how much her visit meant to me. She renewed my spirit.

Jerry repaired the spring while Alice was visiting. While I wasn't pleased about the timing of the work, it was such a pleasant change to have someone to share the frustrations that arose. Again, *everything happens for a reason*. It turned out to be a far bigger job than anticipated. Jerry did the best he could given the situation, and I couldn't ask for more than that. I ended the year with a much improved water source, and hopes that the New Year would bring a change for the better for my life.

Our realtor listing was up at the end of the year. I really hadn't focused on the marketing of the mountain property at all. I told myself it was because I was too involved with the log house. Truth be told, the reason went deeper than that. I hadn't, wouldn't, couldn't let go of my dream. Unconsciously, I couldn't go there, because the hurt was too intense, so I simply lived in denial.

My exasperation over the log house and its builders forced me to take another look at my realtor friend, whose performance had been less than acceptable. Before I committed to a change, I visited his website to check the listing on the mountain property and was stunned. I saw the original picture of the Deltec from July, with the exterior unfinished, staring back at me. I'd sent new pictures, as soon as it was completed, in early August. I was appalled at his obvious lack of attention to our property.

I needed to become more *accountable* for how the property was being handled. I had to let go, so that someone else could purchase it. I committed myself to selling the two North Carolina properties and returning to New Jersey, where I felt I would be nurtured and healed amongst my wonderful friends and in-laws.

The New Year began without much ado for me. A few days into it, little Michelle received some terrible news. After months of chemotherapy, her husband's CT scan showed his melanoma cancer had metastasized to his lung. We were devastated. Surgery was scheduled for a couple of weeks later. Cancer is horrible for anyone and their family, but Mike wasn't even 50 years old. It just seemed extra cruel in someone that young, no different than with Roger. When you're as close to someone as I am to Michelle, it's like the tragedy has happened to you as well.

More tragedy struck the same week, when Master Michele and David's wonderful Golden Retriever, Logan, lost his battle with cancer. I would truly miss his energy in my home away from home in New Jersey. They'd spent a fortune and bought Logan five good months. The hole he left in their hearts and lives would take a long time to fill. He was a very special soul, and we were all privileged to have known him. It seemed like everyone I knew was dealing with loss, grief, and much sadness.

As for a better year, so far 2006 pretty much sucked. I used the time before I left for my divorce hearing to meet with some realtors. With the emergence of a New Year, my business focus was back. I was ready to undertake the mission of selling my dream. It was my reality, whether I accepted it or not. I needed to realize and accept the notion that it was neither *right* nor *wrong*, it simply *was*. While I was starting to recognize it as reality, I was a very long way from understanding and accepting it.

I still hadn't received the fencing, which created panic in me. The frustrations involved with this log house were taking its toll on my sanity. It was one thing to have issues with the house, but the fencing involved my dogs' safety. Finally, I arrived home to find a delivery from the fencing company. I breathed a sigh of relief, since I had to leave in two days. My relief was short lived, because the delivery was incomplete. I called the landscaper and told him I had some of the fencing, but not all. I went into town for posts, so it could be installed the next day – the day I had to leave.

I was so upset, I couldn't think straight. I'd deal with the company when I got back. I was very uncomfortable leaving without the fence installed, but I had no other option. Fate had orchestrated it that way for whatever reason. It was out of my control like the rest of my life. It wasn't installed to my liking, but the dogs were safe and Jodi was happy, which were my primary goals.

This was the first time I'd left the dogs since moving into the log house. When they looked at me with those questioning eyes, my heart shattered. I knew the feelings of abandonment that their eyes reflected. I'd felt that continuously over the past many months. I drove away from the house in tears. They'd been my constant companions, my source of unconditional love, and my angels without wings.

After I cried myself out, I began to focus on my friends. I didn't think about the court hearing, which I'd been waiting almost six months for. I wasn't looking forward to it, even though I wanted to get past it.

I stayed with one of my oldest friends, Pam. We'd ridden horses at the same farm when I was a kid. Pam had been a real support through these difficult months. Recently her adorable mini schnauzer, Wil, had been diagnosed with diabetes. What is going on with all these dog breeds and serious diseases? Pam would do whatever Wil needed. She used the same animal hospital that had treated Logan. We joked that each of my friends owned a wing in their new state-of-the-art clinic.

Pam was concerned about who would care for Wil if something happened to her. She didn't know who would cope with his daily injections, diet constraints, and frequent urination issues, which were all ramifications of his diabetes. I told her I would, no problem. She was thrilled and relieved. So, I became a divorcée and Wil's godmother. I was happy to commit to this wonderful little soul. He'd been Pam's salvation through nine years of the trauma and drama of her life, which was no different than my boys were for me.

I made the rounds of visiting everyone during meals... the great American pastime. Everyone was so supportive, especially my in-laws, Vince and Gloria. Their love and support through this time of conflict with my husband meant so much to me. I had dinners with Gary and Kit and Peter and Amy. Everyone was concerned about my emotional state, given the reason for my visit.

I assured them all I was fine. Their concern made me feel loved. It was wonderful to see all my special friends again, especially Michelle, whose husband was anticipating surgery in a couple of weeks. Michelle was coming to the divorce hearing with me, since she didn't want me to go alone. Because of Mike's medical appointments, she ended up working the day of the hearing. I told her not to worry. It was no big deal.

I spent time with Master Michele, David, and Michele's mother, Marie, who'd just lost Logan. They were dealing with the huge hole he created in their hearts with his death. If there was anyone who understood the pain of loss, it was "yours truly." I was just happy to support them as they had me for all this time.

I met another friend, Melissa, for breakfast at Perkins Family Restaurant, where little Michelle worked as a manager. Melissa had worked for us on the farm forever ago. She asked if I was going to the hearing alone. Michelle confessed that she'd canceled on me. Melissa said she'd join me and Michelle was so relieved. From her sigh of relief, I realized how worried Michelle was about me going alone. What was the dig deal? I certainly didn't see it, but if they were happy... .

Once again, the Universe worked in *perfection*. I'd been distracting myself from the divorce hearing with all my *doing*. When it finally arrived, I had to focus on it. It turned out to be much more emotional than I had expected. It was wonderful to have Melissa by my side. I was so grateful she'd made the effort. There is a method to the madness, even if we don't see it as it's unfolding.

I was struck by how quickly it was all over. A 27-year marriage dissolved in less than half an hour. I was once again, Nancy *Kaiser*. It felt good. I was proud of the name and the family that it represented. It took me weeks to get used to saying and writing it. I couldn't believe how foreign it felt to write it. Old habits die hard, I guess. It required an inordinate amount of work changing everything, but it was worth the time and effort. I would never give up my name again. I know, never say never. But I did, and do still, say *never*!

I had planned on having all of my close friends join me at one of my parent's favorite, fancy restaurants for a divorce celebration. I was trying to make it a positive event and not focus on the negative aspects of it. Because little Michelle had to work that day, I changed the location to Perkins. It wasn't as fancy, but I wanted to include her. The *who* was far more important than the *where*.

Everyone was so encouraging and supportive. I felt so loved. We laughed and shared, while they helped make the most difficult day in my life easier. Again, in perfection, it was a blessing that the divorce had to be filed in New Jersey, and that I had to appear at the hearing. Those reasons guaranteed that I'd go through the trauma with people who truly cared about me.

After we finished our celebration, I headed back to North Carolina. A short while into my trip, I broke out into uncontrollable tears. The realization that I was now divorced, and what that concept meant to me, was overwhelming. Once again, I felt a failure, alone, and a defeated woman. I never believed I would *ever* be divorced. I can't say I hadn't thought of it over the years, during our rough times, but actually get divorced... never. Hadn't I heard that before? What was it? Never say never!

Chapter 6

A Divorcée

I was anxious to see my dogs, but not to be back in the log house. I didn't realize how emotional the hearing would be. I was exhausted as I arrived back in North Carolina. I tried to get my new driver's license on my way through town, but found out I had to change my name with Social Security first.

It was so good to see the dogs. Jodi had taken wonderful care of them. I gathered them and headed off to the Social Security office, an hour away. I wanted to get things changed over as quickly as possible. Although I wouldn't need my passport for Hawaii, I'd feel more secure with one. This was my new project, so I might as well get started.

I called all the credit card companies, insurance companies, mortgage company, Ford credit, brokerage firms, bank, etc. I felt a great sense of accomplishment when it was all done. It is something I will never have to do again. Read my lips: never! All the name change stuff helped to fill my days, but at night I struggled with being a divorcée. It was a word I'd heard many times in my life, but now I was learning the significance of it in my life.

All my feelings of failure and defeat were resurrected. The could'ves, should'ves, would'ves, and what-ifs began again. Intense feelings of abandonment, isolation, and loneliness consumed me. I fought to stay positive and be grateful for all that I had.

The day after Christmas, on the other side of the globe, a tsunami had taken hundreds of thousands of lives and left devastation that was unprecedented in my lifetime. I reminded myself of this terrible disaster and used it to give me perspective on my little, personal disaster. My troubles paled in comparison.

I chastised myself for feeling sorry for myself. After all, I had a warm home, fabulous friends, a supportive family, a wonderful animal family, good health, and an income that met my expenses. In the scheme of things, I was truly blessed.

What I lacked was a husband, which robbed me of feeling loved by that special someone. It amazed me how this one thing caused such a negative impact on my life. I let it taint my life for a long time by giving my power away to it. I allowed it to totally negate all of the blessings in my life shame on me.

I couldn't take back my power until I began to understand and accept exactly what brought me to this place. I wouldn't heal until I learned to let go of equating divorce with personal failure and let go of the pain of being abandoned and alone. I had to let go of the fear! I hadn't a clue how to *let go*.

For whatever reason, it was easier to hold onto all these emotions that brought me such hurt and pain. Healing would never come if I didn't let go of feeling solely responsible for my failed marriage. I had to stop judging the choices and actions of my life. I had to accept that my divorce wasn't good or bad, right or wrong, it just *was*. Sounds simple, doesn't it? Ha! This acceptance, this letting go of personal blame and guilt, is the most difficult thing I've ever done.

What I didn't realize was that until I accepted that my soul had created my life situation, I'd never be able to move forward. My lack of acceptance delayed my healing. At the time, this awareness was hidden from me by my unrelenting ego, which kept me busy with destructive thoughts drenched in judgments that were rooted in my illusion of being *the responsible one*.

Along with the chore of changing my name, I also met with a Re/Max agency about listing the mountain property. A retired CEO from New York City, whose expertise was marketing, owned the agency. This fact, along with their presentation, convinced me that they would be the best group to market my dream. They agreed that an artist's rendering of the house would be a good marketing tool. I'd suggested this idea seven months earlier to the first realtor, but he blew me off.

I contacted an artist they recommended and got current pictures of the Deltec to him. He promised the rendering by the end of February. I'd be away in Hawaii, so they would have to follow up with the artist. They told me: no problem; that's what we're here for. I had finally found someone that would do the national advertising, which was essential. I had great hopes... .

I went to see Stormy a couple of times a week. I always felt better after time on the farm, where I escaped the depressing rest of my life. While I was with Stormy, I didn't let anything else interfere. I got absorbed into the energy of the place. Stormy and the farm renewed me every time.

Many times on the farm, I'd look around the immaculate 33 acres and just smile, because I didn't have to do anything to make it look that way. I just felt blessed to be at such a perfect farm, and told myself how much I deserved this. I perceived it as payback for all the hours, days, months, and years that I toiled caring for horses. I gave myself credit for a job well done, something I didn't do that often. I was rewarding Self. My work with horses was a resounding success in my life in direct contrast to my failed marriage.

Just before I'd left for New Jersey, I'd seen a dermatologist, who removed several lesions on my back and hand. Due to the results, he wanted to remove an additional area. The biopsies came back with differing levels of precursors to the dreaded melanoma. The dermatologist felt I had a genetic predisposition to melanoma.

Because I'm fair skinned, blonde, and very sun-sensitive I figured I was prone to skin cancer. To hear about a genetic component really shook me. When I asked further, he told me that normal people have a 1:42 chance for melanoma. I had a 1:8 or something like that. He definitely got my attention.

I felt blessed to have been made aware of the lesions' presence. I didn't dare tell Michelle what the results were. She would have lost it. Her life had been taken over by Mike's melanoma. She didn't need to fret about anyone else. Knowledge is a powerful tool if we use it. This was a real eye-opener for me.

I learned from my folks' cancers the value of screening tests. Their cancers were too advanced by the time they expressed symptoms. They taught me then, and this experience has taught me further, about safeguarding our health. It is the most important thing we have. I'd just taken good care of my physical health. I had to work harder on my mental, emotional, and spiritual health, which are far harder to heal. This was a very important lesson I was learning.

I tried to read, but still couldn't focus. I bought a couple of books hoping that the right one would kick-start my ability to read. One was by Debbie Ford on shadow work. She'd written the book on divorce that encouraged me early on. I also purchased a book that called to me: *The Power of Now*, by Eckhardt Tolle. You can imagine my disappointment when I couldn't keep my attention on them. I knew they both dealt with important subjects for me, but the time wasn't right just yet.

LETTING GO

Another thing I learned through this period was the affect of music on me. When I wasn't being distracted by television, I'd have music playing. I simply couldn't stand the silence. My ego would really take off in it. Whereas in the past I'd learned the value of silence through meditation, I had lost the ability to exist in the silence.

Different songs had different effects on me. I'd listen to a song one day and would be fine, then a few days later that same song created tears. I just never knew what to expect. I discovered that I did better listening to the oldies station. These songs carried me way back before my relationship with my Ex. They brought me back to the days of high school and horse showing. My mind traveled to happy days with my folks in my life, and I felt whole again.

In late January, we had five inches of snow with sleet on top. It took almost two weeks for the snow to clear from my drive and property. I kept my car at the top of the drive for 11 days until I dared bring it down to the house. Just walking up and down with groceries was a danger.

I'd voiced my concerns about the road and drive in winter, but my realtor friend assured me the access would be fine. I was furious with the realtor, who'd obviously lied and deceived me. Once again, I felt betrayed and disrespected by a friend. The realtor ignored my emails joining my ever-growing list of people who weren't accountable. Why does this keep happening? It's time for it to stop.

As I slipped and slid my way up and down the steep driveway, I decided to report the realtor to the North Carolina Real Estate Commission to help the next person. He was no better than the builders from Hell, who I also contemplated reporting to some authority.

I also had to call the fence company before I left for Maui. They surprised me and said I could return everything. They were very apologetic about their poor performance. It wasn't the response I was anticipating. The gal was very nice and told me to call when I was ready for them to issue a pick-up tag.

I continued to marvel at how difficult *everything* seemed to be for me. I'd never experienced so many frustrations in my life. They were overwhelming and exhausting. Every time I thought they'd stopped, something else would rear its ugly head. I was used to being exhausted from all the farm, hospital, and vet office work. Interestingly, I was just as tired, or maybe more so, in Carolina.

This exhaustion was strictly mental/emotional. For me, this emotional work was far worse. With a good night's sleep back on the farm, I'd be good to go the next morning. In Carolina, I didn't seem to benefit from my night's rest. I felt tired and weighed down all the time, which was oppressive. I was simply in the dark about why, since I kept looking outside of Self for the culprit(s).

My nights before leaving for Maui were consumed with thoughts about my Past. I hadn't focused on my Past lately, but the divorce hearing sent me hurtling back. Up until now, my ego attacked me with my fearful, uncertain Future. Now, it was beating me up with painful doubts about my Past and the choices I'd made.

After reviewing so many of the *bad* times (there's that old judgment again) I felt that the only way I could justify more than half of my life was to fully embrace my belief that *everything happens for a reason* and *for my highest good*. This was imperative. I had to believe that I met this man and fell in love, worked side-by-side for 27 years, moved to North Carolina, and was now divorced and alone, all for *my highest good*. Now, there was a challenge for me to reconcile and embrace!

Although I was consumed with the mundane issues, they didn't keep me from pondering the fact that I was a divorcée. I would watch TV at night and fall into a terrible mind game regarding the situation I was in. I sat thinking about the times when, in anger or frustration, I pondered divorce. When you've been married as long as we had, you have times when the thought crosses your mind. It wasn't anything I thought of as an acceptable solution.

I'd always felt that our love was strong enough to override the disappointment and anger. It always had for me. I blamed myself for giving up the fight for the storybook marriage. I hate fighting, although I'm sure my Ex would tell you otherwise. When I began to realize that the arguments weren't eliciting any positive effects, I stopped.

The most difficult change in my husband was his increased attraction to organized religion. I had an aversion to religion, religious people, and churches. For years, I never understood why. I just knew how I felt and it was strong. As I opened to my spiritual path through my communication work with the animals, I realized that my intense dislike of anything religious had to do with my soul's past lives. I realized I'd been stoned, burned, brutalized, yes, even crucified in the name of religion in many of my past lives. So, you can see my dilemma.

I know my relationship with Bob changed in response to his ever-increasing interest in religion. Over time, it became the main focus of his life. In our wedding vows, we promised not to prevent one another from changing, but to grow with those changes. I had reread our vows a number of times looking for the strength and understanding to get through the hard times.

I must admit there were difficult times, but there were so many more wonderful times. I thought we'd been blessed with our lives together. We had a mutual love of horses and so much in common, despite the fact that he became more religious as

I awakened to my spiritual path. We spent most of our time focused on a common goal, which was running his veterinary practice, equine hospital, and farm. Who could ask for more? The *good* far outweighed the *bad* as far as I was concerned.

Maybe I wasn't looking at our life realistically; perhaps that was my mistake. I know it's one I'll never make again. Of course, there aren't any mistakes, only opportunities for learning. This was by far the hardest learning I'd ever done – and am still doing. For someone who graduated easily with a pharmaceutical degree, I am dumbfounded by my inability to figure out my own life.

Depending on the moment, I vacillated between feeling guilty that I gave up the fight long ago, and wondering if I should have given more credence to my thoughts of divorce. What I never wavered on was my right to feel the way I did towards religion. It was a viewpoint rooted in the traumatic cellular memories of excruciatingly horrible deaths. My inability to let go of my intense negative emotions towards religious people gave me such a feeling of defeat. In the heat of an argument I'd ask my husband, don't you think I want to be able to embrace religion? It would've made my life so much easier. It was an overpowering emotion, which I had no control over. So, I allowed him his beliefs and asked in return that he not try to change me. If he had tried, I would have been a divorcée years ago.

My awakening led me towards a path of non-judgment of Self and others, away from fear and worry, and towards love and acceptance. My husband's Born Again Christian path fed into nothing but judgment and fear. His religion was based on a God that judged and dictated a way of living based on fear of retribution. It was based in separation. If you weren't Christian, you went to Hell, no exceptions.

Just as I didn't want him to change me, I shouldn't change him. Our souls were obviously on differing paths. I tried to figure out why we'd been brought together, because as our beliefs strengthened, our differences seemed to separate us. I had let go of the idea that we would ever be able to compromise our differences on these religious/spiritual issues.

The other area that created stress was his four children from his first marriage. I was not, nor ever would be, a kid person. It just wasn't my nature. Once again, neither right nor wrong, just who I was. I began to recognize a pattern he had involving relationships. He was very intense at the start of a relationship and then cooled off over time, which took a long time for me to recognize.

The damage done to me by this behavior was devastating. His infatuation with me cooled off long before mine did with him. I couldn't understand why I was no longer *the* most important person in his life, since he was in mine. Our passionate infatuation created a terrible co-dependency issue for me. Of course, it would take me quite some time to realize I had an issue. Hindsight is 20/20, and all that.

Over time, this created within me a feeling of competition for his attention. Another of his traits that fueled the problem was his inability to focus on more than one thing at a time. His one-track mind made me feel like extra baggage on family vacations. After a number of failed attempts, I stopped going. My co-dependency made being apart from him torture, but feeling ignored was worse than staying home alone. I confessed how his inability to focus on more than just his kids made me feel, so I wouldn't go anymore.

I'm a firm believer than you cannot affect a long-term change in a person's basic character; i.e., my lack of need for children, my ever-growing spiritual interests, his one-track mind, his diminishing interest in relationships, and his obsession with religion. So, he spent vacations with his kids without me.

My husband's mother had been divorced when he was very young. His biological father had hardly anything to do with him. I knew the guilt that my husband felt over his first divorce. Guilt combined with having been abandoned by his biological father fueled his need to prove to his kids that he wasn't going to repeat the pattern. In reality, he was trying to prove it to himself. It was as if nothing he did was ever enough. I felt sorry that he never seemed to satisfy himself.

It took years to recognize his behavioral patterns that caused me such heartache. The painful memory surrounding the last time I can honestly say I made love to my husband still burns in my mind, and even more in my heart. That vivid memory is one of emotional pain. The physical pain I experienced subsided quickly. The emotional pain I experienced lives in my heart and will until I can resolve the issues behind it.

The beautiful feelings created by our intense intimacy were totally obliterated when my husband went to church immediately afterwards. I lay in bed, in utter disbelief and confusion, that he'd rather spend time with other people. Moments before, I had felt so loved, so special, and so needed. When he left, I felt abandoned and defeated. I deduced that I ranked below church on his list of import. I knew his children were number one.

My self-esteem plummeted. Within minutes my ecstasy turned into terrible heartache and pain. I experienced what I had read about in *The Prophet*, by Kahil Gibran concerning joy and sorrow, and it happened in an instant. I felt so alone and abandoned. I decided I'd never be hurt that deeply ever again. He never knew the effect his choice had on my intimacy issues until years later.

We had sex again, but I never "made love" again. After that afternoon, I no longer felt the ecstasy of making love, which would negate the physical pain I experienced. After that afternoon, there never was anything more than physical pain. I simply tried to fulfill some fantasy of a wife's obligation in the bedroom. I know I'm not the only one who has been misled by this foolish concept.

Eventually, I confessed my feelings to my husband. I'm sure it came up during one of our discussions regarding *my* sexual deficiencies. Back in the day, I was flooded with guilt over my intimacy issues. He told me he'd been thrilled with our love making that afternoon. I asked why he went to church. I was stopped cold by his response. I can still hear it to this day. He wanted to thank God for what we'd just shared.

After I recovered from my shock, I murmured that he should have thanked me. I never have understood why religious people feel they have to be in a church in order to reach out to their Creator. He could have given thanks no matter what his location. It was a lame excuse. His rushing off to church simply left me feeling used and hurt. His explanation just added to my declining self-esteem. My heart was broken in more ways than one.

I'd begun to build a wall of protection around my heart to keep from being continually hurt. The problem with this tactic was that it not only walled things out, but it walled things in. It diminished my ability to feel. I didn't do it consciously; instead it was a subconscious, self-preservation technique. Unknowingly, I'd built a substantial wall, which was completed with that hurtful experience. It proved to be a costly afternoon for us both.

We never felt that ecstasy together again. I judged my husband's choice that night as wrong. He'd made a choice, which I rebutted with a judgment. Choice followed by judgment robbed us of the most treasured moments spent between two souls in love.

Years later, after I stopped beating myself up over my sexual inadequacies, I recognized my husband's dysfunction. He was always surprised when I'd speak about the physical pain I endured for him. Once I discovered the wall's existence, I tried to dismantle it with the help of several spiritual healers. Each had different techniques that they offered. The Berlin Wall came down more easily.

I didn't have much success with the different healers, because nobody can heal you, except yourself. I was looking for healing from outside instead of within. I didn't seek help from my own soul, which is where true healing is generated. I didn't know this back then, but the recent drama of my life has taught this lesson. No one else can do the work for me, or you.

In order to combat the pain of his abandonment, I fortified the wall into an impenetrable fortress. I do believe it offered me some insulation against the full strength of the emotions of my divorce, which was a good thing. I don't think I would have survived the trauma of my break-up if I had to feel more pain than I did. So, *everything does happen for a reason.*

I'd taken advantage of a myriad of methods and techniques, which had short-term effects. To truly heal, I have to discover and resolve the issues behind and underneath my wounds. I am responsible for their creation. I built the fortress and only I can demolish it. Until I can embrace this idea, I won't heal. It's crucial for me to understand the reasons why I've created these wounds. It's all about learning the lessons my soul is trying to teach me.

My willingness to walk the path is what will allow me to heal, to move out of the Abyss and the Tunnel, and to move on with my life. Since we are all One, the same applies to anyone on the road of healing wounds of any nature. We travel the road individually, and together. It's really not about the destination, but the journey along the way.

Although I recognized the motives behind my husband's behavior, it didn't make it any less hurtful. I tried to accept his actions without judgment, but unsuccessfully. His behavior wasn't right or wrong, it just was. It has taken me years of effort to become nonjudgmental, and I'm not truly there yet.

His one-track focus on his kids continued to make me feel like I was insignificant to him. I spent years trying to understand why his feelings for me changed so much. I tried my best to do what I thought was best for us. I worked ceaselessly in our business. I took on more responsibilities than I ever should have trying to lighten his load with love as my motivator.

I never understood why I could do everything else in my life well, except get my husband to feel like he used to about me. My marriage was the most important thing in my life, and I couldn't make it perfect no matter how hard I tried. I have no regrets, because my intent was from my heart. Obviously, my best efforts weren't enough, or right, as far as he was concerned. If they had been, we wouldn't be living apart now.

These were the thoughts I struggled with every night in the log house with my dogs around me. I have come to realize that it wasn't only about me or my failure to provide whatever he felt was lacking in our relationship. After every argument, I asked him to help me deal with what I thought was my dysfunction in order to avert any future problems. He always agreed, but then never did what I suggested would help me, so the cycle continued.

It took me forever to stop feeling so dysfunctional and guilty about these issues. My waning self-esteem added additional negative energy to the conflict over these destructive issues for us. Feeling like I was in a competition was a dysfunction on my part. It was neither right nor wrong, it just was, like his one-track mind.

During all the years, and tears, of living with these issues, I existed within the realm of judgment. Judgment fueled the fires of hurt, guilt, and blame. Remove the judgment and the pain evaporates. Sounds easy, doesn't it? Like learning to let go, which is another one of the hardest lessons to grasp. I have recognized the lesson. The trick now is to accept and embrace it. Once achieved, I will be able to let go of the all the anger and pain and continue further through the Tunnel down my road to healing.

The past was packed with lessons that had been missed, simply because the student wasn't ready. My current situation was providing the perfect time for them. My challenge was to embrace my belief that *all is truly in perfection* in the Universe, and allow it to unfold in its perfection. I stopped questioning my past decisions, because I knew I had followed my heart, which had never let me down before. I just went on faith that it wasn't doing that now, nor would it in the future.

The problem that loomed largest for me was that I still couldn't *feel*. My heart had been broken by the dissolution of our relationship. To survive my pain and grief, I completed the fortress, which surrounded my heart with walls high and thick enough that even I couldn't feel my heart.

My guidance system was down. How was I going to *know* if I couldn't *feel*? I couldn't learn if I couldn't *know*. I couldn't heal if I couldn't learn. It was a vicious cycle. Whatever was a gal to do? Whatever was a soul to do? What a conundrum.

Prior to Maui, I was searching the Internet for houses in Jersey, which helped pass the time. I was frustrated with the slow dial-up connection, but I had no recourse. Someone was trying to teach me patience, but I was just not seeing it. I started to read in anticipation of my vacation. Of course, the topic was paradise, but the mere fact that I could read and retain was encouraging.

Thank goodness, it was finally time to leave for Maui. My conundrums would all have to wait until I got renewed in paradise. Sorry Ego, I'm on my way to the Now. No time for past or future in paradise, only the present moment. It's really all we ever have anyway, isn't it? Think about it. One of these days I'll be ready for *The Power of Now*.

I packed with my boys watching me with very anxious eyes. I had such mixed emotions as I prepared to leave for one of the most special places in the world. One thing I had been right about was my need for Hawaiian healing!

Chapter 7

Sunsets & Whales & Healing, Oh My!

*L*eaving the dogs ignited my still-raw feelings of abandonment. Those questioning eyes were, again, pleading for an explanation. This time I would be gone for a long time. I knew that dogs were creatures of the present moment like all animals, so they'd be fine. I was leaving them in good hands with their new friend, Jodi.

Because of my early flight, I booked a room near the airport and left the afternoon before. My first Valentine's Day without a Valentine was spent in a motel near the Greensboro airport. I couldn't help but see the irony. I spent a holiday celebrating love in the loneliest of places, a motel room. Welcome to my new world.

Early the next morning, I headed toward two weeks bathed in the natural beauty of Hawaii and the company of another human being. I needed both desperately. I killed some time in the airport bookstore. My obvious love of books and reading supplanted my annoying inability to read.

I found some new books by one of my favorite writer/healers, Deepak Chopra. My husband and I had the privilege of hearing him speak at Drew University. Chopra has an uncanny ability to make the most complex concepts easy to understand. I think that is truly one of his greatest gifts. I was eager to read his latest endeavors, but left them on the shelf for another time.

I was thrilled when Marie and Master Michele arrived early enough to enjoy a nice lunch. We had a wonderful visit before Marie and I boarded the plane for the seemingly unending flight from Newark to Honolulu, which totaled 11½ hours. With all the distractions of meals, movies, etc., the time passed. Every time I visit Hawaii, there is a point when I begin to ask myself, "Why go so far?" By the time I get to the timeshare, I've already forgotten about the arduous flight. Having to travel from my location in the Carolina mountains added another significant segment, but it was still worth it.

Hawaii is everything that everyone claims it is, and then some. It is truly paradise. The Pacific is spectacular, the islands each have their own unique energy, and the Hawaiian people are so pleasant and helpful. Having been there twice so recently, I felt comfortable traveling without my Ex. Everything was familiar, plus I had a gal with me who'd been to the Hawaiian Islands over 20 times. I was anxious to see my best friend, Linda, who was meeting us when we landed.

We spent a wonderful time with Linda on Oahu. We met her friend Penny who made living in Honolulu easier for Linda. The next afternoon, Lin took us to the airport for our short flight to Maui. We'd see her again in two weeks.

Once we deplaned on Maui, I headed for the rental car while Marie waited for the luggage. Knowing where you're going is half the battle. My familiarity with the Maui airport was comforting. I drove back to collect Marie and our luggage. I found the luggage – always a relief – and Marie with a funny smile on her face.

As I loaded the car, I asked Marie what was so funny. She told me that our luggage was the only luggage that got off the plane. I looked at her in amazement. The plane was going on to the Big Island of Hawaii. Most of the passengers had gotten off on Maui, but their luggage didn't. So, off we went, with the luggage in tow, grateful for our good fortune. I thought to myself: this *is* going to be a great experience.

I was exhausted from the flight the day before and my intense catching up with Lin. While the room was nice, the view was far from acceptable. We'd bought this timeshare with the guarantee of an ocean view. I was furious at what I saw, or should I say, couldn't see. We had a wonderful view of vegetation and the back of the neighboring resort. This was not what I spent so much money for. Here I was in Maui experiencing the same level of frustration and anxiety I thought I'd left in North Carolina.

I told Marie not to unpack yet, because this was not an acceptable room.

I went to the front desk, but I couldn't speak with anyone until the next day. We settled in for the night, but I was going to do whatever I could to get us a better view. This just wouldn't do. My great experience came to a screeching halt! Linda called to see if everything had gone okay. I told her about our disappointing view and my intentions for the next day.

After breakfast, I set out on my new mission. At the front desk, they pulled up a picture of our view and told me that we had one of the best ocean views. First of all, the view they showed me was not our view, which I showed them with pictures in my digital camera. Secondly, if they thought our view was one of the best, then we had a *very serious* problem. Apparently, all one-bedrooms were on the first two floors, so the presence of landscaping was a given. Obviously, none of this information had been shared during the sales pitch.

After getting no satisfaction at the resort, I moved to the sales office. I explained my grievance, and was directed to a sales manager, Diane, who seemed genuinely concerned. I'd spent a lot of money and felt deceived. She said my agent had left, but not for any wrongdoing. I explained that we'd been in a unit that faced full front to the ocean when we decided to buy, but it was too expensive for us. We were offered a unit at the neighboring resort, and I specifically asked if it had the same view of the water. We were told it would if we bought an ocean view. We bought an ocean view, which wasn't what I saw from my room.

Diane got her superior, who went to see what he could do. He came back shortly and said that just for me.... Where had I heard that before? He'd found a unit with the beautiful ocean view that was in foreclosure. They would take my unit in trade plus more money. Having been deceived so much in the past eight months, it was challenging for me to discern truth from lie these days. I needed time to think about it. I'd already wasted too much time on this while poor Marie was waiting in the room with a view of the other resort. Are we having fun yet? I don't think so.

I brought Marie up to speed and took her to see the prospective unit. The money necessary to make up the difference provided my biggest concern, given my current state of uncertainty. If the mountain property sold, it would be a no-brainer.

Marie and I set about getting a few things at the grocery, having lunch, getting things-to-do books, and talking about plans for the next couple of days. Internally, I was struggling with the decision about the timeshare. I'd just spent unexpected thousands in the log house. Now, I was being challenged with another decision that required more thousands. Marie was so patient and supportive. I was grateful to have a friend with me to bounce my thoughts and fears off of.

Lin called later and I explained my dilemma. Knowing each other as well as we do, I value her thoughts tremendously. My conclusion was that if I didn't take this option, I'd probably never come back to Maui. The timeshare would serve as a source of anger and disappointment at being deceived and disrespected, yet again. If I didn't come to Maui, then I'd paid way too much for two weeks, every other year, anywhere else.

The question I had to answer for myself was could I spend the additional money without internalizing the stress that I would feel doing it? Linda listened to all my musings and shared her thoughts, which were very valid concerns. She could look at it from a much less emotional and more realistic position. She simply helped me look through different eyes. I made the choice to go ahead and spend the money. I was going on faith that the mountain property would sell in the near future.

Linda didn't want my fear of financial obligations to be a factor, so she offered to lend me the money until the mountain sold. Inexplicably, I accepted her offer. I was amazed at my decision to borrow the money. I had never borrowed money or anything else for that matter. I could hear my folks saying, "Neither a borrower nor a lender be." I grew up hearing that.

My folks had always taught me that you don't buy what you can't pay for. What I was thinking of doing was almost that. I could pay for it, but in doing so I would heap mounds of stress on an already overloaded psyche. Linda's offer was a creative way to eliminate the stress factor. Only because it was Linda would I even consider accepting. She was my soul sister. I would do the same for her if our positions were reversed. The love behind the offer touched me deeply. Now, Marie and I could get on with the business of vacation.

My main focus was to see whales. Having a fair amount of experience whale-watching, I knew there was no point going if the water was too choppy. The best viewing is with flat water, so you can pick up the location of the whales when they break the surface to "blow" as they breathe. We were almost a week into our vacation before the winds calmed down enough.

We went in a different direction each day. We'd discuss the possibilities over breakfast either on our lanai (porch) or in a wonderful little spot that my Ex and I discovered called the Castaways, where you can sit for as long as you want in the most spectacular location on the beach. We phoned our dear friend, little Michelle, whose husband was recovering from lung surgery, from time to time. I think her circumstances made us appreciate our good fortune even more. I was having a wonderful time albeit different than my vacations of the past 29 years.

I am enamored with sunsets, and there is no finer place for sunsets than Hawaii. My Ex and I always watched sunset no matter where we were in the world. We had hundreds of pictures of sunsets. I always appreciated and never missed the gorgeous sunsets on our farm, which I missed dearly now. The mountain property, in its perfection, offers sunsets. The log house doesn't. Surprised?

Sunset is a big deal in Hawaii. Resorts blow a conch shell to announce its arrival. Most everyone gathers on the beach to watch the sun drop. Being the honeymoon capital of the world, the beaches had their share of newlyweds. This was the most difficult time for me given my recent divorce. My heart would break as I watched a couple kissing. I couldn't help wonder how long their marriage would last. I remembered my own honeymoon, on Oahu, 28 years earlier.

I felt the sense of wonder that sunsets invoke within me. It's a feeling of being connected, not being so alone, and of being part of something infinite. I never missed a Maui sunset. I used the emotions they evoked within me to work through much of the grief over my lost soulmate. I'd waffle back and forth between sadness and despair, and awe at the beauty unfolding before me. They taught me that sharing moments with someone you love, and who loves you in return, amplifies the experience tremendously. Experiencing the sunsets alone paled in comparison to sharing them with my life partner.

My diminished sense of wonder seeing sunsets alone opened a small window in my being that perhaps one day I might share sunsets with someone that important to me again. Up until that time in Hawaii, whenever anyone dared to suggest a relationship in my future, I screamed, "Never!" Now, I allowed a tiny seed of possibility into my psyche; a tiny seed.

Eventually, the winds stopped and the sea calmed. It was whale time! Marie joined me on my first trip on a fairly large boat. It was perfect. We saw whales quite close to the boat, while still enjoying the comforts of a larger craft. My other three trips were on large Zodiac raft-type boats by myself, because they weren't good for Marie's bad back. Due to their size and speed, you can get up-close-and-personal with these magnificent beings.

Hawaiian law restricts the distance that the boats can approach the whales. They regard the whales' right to their breeding and calving grounds as sacrosanct. Penalties for breaking the law were quite severe, as well they should be. The whales had no restrictions, so if the whales chose to approach you, oh well.

Each trip was as different as the whales that came to *play* with us. My experiences with Atlantic Humpback whales taught me how curious and playful they can be. Each encounter with these gargantuan beings always leaves me in awe of their magnificence. Even the calves were large enough to cause our boat to flip easily. They swam back and forth underneath us. They mini-breached along side of us. They seemed to love to play with the boats, especially the calves. They were no different than a youngster of any species. They lived in pure joy.

I watched mesmerized as one mother was teaching her calf about boats and humans. I felt privileged that a mother allowed her calf to come so close to us. She exhibited trust in us that her calf would be safe. We trusted her that she wouldn't harm us. It was Trust and Respect in its purest form.

One time, a single adult male struck the water multiple times just a few yards from our boat. He slapped with enough force to get our attention, but not enough to cause any harm. He had great aim and control of his giant body. You could sense his power as his fluke (tail) hit the water, which then moved our boat from its ripple effect. It was awe-inspiring! He was telling us the best way he could to move away from the mother and calf he traveled with. His job was to protect this pair.

The contrast between the power and the gentleness of these whales was fascinating. We all knew the damage that could be done with just one misplaced tail or flipper slap, but it never happened, not even with a calf. Their incredible size denotes such power, yet belies the gentleness they radiate.

When you photograph whales, most of what you get, or at least what I get, is disappointing. Every so often you get lucky. I took a picture of a raft-boat like the one I was on with a whale fluking next to it. When whales go into a deep dive, they bring their flukes way out of the water in order to propel the dive. The size differential was stunning. The whale's fluke was almost as large as the entire boat, which left me marveling at the whale's total size. I felt blessed to have captured this picture.

Watching them touched my heart with a sense of joy that had been missing for what seemed like ages. I really needed to feel joy again. I needed to unlock my inner child and be a kid again. I needed to let go of my oppressive sense of responsibility. I felt blessed to be experiencing such cooperation between species. I couldn't help but wonder why two such different species have less trouble respecting one another than beings of the same species, namely humans. Somewhere deep within me is the desire to facilitate respect and trust among all species, thus creating a harmonious existence on our planet for all.

In my animal healing brochure, I defined the purpose of my work as helping to bridge the chasm that has developed between people and animals through better communication. What I was shown on my trips with these enormous, peaceful beings was exactly that. All of our choices, human and whale alike, begins the bridge over a rift that has been forged over lifetimes of abuse and disrespect. It's not only respect for the wild and free, but those animals that have chosen to live with humans. Encounters with exotics on vacations will hopefully create the passion in people to join in the task. These experiences provide the basic structure of the bridge. They are a point from which to start. A beginning... .

When I'm confronted with experiences like the whales gave me on Maui, hope for the future stirs within me. Hope for the future of the world, but it also ignited hope for my own future. These wonderful beings, by sharing themselves, gifted me with more healing than they would ever know. I am eternally grateful to them. Their gift was profound for me on many levels. The winds kicked back up and my whale watching was over, but I couldn't have been more satisfied. I embraced the gift they offered. My Hawaiian Healing had begun.

The only other boat adventure I planned was an all-day snorkel trip around the neighboring island of Lanai. The trip encircled the island, where dolphins are abundant. It was too arduous for Marie in spite of her game nature. I kept watching the weather forecasts to determine which would be the best day for my adventure. Snorkeling requires calm waters and bright sun, which create the optimum conditions for seeing the farthest with the best color. I didn't want to devote an entire day to a trip that would be anything less than perfect, so I waited.

Marie and I drove all over while waiting for perfect snorkeling weather. I began to realize that even in Hawaii winter happens. The weather conditions were very different from my visits in May and September. I actually only swam in the ocean once. Never would I have believed that before I left home. I was an avid swimmer in my youth and loved to swim any chance I got. While the water wasn't that cold, it was churned up by the winds. The biggest deterrent was swimming *alone*, since it just reminded me of that missing person.

One afternoon, I shopped at a store called "Women Who Run With Wolves." Obviously, its name was the attraction. I found two greeting cards that were particularly significant to me. One card dealt with numerology, which is a spiritual science that I find intriguing, but really don't know much about. The number on the card corresponds to your birth date. Mine is 8 and was entitled, Leader.

LETTING GO

Years earlier during a Native American ceremony at the Omega Institute in New York State, the leader gave us all "natural names," which he was given by Great Spirit. My natural name is "Mountain Lion Woman." He prefaced it by saying this was a very powerful name, which immediately intimidated me, but also made me proud to have received such a name. Through more studies of Native American culture, I learned that mountain lion represents, you guessed it, leadership. So, the card was simply confirming information I'd been given years earlier. I hadn't been feeling very leader-like these days.

A second card attracted me with its fabulous picture of a sunrise. The text on the card was incredibly significant, given the recent events of my life. It hangs by my bed, and I cannot tell you how many times I've read it since. It is titled "New Beginnings" and reads, "What may be perceived as the end of something, is the start of something new in your life. What you call a beginning is often the end. And to make an end is to make a beginning. The end is where you start from." The power of these words was startling.

I'd spent all my time looking at the dissolution of my marriage as nothing more than an end. Until I found this card, I never looked at it from the other side. I never perceived it as a beginning. Whenever I'm struggling with life, I take a quick read of the card and shift my focus away from endings. I marvel at how my perception of an event dramatically changes when I simply shift my focus.

Our travels showed us all of Maui's topography – beaches, pasturelands and meadows, mountains, and volcano craters. It is truly unique in the variety it offers. In February, the mountains really collected the weather. We tried to head to the volcano crater at Mount Haleakala several times. It is a spectacular place.

While its natural beauty touched my heart in a positive way, memories of spending time in it with my Ex hit me with mixed emotions. On our first trip for our 25th wedding year vacation, I gave Bob an all-day ride on horses into the volcano for his 65th birthday. I expected a dormant volcano to be black with varying shades of gray. The crater exhibited the most unusual diversity of colors, flora, and conditions. The colors were incredible with shades of muted reds and greens. There is no place else quite like it. It is one of the places where NASA trained the astronauts for the lunar landings. Our ride was nothing short of fantastic.

We were gifted with a second ride by Bob's college roommate, Peter, who lives on Maui. His family is one of the most influential in Maui's history. Peter was a wealth of information. He told stories of his grandfather driving cattle from one side of the crater to the other that were unbelievable. We experienced how strenuous it was to ride leisurely into the crater. The feat of driving cattle for hours on end was nothing short of phenomenal. To help you appreciate his grandfather's achievement: the crater is large enough to fit the entire island of Manhattan inside of it. The time with Peter in the crater was as exceptional to me as the uniqueness of the volcano itself.

Marie and I just wanted to drive to the rim to take in the gorgeous view it offers of the crater, and Maui itself. The rim sits more than 10,000 feet above sea level. I guess Nature figured I couldn't cope with being up there on this trip. *She* must have known the memories were too painful. When we'd see that the top was clear, we'd head for it. Since we lived quite a distance away and conditions change fast on Maui, the clouds arrived before we did on several attempts. One time we got almost to the rim before the clouds shrouded us completely. It was a very scary drive back until we got below the clouds. On my next Hawaiian vacation, after I've let go of my pain, Mother Nature will part the clouds and reveal her beauty.

Another area that played tricks on us was the Iao Valley. The beauty of Iao, while in sharp contrast to the stark nature of the crater, was on the same par with it. It contained gorgeous, luscious vegetation. The Iao Valley is a tropical rainforest that is simply breathtaking. My Ex and I had visited the Hawaii Nature Center in Iao and taken a guided hike with a local naturalist. It was marvelous and very educational as to the multitude of flora existing there. It was another of my treasured memories made with the missing person. I guessed I wasn't supposed to experience this area just yet, either. The clouds and foul weather seemed to always be caught in Iao.

I told Marie I wanted to overnight in Hana, which is my favorite spot on Maui. This was going to challenge my emotional fortitude, but I knew what Hana offered was worth the probable pain. I was up to the challenge. Time in Hana would help me *let go*. The road to Hana is infamous. It is too narrow with a zillion turns and considerable traffic. Marie was up for an overnight, so I asked my sales gal, Diane, for advice. We decided on the Bamboo Inn, since it overlooked Hana Bay. So, our next to last night on Maui was reserved for Hana. I couldn't wait to return to this special, serene portion of Maui. My Ex and I had stayed at the Hotel Hana Maui, so as long as we didn't stay there, I'd be fine.

The weather finally allowed me to book the circumnavigation trip of Lanai. I really pushed myself to go on this snorkel adventure alone. I was way out of my comfort zone, but I felt it was important to begin to live the life I'd been given. I didn't want to give into the fear of going by myself. I had to let go of those kinds of feelings. I had to take these "firsts" head on. I couldn't justify missing this wonderful opportunity, so I accepted the challenge. My space was the last one available on that day. Was it destiny?

As I drove to meet the tour, I was gifted with a most beautiful sunrise. The winds had stopped, the sea was calm, and there wasn't a cloud in the sky. It was going to be the perfect day. These were very good omens, until someone overbooked the trip. They rescheduled me two days later. I was very angry and disappointed. I drove back to the room totally deflated.

My plague of "nothing seems to go right" had followed me all the way to Maui. Marie couldn't believe my story. I worked hard all day trying to look for the positive in the situation. It was a real struggle for me to accept and surrender to what had happened, since the weather was the best of our entire stay. I'd worked so hard convincing myself to do the trip alone that it was hard not to be angry at the outcome. I kept telling myself that *everything happens for a reason*, but the idyllic weather made it really hard to embrace. I eventually recognized that I needed to let go of the anger and disappointment. I had a choice. If I didn't, I'd contaminate the rest of the day.

The weather for the rescheduled trip looked terrible, so I called and told them to forget it, while letting them know how unhappy I was. I closed the book on the failed attempt trying to embrace the notion that I was just supposed to have this adventure my next time on Maui. Maybe then, I'll be able to share it with someone. That thought paired with ideal weather conditions would make it truly perfect. So, I *let it go*. You just gotta believe.

I was filling my memory chest with new, positive memories. My memories of my previous trips to Hawaii were all positive, wonderful memories, but the person with whom I'd made them tainted my recollections. I had to let go of that person if I was going to heal. I'd never get out of the Tunnel until I accomplished that, and I knew it. I wasn't sure how to let go of him without letting go of the memories.

I wasn't aware of how my *doing* protected me from my evil ego, which loved to drown me in negativity. It was back at the log house, while writing, when this revealed itself. I finally allowed myself to *be*, and it hit me that it wasn't the man I had to let go of. It was the negative thoughts and painful emotions that filled me whenever I thought about him. He was an integral part of my memories. That is, the man that he was. I still loved that man and always would. I had to figure out a way to let go of the pain, anger, and grief over the loss of that man. I had to learn to release all those negative emotions, which shrouded my wonderful memories with unhappiness.

My unhappiness was so similar to the dense clouds that kept the spectacular views on Haleakala and in the Iao Valley hidden. Nature was attempting to teach me with a metaphor of my current life. These spectacular places, which had given me fabulous experiences and wonderful memories on my previous two trips, offered me something far greater now. My soul, using these metaphors, wanted me to recognize what I was doing to myself.

Haleakala and the Iao Valley were gifting me with a lesson *if* I chose to acknowledge it. My unhappiness was preventing me from accepting the beauty of who I am and the life I am living. Until I find a way to clear away the clouds of my unhappiness, I'll never be able to see the view and experience the beauty that is my soul. In all honesty, the lesson is just being revealed as I write.

I sit, in amazement, at the wonderment of the Universe. It is so clear to me now, as I recall the experiences. I was so clouded by unhappiness and distracted by *doing* that I never had an inkling of what Mother Nature offered me on Maui. I knew Haleakala was still there in spite of the dense fog and clouds. It is crucial for me to believe that my spectacular life is waiting for me once the dense clouds of unhappiness no longer envelop me.

I learned that lessons are offered all along our journey. Many of them, such as those from Haleakala and Iao, are discovered long after they are experienced. It doesn't matter when you learn them, as long as they are received and embraced. *Everything happens for a reason,* and always at the *perfect* time. I feel blessed to have just recognized this lesson. My challenge is to embrace it and live it. I must let go of my unhappiness. I have to *choose* to be happy. Until I can, happiness will continue to elude me. Until I can, I will not emerge from the Tunnel. Recognition is the first step, so I'm on my way. The depth of my unhappiness is without end and creates my Abyss if I allow it.

Through my years of spiritual learning, I'd heard and read about the need for negatives to contrast the positives. In order for us to appreciate the happy times of our lives, we have to experience the unhappy. My first introduction to this concept came when I read *The Prophet,* by Kahlil Gibran. It is a most wonderful, thought-provoking book. For whatever reason, his writing on joy and sorrow was what struck me the most.

What he shared was that I/we will experience the depth of sorrow equal to the height of joy, and vice versa. His concept intrigued me, but I didn't know why at the time. I experienced a peek at what he was writing about the last time I made love to my husband, but just a sneak peek. Each time I read *The Prophet,* I pondered what sorrow was ahead for me.

When I entered my time of prolonged sorrow, the losses I'd recently been assaulted with, I returned for another read of Gibran. The timing was such that his words struck me to the core of my soul. "The deeper that sorrow carves into your being, the more joy you can contain. When you are sorrowful, look again in your heart, and you shall see that in truth you are weeping for that which has been your delight. Verily you are suspended like scales between your joy and sorrow. Only when you are empty are you at standstill and balanced."

Somewhere deep in my soul I knew this as Truth when I first read it so long ago. Living it brought the knowing from my mind through my heart and into my soul. I now understood what he wrote about. I'd been blessed with joy in my Past, and to balance the crushing sorrow of the Abyss, I have much joy to look forward to.

Life is about balance and nowhere is that taught more than in Nature. Having spent a life serving Nature by helping animals, no one was more aware of this than I. However, when my pendulum swung from the happy to the unhappy, I was completely unprepared. If you can step back from the microcosm of it and look at what I call the big picture, it made sense. Making sense didn't diminish the devastating effect it had on me. I didn't remain in the big picture view very long, my ego always brought me back to my little world and my unhappiness. My job was to get the pendulum to swing back to the center point, where I am at standstill and balanced.

Marie and I headed to Hana, which offered me a coming attraction for a life lived in happiness. The road to Hana is stunningly beautiful, but tiring to drive. We left later than most, allowing us a more leisurely rate to enjoy the gorgeous scenery along the way, which included many waterfalls.

We stopped for a picnic lunch about halfway on the Keanae Peninsula. It is a beautiful spot with crashing surf that pounds up on lava rocks. The contrast of colors was breathtaking: the blacks and reddish browns of the lava rock; the blues and turquoise blues of the water; the white of the crashing surf and all the hues in between. The power of the waves breaking against the rocks and the eternal motion of the ocean left me with a sense of awe. Watching the surf was hypnotic and soothed my much-maligned soul. Spending time in this special place just *being* began my much-needed Hana Healing. While this wasn't Hana yet, it held all the same gifts.

Hana is what Maui must have been like 100 years ago. Other than enjoying Nature, there isn't much else to do. If you want to relax and immerse yourself in Nature, Hana is for you. Hana is about *being,* not *doing.* By the time we finished our exploring, it was time to check-in. The villa was lovely. I left Marie to settle in and went for a walk along the water. I needed to be near the water. My birth sign is Pisces, the water sign: dolphins, whales, waterfalls, rivers, and oceans are my destiny. I soaked in all the bay had to offer. The constant motion of the waves was mesmerizing and brought me to a very calm, serene place. I didn't have any trouble with the silence in Hana.

Another hidden lesson and gift from Maui is being revealed as I write. Silence spent within Nature was totally different than the dreaded silence in the log house. Silence in the log house took me to the Past and Future, which fed my fears and perpetuated my agony. Silence spent in Nature intensifies the present moment, feeds my spirit, and heals my wounds. Silence is silence is silence. It shouldn't matter where I experience it. I needed to recognize this and take back control from my ego.

Until I can embrace the silence of the log house, I need to seek out the healing silence within Nature, which is abundant in the mountains of North Carolina. In order to bathe myself in the natural beauty that surrounds me in the mountains, I must let go of the painful memories, which cloud the beauty and the healing energy it offers me. My pain and unhappiness shroud it from me. I've allowed my trauma to steal Nature's healing that is right outside my door. I have to *choose* to experience my loving relationship with Nature without my shroud of unhappiness. I have to *choose* to accept her gift of healing for my Self, my spirit, and my soul.

Marie watched me connect with the energy of the Bay from the lanai. I was so grateful to Marie, who made it possible for me to be there on that beach. Without her, I would not have come. We sat on the lanai staring at the water with no need to talk. We simply absorbed the gifts that Hana offered. I finally allowed my Self and my soul to *be*. I felt the healing energy I came to Maui for. All of my *doing* had been blocking the healing energy from my *being*.

As I stared out over this most spectacular view, I asked my Self to emblazon it in my mind to be conjured up whenever I needed its healing. I had walked the bay's shoreline, and gazed at it from the lanai, allowing our energies to merge. I was simply one with the bay and Hana, which commenced my healing.

Hana taught me about *being* and *doing*, which were more contrasts. I needed to swing the pendulum between them back to the point of balance in my life. I'd lived most my life in the most extreme *doing* mode. My recent life was trying to bring the pendulum to the *being* position, which Hana accomplished.

Hana offered me a view of what my life would be like if I could only become adept at *being*. My healing came to me in Hana only when I allowed my Self to simply *be*. It was a profound lesson, and one I'd struggle with for some time. Hana opened my awareness to the benefits of *being* and allowed me to touch that supreme state of Presence.

The next morning Marie and I lingered, not wanting to leave the sense of harmony that Hana generates. We stopped by a state park with a fabulous black sand beach. I walked down to the beach and along some of the sacred Hawaiian areas. My soul was bathed in the soothing, renewing energy that is created when Nature and people live in harmony. I felt my emotional wounds starting to heal. Hana gave me hope.

On our way back, we stopped at Mama's Fish House, a favorite of ours. Mama's serves the best fish on Maui, and the view is amazing. It was another of those places that challenged me with memories. On my last trip, Bob and I celebrated his birthday there with Peter and his wife, and his horse vet and his wife. It was a wonderful evening that created a wonderful memory. So, being there confronted me with my demons. Marie and I enjoyed our meal, as well as watching all the sailboarders. Its world renowned winds provide a very entertaining spot to eat. I treated Marie for her birthday, creating new memories.

We headed back to Honolulu late the next morning to spend the day with Linda and Penny. We checked Marie in at the Hale Koa, where she'd be for another two weeks. My trip proved better than anticipated, so I was deeply satisfied. While I didn't look forward to the log house in the woods, I was anxious to see my critters. They had a lovely farewell dinner for me, and then Lin dropped me off for my late flight.

As I sat in the terminal, I gave myself credit for having come, for having cried only a few times, and for making wonderful, new memories. I was proud of myself and it was important for my Self to know that. While I waited at the airport, I bought Deepak Chopra's book on synchrodestiny, *The Spontaneous Fulfillment of Desire*. It was something I used to experience, but seemed to have lost in my current life. Synchronicity, or Chopra's synchrodestiny, was something I needed to attract back into my life.

The return trip seemed never-ending. I was anxious to see my boys, so I drove right home after landing. I was utterly exhausted when I arrived home. My schedule for the trip back showed why – moving to Carolina added a five plus hour segment to my travel. I would, and will, do it again in a heartbeat. Hawaii is that special and deserves all the platitudes it gets, not just for the beauty of the islands and the weather, but for the people, too. The people exude happiness, which I'm making a priority in my life. My level of happiness will be the barometer of healing. Aloha.... .

Chapter 8

Back in The Abyss

*T*he dogs seemed happy, healthy, and thrilled to see me. Jodi had taken great care of them. I couldn't wait to bathe in my big, beautiful tub. Jodi thought the water filter needed replacing, so I changed it first, but while it was filling the flow stopped and started several times. This wasn't a filter issue. The plumber came and replaced the pressure switch, but really felt it was a pump problem, so he called a reliable pump company for me. After the plumber got done, my water flow was far worse, so I ran into town for gallons of bottled water. Welcome back!

My Ex called, asked about my trip, and then the mountain property. I was wondering why he was calling. Ironically, I thought with early birthday wishes for me, which was the following day. He said he was coming to get more stuff from the steel building. I was relieved to hear that. Eventually, he got to his reason for calling.

His next words are burned into my memory much like his confession nine months earlier. "I thought you ought to know I got *married!*" There was utter silence. My mind was racing with the reality of what I'd just heard. He continued, "Well, I just thought it was better than being alone." I thought to myself – now there's a great reason for marriage! I really didn't know what to say as I felt an emotional knife thrust deep into my heart.

I just had to know if my suspicions were correct. I asked, "What's her name?" He only said her first name. I took him totally by surprise when I blurted out her full name and confessed to knowing all about her. It was silent for so long I thought perhaps he'd hung up. Then I heard, "Well, I didn't really know where it was going." In the prolonged silence, I'd almost said, "And why do you think I need to know this?" What a birthday surprise!

Help! I've fallen, and I can't get out. Confirmation of my suspicions sent me hurtling back into the *Abyss*. There was no doubt anymore. I couldn't believe that I had been so completely fooled by this man. All the hurt I'd been suffering transformed instantly into anger. My traumas of the past nine months had created a place of grief, hurt, pain, and suffering that had kept me their prisoner. His call released me from that prison and sent me flying into the Abyss enraged.

The first time in the Abyss I resided there as a hurt, wounded woman. Now, my time there was spent in fury. His admission threw me into a depression so deep that I wouldn't find my Hana Bay view or my Hawaiian healing for a very long time. My mind raced with the realizations that were contained within his latest confession. Obviously, this relationship had been developing for some time, since we hadn't even been divorced two months.

After I came back from wherever his call took me in my mind, I called my father-in-law. After Vince, I called a few of my closest of friends, who'd felt from the get-go that there was another woman. They were supportive and sensed the devastating effect his news was having on my already tenuous emotions.

Gloria, my sister-in-law, called with birthday greetings. I told her about her brother's call and mine to her dad. She said Bob had already called them. Gloria was glad he'd told me. It wasn't news they wanted to share, which I completely understood. Later, she confided that while he was her brother and she loved him dearly, she would never understand what he did to me. I sit at the top of a long list of people who will never understand.

When Vince called for my birthday, I told him I understood why he hadn't said anything. I could tell he was relieved. His concern for my opinion about his silence showed me that our relationship was important to him. It was solid and strong. My in-laws continue to be a constant source of strength for me. Their support has never wavered, and I'm so grateful for their presence in my life.

I don't know why, but I just wondered what this woman was like. Secretly, I guess I was trying to figure out what was better about her than me. Why did my Ex prefer her? What type of woman would cause someone to trash a 29-year relationship? My questions focused on her rather than me and were obliquely asking what's wrong with me. Prior to this call, my thoughts had always been comparing me to no one else. Now, there was someone.

It took me forever to accept that it had nothing to do with my deficiencies or me, but rather with his dysfunction. Once I truly embraced this I'd be able to stop questioning everything I'd said or done. It would take some time until I fully believed and accepted this concept. With his call, my struggling self-confidence hit the skids, sliding me back into the dreaded Abyss.

I had to emerge from the Abyss, because the pump people arrived on my birthday to assess the situation. He felt it was the pump too, but checked the pressure switch and found that it was installed incorrectly. With the switch corrected, my flow improved. How could a pump go bad in six months? I think the dirt in the tanks damaged it before Jerry repaired the spring. The new pump was installed and the water flowed. Now, I just needed my life to start flowing.

So, I hadn't been home a day before I was engulfed in pain and frustration. I was furious with my Ex, the builder, and the realtor. I was annoyed with the landscaper for not getting my new driveway in before winter. I also had the fencing parts to return.

I'd hoped for a little transition time between my bliss on Maui, and my struggles with life alone in the Carolina mountains. I was grateful that the water issue waited for me to get home and that my animal family fared well in my absence. I was trying to find the positives. Life is filled with little blessings if we look hard enough.

I spent part of my birthday composing a letter to my Ex. There were things he needed to know. Obviously, he thought I was "dumb as a box of rocks" and hadn't a clue about his deceit. Initially, I didn't. I was so stunned by his admission of not wanting the house or me that I simply lost my ability to assess the situation. I'd spent my time trying to organize the chaos his decision created in my life.

It was hard to believe I was spending my birthday on such a letter, but for my own sanity, I needed to express myself. Remember his one-track tendencies? With a letter, I felt I had the best chance of having his undivided attention. I wanted him to understand how I'd become suspicious. For whatever reason, it was important to me. Living alone had allowed me to see some of the clues the Universe flaunted in front of me. However, my misguided trust and love for him prevented me from truly seeing the reality of the situation. I'd been living the old adage, "Love is blind."

LETTING GO

After the farm sold, we'd bought him a computer. One afternoon, he said he'd gotten email addresses for some old classmates from the Cornell Alumni website. I thought reuniting with college chums was a good thing. One was an old girlfriend, who posed no threat to me, or so I thought! I trusted my husband, so I never gave her a second thought.

Our first phone bill in Carolina had about 50 calls to a remote computer, so Bellsouth asked me to verify the dial-up number, which was correct. When I opened his email program to check the number, I saw two emails from the old girlfriend, from two different addresses. One address was Albuquerque!

I didn't read the messages, much to the dismay of my friends, but that's not who I am. Maybe that was a mistake, an opportunity for learning, but my integrity wouldn't allow such an act of mistrust then or now. I've maintained throughout this horrible time that I wouldn't allow Bob's treachery to change me. I would not give him that much power. So, I closed the email program and let the knowledge filter into the recesses of my mind. Maybe I didn't want to know.

I still didn't allow myself to see it when I learned he'd been researching Carolina divorce laws. I never put the two together. Writing about this now, I look really foolish back then, but you have to remember I was still trying to reconcile the two different men in my life: the man I loved and married and the man who was tossing me aside. The part of me that had loved and trusted him for almost 30 years was struggling with my current reality. The conflicting and reactive emotions of the moment were hiding the clues from me.

Over the months of waiting for our divorce hearing to be scheduled, he asked one too many times about what I'd heard from the lawyer. Why was he in such a hurry? The only plausible reason was he wanted to begin something new. It was another clue that moved to the back of my mind. My attention was being swept in so many other directions that it was easy to avoid dealing with the thoughts about another woman.

Avoidance and denial are great procrastinators that allow you to live in your own little fantasy world protected from the reality of what truly is. My inability to let go of the love I felt for Bob helped to perpetuate the myth I was living. I kept giving him the benefit of the doubt, basing my beliefs on our past history.

I'd let go of my trust in him rapidly, but the love was too strong to let go of so easily. My love prevented me from seeing the truth of my reality. My growing distrust facilitated my eventual ability to discern the truth behind his choice. I believe the reason for my refusal to accept what was really happening was that I didn't want to believe that he'd rather live with someone else.

Believing that he just didn't want to spend his life with me was the lesser of two evils. This dysfunctional belief fostered by his deceit led me down a path of terrible heartache and suffering. It put me through months of soul-searching that would have been of a different nature if only he'd been honest.

My letter forbade him to have any future contact with me. He'd lost that right, since I didn't allow liars in my life. I felt slightly empowered, since I took back control of the part of my life that involved my Ex. My feelings were headed to New Mexico marking the end of an era that spanned half of my time on Earth.

I did have to communicate with him regarding the dream property, but our communications were relegated to email. I vowed I would never see him or hear his voice ever again. I hoped this would put an end to the pain, but that wasn't realistic. My pain would remain until I finally learned what it was trying to teach me. It would prove to be a long time before I even recognized this.

A couple of days after his latest confession, the phone woke me up. When I heard his voice, I became fully awake. He was having trouble opening the lock at the mountain. Is he crazy? Does he think I care after his latest news? I swore I'd never answer the phone again, unless I knew the caller. His call sent me into abject anger.

The next afternoon the phone rang with a Colorado number. Since I had a friend who lived out there, I answered it. There it was again, his voice! I couldn't believe it. I just listened without saying anything in the spaces he left for a response. Eventually, I heard him say he'd be talking with me soon. In a *very* strong voice I said, "No! I don't want you to *ever* call me again!" There was more silence and I hung up.

I was shaking from the powerful emotions of the moment. It was anger that had to be categorized as rage, which I didn't think I was capable of. I couldn't believe the audacity of him to call. He acted like nothing had changed. What dimension did he live in?

After much time and soul-searching, I finally recognized the *perfection* of it. Being able to tell him to never call me was much more empowering than writing it. I could feel the anger fly through the phone. To hear his voice or see him was too painful and created conflicting emotions. He looked and sounded like the man I loved for all those years and still do love. But, in reality, today's man had lied, betrayed, and disrespected me. That man created such prolonged pain and unhappiness in my life that I won't put myself through the uneasiness of being in the same room with him. I simply won't allow it.

LETTING GO

Hopefully, the sale of the property will allow me to let go of the rage I feel from his betrayal. I'm hoping the release of that dream to another will provide the catalyst for my creation of my new dream. For now, I'm trying to learn patience, acceptance, and surrender, which are challenging lessons for me.

My arrival back in the Abyss sent my ego zooming to my Past. I spent much of my waking time trying to comprehend how I could have been so totally duped by my Ex. I just never saw it happening. I'd been looking at the clues through emotional blinders constructed of Love and Trust. Hindsight has removed those blinders.

I've mentioned before the strange change in behavior that Bob displayed the winter before we moved. I didn't understand why, but I did recognize when things started to change. After his recent call, I knew why. He was beginning a new relationship.

Several months after his new marriage call, the Today show taught me what had happened. The series was on emotional affairs or emotional cheating. I saw my life being discussed before my very eyes. *When the student is ready...* . His affair began over the Internet. Obviously, someone doesn't begin something new if they're satisfied with what they have.

An innocent joke of mine before we moved I now recognized as a puzzle piece my soul had tried to get me to notice. It revolved around my husband's teeth whitening, skin tag removal, and new diet. While out with friends, I teased that he must be getting ready to go back on the market. We all laughed along with him. I didn't really believe it, but it was how it appeared. If it hadn't been Bob, I'd have been suspicious. My thought patterns didn't even go in that direction. Now, who's in denial?

I can't tell you how many times I've heard that joke in my mind since his call. He already had a new interest and was getting improved for her. What really stung was that I paid for half of his improvements. I chastised myself for allowing him to treat me with such disrespect. I felt stupid and ashamed of what I'd allowed. There really was no one else to blame, except *moi*!

I floundered in the Abyss, swallowed up in the past. I relived everything looking for the pieces to the puzzle that I'd missed. My self-confidence took a nose-dive with this recent admission. I spent almost equal time being angry with myself for my stupidity, as I did with him for his deceit.

When my friends learned the latest installment, their commentary was he did it before. I can honestly say it never crossed my mind that he'd do the same to me one day. His first wife had made an abrupt change in religious beliefs, which was ironic in light of my Ex's later religious changes. He said he didn't love her anymore.

Our love was so strong that I felt we were meant to be together. It felt right. The first time we kissed my mind began racing with how wrong this was. This was a married man with four children. My mind said *wrong*, but my heart whispered *right*. My heart had never felt like that before.

I followed my heart that day, and I have no regrets. We lived 29 years together, so I don't think anyone can say my heart was mistaken. A big difference was his first wife knew about me, otherwise the pattern was eerily similar. He'd kept this new relationship a secret from me. I'd given him plenty of opportunities to be honest, but he dodged every single one.

I've learned he was a much more deceptive person than I ever knew. I think he played me to the end. He knew that the divorce settlement would have been much different had I known about the betrayal. My desire for taking the high road and having an amicable dissolution went right out the window when I found out he was married.

My second encounter with the Abyss continued to be focused on the past. My greatest nemesis, my Ego, was preventing me from going anywhere near the Now. It challenged me with all sorts of negative narrative about my inability to recognize what was happening in my life. Intense pain resulted from my feelings of inadequacy.

The only respite I had was during the day when I attempted to deal with the current issues of my life. Not only did I have the unresolved issues with the previous realtor, the builder from Hell, and the fencing company, I also had insurance woes. I'd received a letter regarding the coverage on my dream house. Since we'd stopped construction, they wouldn't renew the insurance. What I thought to be a fairly routine chore turned into something far more. After being told by the Underwriters of North Carolina that they wouldn't handle an unfinished property, I began a very stressful search for coverage.

My search included hours on the Internet, numerous phone calls, etc. After discussing my dilemma with Master Michele, my voice of calm reason, I got the name of the company that her agent had obtained a similar policy from. I worked my way back from her company to a local company that would insure it.

The longer it took for me to find this local agent, the more stressed I got. I felt so relieved when I walked into the agency to complete the application. Throughout the entire episode, I fumed with anger at Bob for leaving me with all of this to deal with. I left the insurance gal's office feeling like I'd accomplished a great feat.

Several weeks later, a letter declining the coverage arrived. The letterhead showed it had come from the Underwriters that I'd first spoken with. I'd discussed this situation with the insurance gal initially. Doesn't anyone listen? Here I go with accountability again. I called her immediately in my quiet desperation. She was the sum total of my many days of work on this very important problem. She'd pursue it.

I kept calling her to find out what was happening. Much of my worth was sitting up on that mountain. I needed to be sure it was safe until sold. After a couple of days, she'd found two different companies that would cover my unique situation. I really couldn't believe my situation was so unique. She was waiting for quotes from each.

Eventually, I filled out a new application and paid a considerably larger premium. I asked if she was sure about this new policy. She assured me the coverage would be written. I can't say I left feeling very confident. A couple of anxious weeks later, I received the policy, which was with Lloyd's of London. No wonder it was pricey. I was emotionally exhausted, but glad to have insurance coverage. Mission accomplished.

I was still concerned about my inability to receive incoming calls while online searching for a home in Jersey. The slow speed of my dial-up connection was a reflection of the rest of my life – out of my control. My hours on the Web did keep at bay the destructive thoughts that filled me in the Abyss. Anything was better than the Abyss, so maybe it was a blessing that the connection was slow. See, I'm trying to make "lemonade." *Everything happens for a reason... .*

I contacted the new realtor, since I was anxious to see the artist's rendering of the Deltec. It was an innocent call, which caused more frustration and stress. It seemed no one had been in touch with the artist, so I called and found out the rendering hadn't even been started. I just wanted to throw myself off *my* mountain, while screaming, "Doesn't anyone do his or her job anymore!" So much for the marketing deadlines that had just passed.

The artist thought the photos I'd sent him looked good enough. Hello! Am I in that other dimension again? I reminded him, as nicely as I could, that we'd had this conversation six weeks ago. He promised it would be done in two weeks in time for the next deadlines. I was furious that the realtors hadn't followed up on this. Their performance so far concerned me.

The painting was ready when promised and was worth the cost both in aggravation and dollars. I hoped it would entice the buyers. Looking at it just made me sad again. I continued to question the reality of the whole situation. After the realtors scanned it into their system, I brought it home. At first, I figured I'd simply dispose of it after the property sold. However, the more I lived with it, the more I began to recognize its significance.

Once I stopped seeing it as my lost dream, I began to see what it truly represented to me. It epitomized my ability to create and manifest. I'd manifested this fabulous place using my love for Bob and our future life together, my love for this sacred mountain, and most importantly, my love for Self and soul as a motivator. It strengthened the resolve I had to find that better dream. It said to me, "You did it before, you can do it again!" In uncovering all of its hidden meanings, I sat in wonder at the perfection of the Universe. While the rendering was commissioned for strictly marketing purposes, it became something far greater and more valuable to me.

I went to check on the property shortly after my Ex left. I wanted to see how much of his stuff was out of the building. From what I saw, he hadn't taken one thing. Who was he kidding? My letter had asked him to clear out the building within 90 days, because the realtors felt it would show better empty. I met Ernie and his crew there to move the garage parts into the steel building.

This was the first time I'd talked with Ernie since Bob's visit. Ernie asked how I was doing. I knew he'd never say anything negative about his friend. I always tried not to put our friends in the middle, then or now. Looking me straight in the eyes, Ernie told me that Bob and the new wife hadn't stayed with them. It touched me that it was important to him for me to know this. I told him that I appreciated that. Not extending an invitation to stay meant that Ernie didn't condone Bob's actions. I appreciated his loyalty.

Due to my disappointment with the latest realtor, I devoted much time checking the accuracy of the marketing for the property. I was out of the hazy funk of my separation with a mission to accomplish. Who else would if I didn't? You're right, no one. I met with them several times brainstorming about how and where to advertise the mountain. I was promised national marketing in key areas.

We worked on the sale of the log house, although my primary concern was the Deltec. I had such hopes for this new agency. I felt, with my participation and direction, we could find that person who'd recognize what I had, fall in love, and complete their mountain dream. All they had to do was put their own touches on the interior. What could be better?

Over time, my enthusiasm for this realtor group began to wane. I found myself constantly checking, reviewing, calling, correcting, and then starting the cycle all over again. I wondered who should be paying who for selling the properties. During one of my meetings with the owner/marketing whiz, I told him I felt like a realtor. He offered me a job right on the spot. I told him no thanks. I was so disappointed and frustrated that my hopes were being crushed so soon.

Towards the end of March, I got one of those thought-provoking calls from Linda, a gal I'd met at a Native American study group. Given my interest in Native American spirituality and my need to meet people of like mind, I'd gone to several of their meetings. Linda called to tell me about a gathering being hosted by a spiritual healer who lived down the road from us. He was inviting folks to join him on the night of the full moon. What she said next really got my attention. She told me I was the first person she thought of. For her to think of me first was quite intriguing, since we'd only met a few times.

I found the healer's website and his practice was quite impressive. Not only was he a spiritual advisor, but a trance channel as well. I read about trips he'd led to different parts of the world. One that caught my eye was to my beloved Banff. I decided this looked like something I needed to attend, if for no other reason than I might meet some other kindred spirits. It would also distract me from the Abyss, which was where most of my nights were being spent.

Happily, my inability to read disappeared after my Maui excursion. It never occurred to me that there would come a time in my life when I wouldn't be able to read. My reading helped alleviate the depression from my Ex's recent news. I was finally reading Eckhart Tolle's, *The Power of Now*. I was taken aback by what I read in the publisher's preface. "It is more than a book; there is a living energy in it, one you can probably feel, as you hold it." I'd read many, many spiritual books and never felt anything quite like it.

I loved the information, but it required time to integrate the lessons. As usual, the timing for me was perfect. I felt like Tolle was writing to me personally. He taught about what I was experiencing, and why I was having so much trouble coping with it. The concepts resonated with my soul. It elevated my self-esteem to learn what had been controlling me and recognize that it wasn't my fault. It wasn't right or wrong, it just was. I finished his book encouraged that I could overcome my greatest foe, my ego.

My trauma of the past nine months epitomized exactly what Tolle taught. When we don't reside in the present moment, we miss out on life, because our lives only happen in the Now. We cannot take action in the past or the future. When we are fully in the present moment, we are *being* in our life. When we're fully present, our ego loses its control over us. The ego exerts control by creating destructive thoughts about our past and future that cripple us. I had to take back control from my ego. *The Power of Now* helped me recognize what was happening and why. It'd take some time before I could wrestle control away from my ego, because it was a stubborn fighter like someone else I knew – me.

My Future depended on fully embracing the lessons Tolle was teaching. My ego was strongest in the Abyss. I needed to find my way back to the Tunnel. Now, I was equipped with more knowledge, so it was just a matter of time, which I had plenty of. I had a tremendous need for Tolle's teachings and will be forever grateful that I listened to my inner voice telling me to order his book so many months earlier. My reading abilities haven't disappeared since.

I began Deepak Chopra's book on synchrodestiny next. My inner being was hungry for spiritual help. I was so thankful to feel interested in something again. I'd been drowning in negativity. I was pleased that I could read in the Abyss, which was definitely better than my first visit there.

I was on the phone a lot after my Ex's wedding news. So many of my closest friends were worried about me. I was surprised at how hard I took his news. As I sat in the Abyss, I recollected so many comments since the whole drama had started. I remembered my friend at the bank, Carolyn, telling me a friend told her, "No man leaves unless he has someone else to go to." I could hear myself telling her, "I just don't think so." Ha! Another one was, "Remember, the wife is the last to know."

My unforgiving ego kept belittling me with thoughts about my failure to recognize my true reality. I just couldn't conceptualize any valid reasons for having missed the signs and clues other than I was an idiot. A fool blinded by trust and love; trust and love that had been betrayed. I swore I'd never let that happen to me again... never ever!

One thing that really helped me was something Linda shared with me. It was a quote in the newspaper about happiness and expectations. Lin said, "In order to be happy, you have to be willing to lower your expectations." I didn't like or agree with it, so she found the paper. It said something like, "In order to be happy, you have to be willing to *adjust* your expectations." Now, that was great!

Well, I cannot tell you how significant that little tidbit was for me. It just kept flying around my head. I hadn't even realized that so much of my pain stemmed from my not being able to adjust my expectations. So much of my unhappiness drew its strength from the loss of my expectations of being married and living on our mountain in our dream house.

My happiness was never going to return until I let go of those dashed expectations. I had to *choose* to adjust my expectations. Or, I could choose not to and continue to sink into further unhappiness and depression. I couldn't wait to tell Lin how instrumental her little saying was to my healing. While it seemed so innocent, I reaped tremendous benefit from it. It was pivotal and in perfect timing. I was thankful that Linda listened to her inner voice and gifted me with another component of my healing.

My motivation for searching for a house in Jersey was no different than when I started searching for my dream property – something positive to focus on. So much of the rest of my days and nights were consumed with negativities. Besides time with Stormy, working on a way out of Carolina was the only other positive thing I focused on. I finally surrendered and let go of my frustrations over the slowness of my Internet connection. My soul was definitely trying to teach me about acceptance and surrender, but as usual I was clueless.

Linda surprised me one day when we were talking about my house search. I was frustrated that I wasn't closer to help Michelle cope with Mike's cancer. Linda's comment really stopped me short. She wasn't sure moving back to Jersey was such a good idea. She was afraid that I'd get myself involved caring for everyone else again. She said I'd spent my life taking care of everyone else: my husband, my animals, and my parents. I never really thought about that before. I just did what I did. After all, I was *the responsible one*. What else would I do?

I was moving back to regain my happiness, so this was about me. Lin's opinions always held a lot of weight with me. I thought about what she said for a long time. This was something about me that I had completely overlooked. I marveled at how blind I'd been towards my own Self. Her comment was the start of my revelation about how totally focused I'd been on others. Her concerns provided a catalyst to get me to focus on my needs, desires, and purpose and opened my awareness to how much I really didn't know about myself.

While I still continued to be supportive of others, I began to devote time to me, which was a novel concept and not easy for me. I began to give some credence to the smoldering thoughts I'd been having about why I was in this situation. If my beliefs that *everything happens for a reason* and *we create our reality* were true, then I wanted to be *alone* in the Carolina mountains. My soul had brought me to this place.

My failure to accept this reality would be at the root of much of my inability to heal. I just couldn't embrace the idea that I did this to myself. After Linda's comments about not being there for my Self, I allowed a tiny speck of possibility to creep into my awareness. Do you think I was so out of touch with my soul that this was the only way to get me to focus on Self? Ya think?

I couldn't argue that my life on the farm had been filled with the all-consuming responsibilities surrounding everyone else: my husband and his practice, the farm and hospital, the animals, and my parents. When I awakened to my animal communication skills, my growing practice was last on the list of priorities. I did feel the work was involved with my soul's purpose for this lifetime, yet it didn't receive the respect and attention it warranted.

I had to confess that my choice not to give the proper time and importance to my new endeavor stemmed from my pattern of taking care of others at the expense of my own soul. If this was part of the reason behind my life alone in the North Carolina mountains, it was proving to be a very costly choice and one I was totally in the dark about even making.

Until recently, I had always felt that I was in touch with my soul's desires. I had to admit, of late, I was feeling pretty out of touch with what my soul wanted. We just hadn't been on the same page lately.

The full moon arrived, so it was time for the gathering down the road. The hosts, Gregory and his wife Sandie, were very warm and gracious. After we introduced ourselves, Gregory led a healing meditation using Atlantean crystal bowls. Each bowl emits a tone that correlates to each chakra – energy center – in the body. They provide vibrational healing when played.

I thanked Gregory for his hospitality and his healing, and then spoke about Banff. I mentioned the incredible energy I'd felt at Lake Louise and its effect on me. I'd never felt a place with more sacred power. He smiled and shared that it was an area where Archangel Michael... I never heard anything else, because every hair on my body stood on end. I felt a buzz through my entire being that was electric. Wow!

The next morning I emailed Gregory and told him I thought we needed to work together. I made an appointment for a few days later. Having felt so disconnected lately, I was pleased that I hadn't missed the message. My message was synchrodestiny in its truest form. I wasn't even very far along in Deepak's book and wham, it happened. My curiosity was really piqued. I felt, dare I say it, almost enthusiastic, and it felt good.

Back home in the Abyss, I was still focused on my Past. All the questions I'd answered came flying back at me. The single-most asked question was, "Why did he ever let you get the house started?" Every time I heard it, I simply shook my head with no reasonable answer. After many months of soul-searching, the only plausible reason was that he wanted to experience building with his son,

Mike. My Ex had moved on while I dealt with the mess his choice left behind. Having lived with me for 29 years, he knew I'd do nothing less.

Almost two years later, I live with the weight of the responsibility of the unrealized dream home around my neck like an anchor that keeps a boat moored. Until my unrealized dream is sold, I remain becalmed. Having the belief that my Ex knew before we left the farm that *he* was moving on, my anger festered terribly in the Abyss. It was an open wound that became infected by his recent marriage news. One of the most vivid and painful memories was of the dreadful auction. Knowing that we'd never be living in our mountain home, he let me sell all of my parent's fabulous treasures.

Many of my friends kept asking how I could sell all those gorgeous things. I simply answered that they really didn't go in a mountain style house. At age 53, I was looking forward to creating the first home I'd ever had any influence over. I wanted to fill it with decor befitting the beautiful Deltec that we'd designed together. The anger I felt from knowing that he knew our dream would never be realized was crippling.

In the Abyss, I felt the pain at the auction as I watched the trappings of my life being disrespected. None of that would have had to happen if my Ex had been truthful. This revelation moved to the top of my list of things I would never be able to forgive my Ex for. Having a stranger euthanize Randy was a close second. I don't believe I'll ever be able to let go of my anger towards him for these extremely painful events.

Somehow or other word gets around. I received many emails of support, along with cards and phone calls from friends back in New Jersey. I continued to visit the mountain property to insure its safety. As I walked around it with my dear Shadow and Licorice by my side, I fought through the depression in the Abyss. Knowing there'd been another woman all along made it even harder to be there. It meant that we'd never really lived on it as a couple.

I spent a lot of time thinking about the man that I'd lived with and loved for so many years. I was trying to glean some sense of understanding, which might allow me to accept the circumstances of our failed marriage and elicit some form of detachment for me. I hoped acceptance would allow me to finally *let go*. My level of anger was something I'd have to come to grips with before I could claw my way out of the Abyss.

I continued my search for understanding, acceptance, and release. I had hopes of leaving the Abyss behind with the help of my new friend, Gregory. I needed assistance from whatever realm to help me process my emotions, so I could let go, move forward, and start the life I knew I deserved. I simply couldn't work this out alone.

I held no expectations for what I might experience with Gregory, so there wouldn't be any disappointments. I may be a slow learner, but I do get it eventually. Down deep, I was so hoping this upcoming session would reveal significant insights for me. After all, my first conversation with Gregory had been *electrifying*. No pressure.

While I fought to survive my second venture into the Abyss, I received a newsletter from an Australian author and spiritual teacher that I'd studied with at the Omega Institute in New York. His name is Michael Roads and his wife is Treenie. They are warm people with much to share about living a fully realized life. I subscribe to their newsletter, which always contains information of great value and keeps me connected with like-minded people. I've gotten to know their U.S. sponsor, Carolyn, from reading the newsletter she organizes. I'd been introduced to Michael through his books, *Talking with Nature* and *Journey Into Nature*. They offered me a new way of participating within Nature.

Michael gave me my first experiences with guided meditation. I had profound encounters that would change my perceptions of life. Over the years, I'd been in touch with them for various reasons. They knew I was moving, but that was the last we'd been in touch. Who would have ever thought that a relationship begun so many years earlier would result in another profound discovery at such a crucial time in my life? Michael and Treenie would have, that's who. Oh, those *coincidences* are *always in perfection* and *always for a reason.*

This particular newsletter of Carolyn's offered me a startling comparison between my life drama and that of Nature. It hadn't even occurred to me until I read Michael's insights regarding the devastating tsunami across the world. I sat stunned as I read his interpretation of the terrible natural disaster. Michael equated the tsunami with Change, big change. For someone who had been struggling with the changes within her life, this resonated with me at a core level.

Michael's column ended with the words, "There are tsunamis designed to make the whole world sit up and take notice, and there are tsunamis - by another name - in your own life designed to make you, personally, sit up and take notice of what is happening in your world. Don't dig in, becoming ever more entrenched. Let go, release the attachments, and allow Change its magic of alchemy."

Earlier in his column, Michael articulated the choice before us: "You can focus on the horror of the endings, or on the power of new beginnings." Ever get the feeling someone is talking about your life? The wave of destruction that affected my recent life was just as powerful to me as the fatal tidal wave across the world. The metaphor was astonishing to me. I didn't die, but my sense of Self, my emotional stability, and my happiness did. These were fatalities of my own personal tsunami. Michael's words were profound for me. The unexpectedness of them made them even more potent.

Getting to know Self is the basis of their teaching. This self-actualization is at the core of my own current life situation. My attendance at their workshop, so many years ago, illustrates that *everything happens for a reason.* I emailed Michael and Treenie, sharing the powerful lesson that their newsletter had for me. Once more, I was thanking them for the profound effect they were having in my life. I explained what happened after I moved connecting the relevance of Michael's tsunami insights. They were sorry to hear of my trauma, but were sure that I would emerge with a more realized sense of the "multidimensional being of light" that Michael teaches us that we are.

I spent countless hours looking at houses in Jersey. Bottom line was they all were incredibly expensive, but I'd never get out of the Abyss if I stopped searching. I was banking all of my hopes for my future happiness on getting back home to the people who cared about me. Seller's market be damned!

A young realtor named Jennifer contacted me, and she helped me search more efficiently. Of course, my biggest restriction was money, but I was willing to spend it for happiness. I wanted one level, and it needn't be big. I wanted to have a little land, but knew I couldn't afford much. I was trying to stay open to the rest, which would allow the Universe to work its magic, which I still believed in. I found three properties that might be worth looking at.

I was feeling so depressed wallowing around my Abyss that I decided I needed a friend-fix. I justified a trip to Jersey to look at property and have my yearly dental exam. My dentist was away until May 2. His schedule meant I'd be in Jersey on May 1, my should-have-been 28th wedding anniversary and also a year since I'd left my wonderful farm. Much later, I realized the magnificence of the orchestration of my trip.

May 1 would be another of the dreaded firsts, perhaps *the* most dreadful one. It was the day that always commemorated the most important event in my life – my wedding. It had been a gorgeous day at Cornell in 1977, which I felt was a harbinger of a fabulous future. Now it commemorated the day I left the safe confines of Fair Chance Farm, which was the last time I'd felt like I had a home.

What better place to spend it than in New Jersey with all the dear friends that I missed so much? I had to agree that my soul got this right. I'd be in need of more than just support through the phone wires and computer screen. So, I created the perfect solution without even knowing it at the time. Imagine what I could do if I was aware of creating? Now, there's something to aim towards.

I planned to stay with Master Michele, David, and Marie. Their house renovation was almost complete, and I was welcome. I really felt this trip would help extract me from the Abyss. Just planning the trip made me feel better. I contacted Jennifer and told her I wanted to get together. I sent her info on the three properties I was interested in.

When Ernie helped move the garage parts in, he'd offered to let me park my horse trailer at his farm. Ernie's farm was designed for parking big equipment and trailers. I called him, accepted his offer, and moved my trailer before I left for New Jersey. Once again, I never expected how emotional this would be for me.

It had been eight months since I moved from the mountain and ten months since I'd known that it was never going to be my home. As I drove off the mountain with my last remaining possessions, I burst into tears, obviously still repressing a ton of emotions over my lost dream. I thought I'd made progress, but I just had so much more to uncover, learn, and let go of. Why was I having so much trouble with this? Well, I was due at Gregory's first thing in the morning. Hopefully, I'd get some answers from him and his colleagues.

Chapter 9

Help Arrives

I want to preface my experiences with Gregory and his colleagues with a disclaimer of sorts. It's a plea to those of you who find this *way out there* to simply read my words without judgment. I'm sharing them because they were real and beneficial to me. Since *we each create our own reality*, I created these experiences for my own growth and healing. It is my hope that my experiences, if read with an open heart and mind, will be beneficial to whomever is ready. I am willing to share the essence of them, but will refrain from sharing the most personal information. My hope is that others who are enduring the depth of pain, unhappiness, and fear that I have can learn from my story and hasten their healing.

There is a risk I take in losing those of you who aren't ready to accept my experiences without judgment, but my story can't be told without the inclusion of my work with Gregory and the Beings that communicate through him. What they taught was integral to my healing and eventual soul's evolution. Please don't let your fears prevent you from finding the truth hidden within you. Remember – absence of judgment!

I headed off to Gregory's with very few expectations. I meditated a little the night before asking for whatever I needed, or more precisely, for whomever I needed to come to help me with my unresolved pain and unhappiness. Gregory records his sessions, which allowed me to listen to the information brought forth over and over. This was a valuable tool, because I heard new things each time I reviewed the tapes. *When the student is ready... .*

This student was over-ready. Gregory's evaluation of my recent life experiences was very insightful. There were some things I wasn't especially pleased to hear. For instance, he didn't feel I was meant to return to New Jersey. I'd learned from my animal healing practice about the accuracy of the information available to us if we only ask, believe, and allow it to come to us. I had lost faith in my own intuition of late, so I was grateful for Gregory's input.

After we talked for quite a while, Gregory began to channel. The room was filled with a most wonderful, gentle energy. I felt completely safe with the entity, or more accurately, the group of entities that introduced themselves as Master Teacher Spirit (MTS). I will refer to them as "he" because the energy felt masculine. He told me so many things that I'd always wondered about. He offered insights on my current situation. He always seemed to know the right time to bring in some humor to break the seriousness of the conversation. I was so blown away by what I had heard. I couldn't think of a single question when asked if I had any: hundreds, but none that slowed down enough for me to grab them.

We said our farewells, and Gregory's consciousness returned to his body. Three hours came and went in the blink of an eye. Three hours that changed my life. It was more than I could have hoped for. Gregory gave me a copy of a book he had written as I was leaving. I was touched by his gesture. I still was having a hard time assimilating all that I had heard about myself.

I began reading Gregory's book, which resonated with me. I felt like I was reading about my Self. Over the years, I'd learned a truism: "Truth isn't truth out of timing." Well, the information that had just come to me was truth in the ideal timing. This student was more than ready, willing, and anxious to get on with it.

I listened to the tapes and heard things I'd missed during the channeling. I'd been somewhat distracted by the feeling of the energetic presence within the room. I felt loved and admired, and also felt a familiarity that I didn't comprehend. When I communicate with animals, I am clairaudient and clairsentient. I hear and feel. The degree of feeling I have is comparable to seeing. I can't describe it any better than that. It's just like seeing with your feelings.

I'd had a few other experiences with channeled Beings over the years. The interesting similarity is their absolute refusal to tell you what to do. They offer insights, but never interfere with Free Will. Sometimes you'd love nothing more than for them to tell you what to do, but that's not how it works.

MTS offered support, explanations, insights, and teachings. I accepted with every part of my being their offer of help. I was anxious to get on with whatever lay ahead for me. I was tired of looking back into my painful Past. I sensed my climb out of the Abyss and re-entry into the Tunnel had begun with this new experience. I called to set up another session.

I was ready to get back to my spiritual path and continue the journey that had been disrupted by my folks' cancers, the move, and my separation and divorce. It was time to put those behind me and look ahead. I felt encouraged that I could achieve this with Gregory and his colleagues' help. How convenient he lived a mile away. Oh those coincidences!

The day before my next session, I jotted down some pertinent questions. As anxious as I was to move past all of this pain and unhappiness, I knew it was unrealistic to think that a few sessions would do it. I wanted nothing more than to discover what my future healing work would be, but I was experienced enough to know that I had to heal first.

MTS had counseled me to *do* nothing. He wanted me to express my emotions in a safe way. He said I harbored rage over centuries that I was trying to release through this recent life experience I'd created for myself. There it was again: *my creation*. I was having so much trouble accepting this. On a deeper plane I knew it to be truth, but on the surface it just seemed unlikely.

MTS asked me to focus on three keys to my healing: Trust, Passion, Purpose. My job was to heal Self. He felt I'd been doing a bang-up job, even though I didn't give myself credit for it. So, what else is new? It's so much easier to help others and facilitate their healing than to help one's self. Hello, why are you *alone* in the mountains?

I finished Gregory's book, inhaling the information. One of the most startling things in it was a picture of a proposed healing center – a round healing center. I brought pictures of my dream house to show Gregory. We discussed my response to the presence of MTS. In the past, I'd sat in awe of whatever Being was channeled. With MTS, I felt like a peer. While I still am in awe of the process, I likened it to a communication between friends. Gregory asked me why I thought that was.

I had to admit that I felt I'd grown as a soul and in my understanding of spirituality. I assumed that was why I felt a peer with this enlightened presence. It was a contradiction to the way I had been feeling about myself of late: no self-confidence, low self-esteem, defeated, a failure at love and marriage, wounded.

The entity that Gregory channeled this time wasn't MTS. I was slightly disappointed, since I'd already bonded with MTS. However, I knew that whoever was speaking could best help me with my work on this day. These entities were feminine. She called herself Meera and offered me more information about where I was from, why I had come, what I needed to do for my Self in this moment, etc. It fascinated me. She answered my questions seeming to know them already, which made perfect sense to me.

MTS came through next. I was pleased to share his energy again. He came to counsel me not to be in too much of a hurry in purchasing another house. He told me things should become clearer in another couple of months; try to have patience. He sensed it wasn't what I wanted to hear and told me as much. He left me with the tip, "Don't be too hasty." Great! I decided to go to Jersey with an open mind and to be more critical. However, I would be true to my heart regardless of where my warnings came from.

In amongst all of this spiritual enlightenment, I still dealt with the frustrations of the physical world. The realtors hadn't done any of the national advertising they promised. I continued to check on the mountain property to be sure everything was okay. Being there still elicited feelings of disappointment, disillusionment, and confusion over the loss of something that had appeared so *meant to be*. I worked on getting the original Maui timeshare changed into my maiden name. Once again, something I didn't think should be a big deal took forever and a million phone calls.

A couple of days before I was to depart for Jersey, Ken called to say they were ready to cut in the new drive. I had been waiting for months, and now they're ready. I told him they had to do it while I was here. I'd learned my lesson with the dog fencing fiasco. I swore I would never have anything major done without being present. My goal was to improve the marketability of the property with the new drive, plus have the advantage of its use for myself. When the driveway was finished, I was relieved to see how much of an improvement it actually was.

Jodi came and I was on my way to New Jersey to find my better dream. I went with a new perspective gleaned from my sessions with Gregory. I would try to *feel* what was right for me and not be too hasty. I drove away in tears with my boys' questioning eyes begging me not to go. Being left and feeling abandoned were still sore topics for me. I knew they liked Jodi, but they loved and wanted me. I explained the reason for my trip, but I knew they didn't care where we lived as long as we were together. They offered such wisdom, but I was shielded from it by my unhappiness. They never stopped trying to teach me.

I felt going back to New Jersey, where all my friends were, would give me a sense of belonging again and solve all my problems. Down deep, I knew it wasn't the "where" that was the root of my unhappiness. My lost dream, my lost love, my living alone, and my inability to accept and surrender to my reality were the underlying causes of my unhappiness. Once again the motel room magnified my sense of loneliness.

My self-confidence was so shaky that I didn't know if I would recognize the right house or not. I just kept thinking about MTS' advice, "Don't be too hasty." I stopped for lunch with my gal pals, and then went on to meet Jennifer, the realtor. Sadly, two of the three houses I was interested in were under contract. I kept hearing, "New Jersey might be what you want, but it isn't what you need at the moment." Gregory had told me about a recurrent theme in his work of just that; "You may not get what you want, but you always get what you *need* from the Universe." Bah, I say!

Jen and I got to know one another a little better. We reviewed new listings on the MLS. There were a couple of things that were mildly interesting. I told her I'd drive past them and if I needed to see them, I'd get her involved.

My friends were my salvation. I needed to refill my tanks with their love and support to get me through the next however many months until I got myself back home. I met Vince for our usual Saturday brunch. I really missed those brunches in North Carolina. We spent a long time talking, especially about my Maui trip.

After I left Vince, I spent the rest of the afternoon with Michelle, Michele, and Marie. They really got me laughing, which was something I very rarely did these days. I was so grateful to have them in my life. They were my newest friends, but they had quickly revealed themselves as forever friends. I was blessed with so many forever friends. Not only did I want them, I needed them.

The next day, I met Pam for breakfast. Pam's dog, my godson, was having a cardiac test in the late afternoon. I pondered the timing of Wil's procedure and my visit. Years earlier, I'd been taught about universal timing: *always in perfection, no coincidences, everything happens for a reason.* I was hoping this wasn't one of those times. I didn't dwell on it, but it did give me pause. Pam and I had a nice visit, but I knew she was worried.

Marie and I drove around and looked at houses, including one Marie wanted me to look at around the corner from them, but it just didn't do anything for me. I could sense her disappointment. None were appropriate. I was getting frustrated and depressed while echoes of "don't be too hasty" rang in my ears.

Help Arrives

I was getting out of the shower when my cell rang. Pam was trying to tell me through her tears that she just put Wil to sleep. My worst nightmare had come true. This was one of those times when I wished I was wrong. Intuition can be your best friend and your worst enemy. I told Pam I'd be right over. She said it wasn't necessary, but I would hear none of that. I'd be there as quickly as I could. A sad little voice said, "Okay, thanks."

When I got to Pam's, we just hugged and cried. It was unimaginable to have the condo empty of that joyful energy. It was obvious from Pam's reaction that my being there meant everything to her. While we had been out of touch for years, we were forever friends. Friends that might not see each other for years, but when you get together, the years melt away. I was so grateful for the perfection of the Universe. There was nowhere else I wanted to be at this horribly difficult time for Pam. Wil was like her child, her companion, and her most loyal supporter. I knew the sense of sudden loss and emptiness she felt. Oh these unexpected events, they're simply killers.

When we stopped crying, Pam explained that Wil had a rare heart condition with no treatment or surgery options. Wil would never get any better. Through Pam's herculean efforts, Wil had merrily survived his diabetes and resulting blindness. This heart condition was the final straw. Pam chose to let go and send Wil Home.

The next day, I ran past the farm to check on my parents' resting places. Everything looked the same as the day we left, except the fencing was in need of repair or removal. It was discouraging to see how little the town did for the farm. I just had to let go of the sadness that welled up in me when I saw this special place being disrespected.

I always left New Jersey feeling stronger and cared about, although I was very disappointed in the real estate aspect. The prices were simply absurd for what they were selling. I thought about all the roadblocks in the house search. My analysis led me to question if I really was supposed to be moving back. While I didn't want to hear it, I couldn't ignore the lack of flow in my search. I've always put a lot of stock in how things transpire. If it's the right thing, things get facilitated and *flow*.

I had to admit there wasn't a special feeling while driving around the county. My special feelings came from the time spent with my friends. If I lived in the area, the need to have to see everyone within a short time would disappear. Each area was at the full swing of the pendulum: New Jersey with all my friends and North Carolina with no friends. My challenge was to try to bring the pendulum to the center, so life would be balanced and harmony could return to my life.

My endearing animal family was waiting for me when I drove in. Their reception made me feel like I meant something to someone. They *never* let me down. I'd started Stormy's training before I left, so the next day I headed over to resume his work. I recognized myself when I was at the farm. His training gave me a sense of purpose. My confidence and self-esteem were fine in the arena of horses, unlike the rest of my life where they were almost non-existent.

A mere two days after my return, I sat staring at a new listing on Jen's website. The house was about three miles from the farm. It had one and a half acres bordering Green Acres (state land), and most all of the big items were newly replaced. Two days! What is the Universe thinking? I contacted Jen immediately and asked her to send me a picture as soon as one was available. Next, I emailed a copy of the listing to my gal pals, who Jen dubbed my posse.

I had to check on the dream property. The dogs loved the mountain, and they deserved some happiness. I made a startling discovery. My mood was... *neutral*! As hard as I tried, I always fell prey to my negative emotions of lost expectations, disillusionment, and betrayal. What had changed? I didn't understand my newfound attitude, but whatever it was, I liked it. I couldn't help but wonder if it had anything to do with the new listing that had appeared yesterday. Funny how my desire to give my dogs some happiness gifted me with the knowledge that something significant within me had changed for the better.

Alice called me from the Jersey house in question. She really liked it and asked if she should look at it. I said sure. I called Master Michele and Marie, who agreed to meet Alice and the realtor. I couldn't believe all this was happening. Alice called saying they could only see the outside until it was officially on the market the following Sunday. Then, why is it on the MLS? I really didn't get this real estate business. My head was spinning with the rapid turn of events.

I went about my business trying to keep from obsessing over the situation. The phone rang. It was my posse. Alice was describing the house and yard. She loved the house and its possibilities. She'd email pictures when she got home. Michele was as excited as Alice. They all thought I should make an offer before it hit the market. I was thrown into what my mother used to call a tizzy. Their excitement was so infectious. I needed to see the house and *feel* the land. They knew what I meant, but... I'd think about it and get back to them.

A moment later the phone rang. It was Michele again. "You won't believe who just drove in the driveway?" So, who is it? It was Heather, who I'd known for years. What *synchronicity*! Heather's best friend was the seller. "No way!" She offered to speak with her friend, Colleen, to see if the posse could get inside before the Open House. The proverbial cosmic 2 X 4 was banging on my conscious mind. It appeared that synchronicity was working its magic. Heather's arrival was a sign that I was supposed to see the house.

I began an inner struggle as to how to manage this last-minute trip to New Jersey. Jodi was away, so I had no one to leave the dogs with. Michele offered to have the dogs stay there, while I was thinking out loud over the phone. In their advancing age, I didn't want to cause any additional emotional stress for them. And, I had three cats to consider. It's hell when you don't know anyone to seek help from. I had only myself to rely on.

My inner demons were rampant with all the reasons why I couldn't return to Jersey. Wasn't I getting the cart before the horse? Just thinking about my only option, which was taking the dogs and leaving ample food and water in the crawl space for the cats had me *way* out of my comfort zone. I tried to calm down, and let my intuition guide me. I'd been waiting for something like this for months. I knew this was about putting me ahead of others. I'd been trying to recognize and embrace this lesson for some time now. The difficult choice was what I deduced to be a test. I wondered if I'd pass this one.

While I ruminated on the decision facing me, Alice sent me the photos of the house and yard. My first impression of the house wasn't earth shattering. It was neutral. The intriguing thing was the presence of a Japanese split leaf maple in the front of the house. Alice knew I'd tried to grow three on the farm before I gave up. There it was in the photo like it was waiting for me. The yard was very attractive. The neighbor houses were close, but along one side there were mature flowering cherry tress. The yard was more promising than the house. I had to *feel* it. Seeing a photo wouldn't allow my guidance system to work its wonders.

Heather could get them into see the house on Wednesday. I had to decide. I chose to put Self first. I had to leave the next morning. Because of the cats, this would be an incredibly fast trip. I knew the dogs wouldn't care. They loved the car, and always, always, just wanted to be with me.

I couldn't help but mutter to the Universe about the timing of the listing. Why couldn't this have come on the market a few days earlier? How inconvenient this was for my critters and me. It would take me months to realize the perfection in the timing. The timing forced me to begin the task of learning to put my needs ahead of others – something that was totally alien to me.

I stopped much more frequently with the dogs on board. Our stops added a good hour to the already long day, but whatever was best for them. My Carolina realtor called to say that someone was going to look at the mountain property the next day. A huge smile burst forth. This was nothing short of miraculous. I just knew this was all happening in absolute *perfection.*

As I continued to drive, I worked hard to keep myself from getting too far ahead of the Now. I imagined all sorts of results from the events unfolding before my very eyes. I'd been waiting, so patiently, for things to begin to flow. It appeared that my wait was over. I tried to guard myself from getting my hopes up too much to avoid crashing and burning if things didn't work out. I fought with my ego, which constantly tried to get me to focus on the future.

It was an exhausting trip. I had a lot of unresolved worry about the strain the trip was having on my old dogs. In reality, they were fine. It was me being stressed by the trip. I found out that the appointment to see the house wasn't until 1 p.m. the next day. The dogs adapted just fine to Michele and David's house. The next morning, I drove past the house on my way to breakfast at Perkins. I didn't feel any real attraction to the house.

Not knowing what to do with my time after breakfast, I took the dogs to the only home they really ever knew. We spent two hours on our farm. They ran all over just like they'd never left. Their joy was infectious. It was thrilling to see them so happy. If nothing else came of this trip, the time spent with my two devoted friends on their farm was enough for me. They didn't know it wasn't their farm anymore. They are such teachers if I'd only watch and listen.

I rounded up the dogs and headed to meet Master Michele and Marie at Perkins, after which Master Michele and I met Heather at the house. I liked the open feeling I got when we entered. Colleen's husband, Rob, told me he was in the middle of replacing the roof. Michele and I walked around all the rooms. The house didn't give me any special feeling. We walked out into the back yard, which was big, fenced, and great for the dogs. I walked beyond the fencing where the property continued into the woods and supposedly met state land.

I needed to be alone with the land to see what it *said* to me. I hadn't expected to find anything with this kind of seclusion for the price. Don't get me wrong; it wasn't special like my farm, but it was acceptable. Rob walked out to show me where the property lines went. I wondered if they'd accept an offer before the official Open House. I figured it would go quickly once it was on the market. I thought I could be happy living here. Rob said, "Think about it and get back to me before Sunday." If Rob was willing, I was offering their price. He was, and we shook hands.

Help Arrives

We walked back into the house and told everyone. They were shocked and happy with our news. It wasn't ideal, but I could make it work. All the signs from the Universe pointed towards that conclusion. I headed back to tell Little Michelle. I will never forget her face when I walked inside and said, "Well, it looks like I'm moving back." She was ecstatic. I don't think there was anyone who wanted me back in New Jersey more, except *moi*!

With that handshake, I committed myself to purchasing an almost $400,000 house. Talk about being over housed! I still owned two properties in Carolina. However, I did have someone looking at the mountain property. The circumstances leading up to this moment just seemed so *meant to be*, which gave me a lot of faith that everything would fall in line and flow.

If anyone would have told me the day we moved that I would be divorced, my Ex remarried, and I'd be buying a house in New Jersey a year later, I would have told them they'd lost their mind. But, here I was doing just that. Of course, I was on the phone to my dear friend and lawyer, Peter, about handling the closing. Having such a close friend as your lawyer is phenomenal. No worries with Peter at the helm. Next, I called my CPA, Milt, with my news. He'd finished the taxes that had been delayed by my Ex's tardiness. We agreed to meet later, so I could sign the forms and get them filed. I'd gone from nothing in my life working to everything seemingly working and quickly.

I tried to catch my breath on my way to meet Milt. I wasn't having second thoughts, but concerns about paying for it. Milt assured me I'd have no trouble securing financing given my assets. I signed the tax returns and headed back to have dinner with more friends.

Alice was thrilled that I'd decided to buy the house. I was leaving early the next morning due to my cats. Since these people were such good friends of Heather's, I wasn't too concerned about the absence of anything in writing. Alice related the story about what happened to her and Roger, when they bought their house. They'd almost lost it to someone who offered the seller slightly more, after their bid had been accepted. Long story short: they ended up in court. Alice was adamant about not leaving without something in writing.

I called the sellers and told them about Alice's advice. I'd leave a $500 check to hold the property, until the realtors got my official deposit and signed contract. Rob said he wouldn't deposit the check. I stopped by their house early the next morning to sign the agreement and leave the check.

The dogs had been pretty anxious staying in someone else's house, but they managed. It wasn't something I wanted to subject them to again, but it had been worth it. Part of my reasoning behind the decision to return to New Jersey to see the house involved regret. If I didn't come to see it, I would never know. I tried to live my life so as not to have regrets. I've learned you can't always stay in your comfort zone without risking regrets.

By moving out of my self-imposed limitations, I obtained something that was of great benefit without any loss of well being for my animals. I'd found our new house. They'd found joy romping on the farm once more. It was a win-win situation. There was a huge lesson for me. I could focus on Self first without causing any undue harm to others I cared about. It was important for me to embrace this teaching gifted by my animals and my soul.

Despite the concerns of floating another mortgage, I was excited about coming home. There were so many things that had to be dealt with. I just needed to take them one at a time to keep from falling back into the Abyss. What, you ask, you've left the Abyss? I have. I extracted myself with the lesson of putting Self first. I've moved along my path of healing, ever so little, but enough to get back to the Tunnel with a light at the end of it – progress. You bet there's been progress and it's about time!

As I drove, I was thinking of everything I needed to do for this house to happen. It was a little overwhelming to say the least. I've always held the belief that there are no mistakes in life, only opportunities for learning. I believe, as long as we learn from them, they have value. I wanted to make sure everything I'd lived through with the log house had been learned and would not be repeated. Stopping every two hours to let the dogs out for a walkabout distracted me from a mind exploding with emotions.

The longer I drove, the more it sunk in what I'd just committed myself to. I sang along with my music for 600 miles trying to keep my ego from scaring me to death with all sorts of fears and worries. It carried me full force into my future. The only time I spent in the Now was walking the dogs. Good thing they came with me.

About halfway along my cell rang. I figured it was someone from Jersey. You can imagine my amusement when I heard my Carolina realtor's voice. I'd completely forgotten about the prospective buyer. The people liked the property and made an offer. I smiled to myself at the workings of the universe. Whoa, what did I just hear? They offered how much? Immediately, my flowing reality screeched to a halt!

My short-lived happiness converted to anger instantly. The realtor was going on and on with a doom and gloom critique of the current real estate market in the area. I told him the offer wasn't worth commenting on. I'd call him when I got back in town. I had a whirlwind of emotions raging inside me: relief, happiness, worry, fear, anger. I just kept singing and driving, driving and singing. So much for flow.

I was driving back on Stormy's third birthday, which brought me back to one of my wonderful memories of life, B.N.C. (Before North Carolina.) Stormy's dear mother, Squiggles, had trouble giving birth her previous two times. It took all of our skills, along with the mare's strength and the foals' fortitude, to insure Squiggles' successful results. Her first two foals were colts. I'd wanted a filly to give me the option of breeding a third generation. Bob didn't want to breed Squiggles again. Her second foaling had been an improvement, so I really didn't understand his concern. I had such a strong feeling of remorse over it, like someone had died.

After *talking* it over with Squiggles, we went ahead and bred her. The result was Stormy; three years ago during a thunderstorm on Mother's Day. Squiggles experienced her most normal foaling of all and achieved her soul's purpose for this lifetime. Stormy is gorgeous in body, mind, and spirit and has been my salvation these past difficult months. Squiggles taught me a powerful lesson, which I used for Stormy's show name, Follow Your Heart.

I spent time thinking about that lesson on my way back from New Jersey. It was important that I not forget her teaching. Now more than ever, I needed to remember to follow my heart. It had served me well four years earlier when I bred Squiggles one last time. Given the fact that I'd been forced to euthanize her first two colts, if I hadn't followed my heart, I'd be without one of the few positive aspects of my life. It was a lesson my soul needed me to remember, especially now, with my life in a turmoil.

We arrived at the log house exhausted. I'd been wishing for something of this magnitude to happen, but now I was confronted by all of the fallout that was attached to it. I couldn't help but think about the saying, "Be careful what you wish for."

Chapter 10

Moving Home

*J*en worked on the contract and gave me the name of a mortgage gal she worked with. She and Peter would be my mainstays in New Jersey. After a good night's rest, I got right at it the next day. I spoke with three different mortgage people. Unlike the mortgage on the log house, this was going to be what Milt called creative financing. For my own sanity, I needed to be sure I could carry the financial load until the dream house sold in the fall. I began creating the reality of selling in the fall.

My stress was mounting, and this was only the beginning. My income source didn't fit in the nice little box that the lending companies wanted. I spent hours on the phone with different brokers. I will say the enormity of the task brought my business mind out of retirement or from wherever it was hiding. I was back to my analytical self. I felt a little empowered and more in control of my life, and I liked it.

Jen got the contract to me, which I returned with the actual deposit check for $1000. Along with Milt, I worked with my friend and financial advisor, Ed, to figure out the best way to finance this house. None of my assets were very liquid, necessitating the creative part of the financing. It was so frustrating thinking about how much money the mountain represented, yet, I had no access to it. The property was free and clear, but the lenders wouldn't allow me to use it as collateral. It just seemed idiotic to me. I kept telling myself it wasn't right or wrong, it just was. So, get over it, *let go*, and move on!

Back in Carolina, I was dealing with the insulting offer on the dream property and the abrupt change of heart about my two properties' values. I had grave concerns about the local housing market. My confidence in purchasing the New Jersey house was tied directly to selling the mountain property. I met the realtor to discuss the situation. I know I sound like a broken record – remember those things? But I had another of those completely unexpected bad experiences.

My meeting turned out to be with the marketing whiz owner and the woman listing agent. The lookers made another offer, which was still insulting. I told the wiz he'd have to call my Ex with any offers since we didn't speak. He'd been trying, but he hadn't gotten any response to his calls. So, what else is new? The two agents began telling me how the market had changed, and I should really consider the offer. They were relentless. It was doom and gloom all around.

I was shaken by what I heard. My ego filled me with fear and self-doubt. Whatever empowerment I might have felt was lost now. They filled me with fears of my Future, of my recent decision to buy the house in Jersey, and of the losses I could expect with the Carolina properties. I felt stunned, so alone, fragile, and defeated. I left there a beaten down shell of the woman that had walked in there only an hour earlier.

I drove back to the log house in tears. What had I done? Whatever was I going to do? Tons of self-doubt and fear overtook me. My negative emotions were back in full control. I called to talk with Master Michele. She is very savvy in things financial, since she used to work in that arena. I needed to talk with someone knowledgeable that I could trust. When I explained what I'd just encountered, she flew into a rage. She told me that what they did to me was an old ploy. They ambushed me. Michele called it Sales 101.

By the time she got done, I felt somewhat better. She was sure they lied about the local market to get me to take the offer on the property. My fear had usurped my ability to use my common sense. I was vulnerable to their attack, because I didn't even recognize it as one. My dealings with people over the past several months were a perfect example of why I preferred animals. I was just better with animals. I trusted them. Lessons were flying all around me, but I was too emotional to see them. I was so grateful for Michele's expertise and her loyalty.

I called Milt about the Jersey financing and told him my tale of woe about the disastrous meeting. He echoed Michele's words. He told me to never go into a meeting alone against two people. I told him I *was* alone: no husband, no friends, just me. I'd received my opportunity for learning. I was touched by his loyalty too. I knew if this was happening in New Jersey, he or Michele would be with me for the next meeting.

Word got out about what I'd just been put through. I got calls of support and disgust at my treatment by the realtors. My friends' calls meant the world to me. They gave me the confidence to make an appointment to speak with the owner alone. I was *very* specific about alone. I had to let go of the memory of the last meeting, so I could engage the realtor from an empowered position. If we were to have any kind of a viable working relationship, I had to show him I wasn't someone he could manipulate. He worked for me not the other way around.

I moved away from my feelings of fear and self-doubt. Now, I was angry at being treated so poorly by someone who was supposed to be my hired hand. I'd learned from the first realtor from Hell about misrepresentation, and I wasn't going to allow that to happen again. I would take back control of this relationship, or I would let go and move on. His response to our next meeting would dictate the outcome.

More frustrations came from the mortgage rates I was receiving. When Milt heard I hadn't found a good rate, he had a bank he worked with get in touch with me. The gal was very nice, but had the same assessment of my income. Neither Milt nor I understood why my income was being treated in the way it was. As much as we didn't like it, what we thought really didn't matter. I felt better when Milt, a seasoned CPA, was as confused about it as I was. It didn't change anything, except I felt less naïve.

I moved forward with scheduling inspections. Even if the house had been new, I had received my opportunity for learning from the log house loud and clear. Whatever could be inspected would be! I asked my friend Frank if he could meet the house inspector on my behalf. There wasn't any way I could get back to Jersey. It gave me peace of mind knowing Frank would be scrutinizing this house for me. I had a great team!

Peter was in the middle of drawing up the contract. As usual, Peter was done with his part very quickly. The seller's attorney was holding things up. Peter was becoming as frustrated as I was. Orchestrating three different inspection companies was no easy task, but I did it. Working on the deal in New Jersey was restoring my feeling of empowerment before my next meeting with the realtor.

I was dealing with the timeshare deal as well. My father-in-law complicated it somewhat, but in a good way when he called about going to Maui next Christmas/New Year's. I called the new resort and found out I couldn't make a reservation until the transfer of ownership was complete.

As with the rest of my life, nothing was going to be easy with this request, but little did I know how long this would take to get accomplished. So far nothing had been changed. The records showed that the unit was owned by my Ex and me. Oh my, this was going to take some time.

I called the title company in California, who I filed the quitclaim deed with long ago, and found they hadn't received needed paperwork from Bob. I sat in disbelief at what I heard. I felt the anger rising within me. With the distraction from the Jersey deal and keeping after the Carolina realtors, I hadn't even thought about the Maui deed.

Our divorce papers directed Bob to facilitate the changeover. I emailed him and explained that his father wanted to use the unit in January, and I couldn't get a reservation until the deed work was completed. I called Vince to tell him what the hold up was, and he offered to call his stepson. I got an email saying the papers would go overnight the next day.

I focused on my car registration next. I'd made the judgment to wait until it was time to renew the registration to change my name. Again, a seemingly simple task turned into an unexpected nightmare fanning the flames of my unresolved anger towards my Ex. The horse trailer was simple, but Ford Credit required the North Carolina Department of Motor Vehicles to initiate the title request. Okay. Obviously, this was going to take some time, so I simply renewed the car in my Ex's name and paid the fee.

Ever since the handshake in New Jersey, my life went from long boring days to days filled with lenders, lawyers, advisors, and friends. It amazed me the change that one handshake created. With all the distractions, I'd been ignoring my dysfunctional French doors until I couldn't any longer. I feared the glass might break trying to close them. Kim's brother, Chris, repaired them without making it an expensive job.

While he was here, Chris helped me move the fence posts to the porch. As far as getting them picked up, the biggest deterrent was my own procrastination. I just didn't want another battle. I was so tired of fighting everybody. Moving the heavy posts outside forced me to call the company. I mustered up all my emotional fortitude and called.

The gal at the fencing company couldn't have been nicer and was happy to issue the call tags. As soon as they had them back, they issued a credit to my credit card. Oh my God, there are people who are accountable out there besides me. My emotional blinders were still fully in place shielding me from the truth and the lessons being offered to me, just like in Maui.

My Ex created more anger and frustration for me over *my* car. Even though my opinion of the *imposter* was pretty low, his message sent me into a fury. He told me, in no uncertain terms, that he would not sign the title as our divorce settlement dictated. He wanted me to pay off the loan first, because it was adversely affecting his credit rating. It was a good thing he lived 1600 miles away, or I might be picking up trash along the highway with the rest of the convicted felons!

When I was told that I was attempting to let go of rage over the centuries, I questioned it. I'd never felt anything that could remotely resemble rage. Well, I had no trouble recognizing rage as it exploded from its hiding place deep within my consciousness. It took me quite some time to calm my rage down into ordinary anger. Anger allowed me to function. Rage simply paralyzed me. I needed to handle this challenge with the same emotional detachment that my upcoming meeting with the realtor required.

This scenario was much more difficult to be detached from. I found it inconceivable that this man, who deceived and betrayed me, was giving me ultimatums. Did he really think I cared if he was having borrowing problems? After what he'd put me through, he should facilitate this for me. This was just more evidence that the honorable man I'd loved was dead. The *imposter* was in for a real shock if he thought he could manipulate me.

He knew nothing about the house deal in New Jersey and never would. He'd given up that right long ago. I had asked my in-laws not to say anything to him, and I trusted them to honor my wish. I told him that thanks to his deceit I had enough trouble paying my bills for six animals, a big mortgage, and myself. He was required by our settlement to do whatever was necessary to turn the title for my car over to me. My car was in his name for a business reasons. Yet another person was not being responsible or accountable. If need be I would seek legal help, but I sent my email off first. Time would tell.

All of these things were taking their toll on me. I began to wonder what happened to the flow that had returned to my life. Instead of the sense of freedom that accompanied flow, I felt like I was wading through quicksand. Ten steps forward, five steps down and backward. Fears and self-doubt were creeping back into my movie.

The excitement I'd felt driving back from New Jersey was disappearing and being replaced with worry. I was barraged with battles on all fronts: the deal in Jersey, the real estate in Carolina, the car, the timeshare trade, the log house. I needed to find out why, so I booked a session with Gregory.

Moving Home

The only thing that helped me stay sane during this time was my animal family. Thank goodness, Stormy was back in training. When I was with him, I was forced to stay in the present moment. Working with youngsters is challenging, but so rewarding when you see their progress. Stormy was in a very receptive mode during this time. Without him, I would have simply lost it and probably given up. Each time I left the farm, he had gifted me with the confidence I needed to deal with all the other anxieties in my life. I was so grateful to have him with me. *Follow Your Heart*!

At home, my dogs and cats supported me, especially the dogs. Their unconditional love just made me feel worthwhile and special. They bolstered my sagging self-esteem. Crystal's purring elicited feelings of calm, peace, and harmony. She slept on the king bed with me every night, which kept it from feeling so big and empty. You wouldn't expect an eleven-pound cat to fill such a void, but she did.

My animals' presence kept me aware of the emotions I expressed. With the dogs' advancing ages, I didn't want to be the cause of any additional stress for them. They picked up any negativity within me in order to protect me. I learned this from my years in the animal communication business. By doing this, they created dis-ease within themselves. Shadow's aging was becoming more obvious, since he was declining quicker than Licorice. Shadow and I had a very deep bond. While I loved Licorice, it was different. I knew Shadow's more rapid decline was due in part to my trauma. I'd learned not to carry guilt over this issue.

When companion animals answer our souls' cries for help, they come willingly and fast with the intent to help us in any way possible. Shadow was doing that for me. I tried to lessen his load by being conscious of my negative emotions. I was doing my best for him as was he for me. I knew negativity would also create dis-ease within me, but it was their well-being I was more worried about. Wonder when I'm going to start getting the "heal Self first" lesson? My concern for their health manifested better health for myself. Whatever would I have done without these animal teachers? Perished, no doubt.

It was approaching three weeks since the handshake in New Jersey, and I couldn't see many results for my intense efforts. I couldn't wait to get some input from my session with Gregory. The timing of the day before my next meeting with the realtor was perfect. Should we be surprised at that? I don't think so.

I think Gregory was surprised to hear the apparent synchronicity of finding the house in Jersey. I described my recent visit to the mountain property and the emotional change I experienced. I wanted to get some feedback on what might be behind my emotional shift. He felt that I was releasing things from the

Past. He advised me to stay neutral just like I felt on the mountain. It was from a neutral position that I would find, heal, and rebuild Self.

Gregory felt that boundaries were at the heart of the myriad of challenges of the past three weeks. My ability to stand up for myself and not be manipulated, and my ability to say no were being tested. I needed to be empowered like I was when I made the handshake in Jersey, not like when I became unraveled by the Re/Max duo. I needed to set my boundaries and stand up for my Self again.

The work I'd stumbled into was deep soul work. It wasn't going to be easy and required commitment. If I were going to truly heal my Self and my soul, I needed to be willing to invest the time and energy required. I knew that I might get the lessons eventually, but allowing Gregory to illuminate them for me really sped up my learning curve. His gifts were invaluable to me. He also spent a lot of time counseling me on how to approach my meeting the following day. It was so nice to have someone to confer with who I trusted... and a man no less. I felt renewed and ready to confront the realtor from a place of power.

My session with Gregory, a visit to my mountain, and some time with Stormy put me in a much better mindset for my meeting with the realtor. I entered this meeting with eyes wide open, ready to meet head-on whatever he was going to do to manipulate me into accepting this offer from Hell. I set the tone from the start.

I had real issues with the listing agent's performance and told him what I thought of her, and the job his agency was doing. I wasn't complimentary. He was busy back-peddling about my comments. I asked him, point blank, if he wanted to sell these listings. Could he be positive about them? If not, then we were done.

I felt I had done all I could to motivate him. I walked out of that meeting an entirely different woman than the last time. I felt strong and in command. I went into the meeting hoping to handle it like Dad would have. He was the consummate people person. I didn't want to go into it from a defensive position. I wanted to get this realtor to *want* to work for me, not *have* to work for me. I had learned the Universal Law of Attraction long ago – *whatever energy you send out comes back to you*. I wanted to create the best results I could. I knew my dad was proud, as was I. The rest was up to the realtor.

I left the meeting and drove directly to the farm and Stormy. I needed the peace and harmony I always felt there. While I had handled myself well in the meeting, it had drained me. I needed to be renewed before I returned to timeshares, lenders, inspection schedules, car issues, and realtors. I recognized the appearance of the New Jersey house as synchronistic, but I started to wonder if it was truly serendipitous.

Moving Home

The difficulties that appeared to be surrounding it caused me to take a second look at the universal influence. I heard Gregory's insight about boundaries in the back of my mind. I surmised these challenges were confronting me to stand up for myself and learn to say no. Okay, I got it. Can we get back to things flowing?

The realtor had made me aware of another potential problem. When they'd spoken, Bob told him he wasn't willing to accept the same offer that I would. Rage – here I come! Who was he not to be willing to accept a valid offer? He hadn't been inconvenienced by the mountain property or its care. I was the one left to look after it. How dare he! I surprised myself at the level of anger that seemed to be hiding inside ready to explode given the least amount of provocation. Maybe I did harbor eons of rage. After I heard my Ex's opinion of what was an acceptable offer, I was back in my battle mode.

It was hard enough to find buyers with offers, but now I had to be concerned about interference from New Mexico. Not in this life! I wasn't giving away my power to him anymore. I called Peter and he got my divorce lawyer on the line. I found out that due to my greater equity I could get power of attorney to accept an offer, but I had to have one before petitioning the court. I contacted the realtor with my news. What a relief. Finally, I'd lost my victim mentality and solved a potentially big issue before it happened.

I got an email saying my Ex would be in Carolina in about two weeks. The thought of *that* woman being on *my* mountain really upset me. I told him that he should talk with the realtor. When I got my emotions back in check and my non-reactive mind functional, I realized he could sign the papers for the car and horse trailer transfers. After a few emails, he finally agreed to sign the car title over.

My frustrations and anger level grew when I decided to put the window screens in for the season. There were 18 screens of which only three fit. I was baffled and livid at the same time. How could this be? I was a fairly intelligent person. I should be able to install screens. I asked Kim's brother, Chris, to come out and have a look.

Chris found that only three windows had been trimmed properly; ironically, the three that I wouldn't open because the TV backed up to them. I called the builder from Hell, who should be providing a warranty, but his phone was disconnected. If my life ever calms down, I will go to court against this guy before I move. He and his con-artist family needed to be held accountable for their actions! As Scarlet said in *Gone With the Wind*, "I can't think about that right now. If I do, I'll go crazy. I'll think about it tomorrow!"

I continued to keep a close eye on the Carolina realtors' performance. It wasn't improving. It appeared they were more focused on my listings, but errors were still rampant. This was prime season in the mountains, and I didn't have time to be wasting. They were advertising audio tours on their website for each property. When I called to hear them, I just freaked. The tour for the mountain property was filled with incorrect information and claims. The log house tour gave information on a different property altogether.

I met with the owner to discuss my findings. He was half an hour late, which really angered me – talk about disrespect. I pointed out all the errors in the audio tours and handed him a list of corrections. I reiterated the website errors. I asked, again, about national advertising. I'd hired them to sell properties. I really didn't care if they liked me. The squeaky wheel, you know.

Things were going better in Jersey on the financing front. Milt's bank came up with the best mortgage rate. The decision was made, which always gave me a sense of accomplishment. I had some hesitation, because I worried that some of the information Milt gave her was inaccurate. I'd learned from the insurance debacle not to feel too sure of a sure thing. I got all the Jersey inspections set up for the same day – no easy task. Then, I got a call from Jen, which sent me into orbit, saying we couldn't do them that day even though it was one of the sellers' acceptable dates. I was furious.

With this recent news and the hold ups by the seller's attorney, I called Rob that night. I was tired of following protocol and getting nothing done. Their realtor was giving Jen fits and none of us trusted her. Before I lost the house, I'd talk with the sellers without the middlemen. I was taking back my power.

Unfortunately, I got their answering machine. My message voiced my concerns. With no call back, I canceled all the inspections. I felt like a fool and told each firm that. They were very understanding and said it happened all the time. Not with me. Rob returned my call and wanted to honor our deal. So, I rescheduled everything and everyone was ready to converge on the house on my behalf. It would end up being five weeks between the handshake and the inspections, which was mind-boggling to me.

I took my title papers and left them with Carolyn at the bank. I hoped to get out of town without an encounter with my Ex. I knew he still had an account at the bank and worried we might cross paths. The Universe was kind and didn't allow that to occur. With all the stresses coming at me from all angles, I really couldn't have dealt with a face to face with the person I felt was responsible for the current state of my affairs.

I returned to a message from my realtor. He needed to talk with me right away! Okay. I hoped he had good news about a possible buyer. Instead I heard about an encounter between the buyers with the insulting offer and my Ex. They'd been on the mountain without their realtor.

My Ex shared his less-than-stellar opinion about the realtor's representation, which I really couldn't argue with. He told them to wait another month and *he* would sell it to them after the listing was up. They went right back to their realtor with this story. She called our realtor, who then called me. He was furious, and I couldn't really blame him. My Ex acted despicably and dishonestly further confirming the veracity of my *imposter* theory.

It was ten days short of a year since I'd heard "I never wanted this house." I sat in disgust, because all of my efforts of the past six months were destroyed in a nanosecond. Bob comes back for a moment and undermines all my efforts to sell what he abandoned and I still loved. I didn't have time for out-of-control emotions. I needed my analytical mind right now more than ever.

I told the realtor I'd get in touch with my Ex and explain how that wasn't going to happen. I needed to restore this agent's confidence and promised to honor our contract. I asked him to let me work this out over the weekend, and then get together on Monday.

It took some time to get my rage back in check. I was so exhausted from all of the stresses I'd been dealing with. I didn't have time to question why it was happening. I just had to deal with it. The "why" would have to wait. Since *everything happens for a reason*, I knew there was one, but my attention was focused on how to clean up the mess Bob had created.

I emailed Bob explaining my conversation with the realtor, along with the effects his meeting with the buyers from Hell caused. I agreed with him about the realtors' poor representation, but explained I'd been working tirelessly to rectify that. We were in peak season and to begin with another agency wouldn't be in our best interest. I'd arranged a meeting with the owner to work through this problem and needed his support.

Bob's reply contained some facts that hadn't been part of the realtor's discourse. Based on his added comments, the prospective buyers were even worse than I'd first thought. He was furious when he heard they revealed his comments to their realtor. They played Bob, and I wondered how he liked it.

I wouldn't sell to people of such low character. The sacredness of the mountain deserved stewards of equal caliber. Bob echoed my feelings. I chuckled to myself, because it was hard not to consider him in the same category as the buyers, which he judged as *bad* and unethical. He also said the car's papers were signed. Whew!

LETTING GO

The next morning, I headed to my meeting. To my disappointment, the listing agent also joined us. I had flashbacks to my last two-vs.-one meeting. I heard Milt and Michele in my head, but it was obvious I didn't have a choice in the matter. We talked for a little while about the two properties, but I sensed things turning.

All of a sudden the wiz told me that he couldn't be involved in all the subterfuge with my Ex. They really liked and admired me, but they wouldn't have any dealings with my Ex. They would handle the log house, but not the mountain property. Once again, I was bowled over by unexpected events. I'd been dumped, again.

I told them they listed both properties or none. The owner was sure to remind me that their agency would retain a fee from anyone they had showed the property to for a month from this time. I assured him that no one they showed it to would be buying it! I walked out with no one to sell two properties in the mountains, and a house in Jersey that I was committed to buy. Is it any wonder why I felt shaken? I felt defeated and exhausted, so I made a quick stop by the barn for some R&R with Stormy.

By the time I got home, I had rallied and was on the phone to an agent Gregory had referred me to. I couldn't cry over spilt milk, as my folks used to say. I needed my undivided attention on the Carolina real estate debacle. I didn't have time to be interviewing multiple agencies. I just wasn't up to it. I was being pulled in so many directions that I felt like a balloon about to explode. Before I headed to meet the new realtor, Jack, I finalized the homeowner's insurance for the New Jersey house.

I had to let go of the frustration and powerful anger that erupted from the depths of my being. I felt disrespected by everyone. I had to let go fast, which I wasn't great at. The man I used to know was stubborn. He could really dig his heels in when he wanted to. I didn't know the *imposter*, but I conjectured he had the same trait.

I surprised myself and reverted to the energy of a person who loved this man. I drafted an email appealing to the man I used to know. How did we ever reach the point we treated each other so poorly? I asked for his help to get the property sold. I told him about my appointment with Jack, and the need to get the mountain property back on the market immediately. I was really proud of myself and my ability to let go, if only for an email, of the pain and hurt I still repressed. I was being pressed tighter and tighter knowing the huge commitment I was finalizing in Jersey.

I met with Jack, who had expertise with large tracts of land. I explained about the Re/Max dumping and my position of authority over the ultimate price accepted for the mountain. I laid it all out for him as honestly as I could. He felt he could sell the properties. I felt relieved when I left. I emailed Bob and asked that he sign the listing agreement before he left. I was very anxious to hear back from him in light of the message I'd recently sent him pleading for a truce. I'd done all I could to clean up the mess.

Had I known what lay ahead each turn of the journey, I'm not sure I'd have continued down the path, and that would have been a huge mistake. Time is an amazing neutralizer. Looking back at my life, as I write, I just cannot believe the trials that confronted me during this stage of my healing or insanity, whichever you prefer. The activity of the moment didn't allow for processing the lessons within each experience.

This realization has taught that it's the experiences and the memories of them that are of key importance. The experiences gift us with the lessons, but the learning doesn't always come concurrently. Later, when we process the experience, we attain the learning, growth, and healing. It's all about our experiences!

I felt fractured and pulled in many directions. The days of wondering what I was going to do with my time disappeared with that handshake. My sense of *knowing* about the New Jersey house was fading and being replaced by doubt and worry. My sense of flow was totally non-existent by now. Thank goodness I had a session with Gregory in the morning.

Gregory and I talked about all that had been happening and my confusion over the circumstances. Master Teacher Spirit (MTS) shared some amazing information with me. It encompassed what I was trying to achieve in this particular life experience. After hearing his explanation, I chided my soul for attempting such a task. I couldn't help but smile at its over-achiever attitude. MTS stressed the importance of being flexible. He reassured me that all was in perfection, and it was time to let the others play their parts.

MTS instructed me to go to the river, because I needed to relax. Ya, think? I understood the metaphor of the river immediately. He counseled, "You need to drift along with the current letting it take you in the proper direction. You need to surrender, to release control, and *let go*." I needed to let the river (my soul) support me. I needed to trust that the river would take care of me. The river would know the proper direction; it would keep me safe.

MTS also suggested that Gregory perform a ceremony on the mountain property to allow its release to new caretakers. He encouraged me to have Gregory's upcoming full moon gathering at the log house. I left Gregory's a bit overwhelmed, but feeling better. There wasn't anything that made the house in

Jersey seem like a wrong decision, which was a relief!

I received an email from Milt's bank gal telling me that my financial information didn't jive with what Milt had told her, so they were rescinding the rate. She sent me an alternate offer, which was much higher. I flew into a panic. Oh, my God! The inspections were the next day, and I'm faced with no lending agreement! I was on the phone to Milt in a panic. He was shocked and would get in touch with the bank. I had to finalize a mortgage quickly.

The next day was one that I will never forget as long as I exist, which is forever. It was inspection day in New Jersey. While I waited for news, I dealt with the mortgage agents trying to secure new funding. Once the inspections were done, I *had* to have my mortgage finalized. To say I was stressed was a major understatement. I was on a seesaw of emotions.

In the middle of this lunacy, I got an email from Bob saying that he would sign the realtor agreement. Yes, one problem down. His email had a much less combative energy to it. I gave myself a pat on the back for having created this new energy with my previous email. I had hopes of a less antagonistic relationship for the remaining time it would take to sell the mountain.

I had no sooner read my Ex's message, when the phone rang. It was Frank. He'd finished with the inspector. Frank's words brought me down from the high of having just gotten the realtor agreement issue solved. The septic system failed miserably, and the inspector found numerous problems. The inspection revealed that most of the supposedly new items weren't. Rob was working without the proper permits, which usurped the inspection process by the Township. Frank and the inspector disliked Rob and felt he was deceitful and dishonest. Here I go again!

The rest of my posse was waiting to hear, so I thanked Frank and got on the phone to Master Michele. Michele's home renovation guy, Joe, was finishing a few items. She'd ask him for a quote to make the house as advertised. Negotiations would be opened. These were big, expensive items that were lied about. I had trouble reconciling this news with the fact that Colleen was Heather's best friend. Welcome to my life these days.

What just happened to my synchronicity, my *meant to be*, and my *knowing*? What the H was going on? The home inspector's office called to give me a preliminary report. I asked her to fax a copy of the pertinent pages, so I could plan my strategy. I wanted to get the information to Peter for his legal input. I felt caught between dimensions: the one with the *meant to be* house in New Jersey, and the other one with the house in New Jersey that failed miserably. I felt like somehow I'd slipped into the wrong dimension.

Moving Home

Jen called to tell me how the morning had gone. I told her I'd already spoken with Frank, the house inspector's office, and the septic company. I had asked Jen to get my $500 check back from the sellers, but she forgot. I was not happy. I hoped she'd go back and pick it up, but she didn't. I couldn't ignore the disappointment I was feeling. I was totally drained from these unexpected events.

The next morning, I took the dogs to the barn. Stormy kept me from the constant litany of negative thoughts circling around the Jersey fiasco. The boys were so happy investigating the farm. I just marveled at how they were so untouched by all the occurrences of the previous day. They were carefree. I so wanted to find some carefree in my day.

From there, we headed to the mountain. I just had to see what kind of clearing out my Ex had done. The dogs were thrilled to be on the mountain. They were oblivious to all the negative aspects that the property represented to me. One of the things I cursed my Ex for was turning a place that was so special to me into a place that caused me so much hurt and pain. Believe it or not, they'd cleaned out a tremendous amount of stuff.

Back in Jersey, Master Michele drove Joe by the house. Since no one was home, he walked around and got up on the roof-in-progress. His findings were disastrous. The work was not up to code. Once Rob put the roofing shingles on top no one would be the wiser, hence his lack of permits. This confirmed the type of individual I was dealing with – one I worked very hard to stay away from.

Given Joe's discovery, I was pretty much convinced this was a dead deal, but I needed to play it out. After the terrible experience with the log house, I couldn't ignore these warning signs. I'd missed many of the signs from Bob and vowed to be more vigilant about the experiences and lessons I created. More lies and deception made me want to run away as fast as I could. However, my desperation to live amongst my friends stopped me.

Gregory, his wife, and a friend followed me to the mountain property. The Deltec was very similar to the healing center plans that they came up with years earlier – uncanny. I knew they would marvel at the sacred energy that was so palpable there. Gregory's ceremony released the property, thus allowing new caretakers to come. I was very grateful for this, because the mountain deserved it. The following night the full moon group would converge on the log house. Not only did the house need the spiritual presence for its success on the real estate market, but my soul needed to be renewed.

It was the summer solstice, so the gathering at the house had the planetary energy of the solstice combined with the full moon. I was a little anxious about having people to the house, but I knew I had to start to be social. How else was I going to make friends? The gathering was a resounding success. I had room for everyone in spite of the large turn out.

Gregory channeled Archangel Michael. Everyone present seemed very pleased with the experience. It really humbled me to think a Being of that importance was actually in my house. It was my first experience with this powerful entity, but it wasn't my last by any means. The thing I was most struck with was his infectious sense of humor. I had hopes that the presence of all these spiritual people and Beings would help move the log house to its next owner.

The following day was a year since I'd heard, "I never wanted this house." Some days it seemed like I'd been alone forever. Other times it seemed like yesterday when I was happy and secure with my life. It was all according to my perspective. So much of what we experience relies on our perspectives and whether they make us feel better or worse. My experience at the gathering made me feel better, so it was a blessing.

I went to work Stormy on the year anniversary, and then on to my mountain. As the dogs and I walked around the mountain, my mind just wandered through the events of the past year, which were still surreal. A year had passed and I hadn't let go of much. I was still stumbling around the Tunnel not sure if I was getting further along it or not.

I knew my work with Gregory was propelling me forward, and I gave myself credit for my progress. I was definitely less depressed than a year ago. While many people applauded me for having dealt with what was handed me as well as I had, I didn't. I was determined to *do* or *be* whatever was required to move past this terrible part of my life, but I just didn't know how. I was still looking for answers in the *wrong* place – outside of Self.

My work with Gregory pointed me inward towards my soul. Secretly, I hadn't been too happy with my soul lately. If my belief that *we create our own realities* was Truth, then my soul created this mess. I just couldn't surrender to, accept, or embrace this Truth. Many events had to unfold to bring me to a place of true understanding. My conundrum was how could I have a belief, yet not embrace it. Doesn't that mean I don't believe the belief? Gives you a headache, doesn't it?

I learned it doesn't mean you don't believe it. What I learned was that experiences are created to allow us opportunities for surrender, acceptance, and learning. The speed with which we learn is relative to the amount of resistance we maintain. At the moment, I was filled with resistance to my learning and towards my soul.

Moving Home

The more I considered the fact that my soul was the true perpetrator, the madder I got at it, me, whatever. My feelings produced a rift between us. The easiest way to dispel the separation was not to acknowledge the creation by my soul. The obvious perpetrator was the *imposter*. The longer I deluded myself with this scenario, the longer my time in the Tunnel would be, and the longer my journey of healing.

I was consumed with the Jersey mortgage issue and the failure of the house inspections. I just couldn't let go of it yet. Mentally and emotionally, I'd already moved back to my friends. I'd gotten out the moving supplies I'd been saving in anticipation of their use. Luckily, I hadn't started packing despite the urgings of some of my friends. I just knew my happiness hinged on moving back. I *had* to get this deal consummated!

Happily, I got a call that the Ford title was in. Finally! I rushed to complete this long-awaited title transfer. The horse trailer title went through without a hitch. As I began the car title transfer, the gal at the office told me that my Ex had to sign the back. Have you ever had the world just stop? I took a breath trying to control the rage I felt. "I had no way to get him to sign the title." I was told he'd have to sign a power of attorney form.

My high from expecting to accomplish this very difficult task turned into a debilitating low. I went back home totally defeated. I emailed my Ex about the additional form to sign, notarize, and return to me. I sent it priority mail with a postage-paid priority return envelope. I figured the easier I made it for him, the quicker I'd get it back.

I met my new realtor, Jack, at the mountain. Oddly enough, the realtor that I filed the complaint about had a prospective buyer and met us up there with them. Unbeknownst to me, he had been up with these people before. I spoke with the people about the house and land. While Jack showed the steel building, the old realtor and I talked. I held no anger toward him. I just didn't get into that energy. It was in the past and I accepted that. It was one of the few things I had let go of.

These were the first really interested lookers. They'd looked at several more places, but hadn't found anything like mine. No kidding! My old realtor was going to work really hard to sell it for me. He thought he owed me at least that much. I figured that was an apology of sorts. Whether the house in Jersey fell through or not, I wanted the mountain to sell quickly.

The effect the Jersey house collapse was having on my burgeoning self-confidence was devastating. My newly resurrected self-esteem was holding its own, because I knew I'd done everything right. All the things that had been missing from my life I was so sure had returned and with them my confidence grew. As those things disappeared, so did my self-confidence.

My anger towards the Carolina builders from Hell motivated me to finally take some action against them. The gals in the court clerk's office had a stack of cases waiting to be heard against them. I wasn't the only one they'd cheated. My case was in three weeks. By then, I'd have things in New Jersey resolved one way or another. Based on the way things were not flowing, my hopes were fading.

I got an email from my Ex that he changed his mind. He wouldn't sign the car over until I paid the loan off. Once more rage was stampeding into my heart. I was sure the new wife convinced him not to sign. I didn't even know her, but I really despised her. So much for whatever good will I'd created with my email regarding the property. To hell with good will; the truce was over. We were back at war. I don't respond well to ultimatums.

I reiterated why I couldn't, and wouldn't, pay off the loan. I'd promised to pay it off after the property sold, and I was a person of integrity, who always kept her vows and promises. The car could stay in his name until then. I didn't have any more time or energy to devote to this idiotic *imposter*, who could obviously be manipulated by the new wife. So be it!

The quote from Master Michele's contractor ended up in the $50,000 range. Peter asked if I still wanted the house. I answered, yes, but my heart really wasn't in it. We agreed to counter with a $35,000 reduction in price. My emotions were so conflicted that I struggled with them all night. By morning, I'd made a definitive decision. I chose not to give my power away to Rob.

I called Peter and told him I didn't want the house! With my call, I let go of the house and my expectation of returning by fall. Well, there it was. The house was not happening. I felt relief along with immense sadness. I felt defeated, but not a failure. Of course, I wasn't even aware of the lesson I was being gifted by my soul's *creation* of the house in Jersey until many months later.

The past seven weeks had been filled with intense mental and emotional stresses from Jersey and Carolina real estate, my Ex, etc. I ended June wondering if I would slip back into the Abyss. I worried about the effect all of this was having on my animals and me, too. I was learning to think about my Self. I was clueless as to the reasons behind my return-home debacle. As you might imagine, I was on the phone to Gregory for some illumination concerning the most recent disappointment. I would do anything to keep myself from arriving back in the Abyss for the third time. *Anything*!

Chapter 11

Family Crisis

I needed to renew my faith in universal influence with Gregory's help. My session was one of insights and healing for me. Gregory felt what I'd just been subjected to was about me settling. He asked if I felt I deserved the best out of life. I did and always had. We're taught from childhood not to be selfish or conceited, and that is correct. However, we get confused with the differentiation between selfish and self-love. This confusion leads those of us desirous of being good and perfect down a path away from loving Self, which took me into the Abyss and the Tunnel.

Settling. There was that word again. Gregory's insight seemed so simple, yet profound to me. Settling was a key player in everything I'd just gone though. I had to admit the Jersey house had been less than ideal. I was so desperate to recover my lost happiness I was willing to make it work. The past year had taken its toll on my self-esteem and self-confidence. What I didn't realize, until Gregory's comment, was my diminished self-worth. I'd completely lost the Who-I-Had-Been.

The disappearance of my identity as the happy vet's wife caused my lost confidence, lower self-esteem, and depleted self-worth. On a very deep level, I believed I deserved the best in life, but I wasn't making choices based in that

LETTING GO

belief. While I never settled in my earlier life, I was willing to settle for less now.

Having been shown this lesson by Gregory, I was ready to accept and embrace it, allowing me to make more beneficial choices in the future. My faith that I'd find that perfect spot was invigorated. I did it before; I could do it again. The key was to recover the sense of joy and happiness that I was bathed in while planning the last dream. I had to let go of my unhappiness in order to resurrect the woman with the power to *create* dreams: the Who-I-Used-To-Be!

Gregory's insight was a huge piece of the puzzle in perfect timing. The themes pertaining to boundaries, standing up for myself, and saying *no* were reflected in every facet of the deal, especially, my ultimate decision to let go of the entire catastrophe. I stood up for myself. My *no* was evidence of the lessons I was learning, accepting, and allowing to act in my life.

My session introduced me to another of Gregory's talents – channeled healing. I'd never experienced channeled healing, so I had no idea what to expect. No expectation was always a good thing for me. No expectation eliminates disappointment. While I wanted information, I needed healing. So, healing I got.

The Being who gifted me with my first channeled healing experience was none other than Archangel Michael himself. This was our first of many exchanges. Michael arrived with that same powerful resounding laugh, which rocked the log house. Humor was something that still eluded me. Michael had me smiling, feeling lighter, and cleared of much of the stress that had consumed me. Everything about me felt renewed.

I left the session with an introduction to the lessons contained within the Jersey house experience and a cleansed being, which allowed me to recognize, accept, and embrace the lessons in their perfect timing. As we've already discovered, recognition isn't necessarily concurrent with the experience.

As with MTS, I was amazed at the feeling I had of this Archangel being a colleague. I gave thanks to an Archangel and to my soul for the experience, and of course, to Gregory. Without Gregory's willingness to share his body with these Beings none of these experiences would be possible. My lesson for the day was to not settle. I deserve the best! We all do! Getting the lesson, reader? I hope so!

I arrived at the log house to a phone message from Peter. My offer had been rejected, so the deal was dead. Talk about timing! Thanks to the healing I'd just received I took the news quite well. I stayed the course in my Tunnel. The Abyss wasn't going to see me back again. I was proud of what I tried to

134

accomplish, of stepping out of my comfort zone, of following my soul's twisted path of teaching, of taking back my power, and surviving to fight another day. My biggest fear now was telling everyone and hearing their disappointment.

The next day was a year since the mountain property had been listed. I tried to let go of my anger towards the *imposter*. The best way to achieve that was a trip to the barn, so I was off with the dogs to deal with "the first day of the rest of my life" after losing the Jersey house. So be it!

Stormy was beginning to offer some resistance to my training, but nothing too unusual for a baby. He was reaching an age when young horses start to test their boundaries, no different than an adolescent boy. Despite the challenges, he enhanced my sense of purpose and self-worth, which I craved of late.

I decided to bathe earlier than usual, which always threw the dogs into a tailspin. While I was in the tub, I noticed that Shadow had gotten up from his usual spot and was standing. While Licorice always did this at the end of bath time, Shadow never did. Dogs are creatures of habit infrequently deviating from the norm. Worry started to creep into my awareness.

Suddenly, I flew to support Shadow as he slumped to the floor. Through torrential tears, I lowered him lovingly while yelling, "No, you can't leave me. I can't let go yet. Please!" I was terrified of losing him. Shadow got up and stood there looking at me as if to say, "What's your problem?" I regained my composure, so I could make a medical assessment. I ran to the phone hoping to catch the vet, who'd already left for the July Fourth weekend. Shadow was by my side looking fine, so I told them I'd just watch him closely.

I'd been trying to prepare myself for his aging for months. When he fell, all I could think of was a heart attack or stroke. My Lab, Ben, had suffered a few seizures in his advancing age, but this wasn't a seizure. It came and left so fast, but was quite dramatic in its effect on him. Talk about unexpected complications in life. I watched Shadow like a hawk for the rest of the night. I tried to prepare for whatever might be beginning, but you can never be prepared for trauma that effects so important and true a friend.

In the morning with Shadow seemingly fine, we headed to work Stormy. As we got back in the house, Shadow slumped to the floor inside the door. I rushed to break his fall from in front of him, so I could see his eyes darting back and forth very rapidly. This episode lasted a slight bit longer, but after it passed he appeared to be fine again.

I called the covering vet's office, but they referred me to someone I didn't know, so I called my dear friend and vet in New Jersey, Gary. I was worried, but not panicked. Panic would have had me seeing the local vet, who I didn't know. Worry allowed me the patience to talk with Gary. In less than an hour he was on the phone with me.

After describing Shadow's symptoms, Gary diagnosed Geriatric Vestibular Syndrome. As soon as I heard it, I relaxed. It wasn't fatal. Licorice had come down with it before we moved and recovered completely. My first experience with GVS had been with my cat, Rainbow, who recovered too. My emotions returned from the edge of disaster with Gary's diagnosis.

We discussed treatment until I could get to Shadow's vet on Tuesday. Gary put me at ease instantly, because I'd known him forever and had all the faith in the world in his expertise. I was relieved that Shadow would recover just like Licorice and Rainbow had. I kept telling myself, "Okay, you can do this."

Shadow seemed totally normal the rest of that afternoon and evening. He'd been going out to relieve himself during the night for months. I heard him stirring around 3 a.m. and started to get up. When he didn't get right up, I looked back. What I saw woke me abruptly from my sleepy state. He couldn't get up. His eyes were flashing back and forth terribly. I helped him stand, but he couldn't walk. I half carried him outside where he immediately tinkled. He needed my assistance the whole time.

We got back to our beds, but my heart almost stopped when I thought about what I'd just experienced. Shadow went back to sleep, but I couldn't. Fear and worry consumed me. Licorice and Rainbow had never been like this. Maybe it wasn't Vestibular Syndrome. I couldn't see his regular vet for another *two* days. Over the next hour and a half, while I obsessed, Shadow vomited and pooped in his bed. All of this compounded my already heightened fears.

I was on the phone to Gary as soon as I thought it wasn't too early to call. He explained that it still could be GVS and that Licorice had suffered a very mild form. Gary felt Shadow's symptoms were indicative of a moderate case. Moderate! Is he kidding? I *needed* Shadow to feel better and fast! Gary gave me some suggestions to help with his symptoms. I was relieved when Shadow ate a small meal and had no trouble drinking.

I had to go into town to get medicines Gary recommended for his nausea. The thought of subjecting Shadow to a ride in the car was worrisome, but I couldn't leave him alone since he might fall and injure himself. Licorice couldn't drive, so it was up to me. There was no one else to help: no husband, no friends, just me.

Getting Shadow into the car was no easy trick with my bad back. The adrenaline from my fear for my dear friend allowed me the strength to lift him into the car. Licorice joined him and off we went. It was a quick trip to the store for whatever I thought I needed for the next few days. Shadow seemed indifferent, so I continued to the barn for some meds that Kim was lending me. The trip was uneventful for Shadow, but all sorts of debilitating emotions were barraging me. Thank you Ego, I really don't need any help from you right now!

Shadow's illness resurrected my feelings of abandonment, aloneness, and isolation. Their rapid reoccurrence showed me I'd merely repressed them. I hadn't healed them at all. For now, my full attention was focused on Shadow. I'd worry about me after I knew he was well. The critical nature of Shadow's condition precluded my lesson about putting Self first. Shadow was my priority. Recognizing the lesson was an accomplishment in itself. Choosing to put another, who was suffering, ahead of me was selfless, which is a good thing.

Well, if I needed something to take my mind off my feelings of disappointment over the busted house deal in Jersey, Shadow's unexpected illness was a perfect creation. I reverted back to my days of caring for critically ill horses. I felt quite certain Shadow wasn't dying, but his condition required my undivided attention, 24/7. I began medical journaling, so I'd have crucial information for Gary and the local vet. Poor Shadow's eyes never stopped flashing for days. I imagined what that must have made him feel like. His world had to be spinning, spinning, spinning. No wonder he was vomiting.

By Monday, the Fourth of July, his appetite dropped off to nothing, which I understood, but didn't like. I tried a small biscuit, but he couldn't chew it. He tried to take it, but simply couldn't. I knew he had to eat, so I got him in the car and went to the store for several different food options. He was such a pathetic looking fellow with those darting eyes. It just broke my heart. I felt powerless.

I stayed by his side ready to assist in anyway I could. He couldn't stand or walk on his own, so it was up to me to get him outside. I used a large towel under his chest to steady him. I saw the humiliation in his eyes when we started to venture outside, but he always allowed me to help him.

All the lifting caused me a great deal of back pain, but I had no choice. I knew my pain couldn't compare to what Shadow felt. I cursed my Ex for putting me in the position of dealing with a very sick dog with no friends to help. He was the perfect person to blame. Might not be the right person, but that lesson was a long way off.

Things had been quiet, fireworks-wise, on my first Carolina Fourth of July. Shadow needed to go out around 9 p.m. Since it had been quiet, I put Licorice out in their yard and returned to help Shadow out the front, where there were no stairs. Well, I no sooner got outside with Shadow and boom! The silence was broken with the typical Fourth of July thunder. While I held Shadow up, I saw that Licorice was terrified. I thought he'd break right through the fencing. As much as I hated to do it, I had to lay Shadow down and rush to help Licorice.

By the time I reached him, he'd urinated all over the porch and was trembling from head to toe! I tried to calm him while Shadow waited patiently for my help to tinkle. After he finished his job, we retreated into the house. Licorice was terrified, and I felt so guilty. It was my job to prevent such things from happening. After I calmed down, I realized I wasn't responsible. I had no way of knowing what was about to transpire. It had been quiet all evening and dark for a while. How could I have known?

Licorice's emotions were fried as were mine. I knew from my years of animal healing this had triggered past life memories of similar terrors. The next day I used one of my healing modalities, which removes past life negative energies. It had proven very effective for my clients' animals' firework and thunder issues. An added benefit was that I had to clear myself before I could work with another soul.

My not yet embraced lesson of putting Self first displayed itself once more. My love for Licorice motivated me to do the healing work for him. I needed it too, but I still didn't love Self enough to gift myself with the healing. He, like his brother, was a fabulous teacher. I often wondered what their opinion was of their slow student.

I worried that my soul, that tricky little bugger, might have created this event to clear my negative energy. I hoped not, but I couldn't discount the possibility. If that were the case, it was important for me to recognize the lesson and honor what Licorice experienced in order to gift me with my lesson. I didn't want anyone to suffer in order for me to learn. It was okay if I did, but no one else. Hello, self-love, remember? Learning in joy, remember?

As I sat with Shadow waiting to assist him, my mind pondered the timing of his ailment. Its appearance took my focus off the disaster in New Jersey and the depression it created. Shadow's illness pulled me out of my unhappiness and into an intensely focused critical-care mode.

My ego kept trying to get me to accept blame for Shadow's condition. The timing of it so close to the end of seven of the most stressful weeks didn't go unnoticed. Energetically speaking, I was sure some of the underlying causes of Shadow's sickness were the negative emotions I'd subjected us to. I'd contributed to his GVS. I was sure of it. If I didn't process my negative experiences, I'd create illness within my own body. This I knew was truth.

Being available to help Shadow allowed me the time to think about the lesson he offered me. We both needed to release the negative energy. I vowed to learn the lessons from the ruined house deal, accept them, and then let go of the negative energy contained within them. I was responsible for my dearest friend's situation. I understood it, accepted it, and released any guilt within my realization. Guilt is just more negative energy. To harbor guilt would defeat Shadow's purpose. It was counter productive. I let go of my guilt.

Finally, we got to the local vet. She examined Shadow and agreed with Gary's diagnosis and treatment. She drew blood and gave me additional medications for him. I was happy to relinquish Shadow's treatment plan to his vet. His eyes were still flashing, but slightly slower. He was such a great patient. The blood results showed a slow thyroid. I picked up meds to correct Shadow's thyroid function.

As long as we were out in the car again, I ran by the barn to see Stormy. I hoped it would pick up the dogs' spirits to go somewhere they truly loved. Shadow, especially, hated being in the house too much. We were used to our life spent outdoors on our farm. I was surprised at the barn that Shadow required less help from me. He was almost able to walk. I figured it had to do with adrenaline, but I thought that was a wonderful sign of progress. His appetite was still not great, but he had started to be able to chew some small, soft treats. Things were moving towards normalcy. He had a long way to go, but I hung onto any semblance of positive signs.

No sooner had I started to feel a little more relaxed about the outlook for Shadow's recovery, when I got an email from Teddy, who'd bought my dad's commercial building. I was stunned with what I read. His message said that Milt's wife, Paula, had died. Talk about unexpected. I'd just talked with Paula the week before. Paula suffered from heart trouble for years, but she'd sounded fine. I knew they had a family wedding in Chicago.

I called Teddy instantly, who confirmed that Paula had died in Chicago. My heart broke for Milt losing his wife so unexpectedly and having the added issue of being away. How horrible! I wanted to be able to be there for Milt, but with Shadow's condition I was unable to go anywhere.

I called Milt's office and left a message with my shock and condolences. I was astonished that this wonderful person, who I'd just spoken with, was gone. Milt had been such a support to me that I wanted to return the favor. Milt called back and was very appreciative of my call. I thanked him for getting back so quickly and wished him strength to get through this. Once again, I felt helpless so many miles away from a friend in need.

Paula's death served to put things in perspective for me. While Shadow's illness was awful, I knew he'd recover. Poor Milt had just lost his lifelong partner of 40-plus years in a moment. I felt lucky. Both Milt and I had been dealt harsh lessons by our spouses.

The magnificent lesson Paula taught was to never take anything for granted for we truly don't know what each moment may bring. My first taste of this lesson came when my soul mate threw me away. I wanted to honor her memory by recognizing her powerful teaching. She was a kind, lovely woman who I will miss.

I found the perfect sympathy card for Milt with a poem entitled, *The Oak Tree*. I grabbed it out of its resting place and began reading. Well, right there in the aisle I began to cry. At his suggestion, the tree that watched over my father's ashes was an oak tree. It was as if my father guided me to this card for his old friend and CPA, which I explained in my note.

Also included were several poems that echo my beliefs regarding death. I knew they were tearjerkers, but I also learned from my traumatic past that tears are cleansing and good for the soul. Milt sent a beautiful note of thanks expressing the benefit he received from the poems and card. Our losses solidified our friendship even more. The only thing that is consistent in life is change.

As I sat guarding Shadow against any injury, I couldn't help but turn my attention to Mike and Little Michelle. Mike was undergoing experimental melanoma vaccine treatments at Sloan Kettering in New York City. I could sit in the comfort of my house caring for Shadow. They had to make many, many trips to the city trying to find an answer to Mike's cancer. A failed house deal paled in comparison to Mike and Michelle's drama, Milt's sudden loss, and the sudden affliction that had sabotaged Shadow's health. Everything is truly relative.

Between Mike's cancer, Paula's sudden passing, the lost house deal, and Shadow's illness, I had no resilience. It was just too much to absorb. Luckily, Shadow was making slow progress, which kept my heart from just crumbling into irretrievable pieces. The intensity of Shadow's care left me spent emotionally and physically.

About a week and a half into Shadow's illness, I finally got to make reservations for Vince in Maui. It actually occurred on what would have been my dad's 88th birthday, which I thought was rather fitting. I had the feeling Dad was behind my triumph. Of course, I was a long way from completing the legal documentation, but I was able to secure space for him during the time he wished.

I spent time reading to keep my ego at bay. Shadow's need for help prevented me from doing much else. I came across a very apropos section in Eckhart Tolle's *Stillness Speaks*. Tolle writes:

"The playfulness and joy of a dog, its unconditional love and readiness to celebrate life at any moment often contrast sharply with the inner state of the dog's owner – depressed, anxious, burdened by problems, lost in thought, not present in the only place and only time there is; Here and Now. One wonders: living with this person, how does the dog manage to remain so sane, so joyous?"

This thought-provoking query was a bird's eye view into the purposeful lives of our wonderful canine and feline companions. I'd counseled others about their secret mission many times. Here I sat confronted by my own demons and the resultant effect on one of my dearest friends. Self-pity wasn't the answer. I'd been consumed with self-pity while I sat in my dark Abyss. Self-pity paralyzes you and serves no one.

Shadow needed me, so I battled to clear self-pity out from my ego. In the intensity of the moment, I didn't even see the powerful lesson that Shadow was offering me, which was to battle just as hard for my Self and soul. I was grateful for Shadow's unconditional love and assistance in coping with the tremendous stress over the Jersey house deal.

The house just didn't matter in light of Shadow's sudden crisis. What mattered was Shadow's continued recovery and future well being. I didn't even want to think about life without Shadow and Licorice. I simply couldn't go there. Talk about being paralyzed with fear. I wasn't ready to let go of them just yet.

Shadow was steadily improving. I'll never know if he was planning his retreat and I stopped him with my plea to stay. Whatever the motivation, it seemed like he was granting me more time. As long as he had quality of life, I wanted him with me. I reiterated my vow to let go at the first sign that he wished to go. My promise to my friend!

Life goes on in spite of whatever crisis is confronting you. My attention was still on real estate in Carolina and Jersey. It'd become clear to me that I wasn't cut out for real estate.

An unexpected email from my Ex turned my attention from real estate. This was an unexpected good one! The form to transfer the car title was on its way.

LETTING GO

What a shock! I'd set my boundaries with my no. My winning empowered me.

My knowingness about Jersey being the best place for me was really damaged by the last attempt. I tried to figure out what I was supposed to learn from it. As we know, *everything happens for a reason* and *for our best interest*, don't we? It just seemed like one big waste of time. If I kept looking, it meant that I didn't have to stay in this place that had brought me such unhappiness. My growing self-doubt was understandable given the unfortunate results.

During the first few weeks of Shadow's GVS, he also suffered symptoms from too much thyroid medication. The over dosage of thyroxine wreaked havoc with our sleep pattern. Some nights Shadow wanted to go out every half hour. The first time he'd tinkle. The next times he'd roam around acting confused. It tried my patience, but my love for him helped me through the worst of it.

I called the vet about checking his dosage sooner, but she said we had to wait. After a few more sleepless nights, I called Gary. Gary felt I didn't have to wait that long. My skills as an animal communicator reside in my ability to *hear* and *feel* what the animals are saying and experiencing. I called the local vet and told her I *knew* it was too much. I needed to test him now! I couldn't put him through anymore discomfort.

Well, my intuition about my dog was spot on. Big surprise! She lowered his dose and Shadow's strange behavior vanished. He was much more relaxed, which meant I was too. I chided myself for not standing up for what I knew to be true. Once more, Shadow was teaching me to say no, to have faith in my *knowing*, and to trust my Self. Shadow was my ever-patient and selfless teacher.

Shadow continued to get stronger and return to his normal self. All the while, he tried to get me to learn to love my Self as much as I loved him. I'd do anything for everyone else but me. I knew for the sake of my animal family's health and well being I needed to start to recognize and accept his lesson. I had worked with many people who'd do anything for their animals and nothing for themselves.

They'd call me to help their animal when it was they who needed the help. The love for their animals awarded them the healing that their own soul cried out for. I was the wounded healer now with my soul crying out to get me to pay attention. It would be a while still, before I'd start to awaken to the truth that had been staring me in the face from the onset. My blinders were still firmly in place, but the holes in them were enlarging.

While I sat pondering the mysteries of my life, I was brought back to the moment with the arrival of my time in court with the builders from Hell. I went to court with the expectation of winning. I was extremely nervous, which sort of surprised me. It was hard to keep my attention on the judge, since he never made one comment, asked one question, or wanted to look at any of the photos I brought as proof. The judge would have to research a few things and mail his decision. I was optimistic that his research would net me a favorable decision.

I left court and headed straight to my salvation – Stormy and the farm. As I drove, I reviewed the court experience and remembered several things that I wished I'd mentioned. My nerves had gotten the best of me and robbed me of my sharp analytical mind. I gave myself credit for taking action and trying to get the court to extract accountability, responsibility, and respect from the disreputable builders. It was a huge task and one that I'd failed miserably at. I hoped the court would have better luck. I brought my emotions back to a place of calm and peace with some time at the barn. Thank goodness for Stormy.

My newsletter from Michael Roads arrived with some startling news in it. Carolyn, who edited the newsletter, announced that she and her husband of 25 years were separating. My unhealed heart broke for her. I understood just how she felt. My separation and divorce were all too recent. I sent her off a quick email expressing my surprise, shock, love, and support. We emailed back and forth quite a bit comparing notes. Here was another soul creating pain and heartache for her Self.

Carolyn was experiencing her own tsunami of change much unwanted and unexpected just like my own. She applauded me for having dealt so well with my situation. I thanked her, but really wasn't so sure how deserving her adulation was. One of these days I would begin to love my Self enough to give my Self the credit it deserved. Michael's teaching was based on self-love. I'd experienced my first encounter with feeling deep love for Self during one of his guided meditations. I hadn't felt that depth of love for Self since that time. Why?

Michael's "consciousness column" was on point for the challenges I was facing. His topic was Trust. I'd lost all trust in my Ex. Even more importantly, I'd lost trust in myself. My loss of trust in Self gave birth to my plummeting self-confidence, self-esteem, and self-worth. It's impossible to love someone you don't trust. They go hand in hand.

The mirror that Michael offered with his column was again in perfect timing. Michael stated, "Trust engenders self-respect and promotes courage. Trust fosters confidence in life, and is an essential ingredient in the growth of your consciousness." Then, the real slap in the consciousness came. "The Truth is that you created the situation you are in, and that you can change it." See, *we create our own reality*. I know this!

Why did it take reading about it in Michael's column to finally acknowledge the fact that my soul created my horrible, painful life experience? All I heard in my mind was, "Truth isn't truth, out of timing." Oh yeah, right! Michael taught the need to "love and trust self" in order to affect the change required to grow within the drama of our lives. "If you are Trusting, there is no anxiety, and no need for hope. Trust transcends hope. There is no truer friend than Trust." Thank you, Michael, for your illuminating lessons and wisdom.

I was dumfounded by Michael's inclusion of self-respect in his discussion on Trust. Lack of respect is my hottest button. Until I read Michael's words, I hadn't even considered the fact that I didn't respect myself. I was the poster girl for respect. I knew I'd lost faith and trust in my Self and in my soul. According to Michael, lost trust equated with lost self-respect. This was an astonishing discovery.

Michael's column gave me lots to ponder. It was a turning point in my perspective on the recent trauma and challenges since leaving New Jersey. I acknowledged my soul's creation, but accepting full responsibility and being fully accountable for *my* creation was still in the future. I had many more lessons ahead to experience before I truly embraced this revelation. For now, it was a numbing epiphany and one that launched my journey towards true healing!

While I pondered Michael's latest teaching, I got an email from Pam. She'd started to scour the country for a breeder of healthy Mini Schnauzers and found one near Charlotte. The breeder was only two hours away, and I'd be happy to go look at the puppies. Pam felt the kennel was too far from me. Are you kidding? To see puppies! There wasn't a better tonic for an ailing heart and soul than the unadulterated joy of puppies. The breeder had a litter that could be seen in a couple of weeks. I felt Shadow would be up to the drive by then.

I couldn't wait to meet the litter and be bathed in their joy. I told Pam that I'd been thinking about coming for a friend-fix and would be happy to coordinate my trip with the time the puppy was weaned. She couldn't believe what I was offering. I'd just solved her problem. Don't you just love universal influence? For Pam, this was synchronicity at its best. We just needed to check out the breeder, and then I'd plan my trip accordingly.

July began with the terror of Shadow's episode in the bathroom and ended with a trip to meet my new godson. Talk about the swinging of the pendulum from pure fear to pure joy. Ah, if nothing else, life and the universe are all about balance.

The trip to the kennel was uneventful. Shadow and Licorice were happy to have a mission, and the puppies didn't disappoint. I sat on the floor allowing them to heal my war-torn heart. I tried to take pictures for Pam, which was a hoot, since they all looked alike and didn't stay still for very long. They were simply adorable.

I talked with Terri, the breeder, and really liked her. Her kennel was immaculate. I was having a blast, but I knew I needed to head back. I called Pam to report in. She was thrilled to hear my glowing report about Terri, the kennel, and the dogs. What a great way to end my couple of months from hell! It was truly a gift from the Universe.

I was grateful that Shadow was returning to his old self, which would allow me to deliver Pam's puppy. Shadow was about 80 percent normal. He didn't have a head-tilt, but he was more unsteady than before. It wasn't weakness, but legitimate ataxia, which meant a residual neurological component. I gave thanks for each day he gifted me with.

I informed everyone that I'd be up as soon as Pam's new son was ready. The house hunt in Jersey continued with a few possibilities, but nothing that really grabbed me. With my lesson of not settling firmly in my psyche, my requirements for my future home had gotten more stringent. When I moved, it would be to the perfect spot. In my depleted emotional state, I really didn't expect to be able to create anything that would even approach my high standards. Despite my knowledge of this, I kept looking. It gave me hope, and something to keep my ego busy.

Chapter 12

Good Deeds

While we waited to hear about Pam's pup, I spent time analyzing my new revelations regarding Self. I realized I had to get back on better terms with my soul. Until I did, I'd never leave the Tunnel. I acknowledged that my soul created this trauma in my life, but I simply couldn't accept and embrace it. Why was this so hard? What was I not seeing?

I started reading Debbie Ford's, *The Dark Side of the Light Chasers*, which is about discovering and working with your shadow self. I'd started it, but then stopped a while ago. With my recent epiphany, I thought it was time to drag it back out. *Truth isn't truth out of timing; when the student is ready*, etc. Well, this student better get ready soon!

Perhaps, my resistance to this lesson could be revealed by some elucidation of my shadow self. We all have one, whether we acknowledge it or not. I began to get the message that until I worked with my shadow side, I'd never find my way through the maze of the Tunnel. My reluctance towards shadow work was rooted in my misconstrued notion about it. I imagined it as the *bad* side of me. I didn't want to admit there was any part of me that was *bad*. My resistance to meeting my shadow self really delayed my healing.

After reading Ford's concepts regarding our shadow selves, I formed a much different impression of mine and the gifts it had to offer. The core of shadow work is that the things that bother you the most in other people are actually the same challenges you are trying to heal in yourself. I reviewed my hot buttons of dishonesty, lack of responsibility, lack of accountability, and the biggie: lack of respect. I just shuddered to think that I possessed these less than ideal traits.

I struggled with my Self and soul for months over this concept. I just couldn't believe that I possessed any of these distasteful flaws. I judged them as *bad* – always had, always would. In order to heal my shadow self and surrender to the gifts it was offering me, I had to reach a point where I dropped my judgment. I had to look at those heinous attributes not as bad, just that they *were;* and that was quite a challenge for me.

Without recognizing and accepting my shadow self, I couldn't heal those facets of my Self that were at the root of the life experience I'd created. Until I embraced them and then let go of them, I would continue to create the same types of experiences in my life. Well, been there done that; don't want to do it again. I needed to learn from and embrace whatever would allow me to change to learning in joy and love. Without becoming intimate with my shadow self, I'd never be able to move forward into a life of joyful creations.

It took many months before I completed the integration of my shadow self. My willingness to acknowledge its existence was a starting point. I dropped my judgments of my shadow and began to study the lessons it held within its grasp. As I'm writing, I am struck with an observation that I never saw before this moment. I had a Shadow in my life, who was my dearest friend. I feared my life without this Shadow. I had another shadow, which I feared allowing into my life.

Both Shadows were integral parts of my healing. I needed to feel as comfortable with my shadow self and its lessons as I was with Shadow and his lessons. They were two different teachers leading me to the same end result, which was a healed soul. My timely interest in *The Dark Side of the Light Chasers* echoed *when the student is ready… .*

My trips to train my biggest angel began to present more challenges. Stormy really started to test his boundaries by displaying an iron will. I knew his father, Inspiration, had a very strong will. Knowing offspring don't only inherit physical attributes from their parents, I tried to finesse Stormy through what I described as his teenager phase.

Due to his intelligence, I knew Stormy was getting bored with the routine in the ring. Because of his young age, his work had to be restricted to prevent any damage to young joints. My conundrum was to keep his mind busy and challenged while working lightly. With young horses you walk a fine line between the two.

It was my responsibly to deal with these challenges with patience, yet firmness. I had to be mentally and emotionally stronger. Part of the wonder of training youngsters was just how you accomplish that. What works well with one doesn't necessarily work with another, which is why horses are never boring. Stormy and I had embarked on a new phase of our relationship. It would be months before I saw the lesson he was offering me. Once more, it would be uncovered in a session with Gregory.

Stormy's challenges kept me present in the Now. In the horse world there's a saying, 1+1-1. The goal is two beings working together as though they are One, which takes years to accomplish. When you finally get the cooperation you're seeking from your partner, there is nothing quite like the feeling of balance and harmony. It is pure joy. The trait a rider seeks from the horse is one of willingness. To know that your horse is willing to relinquish control to you is truly rewarding.

As a species, horses are one of the most willing participants in our lives. I knew Stormy wanted to be cooperative. I attributed his resistance to my control to simply being a baby. Little did I know the powerful lesson he was trying to teach his grandmother. My challenge of encouraging Stormy to accept his boundaries without confrontation continued for months. I kept telling myself I was the more intelligent, so I needed to finesse his cooperation. In the end, I realized what a joke that notion was. More intelligent? Who was getting the lessons being taught? It certainly wasn't me.

I finally received the judge's decision on my small claims case. Disbelieving, surprised, disappointed didn't even approach what I felt when I read the form letter. Apparently, I had not provided enough evidence to prove my claim, so I'd lost! Was this guy kidding? I had all kinds of evidence and proof, which he totally ignored. Once more, another individual was not being accountable, responsible, or respectful. Should I have expected anything different? My repressed feelings of defeat rose to the surface with his decision.

After I calmed my emotions down, I chose to send a letter to this judge. I needed to express what I felt the effects of his unreal judgment were. I brought up the several items that my nervousness had precluded my mention of at the hearing. I explained that if I'd ignored the situation, then I was contributing to the problem. I just couldn't allow their deceit to go unreported. I expressed my disbelief and disappointment with his decision. His decision made me feel like I actually made the problem worse!

Once the letter was sent, I let go of that frustrating chapter in my life. I did all I could to correct a bad situation. I was proud of myself for having tried, for leaving my comfort zone, for putting myself in a position to lose, but coming away having lost with my self-esteem and self-confidence intact. I'd made progress with Self, despite my pitiful attempt to force the outside world to be accountable.

Progress with Self was way more important and gratifying. I took another step closer to accepting the notion that my actions were the only ones I had any influence over. Once I embraced the lesson that I was only responsible and accountable for me, I would accelerate my healing.

Finally, the time to learn from the river had arrived. It was a gorgeous afternoon with the river devoid of people. Gregory and I spent a lot of time just communing with the river and Nature. There wasn't any real need to talk. We let Nature do the talking. The river was very calm, supportive, and gentle. It took no effort other than keeping the float tube facing the proper direction. I allowed the river to direct all else. The peace on the river was therapeutic for my entire being.

Giving my Self over to the river and Nature was nurturing for me. I bathed in the simplicity and beauty of the experience. I relinquished all my responsibilities for those couple of hours. My goal was to learn to trust my soul again and allow it to serve as my "river." I'd do whatever was necessary to re-establish my loving relationship with my soul. I needed to uncover and let go of everything that prevented this reconciliation. The river honored me with a taste of what my life would be after I accomplished my herculean task. The river had been a perfect teacher.

Whenever I'd gotten harsh with myself in the past, I'd get a heads-up message from Mother Nature. She'd send a deer or two across my path. In Native American culture, deer represent gentleness. Whenever I'd see a deer at an unusual time, I knew Mother Nature was saying *be gentle with yourself.* On our farm, we had a herd of deer feeding every night. These were neighbors, our brothers and sisters.

Messenger animals appear and disappear quite suddenly. They are mystical, but of the physical. I recognize them and *hear* their messages. My soul creates them to get me to pay attention. I can't count the numbers of messages I've received in this manner. Many were from hawks, which represent messengers in the Native America tradition. Every time I see a hawk – messenger or not – I lose my feeling of aloneness. We are, truly, never alone, which was a critical lesson for me at this juncture.

Recently, I'd seen a hawk at the log house and my heart smiled. It was my first in this location. Its appearance signaled that my energy had turned the tide from negative to more positive. When I started examining my shadow self, I began to accept that I'd been sending out uncomfortable negative energy. My energetic waves were not conducive to attracting animals or people. No wonder I hadn't made any friends here.

Eventually, Pam heard from the dog breeder. Trying to get a date to pickup the pup became a nightmare. Anyone that trains animals – and we all know I do – has control issues. The trick is to balance them. Where have I heard that before? The dilemma arose over ear cropping. While Pam disliked the idea, she'd been advised that he could have ear problems otherwise. Whenever I hear people thinking they can improve on Mother Nature the hair just bristles on the back of my neck. Terri was very resistant to the puppy leaving before the cropping. The timing of the cropping would put me on the road Labor Day weekend.

Terri allowed me to get the pup, who Pam had named Hans, a few days post cropping, but not until 7 p.m. I couldn't wait to see everyone and give Pam her new son. To be able to be involved with Hans' arrival in Pam's life was a privilege. To be the bearer of such a bundle of joy was just reward for a little inconvenience. Terri's willingness to get a little flexible kept me from being on the highway for the holiday weekend. The downside was I'd be away for Shadow's and Licorice's 14th birthdays, which was a monumental event for me, since I'd never had dogs live that long.

Little Michelle's Mike had finished his experimental vaccine study with no obvious benefit. Michelle and Mike's drama always gave perspective to my own. While I was consumed with my own struggles, they were nothing compared to what Mike faced. A few days before my trip, Mike was to begin an experimental chemo program.

I was grateful that my pharmaceutical education could help clarify some of the medical information for Michelle. I wanted her to realize that the vaccine program might not be the failure she considered it. While they hadn't had the test results necessary to continue, it didn't mean it had been a complete waste of time.

Helping Michelle helped me focus on something other than my own troubles. During my visit I planned to give Mike a lesson in dog toenail trimming. They had two Labs too, chocolate and yellow girls. I was more than happy to do whatever I could to help.

Before my trip, Pam emailed that a check was en route to help with my expenses, and she didn't want any flack about it. I surprised her when I called to thank her instead of arguing about her very kind gesture. One of the issues I'd been working on for a very long time was receiving. I was a born and bred giver. The check arrived and was for much more than I thought she'd send. It challenged my level of receiving, but I dealt with it, let go of my resistance, and deposited the check.

I was concerned about leaving Shadow, but I didn't feel he'd be a problem for Jodi. Having just been through such a rough time with Shadow, it was even harder to walk out the door. I was working at putting my needs first, which was, in retrospect, my hardest habit to break. Being a morning person, I was really being pulled out of my comfort zone having to travel so late at night.

Hans was twice the size he'd been on my first visit. He ran to greet me with a schnauzer haircut and cropped ears. I looked at his ears and my heart shuddered a little. He seemed totally oblivious to them. I got all of Terri's instructions, which took an hour away from my driving in daylight time. I wasn't going to be alone on the road this time. I had Hans.

I called Pam as we headed out of Terri's drive. We got to the motel at midnight. Hans had slept the entire trip. I took him out with his little matching collar and leash not knowing what to expect. Had he ever had one on before? Well, he went right to tinkling. He was really happy to get out of his prison. I hated to do it, but he went right back in so I could check in. I'd never seen such an agreeable puppy.

I'd brought a crate to set up next to my bed. I really expected Hans to be feeling pangs of loneliness having just been separated from his family. He reintroduced me to life with a puppy in a heartbeat. I was putting my things in the bath area when I heard this rustling noise. He'd pulled a wastebasket liner out and was chewing it. Oh my God, he's going to kill himself before Pam ever sees him. I wrestled it away from him saying no! I went back to the sink, and wham, that same sound. I snatched another one from him, and then he began tugging on the electric wires.

I decided he had way too much unused energy. So, we played fetch for quite a while before he got a little food. I put him in his crate next to me. How much sleep would he allow me? After a little stirring, we both fell asleep. The next time I heard him moving was 7 a.m. I just couldn't believe he'd slept for so long. Pam was so very lucky and so was I. Hans was the consummate companion!

LETTING GO

Master Michele had started to give some thought to getting a dog to help fill the void left by her dear Logan. When I was near Baltimore, she called with a few dog questions. She'd actually been to a breeder and found a puppy. I could tell that she really didn't want to hear my non-biased opinion about the puppy she was considering. She was in love and that was all there was to it. When love is involved all manner of good sense disappears. I was a prefect example of that.

I kept Pam abreast of our progress, since I knew she was very anxious to meet her son. I headed directly to Pam's with my treasured bundle of joy. The weekend traffic was light: my reward for a good deed. Pam was walking down her walk as we drove in. The look in her eye when I handed Hans to her was worth ten times any effort I'd put forth. It was, as the ad says, priceless!

It was so gratifying to be a part of giving something so special to an old friend. The last time I'd seen Pam was the evening she put Wil to sleep. The joy in her face as she walked Hans around the place was wonderful to see. He would never replace Wil, but he'd fill the hole in Pam's heart. From my vantage point, he was doing that already.

Hans had been perfect company on the long drive up. His antics in the motel room gave me a sneak peak into my future with puppies. I'd forgotten about puppies. I knew my dear boys would be leaving fairly soon. Hans gifted me with a reminder of the intense observation that puppies demand. I hoped I'd be up to it. After all, I was much older than when the boys were pups. I thanked Hans for his teaching. I knew when it was time, I'd be ready. To live without dogs was unthinkable. Pam couldn't thank me enough for bringing Hans to her. The joy I sensed in her was thanks enough.

After we fiddled around with Pam's new treasure, I headed to Master Michele's house. It was so good to see them again. I couldn't believe the latest addition. He was huge. I took one look at him, then at Michele, and laughingly said, "You're screwed." Michele and David had named their Golden Retriever puppy Kimo. He had a face to die for – simply adorable.

The two homes had the energy of dog in them once more and they were better for it. Kimo, Hans, and I enjoyed our time together. I knew the next time they wouldn't have that puppy charm any longer, so I took full advantage while I had the chance. I was so glad that my friends' hearts would be filled again with the joy and love of Nature's greatest companion. Dogs aren't called mans' best friend for no good reason!

The next morning, I had breakfast with Vince. He was in good spirits. Marie joined me in the afternoon to drive by a couple of houses, but none of them were worthwhile. We headed back to Marie's with a drive past my old farm to check on my parent's stones and trees. There was a huge sign announcing an auction. My heart came right up into my throat. Neither of us could believe what we read.

The rage forming in my solar plexus was about to explode like a volcano. Marie got all excited and thought I should buy it. I looked at her like she was crazy. I couldn't live here again. I let go of the farm when we moved. The farm was the only thing in my life that I'd been successful at letting go of.

When I negotiated the deal with the town for the farm, there was nothing but adoration for the place by the town's administrator and councilmen. Never in any of the conversations was there any mention of chopping it into pieces. As the realization of what we'd just discovered sunk in, I was attacked by my old nemesis: disrespect.

I guessed my issues with disrespect, accountability, and responsibility weren't restricted to Carolina. They were my issues wherever I was. My heart was broken with disappointment and betrayal. I checked on my folks' resting places and around the property a bit, which still looked uncared for.

We headed back to deliver our news to Michele. I felt her compassion for me, but she wasn't at all surprised. I emailed my Ex immediately, but I never received a response. I knew he didn't care a hoot about me, but I really thought he had some feeling for the farm that had been his equine hospital and breeding farm for over 30 years. Apparently, I wasn't the only thing he let go of. He was a master at letting go, which was something that I failed miserably at.

I began my calls to the various township people. I knew they also didn't give a hoot about what I thought. Even if they feigned interest, I'd learned my lesson not to believe a word they uttered. It was important for them to know that they weren't slipping something by me. Never once did I get an apology for their disrespect or their deception.

I was quite blunt with my opinion of what was going on. I reminded each one about my parents' resting places and the written agreement for their continuance. This requirement would have to follow to the next owner. I assured them I would stay on top of this issue through my friends in the area.

No one could believe my shocking news. I managed to get together with all my dearest friends: Gary and Kit, Amy and Peter, etc. A visit with Milt was a priority. I wanted to see how he was coping with Paula's passing. I spent a little time with Teddy at the restaurant, before I met Milt for lunch. Teddy was Teddy. He's a giver of energy rather than a taker and always made me feel better.

Milt was dealing. As we both admitted, you really don't have a choice. I don't think we ever get over a significant loss. I think we just learn to live with it and that takes an inordinate amount of time. I was still trying to learn to live with the consequences of my loss. Milt seemed pretty good, but then got a little teary. I told him I'd learned that tears proved to be very cleansing. They truly allow us to wash away the pain and hurt within our hearts. I encouraged him to let them flow when they came.

Next stop was Little Michelle and Mike's for the toenail trimming clinic. Holly was less worried and more trusting, so I did her first. Mike was right there to see how much I took off, which wasn't much. I prefer to do them monthly rather than risk cutting too much and hurting them. Daisy was a little less trusting, but when Mike told her to behave, she did. Cookies all around for good dogs! I use bribery with all my animal family.

After the grooming work was over, we sat at the table and just talked. Never once did I hear any complaint come from Mike regarding the terrible fate that he'd been dealt. As we talked, I just couldn't believe there was anything wrong with him. I came to help Michelle with the girls' nails, but I received much more than I gave.

The time I got to spend with Mike to witness his acceptance of his terminal illness taught me a powerful lesson about Grace. I'd been struggling for many, many months to surrender and accept what my Ex had done to me, and just couldn't. His betrayal was devastating, but not fatal. I'd survive to fight another day.

Mike's illness was terminal, and he knew it, but didn't let it affect the time he had left. He hadn't given up: he'd accepted and surrendered. He was still undergoing treatment, but he'd embraced his destiny, which was something I'd been unable to achieve as yet. He was a fantastic role model for all of us. I knew Mike would live whatever time he had in the best possible way. He wasn't going to give his power away and let his cancer win.

I challenged myself to try to live up to Mike's example. I vowed not to let my drama steal my power and control my life. Mike set a high standard to live up to, but I had to try.

Mike' teaching was a treasured gift to me. Trimming toenails paled in comparison. Being in Mike's presence opened my awareness to the rewards of living with acceptance and surrender. My time with Mike was priceless and turned out to be the last time I saw him. Precious memories that were truly a gift from the Universe... .

Visiting with Mike and Michelle really put things in perspective for me.

Good Deeds

Everything we experience can be interpreted in many different ways. Perspective determines our responses to our experiences. Change your perspective and the experience changes. Perspective is a powerful tool, which can cripple or fortify us. I'd progressed far enough in my search for truth and happiness that I did recognize how lucky I was.

Although Michelle and I spoke almost every day, seeing them brought home the drama they were living through. My empathy intensified, my gratitude deepened, and I expressed it more freely than before. I began to acknowledge the good things in my life. My appreciation for my good health was another gift they gave me.

As I drove out of town, I called the town councilman who'd been the most instrumental in getting the farm purchased. He fed me lame excuses for the need to market the house with guarantees that they wouldn't let it be torn down, which was my greatest fear. I also learned this wasn't the first auction. Wasn't that nice? They tried before, but had no bids. I felt deceived and betrayed by the township I'd lived in for 27 years.

I was anxious to get back to my recuperating Shadow, but not to all the aggravations of the housing market in the mountains. I wanted to relinquish my mountain dream. I believed I couldn't move on with my life until the dream became someone else's dream. I figured my only hope was to hand it over to the next person, and then I would *have* to let go and move forward. I'd learn much later that my assumption was incorrect.

I was relieved to see that the dogs had fared well in my absence. Jodi had taken great care of them. My putting Self first hadn't worked against me. Maybe my conscious mind would start to recognize the benefits that resulted from my choosing to put Self first.

I launched right back into real estate management with the realtor and Ernie. Eventually, Ernie scheduled the work to clear the weeds and small trees that had started to grow back on the slope. I also needed to grade the roads where the summer storms had washed out areas. Ernie got a crew up to clear the slope. One step at a time.

Chapter 13

The Three Rs – Reality, Reflections & Reconciliation

*A*huge hurricane hit the coasts of Louisiana and Mississippi and her name was Katrina. The devastation to New Orleans and the surrounding areas was unprecedented. With levies crumbling, the area flooded disastrously. Mother Nature destroyed my folks' favorite stomping grounds. The Gulf Coast region was their last road trip before they died. Many of the treasures in the log house came from New Orleans' antique shops. My last post card from my mom and my last letter from my dad came from there.

Along with the rest of the nation, I sat mesmerized by what I saw on CNN. I felt so helpless watching hundreds of thousands of lives being tossed around on the seas of Katrina's devastation. While I lived far from the actual force of the winds, rains, and floods, Katrina affected my life dramatically.

Reports of the damage to the oil industry were sobering. Costs for everything were going to skyrocket. I came to the very depressing realization that I *needed* to stay in the log house. I could meet my expenses in Carolina. The interest in the mountain property had been nothing short of dismal. My belief that it would sell by fall had disintegrated. Coupling my lost faith in selling with increased living expenses from Katrina, I was forced into an executive decision.

I took a couple of days to sit with the choice before I called Jack to explain my thinking and offer apologies, but I had to stay put. Emotionally, this was as devastating to me as Katrina was to the Gulf Coast. My choice wasn't really based in fear, but more resignation. I'd lost faith in my ability to know, and in my soul. These admissions paralyzed me. I was experiencing my own Katrina wreaking havoc and devastation on my psyche, my emotional well-being, and my self-confidence. I felt battered by the hurricane that was my emotional life!

First a tsunami and now a hurricane assaulted my beingness. I couldn't help but think back to Michael Roads' column on Trust. I really had to focus on reestablishing trust in myself, in life, and the Universe, which ultimately meant trusting my soul. Deep down I knew this was the first domino in a series, which needed to be resolved in order for my journey in the Tunnel to make any headway. My soul and I just couldn't reconcile our differences. Gee, I hope your soul can't divorce you!

Taking the log house off the market left me very blue. All my friends were so disappointed with my news, but also very understanding. I kept saying it didn't mean I wasn't coming home. It just meant it wouldn't be this year. Now, I had to face another winter on Timber Lakes Drive – something I'd sworn I wouldn't do. I kept thinking about Gregory's and his helpers' feelings that I was meant to be in Carolina. It always came down to what I wanted versus what I needed. The self-confidence drained out of me.

Resignation doesn't contain acceptance of that which you are resigned to. Without acceptance, no satisfaction comes with your choice. I just felt defeated all over again. I viewed my decision as the best one I could make given the information I had. Emotionally, I was devastated at the thought of not living in the close company of my dear friends.

While I pondered not moving, I got a bill from the insurance carrier for the Deltec. The bill indicated the premium I'd paid was for three months. What? I thought it was expensive for a year's coverage. I was totally confused and got on the phone to the insurance agent. The gal had to look into it.

While I waited for her to research my problem, I began having thoughts about what to do with myself, since I wasn't moving home. I was used to being busy every minute of every day. My new, inactive lifestyle had proved a huge challenge for me. Time had always been my enemy, because I never had enough. It was still giving me fits, but for the exact opposite reason. I had too much time. Oh, that pendulum's always restoring balance. Blast you, Nature!

My thoughts generated the idea of a book. I was blessed with fantastic experiences with animals, animal healing, and the lessons contained within my experiences. It seemed like an interesting idea. It certainly ought to be a consumer of time. Writing might be a good thing to do. I kicked the idea around, but the most I accomplished was gathering my files.

I kept wondering about the auction of the farmhouse in New Jersey while I dealt with the Deltec insurance problem. Eventually, the gal ascertained that the colossal amount of money I'd already paid was only for three months! This answer opened a whole boxful of anxiety and stress and a new search for coverage.

As you might surmise with my recent decision regarding the log house, I scheduled a session with Gregory. I still was so confused by the outcome of my *meant to be* house in Jersey. Coupling that lost expectation with my removal of the log house from the market, I needed some clarification. Between the two, I knew I wasn't going anywhere any time soon, and I wasn't happy, so I sought help from the best place I knew.

The ultimate source of information and guidance should have been my soul, but we were still fighting like spoiled children. Given the situation I found myself in, my soul was definitely winning. I was a long way from surrendering to and accepting my soul's creations. Losing more faith and trust in my Self and my soul had me feeling lost altogether.

As I began to write about the session, I noticed the date of it was 30 years from the day I fell in love. A favorite poem of mine is *The Dash*, which arrived by email the day my cat Merlin died. Months after when I *asked* what I should name Squiggles' first foal, I heard Dash! Instantly, I knew who was back.

The Dash rests between birth and death dates on a tombstone. The poem teaches that the dash is the most important part, because it represents our life. The memories of my dash, the 30 years since that first kiss and my session with Archangel Michael, came flooding back to me. I harbored no regrets about the journey. I could have done without all the pain and heartache of the past 16 months, but I was verging on being able to accept their significance. I patted myself on the back for having lived a decent dash!

I've decided to share a more detailed portion of this particular session to elucidate its significance to me. This session contained so much that turned the tide of my stumbling progress in the Tunnel that I feel a more detailed description might encourage others to seek help from what might seem like an extraordinary venue.

This session with Gregory and Archangel Michael proved to be a turning point in my search for understanding. The information presented shined a bright light on the reasons that brought me to a life alone in the mountains of North Carolina. It provided more clarity than I had hoped for. It spoke of things that I didn't know I needed to do, accept, and embrace. It addressed things that I knew, but couldn't accept just yet. One of which was that I had animals who were ready to leave. I knew this, but didn't allow my heart to accept it.

I tried to tell the dogs, mostly Shadow because he was visibly declining, that it was okay to go. My years counseling others taught me that he read what my heart said not my mind. Until I could let go with my heart, my most loyal supporter wasn't going anywhere. What I hadn't considered was the consequence of their delayed departures. It was delaying others that were waiting to join me. Interesting!

More wonderment presented itself when Michael described my conflict with the Universe and my soul concerning the ever-present issue of getting what I wanted versus getting what I needed. He equated my thoughts of *I don't like it, I don't want it, I want out of here,* to that of a rebellious teenager. As Michael's words rolled from Gregory's mouth, a spotlight shined on Stormy! I never saw it until that moment.

When I mentioned it, Michael just laughed and admired the efficiency of the Universe. All was *always in perfection.* Stormy was training me, or trying to. Michael categorized it as a beautiful fit. While I was doing what I loved to do, Stormy was trying to teach a lesson I didn't want to learn! You've got to have a sense of humor or you will go crazy.

The animal communicator was so in the dark when it came to herself. My blinders were still firmly in place. I gave animals more credit than most. I learned from so many of my own and my client's animals just how integral they are to their peoples' lives. Even I, who attribute so much of my healing to my dear Stormy, was blown away by the awareness I'd just received from Archangel Michael.

Michael also encouraged me to acknowledge and then surrender to my soul's creations. He echoed Mike's valuable lesson of acceptance and surrender. It was coming at me from all directions. When would I ever get it? The Archangel challenged me to seek out the things that would bring me joy, to become *accountable* and *responsible* for my level of happiness, and to *respect* my Self and my soul. He counseled me to be honest with myself about who was the creator of my drama.

Honesty was the character trait I treasured most in myself. My shadow self was working overtime to get me to embrace my hidden flaws and accept the gifts it offered me. These were my Big Four – honesty, respect, accountability, and responsibility! To embrace my shadow, and therefore my flaws, was a tall order. It was exactly what I'd come seeking. It wasn't what I wanted, but absolutely what I needed to begin to accept.

My flitting thoughts about writing a book were addressed, too. Why this surprised me I didn't know, but it did. *They* always knew everything about what

LETTING GO

I was thinking. My soul's creation of living in the mountains was directly related to writing. I was astonished. Michael's bird's eye view into this portion of my soul's creations opened up an entirely new sphere of understanding.

Michael's method of teaching is to present challenges that force you to reflect on resolutions to the issues confronting you. He doesn't simply regurgitate information. It's an exchange that leads down a path of illumination. He shines the light ahead for you, but you find your own way. I felt my shattered self-confidence and self-doubt were at the root of my recent traumas.

In reply to his challenge to regain my confidence, I exclaimed that I'd never lost it to this extent before. He responded, "Good point!" Then he exclaimed, "The depth of your despair creates the height of your joy." I just smiled and said, "Ah, *The Prophet*." You see all the little pieces of our lives do come together in one complete puzzle. Why did I find that particular portion of Gibran's, *The Prophet*, meaningful the first time I encountered it? Did I know I would be living it 35 years later? Makes one wonder, doesn't it? More coincidences and synchronicity.

Michael led me along my path of discovery, learning, growth, and healing. He asked, "Having allowed for an experience that is deeper than ever before, how can you gain your confidence back?" Since I was at a loss for words and answers, he gently said, "By allowing yourself to express your feelings, your creativity, and your discipline. By writing, so your heart can express itself." Wow, the book really was a key, not just a time consumer.

This pivotal session encouraged me to put to rest the conundrum of my experiences being exactly what I asked for, even though they appeared to be just the opposite. Michael said, "The Truth is – when you get enough of what you need, *then* you get what you want!" Aha! Michael asked me what the theme of the past 16 months had been. There were so many I couldn't choose. Michael came to my aid with, *Letting Go!*

Hmmm, letting go. Over the past two years, I'd been in the process of letting go, whether I was aware of it or not. Depending upon one's intentions, it can be an easy, freeing experience, or one that brings you to the depths of despair. I've felt both the highs and lows of it and am still trying to come to terms with the process. It occurs on all levels – physical, mental, emotional, and spiritual. For me, the difficulty arises from whether I'm aware that I'm letting go or not.

The choices of when to let go, and when not to, are neither *right* nor *wrong*, they just *are*. The choice you make dictates the resulting emotions. Releasing something or someone that you consciously choose to let go of, such as my farm, creates a positive emotional experience. Having to let go of something or

160

someone due to another's choice, i.e. my Ex, results in negative experiences. The first step is to recognize the need to let go, then acknowledge that you have a choice – and ultimately, make the choice.

Knowing I'd been pussy-footing around with the book idea for a month or more, Michael sent me home with strict instructions: "Sit at your computer, type the words *Letting Go* at the top of the page, and write from your heart!" Five days after that session, this book was begun. It wasn't the topic I expected, but I hadn't anticipated any of my creations of the past 16 months. Why should this be any different? The journey through my dark Tunnel of grief, pain, anger, suffering, and abject unhappiness began to take a definite turn towards the Light. I just needed the illumination that Michael and Gregory gave me and a swift kick in the spiritual butt!

My initial purpose in writing was to take up time. Quickly, as I recognized the possibilities of uncovering the reasons and ultimate lessons behind what had happened to me, my intentions changed. I hoped to answer my recurring question of "How did I get here?" I wrote to express my feelings and to let my heart unburden itself. I wrote to heal Self and soul.

My purpose for sharing the personal specifics of this session was simply to offer a window to peek through, which might garner similar results for you. Looking outside the box, expanding your comfort zone, and opening unknown doors often leads to some of the most powerfully profound gifts. My challenge to you is to keep an open mind, and more importantly, keep your heart open.

Don't close a door or window of opportunity because someone else's opinion is pessimistic or judgmental. The path to true healing will not reveal itself in the presence of judgment. No one but you knows what's best for you, your healing, and your soul. Follow however and wherever your heart leads. It is the authentic source of your Truth!

Let your heart guide you to whatever assistance will be the most advantageous for you in the moment. Those last three words are critical – in the moment. Do *not* let your ego dissuade you. It will try; take it from one who knows! It has been one of my biggest obstacles.

While it wasn't a conscious choice at the time, the act of journaling my movie became a commitment to my Self and to my soul to discover, learn, and grow from my trauma. My willingness to write about my pain was a monumental act of self-love whether I recognized it or not. To be honest, I didn't. I began writing with limited expectations, because I wasn't going to set myself up to fail. This book arose from that act of self-love, pure and simple.

LETTING GO

In the beginning, my writing happened in fits and starts. Since I had no agenda for a book, I simply wrote when I was inspired, which is the best way to do anything creative. *Everything happens for a reason... No coincidences... We create our own realities... Always in perfect timing... When the student is ready... .*

Back in my everyday world, I was focused on the insurance about to expire on the Deltec dream house. While at the bank, I mentioned the insurance dilemma to my friend Carolyn. She referred me to a fellow who had helped her with a similar situation. I spoke with him and he agreed to research it for me. Here I go again.

I was still light-years away from accepting responsibility for my soul's creations. I felt my Ex's choice had forced me into my thoroughly unhappy existence. His choices deposited me in the Abyss and the Tunnel. His abandonment built the walls of my prison. I felt trapped by the sense of responsibility that wouldn't allow me to walk away as my Ex had to live the life he chose. My beautiful dream now imprisoned me. Until such time that I finally acknowledged the true perpetrator, I'd continue to be a prisoner of my illusion and my resentment for my Ex.

A week after I stared writing, Mother Nature battered the gulf region with yet another powerful hurricane. Rita's destruction meant even greater increases in fuel and utility bills. A startling change in perspective allowed me greater acceptance of my decision to stay in Carolina. Who would have ever expected another storm of this size so soon? The misfortune of the Jersey house deal was transformed into a blessing by two ladies, Katrina and Rita.

My wiser part, my soul, knew what I needed and got me exactly that in spite of our constant bickering. This latest awareness reinforced my belief that there was someone who knew a lot more about what was best for me than the conscious me. *Everything happens for a reason and in our best interest* even though we don't always see it or understand it at the time. My revelation was a perfect example of just what I'd been trying to embrace. Boy, my soul is good! I heard it saying, "Well, it's about time."

While these hurricanes wrought untold pain and heartache on tens of thousands, they served as a catalyst for my ultimate recognition and acceptance of my need to stay in North Carolina. Had the house gone through in Jersey, I would have subjected myself to financial disaster. I'm sure my ego would have thrown me back into the Abyss with all types of fears of my future bankruptcy. I felt nothing short of blessed and had no other to thank than my own soul.

This bombshell initiated the reconciling of our differences. The trust and faith I'd lost in my soul began to return. Trust in Self came packaged with more self-confidence, less self-doubt, and the willingness to let go of the control I'd been so desperately seeking. How could I continue to battle with my soul, when it had brought me to this place of, dare I say it, surrender? Yes, letting go of the struggle with my soul brought with it acceptance of my soul's wisdom. This epiphany gave birth to my ability to surrender. I acknowledged that I was truly blessed and began to embrace gratitude once again.

While I was making great strides with my soul, I was still frustrated with everything that continued to be beyond my control in the physical realm. I was trying to change my opinion of where I was living. I walked around my little acre in the woods and found to my delight I had wildflowers growing all over it. I apologized to the property for having been such a poor caretaker. I changed my perception of the log house in my mind, but I couldn't find room for it in my heart. The sacred mountain property took up all the space. Until I *let go* of the dream within my heart, I will remain imprisoned.

Carolyn's insurance friend found cheaper insurance coverage. When I filled out the application, I noticed the company was the same one that had declined it twice before. He assured me that they would write a policy. I wanted to believe him, but I left his office filled with reservations. Since his office was near the mountain, I stopped to see what progress had been made on clearing the slope. It looked wonderful. I patted myself on the back for perseverance. The mountain was once more presentable.

The next morning, I was ready to find solace with Stormy. We were still struggling with our strong wills, which meant my soul and I were still battling. While I'd acknowledged and accepted the astuteness of my soul's creation of the failed attempt to return to New Jersey, I still struggled with surrendering completely. Trust was returning slowly.

Stormy offered a window to peer through to see my shadow self. His level of objection to my control allowed me an indicator of my own resistance to letting go of control and surrendering to my soul's creations. In spite of our arguing, the barn was where I sought refuge from the frustrations of the rest of my life.

The universe gave me a little peek into the progress I really had made on my fears with a power outage that night. Last year, I'd flown into fear about being without power in daylight! This time I was calm in the dark of night. I surrendered to it, which pleased me. The universe showed me I'd come a long way. I needed to start to praise my progress. I reveled at finding a little piece of the strong woman I used to be. Perhaps, I was finally embracing my core beliefs and trusting Self more.

While surfing the Internet, something (my soul, ya think?) made me check Eckhart Tolle's website. His workshop schedule had been curtailed due to work on another book. A few days later, something made me walk through the book section at Wal-Mart. Well, lo and behold, there was Tolle's new book staring back at me. I just smiled with the synchronicity. It was just what I needed. Okay, I'm starting to get it!

Tolle's second book, *A New Earth*, was in perfect timing. It cemented my practice of living in the Now. This book resulted in my recognizing the need to be the ever-vigilant observer of my thoughts, my ideas, my emotions, and my creations. It compelled me to take control away from my ego and discourage its participation in my life. Tolle helped me remember more crucial ancient wisdom. *When the student is ready... .*

A letter declining the insurance policy for the third time arrived. I just shook my head at the ineptness of all these agents. This was not unexpected, but I was aggravated at wasting so much time and energy. I gave up. I surrendered. They won. I emailed Bob with the news and for once, we agreed on something. Insurance coverage for the house just wasn't an option. It was more than we could afford under the circumstances.

Gregory hosted another gathering at his home. Boy, did I need one. Archangel Michael offered us a healing meditation with the power of the full moon, one of my favorite of Mother Nature's treasures. The full moon swells my heart with feelings of connectedness, not being alone, and being a part of the infinite. Michael's full moon meditation was exactly what I needed and wanted. Gee, I got them both together!

Before I left the gathering, I made an appointment for a session. Lately, I felt like I'd been spiraling backward and downward in the Tunnel. My dislike of the dreaded Abyss inspired my choice to seek additional enlightenment. Gregory had begun as an advisor and counselor for me, but my relationship with him and Sandie had grown into friendship. They were becoming my first true friends in the mountains. Maybe there was hope for me.

My writing began to allow me to step out of the intensity of the moment and observe what I experienced. When I embarked on this creative process, I'd made a commitment to be totally honest about what I observed and discovered about my Self and my soul. To do anything less would make the writing worthless. I wanted to share my feelings about it with whoever came to teach and guide me in my session.

I met a new Being named Jalil. My main concern was the sale of the mountain property. The information I received was very encouraging. Jalil showed me a scenario which I'd never considered. Something he said really touched me deeply. Jalil acknowledged me as "the designer and founder of the energy on the property." His view caused a stirring in my heart.

I'd always given sole credit to Mother Nature for the spectacular energy on the property. To think I contributed to its specialness was very gratifying and humbling. In some way, it made me feel that all my efforts would still have meaning. Jalil guided me to find things to enjoy here in the mountains. My wish for someone I liked on my mountain was predicted. I just had to be patient. More lessons.... .

My friend, Archangel Michael, flowed through Gregory next. I was pleased to hear his booming laugh. It always brought a big smile to my face. His first words were, "How goes the battle?" I was waging battles on so many levels. Another huge smile crossed my face. Humor is a powerful elixir. I admitted my biggest disappointment had been that my dream was unrealized. Michael asked, "Does it matter?" His question stopped me in my mental tracks. I waffled. He asked, "Does it make a difference?" All I could think was *yes*, of course it does, but I knew this wasn't the answer he was fishing for.

He asked in a different way: "At this moment in your life, does the fact that your expectation didn't come to pass – does it matter?" He displayed incredible patience with his bumbling student. He switched tracks a little and asked, "What will be your own frame of mind, when it doesn't matter anymore."

As I pondered that and *felt* the emotion of when it didn't matter, I exclaimed "Oh, yeah." He continued, "Do you see how freeing it feels?" Freedom was precisely what I felt. Freedom resulting from finally having let go of the dream and its disappointments, the weight of the responsibility for its management, and the deep hurt I still harbored in my heart.

What he said next opened my understanding and awareness to a level I hadn't yet experienced. By my continued presence in the area, the appropriate person would be drawn to the mountain property. He stated that had I left, the possibility of that occurring would have been very, very slim. I'd have never thought of that. Also, if I left, I'd never see how my dream unfolded. This was fascinating.

My wish to hand the stewardship of this spot, where my soul had finally felt at home, over to the appropriate person was of utmost importance. Michael opened me to that which had been hidden from my view by those blasted blinders formed from my unhappiness and self-doubt. This new perspective made it worth staying in the log house for however long it took. Michael's insight made my situation much more acceptable.

Once more, I was stunned with the clarity of understanding I was being gifted with. The humor returned with Michael's last question for me; "How's the grass growing?" With a broad smile I answered, "Here and there." It just blew my mind each time these powerful entities would chime in with some mundane comment or question.

Having just spent all this time on issues of supreme importance to my growth and healing, he wanted to bring me back to my everyday life where all the experiences that allow growth and healing happen. Those types of comments always triggered my thoughts that we truly are never alone. They're up, over, around, and under, always watching.

I left Gregory's, gathered the dogs, and headed to the barn. Stormy was really cooperative. The next day was the same. Late October, fall colors, 60 degrees, and a very agreeable horse to ride. What more could I ask for? We rode all around the gorgeous farm enjoying the beauty of the season, the weather, the surroundings, and each other's company. No tedious training, just the pure joy of Nature. It was a memorable day for me. I categorized it as a *Great Day*!

It was 16 months since life as I knew it and expected it to be had ceased. Until this day, I hadn't had a good day, no less a great day. I felt happiness within me, which I'd wondered if I'd ever feel again. I would, and did, that day. I had Stormy to thank for facilitating the arrival of happiness in my life on that Sunday.

It turned out that Mother Nature provided us with identical conditions for the next four Sundays. Each one was a gift, which helped reinforce my newfound happiness. Stormy and I weren't without our disagreements, showing me that I still had issues to reconcile with my soul. The weather began to get inconsistent, but those four Sundays were treasures to me. I was blessed with so many fabulous teachers supporting, guiding, and being patient with me. My gratitude runneth over.

The timing of Stormy's change of heart didn't go unnoticed. I longed for him to let go of his resentment and couldn't help wonder how much had been triggered by my willingness to acknowledge my soul's creations. While I was grateful for his willingness to defer to my control, a day or two doesn't mean much with horses. As winter approached, I wanted to reach a point where he wanted to do what I asked. I needed to stop work on a good note. Horses have phenomenal memories, so it was imperative that he remembered positive ones.

The importance of animals in my life is huge, but I accept that animals are insignificant to many others. I received a poem from one of my horse friends that expresses the value of horses to those who live under their spell. Stormy's powerful teaching, which allowed me to recognize such a crucial component of my own healing, epitomizes what this poem is attempting to teach the non-horse person.

"It's Just a Horse"

From time to time, people tell me, "lighten up, it's just a horse,"
or, "that's a lot of money for just a horse."
They don't understand the distance traveled, the time spent, or
the costs involved for "just a horse." Some of my proudest moments
have come about with "just a horse."
Many hours have passed and my only company was "just a horse,"
but I did not once feel slighted. Some of my saddest moments have
been brought about by "just a horse," and in those days of darkness,
the gentle touch of "just a horse" gave me comfort and reason
to overcome the day.
If you, too, think it's "just a horse," then you will probably
understand phrases like "just a friend," "just a sunrise," or "just a promise."
"Just a horse" brings into my life the very essence of friendship,
trust, and pure unbridled joy.
"Just a horse" brings out the compassion and patience that make me a
better person. Because of "just a horse" I will rise early, take
long walks and look longingly to the future.
So for me and folks like me, it's not "just a horse"
but an embodiment of
all the hopes and dreams of the future, the fond memories of the
past, and the pure joy of the moment.
"Just a horse" brings out what's good in me and diverts my thoughts
away from myself and the worries of the day.
I hope that someday they can understand that it's not "just a horse"
but the thing that gives me humanity and keeps me from being
"just a woman."
So the next time you hear the phrase "just a horse" just smile,
because they "just" don't understand.

–Anonymous

You may want to look closer at your relationship(s) with your own animal friend(s). You might be overlooking one of your greatest allies. Perhaps, one of these wonderful teachers is waiting to enter your life.

Chapter 14

More Heartbreaking Holidays

*T*o give you some perspective, I'm writing six months after that first Great Day. Since then, I've learned so much about the lessons my life experiences were created to teach. By reliving them in order to write, I can see very plainly what I had only a hint of at the time. After my session with Gregory, Jalil, and Archangel Michael, my perspective about not returning to New Jersey changed dramatically. Only a couple of hours after that change, I had my first willing encounter with Stormy in months. I surmised that my soul and I had resolved some major issues immediately upon my changed perspective.

While I hadn't truly surrendered, I had recognized and accepted my situation. Surrender would have allowed me to let go of my unhappiness. In my conscious mind, I accepted my soul's creations. I became accountable and responsible for the circumstances of my life. My reinstated honesty with Self and soul evolved from restored respect for my soul. Like a game of dominos, once one moved, a chain reaction started.

Being gifted with this lesson was the purpose behind why I chose to write. The act of writing allowed the lessons to unfold in their perfect timing. Without writing, I might never have seen them, which would have been a waste of creating.

More Heartbreaking Holidays

My dear Shadow was aging so much more rapidly than his brother. It just broke my heart to see it. He always wanted to be by my side, but the stairs to the office were really strenuous for him. I'd support his butt and give him a push to help with the climb. Actually coming down was worse because he didn't have the strength to hold himself back. Eventually, he had to be restricted to one trip a day. Neither of them liked being out of my sight, but it couldn't be helped.

Shadow also fell on the three stairs from the porch to their yard. He'd wait for me to help him up. He was humiliated by his decline, but accepted it with grace, which was something I still struggled with: acceptance and surrender with grace. Mike and Shadow exemplified grace. I tried to prepare myself for the inevitable, but it was something I couldn't focus on. I just hoped I would *know* when the time came. My confidence was on the rise, but self-doubt still plagued me.

Back in Jersey, Mike received abysmal, heartbreaking test results. His local oncologist would handle future treatments. I felt so useless 600 miles away, but there wasn't anything I could do about that. I'd tried and failed. Let it go! Mike had a hunting trip planned to Mexico the first week of December. It was a yearly event with a close friend. This year was to be no different.

Michelle and I'd been discussing the trip for months. Mike was the only one who truly knew how he felt. He deserved to go for the brilliant example he'd shown the rest of us and for the unselfish life he'd lived. The news about Mike combined with advice from Gregory and his helpers enticed me to take a day off. I went in search of joy and happiness for my Self and soul.

Fall has always been my favorite of Mother Nature's seasons. The dogs and I drove along the Blue Ridge Parkway, one of the most beautiful roads, which I happen to live close to. Think I'll ever start to recognize my soul's wondrous creation? The previous fall, I was in the Abyss, unable to see the beauty in anything. I hoped the Tunnel would allow me to appreciate this most colorful time of the year.

We drove to Grandfather Mountain, whose magnificence called to my soul years ago. I needed Grandfather to breathe new life into my feelings, to awaken my heart, and to find my inner children. I sought peace, joy, and the sense of connectedness, which I always find on this spectacular mountain. I sat on a rock formation on the precipice and simply allowed the energy of the mountain to permeate my Being.

By the time I came back to the car, I felt renewed and whole. It had been a long time since I'd felt so serene. It'd been a *perfect* day. I was encouraged that I could appreciate the beauty of the area, which had been lost after the abandonment and betrayal by my Ex. My ability to begin to let go of some of my overwhelming unhappiness rewarded me with a spectacular day. Unlike my time on Maui, when so much was hidden by the clouds, all of Nature's splendor was in full view now. I felt blessed, thankful, and humbled.

The next day, we went to the mountain property. Feeling renewed by Grandfather Mountain, I decided to see if I was healed enough to handle seeing the fall beauty from the dream house, where I'd expected to admire all the autumns of the rest of my life. I survived the colors of the view from Heaven fairly well, showing me the progress I'd made.

When I got to my driveway, I had cell phone service. What's this? I called, and lo and behold, I heard the house phone ringing. Oh my God, the cell phone worked at my communications-challenged location. I found out the cell company added a tower somewhere along the main road near me. One of my greatest aggravations had been the poor communications here. With my DSL modem and cell service, I had joined the 21st century. I felt a tremendous sense of relief and security knowing I'd no longer be cut off from the outside world.

My decision about a whole house generator required some decisive action. If I was going to spend the thousands it would cost, I wanted it in before an ice storm. My great fear was the power outages that accompanied freezing rain. I called my electrician, Travis, who gave me a quote and installation date.

The week I spent waiting for the generator's arrival brought snow and winter-like conditions. I was relieved that the generator would be here soon. I applauded my decision to spend so much money to gift myself peace of mind. Its arrival was set for the day after Thanksgiving, which I found quite apropos.

I'd been on the phone seeking support from all my dear friends. I think the only one that was happy about my staying in North Carolina was Linda. She'd been worried about my going back to putting Self last. Well, she wouldn't have to worry, because it wasn't going to happen anytime soon. I thought it interesting that she'd been right on track regarding my *need* to return to New Jersey. She didn't think it was in my best interest and neither did my soul, which was painfully apparent by my failed attempt to return.

I kept my ego at bay by ceasing all thoughts of my future home. I started to focus on the positive aspects of the log house and the life that had been created by my Ex's departure. My inner voice kept saying, "Stop trying to change it, begin to respect what it offers you, be grateful, and make the most of the experience." I was grateful, but I guess I just didn't express it enough. I was trying to make the best of it – truly I was.

There are a few perks of living alone, although it's not a choice I'd have made for myself. I ate when and what I wanted. I didn't have to defer to anyone else's schedule. Having been married to a horse vet, my life had been dictated by the health of our clients' horses, which I accepted being a horse lover extraordinaire. Now, I was the ultimate decision maker. The choices I made were mine alone, so no compromise was necessary.

I focused on the pluses and let go of the minuses. With each thing I let go of, I found myself feeling a little less weighed down and more free. I thought about the sense of freedom I felt when Archangel Michael was asking, "Does it matter?" Perhaps, I was truly starting to get it.

With these results, you'd have thought I'd have just chucked everything I clung so tightly to: all the pain, grief, and anger. Wouldn't that have been nice? Maybe, but I wouldn't have learned the lessons they came to teach if I'd let go without thoroughly processing each emotion. Without the learning, my soul would simply create more traumas to challenge me to see the lessons being offered. I needed to make this a one-time journey through the Tunnel. I needed to make the most of my experiences and my creations.

Pam and I had been talking about the ebb and flow of the frustrations and aggravations in our lives. I told her that I perceived a blanket of oppressive energy, which seemed to smother me and then move off for no apparent reason. She claimed the same sensations. I told her it must be planetary.

Pam mentioned an astrologer she'd worked with in Charleston. I asked, "South Carolina?" How coincidental that I'd been in touch with the very same gal. I'd lost her contact information in the confusion of my multiple moves. Pam would see if she could find it for me. I just marveled at the workings of the Universe. Even though I was in the early stages of my writing, I'd begun to pay more attention to the creations in my life. Each had a specific goal or purpose.

I checked with Gregory, and he confirmed our suspicions. Mars was in retrograde. Planets in retrograde always seemed to elicit unpleasant energy for everyone. Gregory said his phone had been ringing off the hook with people in need of help. I smiled with the resurgence of my ability to *feel* and sense things, which was another sign of my progress.

Pam got back to me with the astrologer's email address, so I ordered a reading as a Christmas present to myself. I'd done one some years ago at the Omega Institute, which had been memorable. Given the drama of my recent life, I thought some understanding of the astrological influences might prove useful.

LETTING GO

The day before Thanksgiving, I went to the mountain property to check on things. I crossed paths with four – count them – four deer. Well, do you suppose I got their message? "Chill out, calm down, have faith, trust yourself, be gentle with your Self!" It was as if my soul was screaming at me with their timely appearance.

As I drove home, I remembered spending Thanksgiving with Barbara and Ernie the year before. I recalled my traumatic drive past the road leading to the mountain property and my hysterical, emotional response. This time, I actually walked around the property. While I felt sad, I didn't burst into uncontrollable tears. Yes, I'd made progress, and more than I gave my Self or my soul credit for.

Just in case I wasn't getting it four days later, two deer ran up the slope by my old driveway. I very rarely saw any deer near my house huddled in the woods. I just smiled and thanked the Universe and the deer. I did get the message, but thanks for making sure. It was nice to have animal messengers back in my life. They gave me hope.

Thanksgiving morning I gave thanks for my friends Gregory and Sandie, who'd invited me for dinner. I'd been in the log house a little over a year and they were the sum total of the new friends I'd made. I was grateful for all my dear friends scattered around the country, my family, and animal family.

I worried the nasty winter weather might postpone the generator installation, but Travis made it. After he worked for a bit, I asked about the propane hook-up. I wrongly assumed Travis did it. I immediately called the gas company, but they couldn't come for three weeks! My heart sank. Three weeks would be flat in the middle of winter, which was just what I'd been trying to avoid.

I was so frustrated that Travis hadn't said anything. Of course, I didn't ask either. I was learning to be more accountable. Thank you, Shadow Self. I just had to let go of the frustration and conjure up some more patience. Travis would have to come back after the gas company hooked in. I asked Travis to check my septic pump to be sure everything was in order. I'd never had a septic pump and wanted to avoid any surprises in the dead of winter. All was in order: another possible annoyance avoided.

I worked with Stormy whenever the weather allowed, but I knew our days were numbered. I'd be satisfied with our progress whenever I was forced to stop for the winter. I busied myself with Christmas gifts for all my dear friends, who'd been so instrumental in getting me this far in my struggle.

An old friend, Barbara, called with heartbreaking news. Her husband, Joe, had been diagnosed with liver cancer in July. I almost couldn't speak. I'd been having a lot of thoughts about calling Barbara lately and had ignored them. The mundane responsibilities of my own life were no excuse. Barbara taught me a powerful lesson about listening to my inner voice and acting on it. Had I known why Barbara was on my mind, I'd have called in a heartbeat.

Barbara told me Joe didn't want anyone to know, so I wasn't able to offer him my support and love. I offered it to Barbara. I was distraught to hear about Joe's sad news, but so grateful that she chose to call me. We went way back. She had offered her love and support in my direst of times. I told her to call me anytime day or night if she needed an ear. I wanted to reach right though the phone wires and give her a big hug.

Once more, perspective flowed to the forefront of my awareness. I had issues, but little Michelle and Barbara really had trauma. My drama certainly took a back seat to that of my two friends' traumas with their husbands' terminal cancers. I found it inconceivable that all this was happening to my friends.

Two days after Barbara's unexpected news, Mike left for Mexico. Since we talked almost daily, I knew Michelle was really concerned. I was so proud of how she handled giving up ten precious days of life with her husband. Her strength to let go for this period allowed him to create wonderful, last memories. While I'm against hunting, as you can imagine, I told her to tell Mike I hoped he got his deer. This was obviously something of great importance to him.

My greatest worry was what would happen when he got back. I felt the trip had been so vital to him that it gave him a goal to stick around for. I wanted to warn Michelle without compounding her stress. I didn't want her to be shocked if he began to decline rapidly after his return. She had the same fears and was appreciative of my sharing mine. All we could do now was wait and get ready for the approaching holiday season.

Trying to get into the holiday spirit was going to challenge me to begin with. With all these ill friends, it was even more difficult. I'd only had my tree and treasured ornament collection up once since my folks died in 2000. I'd forced myself to decorate the house for the last Christmas on Fair Chance Farm, although my heart wasn't in it. The holidays just weren't the same without my parents. They'd made all my Christmases wondrous.

I convinced myself it was time to let go of my Christmas pasts and experience Christmas now. I gathered all my boxes of treasures, got the Christmas tree out of its home in my horse trailer, and went about decorating despite the sadness that permeated all our lives. I played Christmas music, sang along, and actually had an easier time than I anticipated.

Seeing the ornaments that my mother had given me, some more than 30 years ago, brought back cherished memories. I was quite surprised that the hundreds I'd bought on vacations with Bob didn't bother me. I loved my tree. It was up, and it hadn't assaulted me with sadness. I gave myself kudos for being willing to take the chance that it might bring me more pain. Internally, I must have let go of more stuff than I'd thought. This was a pleasant discovery. The famous Christmas letter would be next on the list of must-dos.

December started with terrible weather – primarily ice. No wonder I'd had fears of ice and power outages. Maybe my intuition was returning. I let the aggravations of an installed but non-functional generator, unsold mountain property, and winter weather dampen my holiday spirit. I worked on my cards and gift-wrapping while I waited for Ernie to commit to moving the panels and for the gas company to hook up the generator.

The one crowning positive during this dismal time was what Mike accomplished. He'd gotten his deer. We all thought he'd come back early. I think Michelle secretly hoped so. As the days passed, it became clear that Mike was there for the duration. He stayed the full ten days with his best hunting buddy, Marshall.

I hadn't been out in several days due to my icy road. Neighbors were going in and out for work, so how bad could it be? As Mike was en route back from Mexico, I was about to embark on my own adventure. The dogs and I piled into the car and got up the drive without a problem. Thank goodness for four-wheel drive – a necessity at the log house. We headed slowly and carefully down my road. The further down the road I got, the more treacherous it became. There was no turning around.

I was terrified and panicked – so much so that I felt nauseous. What was my greatest fear? Shadow could never walk back up the road. It was a half mile and ice-covered. I was frozen with fear, much like the road from Hell was with ice. I began to cry as everything just caved in on me. I shook it off and told myself I didn't have time for this meltdown.

As long as I was this far, I continued into town for supplies. The main roads were perfectly fine. This realization kicked off a bout of anger at the realtor who got me involved with this road and *the* inescapable person to blame, my Ex! As you can see, I was still working on accepting and surrendering to my soul's creations.

When my problem-solving sanity returned, I set about finding a solution. I went to an auto parts store to get something called V-cables to provide traction on ice. Why did all my dramas seem to happen on Saturday? I had half an hour to get to the parts store. These V-cables were something that I could put on and take off. They were just what I needed. I was never so happy to spend $116. They were a cheap investment in peace of mind. Of course, they still had to be tested on the road from Hell.

With the acquisition of my cables, my anxiety dropped immensely. The dogs and I went about our errands, including a visit to Stormy. Our training had been stopped by the advent of winter, but I went out a couple times a week to show him I was still a part of his life. The dogs and I headed back to the log house armed with, hopefully, the answer to my prayers.

Although a little troublesome to get on, the V-cables were a godsend. I held my breath as we started back up the sheet of ice that was my gravel road. The car just grabbed its way back up. As I parked by the house, I finally began to breathe. I was filled with an overwhelming sense of success, satisfaction, and, are you ready, confidence! Confidence translated into empowerment. I had saved us!

Given the intensity of my terror on the road from Hell, I called in the troops and made an appointment with Gregory. This powerfully frightening incident proved an equally powerful teacher. As with most of my learning, it would take time and outside assistance to enable me to see the lesson. Once uncovered, I vowed to embrace the lesson about controlling my reactive emotions in order to access the powerful problem-solving part of my brain. If I could only learn to have more control over my paralyzing negative emotions, I could eliminate the need for these types of teachings, which was the pot of gold at the end of the rainbow, or Tunnel. I couldn't control what I didn't understand.

This was another session combining information and direct healing. The primary Being that worked with me was named Quan Yin. She is Asian, as the name suggests. Later, I learned that she is renowned in the Buddhist tradition. Her healing was nothing short of incredible. The lifetime from where my recent terror had arisen was painful to relive, but imperative to let go of. As I released the repressed emotions stored in my lower back, the area severely injured in the past lifetime, it eliminated the physical pain in this lifetime. I know you're confused and skeptical. Years ago, I was too. Remember, I'm the left-brained pharmacist.

Over the years, I've been gifted with the reduction or complete disappearance of physical pain in response to healing of stored negative emotions. It is the foundation of the healing modality I practice called Spiritual Response Therapy. In the beginning of my spiritual awakening, I required lots of physical confirmation. I was the biggest skeptic alive. I needed proof and got it, since we always get what we need.

LETTING GO

Without Quan Yin's willingness, I might never have recalled this extremely traumatic lifetime that was the root of so much physical pain in this lifetime. She also shared invaluable insights about Who-I-Really-Am. I realize some of you are thinking, "Here we go again." I encourage you to keep your heart and mind open. I did, and got a most wonderful gift.

Archangel Michael arrived with a discussion about the planetary influences I'd sensed of Mars in retrograde. He had encouraging information that the constraints of those energies would recede sooner than expected. He also applauded my writing and wanted me to be as pleased with my progress as my teachers were. He left me with the words, "All is well!" Later that night, Gregory had another gathering before he and Sandie left for the holidays. It was the perfect end to a very healing day. I was truly blessed.

The next morning I rose very early to meet Ernie to move the Deltec garage panels inside. It was in the 20s and windy as I worked to uncover the panels, which turned into a huge task. The ice accumulated on top had frozen the tarps to the panels. It took almost the hour to uncover them. I used a hammer to break up the ice.

With each hit of the hammer, I released more of the anger and rage that filled my being, which was directed towards the person responsible for what I was doing – my Ex, who else? I still hadn't accepted my soul's part in my life yet. I recognized the concept, but still blamed the *imposter*.

With each swing, I acknowledged my anger towards my Ex. By the time the tarps were free, I'd let go of a ton of rage. *Everything does happen for a reason*, which I am only seeing now. Once more, the benefit of writing revealed itself. I was too emotional that morning to see the gift being offered of releasing more repressed rage.

Ernie arrived an hour late with three men. They moved a couple of the panels in by hand, but didn't have the strength for anymore. Ernie seemed surprised at their weight, despite my warnings. The remaining panels were dragged in by his truck. With the panels out of the weather, I wouldn't have to come over every time the wind blew or the snows fell. It'd only taken me four months to get this accomplished, so I applauded my persistence.

As it turned out, the next day brought absolutely ghastly sleet and snow, and I couldn't ignore the perfect timing of the wall panel mission. With my new revelation regarding the beneficial rage release, I have let go completely of any residual frustration I was harboring toward the experience.

Soon after this accomplishment, I got a call from the township informing me of a buyer for my old farmhouse. He wanted to ask me about the history of the house. Would it be all right if they gave him my phone number? Yes. The new owner seemed to respect the house and its significance. He wanted to know everything I knew about it. He wasn't aware of any restrictions regarding my folks' resting places, but welcomed me any time.

I was relieved and grateful for an appropriate person to return the place to its former condition. It had attracted someone to it who would respect and honor it. The appropriateness of the farmhouse's new caretaker encouraged me that the same would happen for my abandoned Deltec on the sacred mountain property.

The gas company was due to hook up the generator, and I was thrilled when I saw their truck. I called Travis, who said he'd come the next afternoon. I'd finally have an operational generator, and an unbridled sense of security and the recognition that I'd done something for myself. This was an act of self-love, so I had much to celebrate.

While I was celebrating my little successes, Michelle and Mike were approaching the holidays knowing it would be their last together. Michelle shared with me her wish that Mike live until their youngest son, Mikey's, 21st birthday in mid-January. I immediately said, "Well, if he stays that long, Mike better stay for your 50th two days later!" I saw in Michelle's secret hope that same trait I possessed of putting others first. I smiled at our similarities. I only hoped Mike would gift her with his presence on her birthday.

The holidays were a real test of their strength and fortitude. Michelle epitomized the vow of "in sickness and in health." I was so proud of her for honoring her vow. My current life situation was instigated by a broken vow, so to see someone live up to their vows was heart-warming. I felt blessed to call her a forever friend. She was, and is, one of my heroes.

December's ice and snow proved challenging for all of my family. While the snow wasn't deep, its combination with sleet and freezing rain turned my acre and the road into a glacier. The dog yard was abominable. I took my ice chopping apparatus and broke up about one third of the yard. I thought if it weren't so smooth it would make it easier to walk on. It helped Licorice a little, but it seemed to be worse for Shadow. He was so unsteady that he couldn't cope with the clumpy snow. I went back out and moved all the clumps to the sides to make it safe for Shadow.

After almost falling while struggling up and down the glacial drive, someone told me about things called ice walkers. They sounded very much like my V-cables, but for shoes. I was telling Master Michele about my horrible glacier. I swore I wouldn't live here another winter. I just wouldn't!

I mentioned the ice walker things for my shoes. "Don't buy them, we have an extra pair and I'll send them right down." Well, now wasn't that convenient. They're an absolutely fabulous invention called Yak-Tracs. Once more, I sent thank-yous to whomever was clever enough to figure these out. The security I felt with these on was wonderful. I wished they had something like it for my dog friends.

The terrible conditions lasted for most of December. Because of Shadow's feebleness, he couldn't walk up to where the car was parked for three weeks. Shadow was distraught. He obsessed each afternoon by walking around and glaring at me as if saying, "Let's *do* something." I had runners all over the first floor, but he'd still slip when he tried to play. It was heart wrenching. His mind was young, but his body wasn't. He reminded me of someone else – talk about reflections!

Mike's oncologist had planned a three-day hospital stay as soon as he returned from Mexico. Poor results turned into a much longer stay. The news wasn't encouraging. Michelle and I spoke whenever she had a chance to call. Eventually, they released Mike, so he'd be home for Christmas. Mike's condition put a real damper on any holiday spirit. I couldn't wait for them to be over.

I was receiving wonderful gifts from my friends, which helped resurrect some holiday spirit. FedEx needed me to pick up a package because of my icy road from Hell. When I got to the depot, one package was really five. I felt so loved to be receiving all of these gifts. Getting them down the steep, icy drive was no easy job. However, with my handy-dandy Yak-Tracs, everything made it without any breakage.

My UPS driver called me with the same complaint, so I agreed to meet him down by the main road. He had several boxes including one that held a Spruce tree that my sister-in-law sent, which made me smile. The lovely treasures pulled me right out of my anger at the condition of the drive and gravel road. I was blessed with wonderful friends and family.

I marked my 18-month anniversary in Carolina with a very upsetting phone call from Chuck, the builder from Hell. He had a buyer for the two lots next door, which I held a right of first refusal on. He needed me to sign off on them immediately. I wanted to scream, "Who cares!" I didn't say much besides how treacherous the road was.

I sat miffed that this deceitful person, who treated me like dirt, lied to me, cheated and betrayed me, now demanded that I do anything for him and do it fast! Have we slipped over into that other dimension again? I reviewed my right of first refusal papers, which said I was supposed to get a copy of the contract stating to whom, for how much, and for what intent the lots were being sold. I decided to forget about it until after Christmas, which gave me a few more days to stew. I hated having unpleasant things hanging over my head.

The next day was Christmas Eve and my drive was actually quite passable as I headed to see Stormy with tons of holiday apples and carrots and a gift for Kim. After the barn I went to the movies, then bought something for my Christmas dinner alone. The "feel-good movie of the year" turned out to be a huge mistake. Ninety-five percent of the movie was humorous; the remaining five percent ruined my day.

Unbeknownst to me, the mother of the family was fighting breast cancer and died at the end of the movie. The movie ended with the family gathering for the following Christmas holiday, minus one. I could have killed all of the people who did ads and interviews for this movie and never mentioned this part of the story. I left the theater in tears. It was so real for me, knowing Michelle's family was facing this identical situation. This feel-good movie threw me into a terrible depression.

I wanted to fix something special for Christmas dinner, so it would seem festive. I found a small rib roast, which was perfect for one person. The dogs greeted me as I brought my bags in from the store and I made a startlingly discovery. There was no roast in any of the bags. I checked the car, but it was nowhere. I was furious at the cashier.

My car had been needing washer fluid for days, so I decided to put some in. I'd taken off my Yak-Tracs, but felt it would be safe on the flat drive. Wrong! As I lifted the hood, I fell flat on my left side. The jug of washer fluid flew out of my hand. As I lay in front of the car, I heard the plastic jug sliding, sliding, sliding.

Well, the anger over the dismal movie ending and the missing roast morphed into rage. Trying to control my emotions, I pulled my Yak-Tracs back on and went to find the washer fluid. I wasn't going to be defeated! I saw it far down the slope, past the spring, and on someone else's land. I retrieved it, climbed my way back up, filled the reservoir, and went into the house with a teeny sense of triumph over the elements.

As I sat on the stairs to pull off my boots and Yak-Tracs, I burst into tears. The poor dogs didn't have a clue. They hovered around telling me everything was okay. It wasn't. I'd been trying so hard to accept everything around me. I hadn't been allowing myself to express my true feelings. I've learned that if you don't express your feelings, you repress them. I was kidding myself about accepting my circumstances. I saw the wisdom in the failure of the Jersey house deal, but I didn't like my location on the road from Hell or my soul's creations of the past eighteen months.

I shed torrents of tears for Little Michelle and her family, for Barbara and her family, for my aging dogs, and for myself. The unexpected sadness in the movie, the missing roast, and the fall on the ice were catalysts for this release. I was so unhappy about where I lived. I tried to accept that this was what I needed. It just wasn't what I wanted. It was as though the place where we store these repressed emotions simply had no more room. I'd reached its capacity and it erupted. When I was done, I felt empty. I had hit bottom.

Christmas was above freezing and rainy, which meant improved conditions on the gravel road and driveway. After my meltdown, I wasn't going to chance another movie. I began to realize how much empathy I had for Michelle. I saved all of my gifts to open on Christmas morning. Their places under my tree made it look a little more like the Christmases I remembered.

Since the dogs couldn't play with toys anymore, I gave them special treats and spent time on the phone with friends and family. It was a long day, but I got through my second Christmas alone. It was an improvement over my first one, which had no tree. I longed for the Christmas when I would feel holiday spirit in my heart. For now, I did my best with what I'd been given.

I screwed up my courage after Christmas and called Chuck. What a relief; I got his machine. About an hour later Chuck's realtor called. I told him what I needed before I signed anything, which included payment of the builder's share of the spring repair bill. I wasn't too pleasant with this guy. He'd try to reach Chuck and bring me the necessary paperwork. I told him I wouldn't sign anything without the repair bill payment. He understood.

In the afternoon, the realtor showed up. Chuck had agreed to pay the bill. I explained my experiences with Chuck and his family. I wanted him to understand why I'd been so contrary and demanding on the phone. He thanked me for taking the time to explain. He said he really didn't know his clients. I told him he was lucky. They'd treated everyone so badly in this area that they'd moved on to new victims in Fayetteville.

A couple of days later it was time for my astrology reading. Over all, it was very encouraging information for my future. Whew! I don't think I could handle too many more unexpecteds, complications, hold-ups, etc. One of the most fascinating insights had to do with Saturn's cycle and its influence on my life experiences.

More Heartbreaking Holidays

While this is more information of a personal nature, I'm writing about it in hopes of lending credibility to the effects the planets have on our experiences. I know many people scoff at astrology and make jokes, but please reserve judgment until you've read what the astrologer taught me about Saturn's influence on my life.

Saturn has a 29-year cycle, which came to its end in the summer of 2004. Saturn had been in my fourth house: the house of home and family. Prior to the reading, I had emailed Monica about my marital break-up, so she asked when I first knew the marriage was dissolving. I responded June 22, 2004, which coincided with the end of Saturn's cycle and its departure from my house of family. The astrologer asked when we were married: in 1977, but we fell in love in 1975, which was 29 years before as Saturn entered my fourth house of home and family.

Even I, who believed in planetary influences and feels their energetic influences, was astonished. There was no coincidence here. I hadn't a clue about Saturn, its cycle, or where it was in my chart. Yet, the beginning and end of the most important relationship in my life coincided exactly with the cycle of Saturn in my fourth house of home and family. You can't make this stuff up.

If anyone needed proof of the veracity and impact of the heavenly bodies upon our life experience, this was it. This wondrous discovery made me even more encouraged about the rest of the insights the astrologer shared. I was anxious to get her CD to hear what I'd missed over the phone.

I was filled with a huge amount of relief. At least I wouldn't be fighting planetary energies. I was busy enough fighting my soul and its creations. I marveled at the orchestration of the Universe in reconnecting me with the astrologer in order to gain this uplifting information. I'd made a wise choice to gift myself with a reading for Christmas. Putting Self first wasn't such a bad thing. With experiences such as this, I actually might start to embrace the lesson. What are the odds that Pam and I would know the same astrologer? Pretty low, but we did.

My roller coaster of emotions was back. My uplifted feelings post-astrological reading plummeted with a call from little Michelle. Mike was back in the hospital. Then a call from Gloria informed me that Vince was having eye and respiratory problems in Maui. I called Linda in Honolulu to alert her in case Vince needed help.

I'd been thinking a lot about Barbara in Florida, so I figured I'd better call. Her soul had been calling out to mine, since she was having a really down day, as she put it. I was glad I hadn't ignored my inner voice again. We talked for quite a while. Joe wasn't doing very well. I felt so sorry for both my friends. All I could do was be a sounding board for them. Barbara sounded better when I hung up, which made me feel better, too.

The next day was New Year's Eve, so I called Linda. They were experiencing something they term *vog*, which is ash from the active volcano on the Big Island. Combined with unusually high humidity, the vog was giving everyone fits on all the islands. She was sure this was what Vince was suffering from.

I called Vince and Gloria next. While Vince appreciated the information, he'd already decided to leave Hawaii. He wouldn't even get to use the timeshare. I couldn't help but think about all that work to secure the space for him and he was never even going to check-in. If Vince hadn't wanted them, I'd never have realized the problems with the transfer of ownership and eventual deed changes. It ended up taking more than a year to actually receive the deed, which I still find inconceivable. Without Vince, it could have taken even longer. *Everything does happen for a reason… .*

I headed to the mountain property on New Year's Eve. I hadn't been there since the enormous winds just after Christmas. There were branches down, but I'd save clearing them for another visit. The dogs enjoyed their time snooping all around. Happy New Year, boys! I stopped to wish Eunice a happy holiday.

The boys and I headed back to the log house to spend the last day of 2005, which was a year to forget as far as I was concerned. Michelle called during the evening from the hospital. Mike's test results were dreadful. The cancer had spread to more areas. I just wanted to hold Michelle. The best I could do was to hold her in my heart.

Mike's medical battle had ended. There'd be no more hospitals, no more treatments, no more tests – of which he'd had hundreds. Mike came home on hospice care. No one knew for how long, but we all hoped at least until the birthdays were celebrated. Michelle was a devoted life partner. Mike was very lucky, and I knew he knew it.

Chapter 15

Saying Good-bye

*L*ast year I'd wished for 2005 to be kinder than 2004, but it wasn't. This year didn't stand a chance with the impending loss of Mike to cancer. Pessimism replaced any semblance of optimism I might have had. Following Tolle's teaching, I stayed in the present moment. My Now was consumed with Mike's final days.

I relied on Michelle to keep me informed, because I didn't want to be intrusive. She'd call when she could, and I'd relay the information to our gal pals. While I loved Michelle dearly and wanted to be there for her, my first responsibility was to Shadow, who was steadily declining. I asked Jodi if she'd be available on a last-minute basis. She would – one problem solved. So far, 2006 pretty much sucked! Maybe 2007 would be better.

My dermatologist found another suspicious area on my back to biopsy. I was more concerned about my nose's exposure from the summers of my early childhood. He prescribed a topical prescription that enhanced the skin cells' own immune system by increasing interferon production. My pharmacist brain liked the mode of action.

I was being proactive with my health. I was being accountable and putting Self first. All my lessons rolled into one choice. I was getting better at this and

I had Mike to thank for my increased vigil on skin cancer. I wasn't going to let his experience go for naught. If the doctor had any doubts, I wanted it gone: no questions asked, no guessing, gone!

I busied myself with writing and the mundane issues of life, all the while focused on Michelle and Mike. I was making a conscious effort to accept my soul's creations. Apparently, the log house was where I needed to be to heal. I didn't know where I wanted to be. This becomes a real problem when you believe that *you create your reality*. It's hard to create something you don't know about.

Working to stay in the Now, I kept my focus away from my Future. I believe that once I've handed the mountain property to the next person, I'll be free from the obstacles that block my creative abilities. The log house was created for me to work through my "dark night of the soul," without the distractions of others' needs. My soul couldn't trust me to bring about the intense healing that I'd come into this life to accomplish any other way. Based on my past performance, I understood its creations. I didn't like them, but I began to understand them thanks to my writing. The more I wrote, the more I awakened.

January 11 was the one-year anniversary of my divorce. It was a difficult day to commemorate. I still looked at it from the perspective of an ending rather than a beginning. The numerology of the date, 1/11/2005, was one. The numeral one signifies new beginnings, which was more proof that I needed to change my perspective. It had been a year, and I hadn't referred to myself as being divorced or a divorcée as yet. In some strange way, I thought of myself more like a widow; I wasn't in the legal vernacular, but in the spiritual sense I was.

I wanted to seek solace and support from Grandfather Mountain, but Mother Nature wasn't in sync with my plans – it was raining. I took the dogs to Kilwins for ice cream and homemade fudge instead. With spectacular weather the following day, we headed to Grandfather. It was glorious and virtually empty of people. In every direction the views were simply magnificent. To be alone on its precipice was miraculous.

There were no distractions as I allowed the energy of that sacred spot to flow into me. I needed its essence so much that day. Between my divorce anniversary, Shadow's obvious deterioration, and Michelle's agony over her impending loss, I was emotionally weary. Grandfather restored my energy. I created a special memory for myself of being alone with this divine, ancient mountain. I gave thanks to the mountain for facilitating the release of much of my pent-up sadness and anger.

The famous naturalist John Muir suggested, "Climb the mountains and get their good tidings. Nature's peace will flow into you as sunshine flows into trees. The winds will blow their own freshness into you, and the storms their energy, while cares will drop away from you like the autumn leaves."

As Grandfather Mountain's healing energy flowed into me, it allowed me to let go of that which didn't serve me. It had done an impressive job, since I felt lighter than I had in ages. The dogs had a blast in a picnic area, but as I watched Shadow, I couldn't help but wonder when his soul's departure date was. I had so many good-byes ahead. Don't do it! Don't go there! Stay in the Now!

Mikey's 21st birthday had arrived and Mike was still alive, so Michelle's wish had come true. Two days later, she turned 50 and the whole family celebrated. I knew how hard these days were, knowing they were the last birthdays they'd celebrate with Mike.

I met Gregory's wife, Sandie, for lunch one afternoon. It was my first friend date in Carolina. It was so nice to actually go out to eat with someone. I hadn't realized how special those times were back in New Jersey. I would never take them for granted again.

My old friend, Kit, called to chat and asked if I'd known Bob's new wife had died. Bob had called my Jersey vet, Gary, to ask a dog question and told him. After we hung up, I sat there and felt absolutely no sympathy for my Ex, which was unusual for me. I'm the most compassionate person towards other people's pain. I was glad her battle with cancer was over, but that was all I could give of myself. I couldn't help but wonder if it was worth what he gave up for less than a year of marriage. I wondered, but as Archangel Michael would ask, "Does it matter?" I'd no trouble answering with a resounding, "No!"

Michelle called late and told me that Mike was very bad. I knew from her voice that Mike's fight was going to be over soon, so the next day I alerted Jodi and updated the gang.

A county health department fellow, Jeff, came to my door. He was marking the two lots that had been recently sold. His description of the property line confused me, so I followed him outside. My line was almost on top of my house! All of a sudden it hit me: that lying builder had screwed me again. If this were true, it meant the top half of my $3000 drive and part of the dogs' yard was on someone else's land.

Well, talk about meltdown. I just lost it. I was so embarrassed for trespassing on someone else's property. I, the pillar of respect, had disrespected their boundary. Of course I'd done it unknowingly, which Jeff kept reminding me while trying to calm me down. My ego took off with the latest deception.

LETTING GO

If that news wasn't bad enough, Jeff then told me that my septic system wasn't inspected. This pushed me over the edge. I spent the rest of the day in absolute fear, anger, rage – you name it. I had a complete and total emotional meltdown so intense that I felt disgusted, paralyzed, nauseous, and so very, very disillusioned.

I thought I'd moved away from learning in fear. I'd worked so hard to extricate myself from these types of occurrences. What was I going to do? I got right on the phone to my voice of reason and sanity, Master Michele. She was mad at how poorly I'd been treated by the people in North Carolina. I realized the realtor was just as delinquent as the builder for this debacle. We discussed my plan of action and I felt better when we hung up.

Sitting alone in the log house, everything just crashed in on top of me. My ego ran rampant with all sorts of fears and terrible consequences that might arise from my mistaken property line. I just didn't have the strength to fight it. I couldn't sleep all night. I called my surveyor to survey my acre. I hadn't done it before because the lots seemed so straight-forward. They were six weeks behind. I needed to get this resolved soon. It was as if whatever progress I'd made in the past couple of months simply vanished.

Jeff and another county agent, Andy, came back out. Andy was the person who mapped septic systems. He walked around, but couldn't find any septic fields for the lot my house was on. They went behind the house to look at the septic tank. The septic alarm wasn't up to code, so I needed it corrected and then inspected. Jeff opened the tank and saw it was ready to overflow. I told him I'd had the electrician check the pump last month.

He found a breaker that was off and as soon as he switched it, the alarm starting blaring. What a stupid system. If the power is off, not only doesn't the pump work, but the alarm doesn't either. Relief came over me as the level of yuck was receding fairly quickly. I didn't think it could get any worse, but then we heard Andy calling. There was yuck seeping up in the driveway.

Great; I had a septic leak and a not-inspected septic system. My heart sank. How did the county issue an occupancy certificate if the system wasn't inspected? I'd have to take that up with the building inspections office, so I called for the inspector's name. Once more someone wasn't responsible – my ever-present nemesis.

Jeff and Andy suggested I have whoever came out to fix the leak dig around to locate the rest of the piping. Who was paying for that? The county didn't do its job. The builder didn't do his job. "How come it's my expense?" They just shrugged their shoulders and expressed their sorrow over my misfortune. I

186

headed in to call a repairman for the septic leak and my electrician.

With my emotions somewhat in check, I was coping better with the recent lemons the universe had handed me. Understanding the recent events was something altogether different. The next morning, Jeff called with somewhat good news. The septic system on my other lot had been inspected. With this information, Andy was able to locate the map of that system in the county's files. Of course, it still meant the system on the house lot hadn't been inspected.

The realtor's ineptitude and Chuck's deceit could prove to be very costly if the new owners disallowed my use of the $3000 drive. If so, it wouldn't increase my property value at all. When the time was right, I'd deal with the realtor, builder, and county about this mess. For the moment, I worried about Mike and Michelle and waited for the septic repairman.

Later that morning, I got a call from Michelle's close friend, Joann, and I knew. She said Mike had died around 10 a.m. I told her to tell Michelle I'd be there as soon as I could. Since Shadow was holding his own, I called Jodi. I took a moment to gather myself before I made calls to the gang. I was planning to leave the next afternoon and stay in Virginia.

The septic company called next and postponed to the next morning. When no septic people showed again, I called their office. They weren't going to make it. I explained that I had to go to New Jersey for a funeral. The gal assured me that they would be out the next day. I hated to leave Jodi with issues, but what choice did I have?

Jodi arrived and I discussed how Shadow had been, thanked her for her help, and left with apologies for having left her with problems. I walked out the door feeling true remorse for leaving the dogs. Although Shadow had been the same for a few weeks, I sent a silent request to him to please stick around. "Please don't leave without me. Please!" I told him I'd understand if he felt it was easier to leave without me around. I'd rather he didn't, but I'd accept his choice.

For the next week, I'd be Michelle's caregiver. I got to the motel and just crashed. I needed a good night's rest before I hit the hotbed of sadness in Jersey. I was staying at Pam's, since she lived close to Michelle. Spending time with Pam and dear Hans was something I was looking forward to. I knew Hans' jovial nature would counterbalance some of the sadness surrounding the reason for my visit.

Depending on Michelle's needs, I'd try to see some friends, who I couldn't wait to see – but Michelle was my priority. I left all my troubles behind: washer mold, leaking and not inspected septic, and worst of all, the property line deception. They'd have to wait. These were maddening, but nothing in comparison to what Michelle and her family had to contend with.

I drove straight to Michelle's. Getting out of the car, I thought about the last time I'd been there and focused on that memory of Mike. I was so grateful that I'd created the memory. Their home was filled with family and friends. It was obvious she wouldn't be dealing with this loss alone. Michelle seemed better than I expected. I knew she was still in that shock stage that happens after a deep loss, which is a protective mechanism to assist our psyche. I met many of the people she talked about, so I could put faces to names now.

The viewing was the next day from 3 to 8 p.m. I was concerned with the length of time and that there was no break, but Michelle scheduled it that way. I was worried about the stress on her and the boys. Since she wasn't alone, I headed back to Pam's, so we could visit a little. I was tired from my long drive and the chaos in Carolina.

I got to the funeral home promptly at 3 p.m. I gave Michelle a big hug, spoke with the rest of the family, and took up my position behind them. I was there for the duration for whatever Michelle needed. The place was packed. There was a steady stream of people until almost 7:30 p.m. I was nothing short of astounded. Michelle stood to receive all the condolences. Once or twice she sat for a few brief minutes. I sat behind her, we'd chat a little, and then more people would come. It was an amazing thing to experience.

I watched over 700 people offer the family their sympathies. Mike had been involved with Little League for more than a decade and a half. It hadn't occurred to me, until they started pouring through the receiving line, just how many people Mike had touched. If Michelle heard it once, she heard it hundreds of times, "You don't know me, but your husband coached my son(s). Mike was a great coach." It was so heartwarming to see how many people appreciated the effort Mike had made, the time he gave, and the role model he was to these boys. What an influence he'd had on so many lives.

Sitting for hours watching all the different folks, I was struck by the inability that most men and boys had in expressing their emotions. The guys seemed so uncomfortable expressing concern and support. It was fascinating to watch from my little back seat.

I was so proud of Michelle. I didn't know how she could stand there hour after hour. Every so often, she would lose it with certain people, especially the owners of Perkins where she'd worked for almost 30 years. They weren't just employers, but old friends who'd been tremendously supportive throughout Mike's ordeal. In times of great sorrow, you drop your guard with good friends and become vulnerable, because you trust them to take care of you. You put your heart in their care, you let go, and the tears flow. It's cathartic.

From time to time, I came out from hiding to say hello to the people I knew. They were few in number, so I mostly stayed in the background helping Michelle get through the most difficult thing she'd ever done until the next day's extraordinarily difficult thing – the funeral.

I fought hard to control my own tears. I didn't want to add to her struggle. When the funeral home cleared out, Michelle went to the casket by herself, and I lost it. I wanted to join her and tell her it would be okay, but I didn't want to intrude. It just didn't *feel* right. I went with my intuition and stayed where I was. She looked so small and so alone. My heart just broke for her. Eventually, she came back and sat down. I put my hand on her shoulder with my face full of tears. It was cruel to lose such a wonderful man so young.

In a little while, Mikey went up. I said to Michelle that someone his age shouldn't have to be doing this. She went and knelt with him. More tears poured from my eyes. I just couldn't help it. The scene was repeated with their oldest, Cip, who I was most concerned about. He was the baseball player and shared his dad's passion. Mike's father had died quite young, so Mike had stood in Cip's and Mikey's shoes years earlier.

The funeral home staff finally ushered us out. I think Michelle would have stayed with Mike for the night if they'd let her. I went back to her house, which was filled with good friends. I really didn't know how she withstood the five hours, but she did. I stayed for a little while and then headed back to Pam's, utterly worn out.

The funeral home was packed by the time I arrived. My angels saved a single seat for me just inside the door. It was perfect. I could see all the family in the room with Mike. I needed to be able to see Michelle. Marie joined me. She and Master Michele had come to the viewing without David, because he was very sick. Michele wasn't well either, so she passed on the funeral.

It was a beautiful service. Marie joined me at the cemetery and I was so grateful for the company. When I saw Mike's gravesite, I thought, how perfect. It was right next to the woods. When I saw Michelle later, I said, "Great location! Mike will be hunting in the woods." She said that was why she'd bought it. I hoped she'd gotten two and she had.

Apparently, the previous owners now lived in Florida and put them up for sale the week before Michelle came looking. The location was just up the slope from where Mike's father was buried. *Everything happens for a reason… .* Really it does!

LETTING GO

I went on to Michelle's while Marie went back to tend to her sick family. The house was filled to the brim with both people and food. Michelle wouldn't have to cook for weeks. I got to know her close friends and realized that I didn't have to worry about her being alone. Seeing all the people who turned out to honor Mike and show their support and concern for Michelle and the boys spoke volumes about the kind of people Mike and Michelle were.

I headed back to Pam's in the late afternoon. I knew Michelle would have things she'd need to do, so I took a couple of days to see some other friends. I talked with Michelle several times a day to see how she was holding up. Quite remarkably, I thought.

We met for lunch two days later to talk. It was nice to be alone and share some quiet time. I told her I didn't know how she'd done it. She simply said, "I had to, for Mike." I understood just what she meant. She wanted to display the same courage and grace Mike had throughout his entire ordeal. I knew his spirit was all around both days and he was as proud of Michelle as I was.

My dear friend surprised me by taking me to lunch. She told me how much she appreciated that I'd come so far to be with her. I didn't think I'd done anything out of the ordinary. There wasn't any other place I wanted to be at that moment in time. I was just thankful that Shadow had allowed it.

Although I hadn't known Michelle for 40-plus years like Linda, Pam, and Amy, we'd quickly become forever friends. I was convinced that we'd found one another, so we'd be there for each other during our darkest and most needy of times. It was synchrodestiny at its finest.

A few years earlier, after Mike's first surgery, Michelle and I saw *Wicked* on Broadway together. It is one of my most treasured memories. The soundtrack conjures up wonderful memories of better times. We had a perfect lunch followed by a wonderful musical as only Broadway offers. In the song, "For Good," Stephen Schwartz's lyrics exemplify my belief about why Michelle and I are such close friends. It was our destiny.

I've heard it said
That people come into our lives for a reason
Bringing something we must learn
And we are led
To those who help us most to grow
If we let them
And we help them in return

190

Saying Good-bye

Well, I don't know if I believe that's true
But I know I'm who I am today
Because I knew you
Who can say if I've been changed for the better?
But because I knew you
I have been changed for good
It well may be
That we may never meet again
In this lifetime
So let me say before we part
So much of me
Is made of what I learned from you
You'll be with me
Like a handprint on my heart
And now whatever way our stories end
I know you have rewritten mine
By being my friend

Sometimes it makes me cry, but other times it elicits fond memories of seeing *Wicked* twice with Michelle and Bob. I believe it epitomizes both relationships, but especially with Michelle, given the timing of our deepening friendship and our life traumas. Our souls created each other to enable us to deal with our tragic losses. Our souls made excellent choices. Together we've been up to the task.

Having spent 29 years with Bob, I couldn't ignore the significance of its meaning for our relationship, which was the most significant of my life. The more I healed, the less anger I felt, which allowed me to acknowledge his importance in my life. My husband definitely "left handprints on my heart." It was the *imposter* that had broken it. I'd finally begun to differentiate between the two. There is a third verse of this song that is particularly applicable to our relationship.

And just to clear the air
I ask forgiveness
For the things I've done you blame me for
But then I guess we know
There's blame to share
And none of it seems to matter anymore

It contains the answer my Archangel was hoping for; "None of it matters anymore."

In the beginning of my journey down this dark road, I assumed much guilt and blame. I felt I must not have been a good enough wife, friend, or lover. I've moved past that to a place of understanding the creation on a soul level. I do acknowledge and thank the part his soul played in my soul's creation. Without his deception, betrayal, and abandonment, I would've never landed in the Abyss. The resultant depression in the Abyss forced me to confront my demons and learn my soul's lessons. Through my writing, I've learned from those demons and have worked my way along my Tunnel towards the Light of healing and growth.

I picked Michelle up for brunch the next morning. I wanted to keep her distracted from the darkness of her reality. Mike's hunting buddy, Marshall, called to say the taxidermist had the deer head ready. Marshall had explained Mike's situation when he dropped the head off. The sympathetic fellow said he'd get it done in a month instead of a year. What a shame he'd missed Mike by a week. I figured this would be emotional for Michelle, so I'd stay till Marshall came. This was why I'd come so far.

We had fun shopping at a bookstore after we ate. The day seemed like one from our past. The fun ended when Marshall arrived. While it hurt me to see this beautiful animal's dead eyes staring back at me, I was happy that it had given its life to Mike for his last hunting memory. He had given so much of himself to his family and community. I accepted the gift that Nature gave because he deserved it.

I left Michelle with Marshall. I was leaving a day earlier than planned, because of a snowstorm forecast. We held each other tight and long, which spoke volumes without words. Neither wanted to *let go* of the other, but our current reality was we lived 600 miles apart. I met Alice, Marie, Master Michele, David, and dear Kimo the Happy, for my last dinner before leaving.

Chapter 16

The Gift of Good-bye

Half an hour into my trip home, the rain began and remained for most of it. Exhausted from the emotional toll of my visit and driving six-plus hours in rain, I hit my motel bed and never woke up until morning, which is unlike me. Normally, my old back wakes me through the night. The strain of my visit was quite obvious.

I was frustrated arriving home to find that the snow event had now disappeared from the forecast. I'd driven in all-day rain on Saturday in order to miss driving in snow on Monday. I'd been home a couple of hours when Kim called to see if I was back yet. Stormy wasn't feeling well, so I grabbed my oral colic medicine, loaded the dogs in the car, and headed to the barn. I knew the dogs would be really happy to go to the barn.

When I got there, Stormy appeared genuinely happy to see me. Kim had given him some injectable pain meds earlier in the day. There'd been more than a 20 degree drop in temperature in the past 24 hours. Horses usually drop off their water consumption during sudden changes in temperature, which results in constipation. His most recent manure was tighter than normal, which fit with the weather changes. The fact that he'd made manure through the day was encouraging.

Even though he looked pretty bright, I gave him the colic medicine, which contains a sedative and several ingredients for digestion – one that helps with gas build-up. He gobbled up the carrots I brought, so I knew he didn't feel too bad. The dogs got out for their usual romp. Shadow looked happier and younger as he tried to smell everything.

I didn't realize how tired I was until I headed back to the log house. During half-time of the Super Bowl, Kim called to say that Stormy seemed much better. She thought he'd been depressed by my absence. It sounded nice, but I've been around horses for way too long to aggrandize myself with that notion. I knew Stormy liked me. I'd been his person since he foaled, as well as a tremendous source of treats. It stroked my ego to think he missed me, but I knew it was the drop in temperature that caused his troubles.

If the snow hadn't been forecast, I would've been on my way to the motel when Kim called. I released my frustration and replaced it with gratefulness that I was where I needed to be to bring Stormy the medicine that would guarantee his continued recovery. *Everything happens for a reason… .*

I kept in close touch with Michelle. It would take forever to accept Mike's loss. No one knew that better than I. I called Barbara in Florida, whose husband was battling liver cancer, and she was holding her own, too.

I had to keep pushing myself to do things, because I was utterly exhausted. The emotions of the trip had taken their toll. I just didn't have much reserve lately. I was meeting with Gregory in the morning for some enlightenment on the recent problems with the log house property. I thought I'd worked through everything with it long ago, but obviously not.

As always, the insights were interesting and thought-provoking. Shadow was among the topics along with a trip that Gregory was planning to Sedona and Mt. Shasta in late May. These are two powerfully spiritual places that I'd wanted to visit for years.

I knew Shadow's departure was inevitable, but I just hadn't seen or *heard* his request that tells me it's truly time. I'd been telling him I'd be all right if he needed to leave. After all, he'd been by my side for well over 14 years. He'd been selfless and I owed him nothing less.

I'd given my word that I would never allow any of my animal family to suffer on my behalf. With my diminished self-confidence, I was so worried that I wouldn't get his message. He seemed to have survived my absence quite well, so I felt good about my decision to go to New Jersey.

After my session, I headed to the barn to find Stormy fit as a fiddle. The dogs spent some time flying around sniffing everything in sight. Their eyes, ears, and bodies were aging, but those noses – oh, those Labrador noses were as sharp as ever. It always lifted my spirits to see their joy on the farm, because at home they mostly just slept. The only time they really seemed happy was at the farm or on the gorgeous mountain property, much like their person. Watching them so happy made me happy.

I'd been trying to make a decision about Gregory's trip for months. My hesitation was rooted in concern for the dogs and money. The uncertainty about the dogs' future was the far more important concern. The trip was three and a half months off, so I figured that Shadow probably wouldn't be here, although he had surprised me so far. If he was, he'd be so feeble that I wouldn't leave him for two weeks. If he weren't, then I'd worry about leaving Licorice alone, albeit with Jodi.

Remember me, *the responsible one* – the one who puts herself last? I knew this was another of those tricky little tests my soul was giving me. I'd been mulling all this over after my session with Gregory. The deadline for joining the group was approaching, so I had to choose. I awoke with the decision made. I chose to put Self first and give myself the gift of healing that such an experience would elicit. I knew my soul was proud that I'd passed my test. I informed Sandie that I'd be going.

After writing for a while, I was ready to head to the mountain. As we came downstairs, Shadow's hind end seemed very bad. They went out to tinkle, and I heard a noise. Shadow had fallen on the porch stairs. His couldn't hold himself up. Was this my very obvious message already? Our eyes locked and I *heard*, "I can't stay any longer. It's time. I have to go."

I burst into tears at the thought of what this meant. I'd been dreading this moment for months, years if truth be told. I remembered hoping they'd live long enough to move to the mountain. After I regained control of my emotions, I decided to still go to the mountain. I knew the vet office was open long enough to give Shadow one last visit to a place he loved.

I fought so hard to keep my tears from flowing. I didn't want to alarm the boys. I rationalized that the drive to the mountain would give me time to be sure. This was a bit of avoidance and denial; two friends from my Past that I was still trying to learn from. With that look, I'd received the *knowing* I'd been waiting for. Nothing was going to change that. What I needed now was the courage to make the call.

My heart wanted to give Shadow a parting happy memory. He had no lost expectations, so his time on the mountain had always been spent in joy. I wanted to give him joy one last time for all the years of joy he'd given me. I needed to make that last happy memory. The importance of memories was a lesson my folks' deaths had taught me well.

We arrived to find that someone hadn't put the locks back properly, which meant I couldn't take down the chain. I froze. I was determined to give us this last visit. I remembered how tenuous the one post was in the ground, so I simply pulled it out and drove up. Nothing was going to stop me. I could see the weakness in Shadow, albeit, not as noticeable due to the adrenaline of the moment.

I made the fateful call from the house looking out over the spectacular view that was supposed to be mine for the rest of my life. In retrospect, I think the incredible power that I sense from the mountain gave me the courage to make the call. I was supported by that special place where my soul felt at home.

They'd be able to see us in a little over an hour. Before leaving, I took time to tell the dogs what was happening. I knew Shadow knew, but I wanted to be sure to give Licorice the opportunity to tell his brother whatever before they separated. Of course, I drove back to the log house an emotional mess. Tears flooded my face.

We headed to the vet office and I walked the boys outside until they called for me. I put Licorice back in the car with my heart breaking at the thought of their parting. I wasn't sure how Licorice would deal with his loss. They'd been inseparable since birth. But, Shadow had made his choice and that was all that really mattered.

Unlike horses, dogs are given a sedative first, then the euthanasia solution. I sat with Shadow in my lap for almost a half hour while the sedative took hold. This was the longest, most excruciating half hour of my life. I tried so desperately to be strong for him. I was saying good-bye to the dearest and most loyal friend I had. I owed him an easy transition.

My mind raced with all manner of images of our almost 14½ years together. He was there for every foaling, every horse we lost, and every one we saved. He helped me feed, turn out, ride, muck stalls, and do office work. As he lay in my lap, I remembered the years I spent sitting on the floor with him in my lap watching TV.

Bob used to laugh when Shadow would stare me down to the floor. He'd sleep in my lap for hours. Now, he was back in that lap for the very last time. Despite the sedation, he was still trying to console me. I understood this better than anyone, given my years of experience in the animal communication business. I was trying to be happy for him in spite of my complete and utter anguish.

My mind flashed to Licorice all alone in the car. Being alone was a tremendously big issue for me. The sedative finally had Shadow quiet and very relaxed. For me it had taken forever! The vet administered the final medication. I completely lost it as she began to inject the solution. Shadow made a blood-curdling cry that ended in almost a howl. I hugged him even harder and told him it was okay to go. I'd be all right. It was a horrifying sound that I will *never* forget.

After it was over, the vet told me that dogs with brain tumors make that cry. Really? A brain lesion explained why he never recovered fully from the vestibular syndrome. I felt relieved that I hadn't known before. I might have made a decision to send him back to Spirit prematurely based on an x-ray rather than his request. Once Licorice left, I would scatter their ashes on our old farm.

I'd had a good deal of experience helping animals transition. It was something Bob did many times over 30 years. A large portion of my animal communication practice was involved with euthanasia, so I was privy to knowledge the average person wasn't. I'd been present with many, many animals as their souls released from their physical bodies. There are no words to express the joy, exhilaration, and freedom I felt from their spirits when I was telepathically connected at the exact time of release. It's unlike anything I've ever felt in physical form.

Despite my expertise, I'm still unable to cope with the grief involved when I lose my own. My grief has never allowed me to share their unbridled joy and exhilaration. I know in my heart that my dearest friends are experiencing that fantastically freeing feeling too, which brings me some sense of peace.

I sent Shadow into the Light just as I did both my parents five years earlier. I told him to look for Gramp. No one loved dogs more than my dad. I have great comfort knowing that they found each other in Spirit. My dad loved Shadow the Perfect, almost as much as I did.

I got to the car, gave Licorice a huge hug, and just cried. My heart was broken with a colossal hole in it. My heart chakra was closed with the intense emotions of loss, grief, pain, and sadness. Now, I had to face going back to the log house minus dearest Shadow. I ran a few errands because the prospect of arriving at the log house without my soulmate was too painful. I needed a little avoidance just for a while.

I worked very hard to contain my emotions for Licorice. He was grieving the loss of his brother as well. In all the years, there had never been even the slightest disagreement between the two. Thank goodness for Licorice; I simply could not have walked into that house without him.

Sending Shadow home was the second time I'd had to face this most painful task alone. As hard as losing Randy was, Shadow's loss was even more heart-wrenching. I felt empty. As much as I loved Licorice and appreciated his being there, Shadow's loss left me feeling totally distraught and alone. Shadow and I were *one*.

I emailed my friends about my tragic loss and the phone started ringing. I received a tremendous amount of love and support from everyone. Pam called in response to my call the day before. She knew something was wrong when I answered. When I told her, I felt her pain and empathy flying through the phone wires. I knew Shadow's leaving provoked her overwhelming sense of loss of her dear Wil. In spite of the arrival of her terrific Hans, Pam still hadn't been able to let go of her grief over Wil's transition.

Master Michele called and she, like Pam, still struggled with the loss of their dear Logan just a year ago. All three dogs taught so much and offered themselves without condition. All they wanted to do was take care of us, make us joyful, and love us unconditionally. I honor and salute all three. To our forever friends: forever thank you!

When Little Michelle called, we both just cried. I could feel each of us reaching through space trying to comfort the other. We were two souls trying to face our future lives without the most important beings in those lives. To think that we'd be suffering such tragic losses so close together seemed surreal to me. But, we were. We would help each other in any way possible.

A few days later, I got a thank-you card from Michelle for making the trip to Jersey. When I called to thank her for the card, I told her we really had to thank Shadow. I wouldn't have come if I thought he was so close to leaving. His choice to wait was his last gift to me and I guess to Michelle, too. I truly believe in my heart that he knew how much I needed to be there for Michelle. Being the selfless soul that he was, he waited for me to come home, which allowed me to be with him. He gave me the gift of good-bye.

My heart went out to all my friends who were struggling with their own traumas. Once I became less emotional, I couldn't help being amazed that once again I was being forced to deal with a highly traumatic event totally on my own. This seemed to be a recurrent theme of mine lately. I was forcing myself to depend on my Self. I do firmly believe that *we create our own reality* in order to learn. I just hoped that I would hurry up and get the lessons, so I could stop creating so much pain for myself.

As I moved out of the extreme emotions of the moment, I was able to look at the orchestration of it and say once again that it was in perfection. I'd always worried that something might happen to one of the dogs out of regular hours and I'd have to use a vet that I didn't even know, or the drive and road wouldn't be negotiable due to ice and snow, or any of a million possible scenarios that would compound the stress of the moment.

Mostly, I was afraid I wouldn't allow myself to hear or see his request due to my dependence on his love and support. I feared my inability to let go of him would prevent me from granting his wish. In reality, I had no trouble receiving his message. It came thorough loud and clear. My unconditional love for him gave me the courage to *let go*. Love is the most powerful of energies. It obliterated any feelings I might harbor of not letting go.

I couldn't ignore the timing of his choice to let go with mine to join Gregory's trip. My decision gave me something positive to cling to while I struggled with Shadow's death. I do believe we are all connected. Like the ripples on a pond from a pebble, our thoughts and decisions affect everything and everyone. I believe the closer an individual is in our lives, the quicker and more significant the consequences. This universal view is the foundation behind synchronicity.

Our choices appeared to be almost simultaneous. It was as if once I passed my *test*, Shadow knew he could leave. He realized I'd learned, grown, and was healing. He knew I'd be okay. Shadow's decision proved to me that I was more healed than I gave myself credit for. Being the loving, selfless soul that he was, Shadow wouldn't have left unless he knew I was ready to let go. Knowing that gave me the fortitude to look forward to a life without him by my side, which had seemed inconceivable to me.

The next morning at breakfast, I burst into tears. Jodi had given me an adorable ceramic plaque for Christmas with a girl hugging a yellow dog. It was called True: Truly a Friend. It sits next to my "Sometimes on the way to a dream..." plate. I saw me hugging Shadow, which was something I'd never have the privilege of doing again. I'll know I'm healed when I can look at this treasure with a smile instead of tears. For now, I marveled at the synchronicity of Jodi's gift.

Licorice and I went back to the mountain the next day to begin the dreaded firsts. The first time I looked in the rearview mirror and only saw a black dog brought hoards of tears to my eyes. The missing energy was palpable. All of a sudden I heard Mandy Patinkin on his CD singing "Me and My Shadow." Unconsciously, I began to sing to my ever-present Shadow, who no longer graced me with his company. Through even more tears, I quickly moved forward a song.

Poor Licorice just sat there all alone listening to me wail. Now, I had two songs that I couldn't handle: Mandy's, "Shadow" and Josh Groban's, "Broken Vow." One of Josh's CDs was in the car, too. His beautiful hit song, "You Raise Me Up," brought me to tears, but I wanted to listen to it. It honored Shadow's significance to my life. "I am strong when I am on your shoulders. You raise me up to more than I can be." Shadow had done this for me for all our years together, but none more importantly than the past almost two years since I fell so helplessly into the Abyss and the Tunnel. As you can tell, music touches my soul and elicits very strong emotions, which can be quite cleansing.

I walked around trying to experience the mountain without Shadow. Licorice was checking things out, but there was a noticeable lack of elation in his demeanor. He was grieving as well. Anyone who thinks animals don't feel emotions or have souls has never spent any time with them. They would just need to be with Licorice and feel his obvious pain. He was going through his own set of firsts.

We didn't stay long, because it was too hard. My raw emotions over Shadow's loss brought my unresolved pain over the lost husband and mountain home flying up from wherever they'd been hiding. Obviously, there was much I hadn't let go of. Shadow was helping me to acknowledge this. Shadow was ever the teacher and devoted helper, regardless of where his spirit resided.

Licorice and I headed back to the log house to continue our grieving process. As much as I wanted nothing more than to sell the mountain property and get on with whatever my soul had in mind for me, I really didn't care at the moment. My mission right now, which demanded all of my attention and strength, was to learn to let go of Shadow. I had to let go of him physically, but I would never let go of the memories and lessons he honored me with.

Over the next few days, Licorice and I tried to get accustomed to the log house minus the energy of our dear missing friend and brother. Licorice was visibly sad. I tried my best not to make it any harder on him, but I just couldn't stop the tears.

As with Little Michelle, Pam, and Master Michele, Shadow's death brought to the surface all of the unresolved emotions of my lost marriage and my lost dream life. I'd worked so hard over the past 21 months letting go of so much pain and unhappiness. Obviously, I'd hid more than I'd released. Shadow helped me recognize that I still had a tremendous amount of healing ahead of me.

Of course, I had nothing but memories flying around of my departed friend. I remembered when I first saw Shadow at the breeder's house. I was still distraught over the loss of my first Lab, Ben. I couldn't let go of Gentle Ben. I decided that perhaps I'd better look for another Lab, since I wasn't getting any better dealing with my grief.

There I sat in the middle of ten Lab puppies: three yellow, six black, and one chocolate. I defy anyone who is a dog lover to be unhappy around puppies. It's impossible. They are bundles of joy. They were a little over a month old. I found the one available yellow male. He fit in the palm of my hand. I looked him directly in the eyes and asked him, "Do you want to come home and love me? I need someone to love me." Our hearts met and our souls *knew*.

For more than 14 years, Shadow did nothing but love me without condition to the very end. I had chosen the name several years earlier since Ben followed me everywhere as my ever-present shadow. I'd thought Licorice was for my folks, since their Lab was aging, but they'd bought Sweet Licorice to keep Shadow from being lonely. Fate stepped in and assured that we didn't miss the other soul that had chosen to share his life with us.

I was so grateful for Licorice's company and support as I tried to cope with the pain over his brother's loss. I would have never thought that I'd rather lose Shadow first, since our hearts were one. I'd have been even more grief-stricken if I didn't have Licorice with me. The reason for my parent's purchase to alleviate loneliness has proven to be quite prophetic. We will process the loss of Shadow together. Hopefully, Licorice will stay a bit longer to allow me the time I need to recover from this tragedy.

A few days after Shadow's departure, we had the deepest snow of the winter – about ten inches. I couldn't keep from feeling almost happy that Shadow didn't have to cope with it. In the icy weeks of December, he'd struggled outside. It had been hard to watch him without thinking back to the dog that used to fly around the big paddock on the farm chasing down every Frisbee thrown. Where did the years go? They'd simply evaporated. As much as I hated losing him, I was thankful that he chose to go before this heavy snow.

During the Saturday snowstorm, the vet office called to say Shadow's ashes had arrived. I was uncomfortable with Shadow's ashes sitting on a shelf. (My parents' ashes were my first experience with this: I picked them up as soon as I knew they had returned.) It took until 2 p.m. on Monday before the road and my drive were plowed out.

As soon as I was free, I made a beeline to bring them home. My reaction to his ashes really surprised me. I knew they weren't him, because his energy had been released from that body days earlier. I had a tremendous need to have his remains in my possession until they could be returned to his farm. I guess I needed to be sure the body that housed that special soul was respected. I placed Shadow's ashes on the fireplace next to a favorite David Dalton photograph of him. I feel like he's still with me when I look at them. It's my shrine to Shadow, The Perfect.

Chapter 17

Thanks to Shadow

Pam and Michelle sent identical sympathy cards. The Universe was making a point. It read, "Pets teach us to live in the now, to enjoy life as it comes to us, and to love without asking questions. They teach us what's most important in life…" These lessons are so easy for them to teach, yet so hard for us to learn. I'd been struggling with embracing these lessons since I moved.

As I sat with Licorice, I couldn't help but contemplate what Shadow had taught me about: trust, loyalty, forgiveness, selflessness, devotion, and the most essential lesson of all, unconditional love. The trouble with people is that we all have agendas. Shadow's agenda was my agenda – time to feed the horses, okay; going in the car, great; being left at home, not so great but whatever you want. The only time he ever exerted his will was when he insisted on curling up in my lap.

Living fully in the moment was simply the way he lived. He didn't have to work at it. Living in the moment allowed Shadow to love unconditionally. The present moment is free from grudges of the past and expectations of future dreams. It dawned on me that to love without condition you have to live in the Now! Shadow was a shining example of the ideal. I vowed to honor Shadow by striving to express unconditional love first and foremost for my Self, and then for others.

As Licorice and I dealt with the sorrow from Shadow's death, I couldn't help but think about the other soul mate I'd lost. My Ex was the antithesis of my dear Shadow. My Ex had deceived, betrayed, lied to, and disrespected me. His love came with lots of conditions and was withdrawn without explanation. I admit that my love hadn't been unconditional either. His treatment of me has polluted my memories of him and us.

As crazy as it may sound, I still love the man who loved me. In some bizarre way I still feel that person exists, but not in this realm. The thing I couldn't let go of was the *imposter* in New Mexico. This imposter interfered with my ability to mourn the *death* of my husband. Until Shadow died, I could only guess at how different my mourning would have been if my Ex had died like Michelle's husband just had. I'd spent almost two years trying to reconcile this issue. With Shadow's passing, my speculation was over.

Shadow was the next most important being in my life. My mourning for Shadow was what I should've been able to do for my husband, but couldn't. Bob's actions robbed me of that. Shadow hadn't a deceptive cell in his being. He was pure, unadulterated goodness. His love for me never diminished. I have no doubt his choice in leaving was based entirely on me and not him, which was in sharp contrast to the man that had vowed, "Till death us do part."

I sat in wonder at the belief that humans are the more advanced species. "Advanced at what?" I wanted to ask. Certainly not in the treatment of others, in maintaining promises or vows, and certainly not in the ability to love without condition. Even in death, Shadow was still teaching. He allowed me to mourn free from blame and judgment, and to surrender to and accept his choice.

Choice coupled with acceptance opened me to a healthier type of grieving, and for this I will be forever grateful. Shadow answered my question so many years earlier, "Do you want to come home and love me," with more than 14 years of nonstop unconditional love. I will never forget him or his lessons because we maintain a love bond that crosses all realms for eternity.

Being given the gift of choice was what seemed to be the core difference between the experiences. My Ex's deception and dishonesty robbed me of choice. I firmly believe that if he'd just been honest, I'd have been able to accept and surrender to his choice by now. Due to the absence of choice, I'll never be able to truly know, so I harbor a great deal of anger and resentment towards him. My job is to reconcile these feelings, so I can finally *let go* and move forward.

My supposedly less evolved Shadow granted me choice. I've always said I'd rather not have to make the euthanasia decision for an animal friend, but that has never happened yet. I now recognize that making that decision contains the gift of choice within it.

I could've chosen to ignore Shadow's request and not let go, but instead we made the choice together, thereby respecting one another. Shadow's obvious love and devotion allows me to remember him with only positive memories; nothing is tainted.

I've had a choice of my own glaring at me for months, yet I didn't seem to be able to make it. I needed to consciously *choose* to let go of my contaminated recollections. It's my choice and only mine. Until I did, I'd never be able to emerge from the Tunnel. My unadulterated mourning of Shadow's death imparted a great deal of perspective on this unsettled issue. Maybe Shadow would help me make that crucial choice soon.

I couldn't help but notice the contrast between Shadow's passing and Ben's, years earlier. When I lost Ben, I couldn't look at anything that reminded me of him. With Shadow, I looked at pictures of him around the house and found peace in them. I tried to figure out why.

I'd learned so much during the years between their two deaths about life and death, our souls, etc. But mostly, it was because Ben's death was unexpected, and I couldn't accept and surrender to it. Although he was 13½ years old, he hadn't been visibly declining like Shadow. He just got ill and a day or two later it was time. I wasn't prepared when I saw the look and *heard* his request, which was my first telepathic communication, although I didn't realize it at the time.

Shadow's aging allowed me to process some of the emotional turmoil that lay ahead for me. It was similar with my folks, who I knew were leaving soon. Shadow and my folks allowed me the time I needed to accept the inevitable and get ready to let go. Once more, acceptance appeared to be a key.

I thought about the pain that my three friends, Little Michelle, Master Michele, and Pam were experiencing. My pain was just as real, but the difference was that I was able to accept Shadow's passing. The timing of his transition followed the natural order of life. He'd lived a long life free from any suffering. My three friends weren't gifted with transitions that were natural. All three souls died too young.

The startling realization I made while I thought about these three departed souls was how well they each had accepted and surrendered to their fates. It appeared to me that the inability to surrender and accept the inevitable kept the pain alive for my dear friends. Their inability to surrender perpetuated their inability to fully let go.

I hoped that once we could look at our losses through eyes without judgment, we'd move through the pain more quickly and easily. We needed to accept that our losses were neither right nor wrong, they just were. We needed to draw strength from the grace that each of our loved ones had displayed in their passing. It's said time heals all wounds, but not without acceptance and surrender, which is just one wounded woman's opinion.

My greatest supporter, Licorice, definitely felt a need to watch out for me. I think his brother must have told him how much I'd need him. He became my new shadow. It was really cute and made me smile a little.

I was having trouble with all the firsts. The first time I stepped out of the bathtub and didn't have to step over Shadow. The first time I made my homemade dog food for one dog. The worst was when I washed the dog beds and stored the extras. I was bothered terribly by the open space where Shadow slept. The empty corner next to me just broke my heart. After a couple of days, I moved Lic's bed there. He looked at me and settled down in it knowing I needed him to sleep there.

Everyone knows by now that I believe in reincarnation, so you must be wondering why I was so heart-wrenchingly sad about losing Shadow. When Shadow came home as a pup and I asked if I'd known him before, I *heard* Tina. The only Tina I knew had been my first best friend, who died when we were six years old. Tina had been my first encounter with death.

Since she was human, I thought I'd heard wrong. I was *told* that Tina had come into her soul's first human incarnation. Feeling unprepared for a human life experience resulted in her early departure. I am of the belief that Tina/Shadow, through the life we just shared, is now equipped to evolve into a more successful human incarnation. The soul is ready. It brings me great satisfaction to think that I may have contributed to his/her soul growth.

Helping beings evolve is a purpose we all aspire to. I've been privileged to help several of my animal friends achieve their soul's purpose and there's nothing more gratifying. The down side of Shadow's soul's growth means we won't be together again in this lifetime, which heightened my grief.

There's a poem that reflects Shadow's importance to me, which my friend, Melissa, gave me as a moving away present. Her husband carved a picture of my old Lab, Ben, and this poem from one of my Christmas cards on a wooden plaque. It represents love on so many levels and sits on my fireplace guarding Shadow's ashes. Who'd have thought when I found this Christmas card so long ago that I'd be reading it over and over in floods of tears?

I figured the author had a little creature, which had followed him or

her just like Ben, Shadow, and my dear Licorice followed me – "up my butt!"
The poem reads:

When God had made the earth and sky,
The flowers and the trees.
He then made all the animals,
The fish, the birds, and bees.
And when at last He'd finished,
Not one was quite the same.
He said, "I'll walk this world of mine,
And give each one a name."
And so He traveled far and wide
And everywhere He went,
A little creature followed him
Until its strength was spent.
When all were named upon the Earth
And in the sky and sea.
The little creature said, "Dear Lord,
There's not one left for me."
Kindly the Father said to him,
"I've left you to the end.
I've turned my own name from back to front
And called you dog, my friend."
–author unknown

I will never be able to thank Noah enough for saving us from a life without animals, and dogs in particular. They are skilled teachers, devoted and loyal lovers, simply angels without wings. The thing I miss most about Shadow is having those deeply loving eyes looking back at me telling me just how wonderful I am and how much I'm loved.

I have great comfort in knowing that Shadow led a wonderful long life mostly running free on our farm in New Jersey. We took care of one another in the good times and the hard times. Our love for each other never waned. I miss that love so terribly, especially now when I need it the most. I was grateful he stayed as long as he did. I am proud to be the person he chose to share this life experience with. I think we are each better souls for having lived with and learned from one another.

There is another heartfelt poem that hangs on Pam's wall with a picture of her lost friend. It had been a gift to honor Wil's presence in her life. I read it again on the website for the pet crematory that handled the vessel that housed Shadow's spirit.

"The Rainbow Bridge"
There is a bridge connecting Heaven and Earth.
It is called the Rainbow Bridge because of its many colors.
Just this side of the Rainbow Bridge is a land of meadows,
hills and valleys, all of it is covered with lush green grass.

When a beloved pet dies, the pet goes to this lovely land.
There is always food and water and warm spring weather.
There, the old and frail animals are young again.
Those who are maimed are made whole once more.
They play all day with each other, content and comfortable.

There is only one thing missing.
They are not with the special person who loved them on Earth.
So each day, they run and play until the day comes when one
suddenly stops playing and looks up!
Then, the nose twitches! The ears are up! The eyes are staring!
You have been seen, and that one suddenly runs from the group!

You take him or her in your arms and embrace.
Your face is kissed again and again and again,
and you look once more into the eyes of your trusting pet.
Then, together, you cross the Rainbow Bridge,
never again to be separated.
–author unknown

I'd learned over the past two years the importance of releasing my grief, pain, and sorrow. While letting go of all these intensely negative emotions wasn't enjoyable, I knew it was necessary in order to emerge with a lighter spirit. Whatever it took, I wanted to process my deep sadness as quickly as I could, so I'd be able to recall my thousands of memories of Shadow with joy and happiness. I didn't want my sadness to rob me of my wonderful recollections like I'd let my anger and resentment towards my Ex rob me of 29 years of wonderful memories. I'm trying to learn, Shadow.

Through my tears, which will last a very long time because I miss him so, I say, "It was an honor to be your student, your teacher, your caretaker, and your friend. Be well, old friend. Your brother, Sweet Licorice, is up my butt! I'll meet you in my dreams. Our cherished memories will always keep you in my heart. For now, I have to *let you go!*"

I'd feared Shadow's transition for years and now it was over. I couldn't help but analyze the depth of my pain, given the fact that I'd constructed a supposedly impenetrable fortress around my heart for protection. My architectural wonder hadn't worked with Shadow. In fact, I began to realize that my love and emotions for animals weren't diminished at all by my wall. I loved them freely and deeply and felt the same in return. I thought long and hard about why. There had to be a lesson looming in there somewhere.

I compared my experiences with animals and people. The basic difference involved *trust.* In general, I trusted animals, but I didn't trust most people. I loved both, but I didn't trust both. People had hurt me. People had lied to me and one recently had betrayed, deceived, and abandoned me. I could honestly say that no animal had ever done that to me.

Of course, I'd been hurt when they died, but that wasn't the kind of hurt I'd experienced at the hands of humans. It was definitely about trust. Trust removed the armor around my heart and allowed the free flow of emotions. This was quite an epiphany!

I was reminded of Michael Road's insights pertaining to Trust. "Trust fosters confidence in life. There is no truer friend than trust." If I could learn to Trust my Self and my soul, and then move on to other people, my fortress would cease to be.

I thought about David Roth, who I was also introduced to at Omega. I loved his music because his songs are so well written. In "Till You Give It Away" he sings,

> But the wall I built around this heart protected me
> It was constructed out of innocence and pain
> And now it's taking every ounce of strength I have
> To pull it down
> But I'm determined that it won't be built again

On the same CD was another very significant song for me. "Looking In For Number One" really echoed what my process of writing had developed into.

> I tried so hard to get in touch
> And then one day out of the blue
> My inner voice came calling through
> "You have the answer in your heart
> Try looking in, that's where you start."

Thanks to Shadow

I used to jump at my conclusions
Now, I'm taking leaps of faith
Getting all my answers questioned
Looking in and seeing straight

I offer examples from songs, books, and newsletter columns as a sampling of where I uncovered wisdom meant for me. It was everywhere around me. I simply had to open my eyes, ears, and heart to *see*. Our souls create assistance and guidance in many diverse forms. They are tricky little devils, so be aware. *When the student is ready... .*

Having undergone so much loss in a short time, it was all I thought about. I counted the losses and was shocked at the number of significant souls that had disappeared from my life: eleven in five and a half years. It was unreal. I'd lost five people: father, mother, aunt, uncle, and husband. Missing were six animals: four horses – Junior, Dash, Squiggles and Randy; Lucky, the black cat; and dear Shadow.

No wonder I felt alone. It appeared as though I was shedding my previous life. Why? The metaphor of the caterpillar and the butterfly popped into my head. I did feel stuck in a cocoon and unable to complete my metamorphosis. Not only was I in a Tunnel, but I was in a cocoon, too. No wonder I couldn't see the Light!

The events of Shadow's passing were the only part of this book that I wrote in real time. By the time he chose to depart, I'd been writing for almost five productive months. My writing allowed me to make substantial headway on deconstructing the blinders that I thought kept me protected from my pain. In reality, all they did was prolong it.

Shadow's death was devastating for me. I'd learned the benefit of expressing my emotions through journaling, which allowed the acceleration of processing my pain. I needed to move through this excruciating pain as rapidly as possible, so I chose to write about it as soon as I could.

Expressing my feelings was so painfully difficult, but I pushed my way through the torrents of tears knowing that my tears would cleanse my grief. The day I finished writing the Shadow pages, I had two deer visitors telling me to be gentle with myself. The *be gentle* message was fitting given the toll the Shadow pages had extracted from me. I took Licorice to the mountain hoping to get some strength from it and it consoled me like an old friend would.

While I was learning about life without Shadow, Gregory introduced me to a woman from Norway who was joining us in Sedona and Mt. Shasta. She also rode horses and was studying animal communication. We decided to ride on our free day in Sedona, so I began researching trail companies.

To ride in such powerful energy would bring an enormous amount of healing to my wounded heart and soul. When I'm on a horse, I am the closest to touching that place deep within me where my soul resides. The planning brought me out of my deep grief and sadness, even if for only an hour or so.

Even though I was looking forward to this trip, my grief didn't allow me to fully feel the joy I should have. The locations we were to visit are some of the most spiritually powerful in our country. To experience them with friends was simply perfect. I should've been totally jubilant, but I wasn't. I looked forward to the experience, but my sorrow wouldn't allow me to feel the joy. I knew, given time, I'd begin to appreciate the experience that I'd chosen to gift to myself.

Leaving the excitement of my future adventures and returning to the frustrations of the present, I met my realtor to discuss the lots next door. His partner joined our discussion. Neither of them could believe my saga. The bottom line was that I needed legal counsel. They also felt the realtor's representation was in question. I left with advice about how to proceed and recommendations for lawyers.

My focus on property problems and the arrival of new computer equipment pulled me out of my doldrums. I'd been nothing but blue since Shadow's death. I tried very hard not to cry around Licorice. I cried the longest and hardest in the bathtub where I was out of sight.

Shadow's transition had totally distracted me from my problems with the property lines and septic. I thanked Shadow for putting things in perspective. While I'd had an emotional meltdown over the news about my property line initially, Mike's and Shadow's deaths made my boundary troubles seem trivial.

The completion of writing about Shadow coincided with the resurgence of my property line situation. It was as though my soul knew I'd processed enough pain to cope with the frustrations of the log house location once more.

The new lot owners' realtor called saying they weren't concerned about the new drive or the dog yard. I told him I was very upset about trespassing, but I'd done it unintentionally, because I'd been deceived. I was greatly relieved that they would grant me an easement, which was the good news. My future use would be guaranteed. Always mistrusting people, I'd believe it when I had the legal papers granting it.

The bad news, which I never seemed to be prepared for, was that they were building two houses, which meant I'd have a house right next to me. My heart sank with that news. Instantly, I feared the effects on my property value.

Thanks to Shadow

My birthday coincided with the one-month anniversary of Shadow's death. It had been a difficult month. The weather was good so I was off to the farm. Stormy gave me a gift by being great to work with. I couldn't wait to get him back into training. As spring approached, my prospects of that happening improved. I stopped at the florist for two birthday arrangements. They were beautiful and made me feel so loved. I got calls through the day from numerous friends and family. I was blessed in so many ways.

I began to look at Jodi's plaque and smile with fond memories of my lost friend. I'm not saying that I didn't shed tears over Shadow now and again, but I could look into those penetrating eyes in my David Dalton photograph without bursting into hysterics. Instead of intense pain, I felt supported and humbled for the part he had played in my life and my recovery. I couldn't have achieved this level of acceptance and surrender to his loss without having expressed my pain through my writing. It was absolutely cathartic. To have dealt with Shadow's transition in such a rapid manner was truly a gift. I knew Shadow was proud of me as was my soul.

The coincidental timing of my writing facilitated a tremendous dumping of anger, resentment, grief, sadness, sorrow and pain, which was unknown to me at the time. I'd been writing about the marriage call just prior to Mike's funeral, which was immediately followed by Shadow's loss. Once I finished the Shadow pages, I launched back into writing about the trauma that landed me back in the Abyss. The journaling of that right on top of Shadow's death was enormously challenging.

I was forced to face all of the demons that I'd been repressing since my Ex's call a year earlier. The timing of this creation allowed me to let go of a humongous amount of negative emotions. Through processing my grief over Shadow's loss and my resentment and anger at my Ex, somewhere amongst all of those destructive emotions, I finally surrendered to my soul, its creations, my pain, and my path.

My anguish over Shadow's loss enabled me to relinquish the residual grief I still harbored over the loss of my husband. My writing about the call allowed me to let go of the cache of anger and resentment aimed not only at the *imposter*, but also at my soul.

The volcano erupted spewing forth all manner of darkness, to which I'd been clinging. As my mourning progressed, so my healing progressed. The act of letting go of my grief over Shadow's passing, my anger and resentment for the *imposter*, and my lost confidence in my soul, sped up my sojourn down the Tunnel towards the Light.

Chapter 18

A Shift

*T*he week following my birthday brought with it that harbinger of spring hopefulness. I began to look around my little acre through different eyes. I got more grass seed, scattered it about, and covered it with straw. I seemed to care about it. I'd been working Stormy from the ground with great results, but I needed more consistent weather before I attempted riding again.

I still had issues, but I seemed to be handling them better. My expensive generator wasn't exercising itself like it was supposed to, so I was waiting for Travis to check that out. I still had the situation next door with the proposed two houses, plus the not-inspected septic system. In spite of all of these concerns, I felt less weighed down. I credited much of my lightness to the pleasant weather.

Before Mike's death, I'd begun reading *How Did I Get Here?* by Barbara DeAngelis. My reading ceased when Mike and Shadow chose to transition. Since my mood had improved, I finished Barbara's book. It was another of those *in perfect timing, when the student is ready*, happenings. What she shared was profound and priceless for me. It was so transforming that I actually sent an email to her, which was a first. Her candor was inspiring and heightened my sense of hope for what I felt had been a shift within me.

The mild spring weather disappeared the following week, but my new mood didn't. By mid-week, I couldn't ignore my improved attitude and energy. It was subtle, yet profound. When you feel so bad and so low for so long slight changes seem monumental. What kind of changes, you ask?

Well, I found myself with a smile on my face, which I hadn't worked to put there. I noticed that I was laughing at comedic instances on TV. I started to acknowledge the beauty around me in Nature. I actually admitted that I liked the log house, just not its location, which was a huge change. I also began to refer to my Ex, the *imposter*, as Bob again. The utterance of the name Bob took place without any negative energy attached to it. This was *very* significant to me, since he was at the center of my trauma.

I felt lighter, freer, and more content. I was almost happy. These were small but quite perceptible clues to me. I didn't dare mention them for fear of scaring them away. Since my self-doubt was still lingering around, I set up a session with Gregory to investigate my newfound attitude.

The log house was still causing aggravation. Travis discovered the generator company had installed an improper fuse, which had blown. The county was demanding that my septic line be located before they'd issue a building permit to the new lot owner. I amazed myself with the way I was handling these frustrations. It was totally different than before.

I still felt frustrated and aggravated, but I didn't relinquish control of my emotions. I'd lost my out-of-control, reactive, meltdown mentality. I found it absolutely intriguing. I hesitated to mention my change to anyone. I didn't want to jinx it. Even cleaning the snow off the porches was done minus the anger, which had accompanied it before. I felt like I'd let go of my internal battle.

I felt my new improved Self was a direct result of my final act of surrendering to my soul. With surrender, I'd shown respect and trust for my soul. With these two critical components restored, my return to wholeness and a balanced life was secured.

The winter snow, sleet, and ice of almost-spring allowed me a lot of time to write. I sent the Shadow pages to several friends who'd expressed an interest in them. I'd never shown anyone my work before. I thought my willingness to share what I'd written was a barometer of my burgeoning self-confidence. I was putting myself and my writing out there for the world to see.

Of course, these were my dearest friends, so it wasn't like I'd sent them to a literary critic, but I still gave myself credit for sending them out. I was getting wonderful reviews from everyone, which was so encouraging. Next, I sent the pages about the marriage call at Pam's request.

The fascinating thing was the emotions they ignited in almost everyone. It seemed like my writing, my story, was eliciting a release of repressed emotions from the readers as well as the author. Hearing each person's thoughts about my writing broadened my perspective about the effect my writing might have on others.

My writing changed from just writing to heal myself to writing for those who've experienced similar traumas. My friends were teaching me a valuable lesson. Maybe this was meant to be published? Time would tell. *When the student is ready... .*

My session with Gregory was six weeks to the day from Shadow's death. It seemed the new mood and lightness that I sensed was valid. Quan Yin, and then Archangel Michael, joined me. The changes as explained were two-fold: planetary and personal. On the broader plane, Mercury had recently gone out of retrograde, which was always a relief no matter who was in retrograde. Mother Nature was entering her cycle of spring: a very positive time of rebirth and growth.

Both of my teachers were in agreement that on a personal level, I had cleared a tremendous amount of negativity. My writing was the main facilitator of my release. They both agreed that this would continue as long as I allowed it. I needed to give myself permission to move forward. They felt I'd done just that with my commitment to write and by writing my absolute truth.

Michael exclaimed that I was the most positive I'd been since we began communicating with each other through Gregory. I smiled and thought to myself it wouldn't have taken much to be considered more positive. He was absolutely right though, I was brimming with positivism.

He informed me that I'd achieved one of my missions for this lifetime through my writing. To hear that I'd attained my goal elicited a tremendous sense of pride within me. I was six months into my writing and 21 months from my Ex's confession that he never wanted, yada, yada, yada.

While those months were the most painful and threatening of my entire life, hearing that I'd attained this phenomenal goal, I felt it was all worth it. I was amazed that I'd succeeded in a relatively short period of time. While I was living through it, it felt like time crawled. It seemed like eons since I'd been happy on my Jersey horse farm.

Michael assured me I'd never have to go through anything like this again. What a relief. It had been the most encouraging session with my two colleagues. My change, the new me, was for real and it was the product of actual healing. At one point, Michael asked if I felt I'd been reborn through a tube. I told him absolutely, but through a Tunnel.

A Shift

Later, Licorice had some trouble coming down the stairs, and I worried if this was the start of his deterioration. My unadulterated feelings of self-confidence and empowerment, which were ignited during my session, overpowered my worry about Licorice. Nothing was going to bring down my renewed sense of self-confidence, self-respect, and self-esteem. They'd all been recovered from the depths of the Abyss. I thanked my soul for not giving up on me.

Once more, I trusted and respected both Self and soul. I wasn't naïve enough to think I was finished. I knew I still had more lessons, learning, clearing work, and healing to do, but the hardest part of it had been done. My feeling of success and my sense of accomplishment boosted my entire Being. My heavy heart had been revitalized. I was elated with the validation of what I'd been sensing. I was back!

Also that afternoon, I received a package I wasn't expecting. It was from my friend, Bert, whose mare I'd foaled numerous times. I unpacked a gorgeous Baccarat crystal of a Labrador. The note read, "Shadow is with you always. Love, Bert." Well, I burst into tears for the memory of my missing friend and for the outpouring of love and support from Bert. It was such a thoughtful gesture.

This wasn't the first gift to bolster my spirits, since I'd lost the perfect dog. My best friend, Linda, had sent me a silver necklace with a sitting dog, which reminded her of Shadow. I was blessed with such wonderful friends and I missed them so much.

The next day Licorice was hesitant coming down from the office again. My heart sank. Was it starting? I helped him like I'd done with his brother so many times. Licorice wasn't nearly as cooperative about being assisted as Shadow had been.

The following morning, he was lame in his left front leg. I had some analgesic tablets, which I started and he improved. We'd had more snow, sleet, and ice, so I thought perhaps he slipped when I wasn't looking. As long as the meds kept him sound, so be it.

I continued to marvel at my optimistic mood. I caught myself smiling and actually laughing without constraint. I felt so much different than I had for the past almost two years. My heavy heart was lighter, more open, and less tight. I was becoming upbeat! I was on a writing rampage. When I wasn't writing, I was reading.

I still had nuisances with the log house, such as the humidifier that hadn't worked properly in the two years since it'd been installed. I'd been waiting for months to get that rectified and for Travis to replace my blown generator fuse.

I still had all the drama of the property line and septic issues. I was still waiting for the surveyor. Any one of these things in the past would have set me off on a tirade of insanity. Now, I dealt with each of them in a rational manner. The way I used to respond B.N.C. (before North Carolina).

I kept in touch with Little Michelle almost daily. She was back at work and fearing her customers' questions about where she'd been for so long. I tried to encourage her over the phone as best I could. She was coping, but it would take forever.

I trained Stormy from the ground, waiting for four good weather days in a row to attempt riding. I needed them more for my aging body than his mind, since he was being very cooperative. I'm sure my new attitude had a lot to do with his more positive attitude. I'm always my happiest at the barn.

I ordered window screens, so I could bring fresh air in the house in the mild weather. Instead of obsessing over the builder from Hell, I ordered them without any negativity about the reason why, which was very different from my past two years. I really had lost the feeling of fighting everyone.

Finally, I heard the generator exercise itself, so I knew Travis had been by. The heat guy came with a larger nozzle for the humidifier and my screens were ready. I marveled at how things were beginning to come together. I was amused with the new me. I smiled and just felt good. Using the tools my brother gave me, I installed the screens easily, which fueled my confidence.

My friend Kathy's Labrador had come into heat, which improved my mood even more. She was bred on the next to last day of March, which meant she should whelp during my trip. Kathy said they'd check for pregnancy in 25 to 28 days, which was more of a formality for me since I just *knew* Dini was pregnant. This was in perfection considering my loss of Shadow almost two months earlier. I had the trip and my new family to look forward to.

I'd found a concert in Jersey I wanted to attend in late July, so I made arrangements with Jodi. I was really in need of a friend-fix. What I didn't realize until much later was that the trip would coincide with the time the pups would be ready to come home, if all went as hoped. Once I recognized the synchronistic timing, I was enthralled with the orchestration of my not-so-distant future.

If all transpired as anticipated, my healing would culminate on my upcoming trip to Sedona and Mt. Shasta, according to my last session with Gregory. I would re-emerge from my dark night of the soul as the butterfly of my metaphor. The butterfly would be getting a new family to join the new life her soul was creating. *Everything happens for a reason,* and *for our highest good.*

A Shift

I know you're wondering what happened to staying in the Now. I knew I was getting ahead of myself, but it had been so long since I'd had anything to look forward to. I was experiencing optimism again and it felt good.

I began April with such a renewed sense of Self. I compared my present mood to that of the previous year. I was like two different people. Nothing had changed but my attitude and perspective. I had a stronger, more balanced psyche, which my soul tested with a severe thunderstorm.

Simultaneously, I heard and felt a tremendous lightening strike. I knew it had struck very close. Thank goodness, I'd gotten the new computer turned off! Licorice began trembling and salivating, and I almost followed suit. I comforted him and "asked" that we not have any more close hits for my friend's sake.

The storm passed quite quickly, but left my electronics in ruins. The old TV, the new cordless phones and my new DVD/VHS player were dead. It appeared the satellite dish worked, since it was searching for a signal. I just had to know, so I cautiously turned the computer on. All the new equipment worked, except the DSL modem. The TV still hadn't located the signal, so I called the company but the tech couldn't fix it. I found two huge gashes on the tree trunk above the dish and the dish looked split apart. Unreal!

It began to sink in that I had no television, which had been my babysitter for the past two years. My land line and cell phones worked, so I could reach the outside world. My computer worked, but not my other babysitter, the Internet. My CD player and radio worked, so I'd have the company of music.

For a short time, I was aggravated with the damaged equipment and the costs to replace them. The new me recognized how lucky I'd been, since neither my animals nor I had been injured. The woods and the house hadn't caught fire. No tree had fallen on my house or car. Yes, there was damage, but it was incidental compared to what could have been. I could replace electronics. I could never replace my cats, Licorice, or myself.

It didn't take me long to feel this way, which really surprised me. If this had happened last year, I would've been angry beyond belief and paralyzed with fear about being without TV or the Internet. This year it was an annoyance and nothing more. This was a stunning revelation for me.

Less than 48 hours later, everything was functional. Things were definitely looking up, but mostly my ability to surrender and deal in an efficient and non-emotional manner. I gave myself kudos for passing my soul's little test, which was something I needed to do more of.

Gregory wanted to do another releasing ceremony on the mountain property. While the previous year I was incapable of speaking, this year speaking was essential in order to release the property. It was imperative to say good-bye to this sacred spot, while calling forth its new steward. I began speaking to those gathered from the unseen realms and to the mountain.

When I was directed towards my mountain, the tears started. My heart burst open with the love I held for this special place. I thanked it for the experiences and lessons it gave me. The realization that I was letting go of not only this beautiful location, but also my fantastic dream initiated even more tears. *Letting go* was rooted deep within my heart and soul.

After I finished, I cried for all my losses over the past six years. I was ill-prepared for the intensity of the emotions that engulfed me. For months, I deluded myself that I was detached from the property. It was so obvious that my heart wasn't until now. This ceremony enabled my heart and my soul to finally let go of the mountain where they felt so at home.

Through my tears, I heard that familiar booming laugh of Archangel Michael. I began to smile and remember his profound question, "Does it matter?" Not only had he joined me at this most emotional event, but Quan Yin had come before him. Inaha, a Native American grandfather who'd led the first ceremony, led this one as well. I was humbled that these new friends wanted to share this epic occasion with me. Their guidance and insights had been essential to me. I *let go* of my dream fully and completely.

As I got to the car, I inadvertently called Licorice "Shadow." In that instant, I knew Shadow had been among those there to support me during my intensely emotional farewell. It was a beautiful day to say good-bye to a dream. Even if I couldn't see most of my supporters, I could *feel* them. I was blessed. The mountain was free now to attract its new caretaker.

When I got home, I applauded my courage for letting go of that which had been my creation and my focus for the past five years. It wasn't like I'd replaced one dream with another. I had no idea what my future held. My release of this sacred mountain by my heart and soul offered up more evidence that I'd finally surrendered to my soul. I trusted and respected my soul and its creations once again.

The day after the ceremony Licorice was acting very strange like he was in pain or stressing. His hind end seemed to be weaker. Whatever emotional stability I'd gained was lost to me now. My heart froze. I couldn't lose Licorice just yet. I wasn't ready.

I called the vet for an appointment and started to cry with the thought of another good-bye. I'd just had to say one good-bye yesterday and I wasn't very good at them. You'd think after all of the good-byes suffered in the past six years, I'd be a pro.

After half an hour, Licorice seemed to relax, so I told the vet office I'd watch him and call back if anything changed. Luckily, he stayed fine. To this day, I have no idea what it was. Maybe he was beginning a process to leave, but my emotional storm convinced him I couldn't be left just yet. Whatever the case, I am so grateful he stayed.

I'd been waiting to hear from my CPA, Milt, as the tax deadline drew closer. I found a message on my cell when I got done working Stormy. Milt was out, but his assistant, Jill, told me it had to do with the withdrawal from my annuity and the penalty involved. I almost drove off the road. What penalty? I didn't know anything about a penalty!

Well, lightning strikes, fried electronics, and dead phones were nothing compared to this news. Jill would have Milt call as soon as he returned. I couldn't wait that long. I called my financial advisor and friend, Ed, who said I needed to get the exact facts from Milt first.

Milt called and explained there was an IRS penalty for an early withdrawal, which was news to me. I explained that I'd taken the money out for the down payment on the Jersey house. Milt said I might not be penalized then. Well now, this sounded more like it. I wouldn't owe anything if the penalty was waived. I focused on the scenario of owing nothing, which sounded so much better.

The forecast was looking good for the week, so I planned to finally get on Stormy. He'd be a good distraction from my tax fears. He was a little grumpy to start, but worked through it. Considering how long it had been since I'd ridden him, I was pleased with his behavior. As long as we ended better than we started, it was a win.

Sandie and I went to an early movie and then dinner. I left Licorice at the log house alone. He'd hardly been by himself since Shadow died, but I knew he needed some practice before my trip. He had to learn to be alone. I knew all about that lesson and it's one of the hardest to learn.

Spending time with another human was a real treat for me. I felt I'd really found good friends in Sandie and Gregory. When I got home, Licorice had been alone for almost four hours. He was panting pretty hard, but he settled within 15 minutes. All in all, I felt he'd done quite well.

I'd been having thoughts about hanging a bird feeder. Something or someone was nagging at me to get one. I got home with my bird stuff to find my tax returns waiting. I was hit with the worst scenario and had an emotional meltdown. I had the funds to pay it, but the knowledge that I couldn't use my own money without a significant penalty paralyzed me with fear. What happened to my light, confident attitude? It vanished in a flash.

I had the worst night's sleep in a long time. I was battling my old nemesis fear once again: specifically fear of my uncertain financial future. I thought I was done with this. The whole night, I was telling my ego to stop it. Go away! I wasn't going to give away my power anymore. My self-talk was great, but it wasn't working.

I wrote for most of the morning trying to keep my ego at bay. The weather was spectacular, so I headed to the barn hoping to find some respite from my fears with Stormy. I was always able to rid myself of my inner demons when I worked with Stormy. He was excellent. My animal family was supporting me through my emotional backslide. I was eternally grateful for their presence in my life. They always brought me back to a place of balance.

I called my voice of reason, Master Michele, to help abate my financial fears. She calmed me down and I was able to overpower my ego and its fears. I couldn't have done it without Michele's concern, support, and love.

I worked the numbers and discovered that I'd really only paid four percent of the monies taken, which was so much more acceptable than ten percent. If I took it even further, the annuity had earned eight percent, so I rationalized that I hadn't lost four percent, but instead earned four percent. It's the glass half full concept. It was my old friend, perspective, again.

Once I'd calmed down and gained control of my emotions, I could use my non-reactive mind to problem-solve and change my perspective. In reality, the facts hadn't changed, but my response to them had. With my new perspective, I let go of my fears.

I was truly shaken by my regression back into my old pattern of fear and reactive, out-of-control emotions. I thought I'd moved out of the trauma/drama learning mode. I was relieved to have worked through it, but disheartened that I'd been pulled back into it so easily and rapidly. Gregory was away in Florida, but I scheduled a session upon his return to help me investigate this latest stumbling block.

Chapter 19

Quizzes

I spent most of my time writing or reading new books I'd found to enhance my journey through the Tunnel. I was beginning to anticipate an eventual end to my time in the Tunnel. I'd found a changed awareness within. I began to consider my failed marriage and dashed dreams as a beginning rather than an ending. The glass half full instead of half empty. I'd always been a half full kind of gal until my life went spinning out of control. The return to a more optimistic approach to my experiences was refreshing, even though I'd had my recent financial challenge.

My new birdfeeder was getting busier as I watched goldfinches, chickadees, cardinals, juncos, and more. My appreciation for the beauty of Nature had returned. I'd lost it in the Abyss and the Tunnel. I'd made the right decision to listen to my little voice that kept harping at me to get a birdfeeder. I was feeding the birds, and they were feeding my spirit. I knew I was the bigger winner.

I begin each day with healing techniques for friends, family, and myself. With my renewed self-confidence, I began to carry on some communications of my own with the unseen realms. I hadn't done anything of this sort in a very long time due to my depleted self-esteem and self-confidence. After my routine, I started to ask questions again. The veracity of the information I heard was acknowledged within my heart chakra. I have never heard anything that initiated any thing other than positive feelings.

When I asked about my recent fall from grace over my financial fears, I *heard* that my soul creates not only experiences to teach me lessons I need, but experiences to test whether I've truly learned them. Quizzes, great! This insight definitely resonated with me. Our souls have quite an agenda for us.

Gregory was back and my session didn't necessitate any channeling. When Gregory asked how long I'd battled my fears, I told him probably 24 hours. He just smiled and applauded me for the speed with which I'd made my recovery. He reminded me of how long it used to take to regain control of my emotions. I agreed, but told him I expected not to have lost control at all. He just smiled and said, "You're human." I'd thought I'd dealt with my need for perfection years ago. I was still being challenged with the lesson of giving myself credit for a good job, which is about loving Self.

We spent the remainder of our time discussing my writing and the resultant progress with my healing. We actually talked about it as a book instead of a personal journal of healing. Verbalizing my work as a book made it more of a reality to me. I wanted to get caught up to current time before our trip to Sedona and Mt. Shasta.

The weather was stormy the next day, so I spent it writing. When the rain stopped, I headed for my mail. My male cat, Butch, came to greet me and was very wobbly. My heart seized up. My first thought was geriatric vestibular syndrome, but I didn't see any rapid eye movement. I called the vet, but they were closing shortly and referred me to another practice that was overbooked. Oh Gary, where are you when I need you? You've really spoiled me.

I asked the covering vet office if I could leave him. Butch needed to be seen. The gal said that would be fine. The vet called later to ask if I had any pesticide Butch could have come in contact with. I said, "No." His blood tests were all normal. I learned that there's another type of GVS, which doesn't have the eye motion and the vet was leaning towards that diagnosis. He wanted to keep Butch for observation, which was fine.

Since I analyzed all of my experiences and creations these days, I set right about examining this one. I'd dealt with Butch without an emotional reactive mode. In doing so, I was able to use my medical expertise with animals to evaluate him quickly and reliably. When I had to go to someone I didn't know, I didn't get crazed, which I'd have done a year ago. I credited myself for better control of my emotions and for making a sound decision.

I was concerned about the cost, but I didn't allow my ego to pull me back into that mindset. For that fact alone, I gave myself a hardy "Way to go, gal."

I'd passed my test! I wondered how many more quizzes I'd be confronted with before my soul was convinced that I'd really learned my lesson. Time will tell.

The next morning brought good news about Butchie. He was eating, drinking, and grooming himself. And, I was sure, purring too. My good news day turned around with an email from an old friend who was a small animal vet in Jersey. I'd known Tracie since she was a teenager and had done a lot of communication work with her animals over the years.

Tracie informed me of the death of her horse, Major, who I'd worked with often. The loss was sudden, unexpected, and traumatic for Tracie. My heart broke for her, since I knew only too well the pain of loss. She'd been after me for a long time to talk with her animal family, but I just wasn't ready. She was always gracious and accepting of my refusal. My improving self-image and self-confidence allowed me to consider her request now. My empathy for her loss outweighed my fear of making a mistake. I told her I'd see if we could get permission to talk with Major. In my entire career, I'd only been given permission to talk with animals that had transitioned a few times.

My new attitude had me thinking I might be ready to return to my healing practice. I wouldn't consider it until I felt 100 percent. I owed that much to the animals, the clients, and myself. When I let my mind wander into the future, I mused that I needed to start back with what I knew, namely, working with animals. I'd learned that much gets facilitated to help you negotiate your soul's true purpose. I interpreted this as a creation to alert me that my return to my work wasn't as far off as I'd imagined.

Two days and Butch was ready to come home. The vet told me, "He's a great cat." I agreed that he was a *great* cat. All my animals were great. I was amazed, confused, and grateful for Butch's apparent complete recovery. According to my bill, he hadn't received any medications. How did he recover so fast without any treatment?

Well, whenever circumstances like this occur, I can't ignore the inconsistency. These were glaring creations to me. I intuited Butchie's attack as being totally about teaching me. I was happy I'd gotten Butch's lesson quickly, so he didn't have to suffer much. I'm sure this was another quiz.

In the afternoon I had a subtle, yet significant thing happen as I changed my bath towels. I'd been discovering all sorts of changed responses due to my healing sense of Self. These towels hadn't been used since I'd left Jersey. When I hung them up, I saw the monogram, RMN. I stopped dead and started to take them down, but stopped. I looked at the monogram and thought, "It doesn't matter."

I knew Archangel Michael was proud of me. I was, too. This was a huge accomplishment. If I'd taken these out even two months earlier, I probably would have taken a scissors to them. I wanted to share this just to illustrate how such a simple act can turn into a powerfully significant lesson or clue. Don't overlook anything you experience or create. Everything is significant even the tiniest of occurrences.

Early the next morning, we had strong thunder. Licorice was much better than after the lightning strike but still nervous, so I cleared him again with spiritual response therapy (SRT). I tested him for vibrational remedies for nervousness with loud noises and being left alone. I'd used flower essences and gem elixirs often in my practice to enhance the clearing work of SRT. I knew they were potent agents and I wanted something for Jodi to give him while I was away. I was on a spiritual roll, so I decided to take a leap of faith and communicate with Major for Tracie. I got permission to talk with Major, which took me by surprise. He felt and sounded great.

After the communication, I asked my helpers for additional information about Major's death. This type of information is channeled as an automatic writing. I was startled when the message started with a greeting for me. I'm sharing it as encouragement to others, who might care to seek information from unusual places. "Dear One, you have been missed. We are so glad you are back to your path. We know of your personal traumas and applaud your commitment to learn and grow from them. Your compassion for your friend is a just catalyst for your return to your gifted work. Welcome home!"

Those words had a profound effect on my entire being. I felt as though I'd truly come home from being lost. This message encouraged me that my successful navigation of the Tunnel was inevitable. I could see the Light at the end of it now. The emergence of the butterfly was in my near Future. I felt so humbled and blessed.

As it turned out, Tracie and I had trouble getting together since she was incredibly busy with a vet practice, husband, two children, and numerous animals. I finally just mailed her the communication. I knew that if she had needed to talk to Major, she'd have gotten back to me sooner. What she needed was in the channeled message. This was simply another example of the discrepancy between wanting and needing.

I felt really good about myself and the ease with which I'd accomplished the communication and insights. My self-doubt took a big hit. I wanted to continue along my path following the light that now illuminated my journey. I felt empowered again. I felt self-respect and self-love.

My spiritual journey with Gregory, Sandie, and the three Scandinavian gals was less than a month away. I was writing like a banshee to reach my goal of being caught up by the time I left for Sedona. I liked goals.

The month of May began with what should have been my 28th anniversary and the two-year anniversary of our move from the farm. What I needed was to get through the day without any regression from my new mood. Master Michele and I talked for quite a while in the morning. I'd had calls from other friends the previous two days as well. I appreciated everyone's concern for my emotional well-being.

I spent the afternoon *doing* to keep my ego from trying to drag me back into my traumatic Past. It had been under control lately, but I didn't trust it. Gregory was in Denmark, so Sandie met me for a movie and dinner, which was a good distraction.

We saw *RV* with Robin Williams and I laughed from start to finish. I hadn't laughed like that in two years, which proved that my heart was healing, since it allowed me to feel happiness and acknowledge humor once again. I think living in the camper for five months gave me even more of an appreciation for the movie.

Dinner was excellent, but the friendship I was developing with Sandie was the most pleasing for me. Being able to share time with someone was something I'd lost two years earlier when I was abandoned by the *imposter*.

They say you don't appreciate what you have until you lose it. I thought I'd appreciated my husband, although he must've disagreed based on his behavior. What I didn't realize was the depth of my friends' worth to my life. So, I got through a significant date quite well.

During my morning meditation time, I heard a message while focused on my divine flame, which is the spark of the Creator that resides within our heart center. The message said, "As the divine flame grows and increases, the fortress around your heart melts. You don't have to tear it down."

Since I'd been focusing on increasing my connection to the divine, I'd been unknowingly dismantling the fortress around my heart and allowing myself to feel again. I was so pleased to hear an unsolicited message. All we need to know is truly within us if we only allow ourselves some silence.

I smiled with the recollection of my favorite of Aesop's Fables, "The Wind and the Sun." I continued to be amazed at the relevance of things in my later life that had been significant in my earlier life, despite not understanding their importance at the time. This was just another of those incidents. The fable teaches that strength comes in many forms.

"The wind and the sun were disputing which was the stronger. Suddenly, they saw a traveler coming down the road, and the Sun said, 'I see a way to decide our dispute. Whichever of us can cause that traveler to take off his cloak shall be regarded as the stronger. You begin.' So the Sun retired behind a cloud, and the Wind began to blow as hard as it could upon the traveler. But the harder he blew the more closely did the traveler wrap his cloak around him, till at last the Wind had to give up in despair. Then the Sun came out and shown in all its glory upon the traveler, who soon found it too hot to walk with his cloak on."

As a child, this story opened a new awareness within me. I learned that strength could be coupled with gentleness. They were not mutually exclusive. It's the only one of Aesop's fables I've remembered.

As I've cautioned before, don't take anything for granted. Anything that touches you is of consequence. I hadn't thought of this fable for years until it popped into my head after my message about the fortress around my heart.

I'd spent years trying to dismantle my wall with the help of many talented healers when all along the fable of "The Wind and the Sun" was waiting to illuminate the lesson. My attempts using the wind techniques were about as effective as the Wind on the traveler. All I had to do was invoke the sun techniques available within my heart. My divine flame, through its gentle, yet powerful ways, would remove the prison that surrounded my heart. The needed protection and the reasons for that protection were gone. All that was left was the fortress, my prison.

Once more, I'd been looking for help and answers in the wrong place just like the song said. I'd sought them outside of Self when all along they were within. When you least expect it, the wisdom appears. Stay aware. Be vigilant.

Along with my newfound revelation about the fortress, my interest in spending time with my little acre increased. I was starting to care about the acre. I'd poured my heart and soul into my Jersey farm for almost 30 years. I'd fallen madly in love with the mountain property and respected it deeply. It was so unlike me to not respect the land I lived on. I apologized to the property and began to feel differently about it.

I knew it wasn't a long-term house, but I did appreciate it as a house to write in, a place of transformation, and a safe haven to heal in. I knew my renewed sense of self-respect and the melting of the fortress were at the root of my ability to appreciate the acre and log house I'd bought as a last resort 21 months earlier.

When I wasn't training Stormy, I was writing. My mood was definitely on the upswing, but my success at getting things done hadn't improved. The generator still didn't work properly, so I was waiting for Travis. The surveyors still hadn't called with a date. The weather held up the survey crew, so all I could do was wait and learn more lessons in patience. My reactions to the delays were much less intense.

I went to work Stormy and found him lame. Kim said he'd run like a fool the day before. I just accepted his soreness and didn't launch into uncontrollable fear, which I'd have done six months ago. We gave him some pain medicine and let him rest. The next time I came out he was fine. I was really pleased that I'd handled it so well emotionally. This was another big clue to the depth of the recovery I'd made. I responded to the challenge, assessed the situation, and used my expertise to solve the problem. No meltdown, no out-of-control ego telling me I had a fatal problem.

My emotions were in-check, allowing my mind to process and deal with the lameness. It was so rewarding to acknowledge the progress I'd made. I was learning to give myself credit for things. Since *everything happens for a reason*, I took this as another quiz from my soul simply checking its student's progress. I think I got an A!

I only had a week and a half until my trip. I called the surveyors to try to get them out beforehand, but I couldn't. I did get them to commit to the day after my return. Well, I'd see if that happened.

I mailed the pages about Mike's funeral to Michelle. I'd asked her if she thought she was up to reading them. Even though they were *my* impressions and experiences, it concerned something very personal to her. I wanted to be sure she was comfortable with what I'd shared before it ever got into print. I secretly hoped they might help her process more of her pain and grief.

It was Stormy's fourth birthday, so I went to see him with treats, even though the weather wouldn't let me ride. I'd missed his birthday last year with my trip to buy the Jersey house. I didn't want to miss it this year. I couldn't help but think back to the dinnertime four years earlier when Squiggles' started to foal. It's the most exciting and most stressful time.

I missed that in my life dearly. But, there is a time for everything and my time for foaling was over. I accepted that when I made the decision to sell the farm. I have no regrets. After our celebration, I got back to the log house feeling better than when I'd left.

The next day was spectacular for riding. Stormy was a little disagreeable to start, but ended well. On my way home, something ran across the road. What a shock. I called Kim and found out there were coyotes around.

I'd been day-dreaming about what a spectacular day it was, which was new for me. I was expressing my gratitude for the day, my horse, the beautiful farm, and my life in general. The appearance of a "relation" I didn't even know lived around here was significant to me. I knew in the Native American culture coyote represented the trickster. I wasn't sure of its significance for me, but I did acknowledge it.

At home I reviewed Sams and Carson's *Medicine Cards* about coyote medicine. It told me that coyote appears when things get too serious. The message is to lighten up and laugh. Well, my life had been nothing but serious for the past two years. Laughter had been noticeably absent from my repertoire of late, although it was slowly returning.

My second source, *Animal Energies*, by Gary Buffalo Horn Man and Sherry Firedancer, taught, "Coyote is our mirror for the lessons we need to learn in order to walk a good, sacred road. You are being asked to look at something you've been avoiding." Coyote's quick and startling appearance on the road couldn't be ignored.

I knew my time in the Tunnel was coming to an end. My attention would soon be focused on my spiritual path and healing practice, which is my path down "a good, sacred road." I felt ready to move forward in my growth, but I had some trepidation. It was uncharted territory. I'd gotten my Self this far. I wasn't going to avoid my future path any longer. If there was anything I'd learned from the emotional upheaval of my past two years, it was to address my path and purpose head-on, giving it the priority that it deserved. I owed my soul nothing less.

I realized I wasn't going to get caught up with my writing before leaving, so I let go of the notion easily and without regrets. An unrealized goal in the past would have given me grief. Today, it just didn't matter. I could hear Archangel Michael laughing wherever he was. His student was definitely getting it. I began to acknowledge that it's easy to let go when something doesn't matter. Oh, these patient teachers.

I made a trip to the mountain property to check on things. All was well. Since the releasing ceremony, I was able to be on the mountain in a more peaceful way. I still absolutely loved it, but from the perspective of a visitor, not a caretaker. My new mindset made the time I spent on it even more special.

I savored it more and was filled with gratitude for all I had learned from the experiences it had given me. I was anxious for it to attract its new steward, not just because I wanted to be free of it, which was true, but because I wanted it to move into its future as well. It was time for both of us.

I stopped at Ernie's office to visit with Barbara. She was glad to see me, but was having a hard time with her mother's death. She asked if I knew that

Bob had been here in late January. I was stunned. It must have been when I was at Mike's funeral.

I didn't know why, but it really bothered me that he'd been in the area without my knowledge. I guessed my "it doesn't matter" lesson wasn't completely integrated yet. I wasn't happy that I allowed his visit to bother me. It was a clue that I still had healing work to do. I was disappointed, but let it go before I got upset. The amount of time it took me to let go was shrinking, which was a sign of the tremendous amount of healing I'd accomplished.

When I arrived home, I found Butch with a nasty looking hole on the top of his head behind his ear. I headed straight to the vet. He couldn't have picked a worse time with my departure in five days. They cleaned it out and sent me home with antibiotics for him. At least he didn't need stitches, a drain, or a collar. I added topical comfrey salve to his treatment, which promotes healing. I knew Jodi would be able to give him the antibiotics.

The day before I left I went to the barn with treats, cleaned my tack, told Stormy I'd be away, and that Kim would ride him, so I wanted him to make me proud. My plan to have ridden a lot before I left just never materialized. I wanted to be fit for my ride in Sedona but I wasn't.

I checked in with Barbara in Florida, whose husband was fighting cancer. Her news was pretty dismal. Joe was confined to a wheelchair now, but trying some new chemotherapy. He was a fighter right to the end. While we were talking, he wheeled into the room, and we said hello across the room. I told Barbara I'd be on my trip, but to call if she needed to talk.

I held off getting the suitcase out as long as possible because it would unnerve Licorice. I had a chat with him about my trip. I knew he had some lessons of his own to learn about being without me. I went to bed pondering what experiences lay ahead for me.

My almost ten-year interest in visiting Mt. Shasta was about to be realized. I'd had a desire to experience the energy vortexes reported to be in Sedona as well, but Mt. Shasta was the destination I was most looking forward to. I didn't understand why, but I just *knew* it was a place I needed to see and feel.

I was about to embark on the gift that I'd chosen to give myself the morning Shadow chose to leave. I firmly believe that my decision to take this trip was the catalyst behind his decision to go. This belief lent even more significance to my trip and now it had finally arrived, which was the good news. The bad news was I was leaving Licorice for the first time without his dear brother, but I knew he'd be just fine with Jodi.

Chapter 20

Sedona's Gifts

I hated leaving Licorice and his questioning eyes behind, but I knew I was headed towards a vital part of my healing process. About ten minutes into my drive I saw a rather large, odd-looking bird fly across the road. It had to be an owl, based on its size and shape. This was a very unusual time to see a night hunter.

I'd only seen an owl twice on my farm in 27 years. I remembered that owl medicine had to do with deception and magic. I asked if owl had a message for me. What I *heard* was, "There is magic all around. Stay Alert. Be Aware. Don't miss the hidden magic." Okay!

I came to an area with wonderful long-range views of the mountains, which was especially breathtaking due to the fog in the valleys. What was even more noticeable was that I *felt* the beauty within my heart. My heart chakra was actually open and free. I hadn't experienced this in almost two years. It was a significant clue that my healing had come very far. I was really excited about the experiences I was traveling towards.

The rest of the trip to the airport flowed. The flight was fine and I arrived at the Phoenix hotel no worse for wear. When I stepped out of the terminal into the heat of Phoenix, which was near 110 degrees, I almost went back and got a plane back to the mountains! I was feeling a 60 degree temperature change, and it was stifling. If I heard one more person say, "Oh, but it's a dry heat," I'd scream. Dry or not, it was hot!

The driver from the hotel said my traveling companions were waiting for me. They met me in the lobby as I was checking in. They all seemed very friendly and spoke fabulous English. I put my luggage in the room and then headed off for some lunch with my new friends.

Gregory and Sandie arrived a few hours after I did. At an orientation meeting, Gregory channeled a message about the purpose behind our upcoming journey. It had been a wonderful day, since everything had gone without a hitch. It was a good omen for the remainder of our time together.

The next morning, we were on our way to Sedona, the first stop on our spiritual adventure. You could feel the buzz of anticipation in the car. Half of us had been to the area. The rest of us didn't know what to expect. I knew I wasn't a fan of heat or arid regions. While I wasn't attracted to the conditions, I still appreciated the beauty of Nature in the desert; just don't make me live there!

While my heart was anticipating Mt. Shasta, I stayed in the present moment and heeded the message of the owl to stay alert. There is no other place to be aware than in the Now. So, Mt. Shasta would have to wait until I had experienced all that the Sedona desert wanted to share with me.

As we approached the Sedona area, the famous Red Rocks began to appear. They were quite impressive. I could see why people gravitated to Sedona on physical appearance alone, regardless of the powerful energies felt there. It was definitely more beautiful than anything we'd seen on the drive from Phoenix.

We stopped by the Chapel of the Holy Cross, which was perched between two amazing red rock formations. It was busy with people, but within the Chapel still retained a serene, reverent feeling. I'm usually not very comfortable in a church, but this place filled me with a lovely feeling of natural spiritual energy, rather than one of religion. My only explanation was the existence of the energy vortex located beneath it.

We checked into the Hampton Inn, and then drove to a popular location above Sedona to watch the sunset. It was a soft, filtered sunset bringing a close to our first day filled with present moment experiences. The other good news was that it was a little cooler in Sedona – only in the 90s!

We headed off after an early breakfast to hike to an energy vortex called the Seven Sacred Ponds. I was so ready to be with Mother Nature. I feel the most spiritual when I'm walking amid all that she has to offer. It was a nice easy hike through incredible red rock formations. We saw images in the red rocks looking back at us.

Due to the dry conditions, the ponds weren't very full and resembled puddles to me. What they lacked in water, they more than made up for in palpable energy. Gregory channeled that each pond contained healing energy for a virtue or trait. Ah, the seven virtues. I hadn't even considered that.

The first was innocence, next came intelligence/wisdom, the third held love, the fourth offered honesty/integrity, the fifth contained patience, the sixth held pride balanced with humility, and the seventh gifted us with ecstasy/bliss/joy.

We were instructed to place our hand in each of the seven ponds and then place the water in various locations on our body in order to receive its healing gift. I joked with Sandie that I needed to bathe in five and seven especially.

We were given permission to take a stone from this powerful and sacred site to serve as a reminder of the virtues that had been replenished within us from these seven sacred pools. This was an energy vortex of feminine energy creating a place of gentle and nurturing sensations.

Next, we stopped for lunch at a mall featuring local artisans' galleries. My roommate, Synnove, had been in touch with a local Indian artist named Bearcloud. She'd arranged to spend our free day with him rather than ride with me, which I understood.

Bearcloud's gallery was in this mall, so after lunch we decided to find it. I'd visited his website months earlier and found him to be quite talented. But, the last thing I needed was more artwork for my crowded walls.

As I walked around the gallery, I marveled at the intricacy of his paintings and the hidden images within them – "the hidden magic." I was doing just fine until I came across a painting titled, *On the Wings of an Eagle*. Well, it just pulled me deep into it. The fascinating thing is how his paintings respond to light that's directed towards them with a dimmer switch. The painting transforms itself before your eyes in the changing brightness of the light. Synnove saw my attraction to the Eagle painting and asked the salesgirl to show me the lighting effect. The painting came to life right in front of me.

The salesgirl, Donna, noticed my keen interest and began to tell me the story of the painting. As I listened to her interpretation of the painting, the hair began to stand up on the back of my neck. All I could think was, oh no! It was as though Bearcloud had painted this about me. It reflected my story of the past two years.

Donna showed me the hidden images, which turned Bearcloud's painting into a reflection of *my* life. When she showed me two mountain lions and two maidens forming the wings of a butterfly signifying transformation, I was a goner. My whole body was tingling. I just couldn't ignore these intense physical sensations. I was electric again like my first encounter with Gregory, and look what that led to. I had to honor what I felt.

The metaphor of the butterfly, which I'd intuited during my writing, was staring me in the face from Bearcloud's painting. I knew I was soon to emerge from my cocoon in the Tunnel. This spiritual adventure was enabling the chrysalis to grow and evolve.

I told Donna briefly about my healing journey of the past two years and the significance of the painting for me. I explained that I'd been given the natural name, Mountain Lion Woman, in a Sweat Lodge Ceremony years earlier. I shared my feelings of being carried "on the wings of eagles" by my friends through my dark night of the soul and how the butterfly metaphor emerged from my writing. It was all there in Bearcloud's painting. This was no coincidence.

Each of our band of spiritual travelers had been attracted to different paintings reflecting our different healing journeys. No one in our group could believe what just happened, least of all me. I decided this painting was meant to remind me of the difficult and miraculous healing and transformation that I'd achieved in a relativity short time frame. It would be a constant reminder of the power contained within my Self and soul.

Synnove had convinced Bearcloud to lead a Sweat Lodge Ceremony while she was in Sedona. She asked if we might also attend, which he eventually agreed to. Having had such a powerful experience with his art, I was quite anxious to meet the man himself. The sweat lodge would be held on our last night in Sedona. It would be a fitting end to our free day and my riding adventure in the canyon lands of Arizona.

Gregory had decided to ride with me. I'd committed to ride months earlier, even if I had to ride alone. It was one of my examples of putting Self first and not settling. I knew my teachers were as pleased as I was. I was delighted with Gregory's decision. We ended our shopping spree and headed back to prepare for the Grand Canyon, which was next on the agenda.

I'd never been to the Canyon before, but I'd driven past the road leading to it with my mother years ago. My mother wasn't a person who was comfortable in Nature, which considering the daughter she gave birth to, was ironic. When I mentioned wanting to see the Grand Canyon, her response was, "Why? It's just a big hole in the ground."

I just let it be and figured I'd get to see it eventually. Little did I know it would take me almost 40 years. She was right. It *is* a big hole in the ground, but a hole with immense power and beauty contained within it.

Our plans were to hike one of the trails, but we never got too far along. One of our group had an intense traumatic response to the trail, even though it was very well established and wide. I knew she had triggered memories from one or more past lives when she'd been injured or died from falling from a similar place. She tried, but her fears were too real, intense, and overpowering. The empathy we felt for her was as strong as her fear.

As we headed back up the trail, I saw a mother goat with her kid lying out on the top of a rock formation. They were as comfortable as could be sunning themselves. I thought about the sharp contrast between their comfort on a rocky precipice that was far more dangerous than the trail we were on, and our friend's debilitating fear on our more protected trail.

Animals live fully in the present moment and in doing so they aren't as affected by fears from past experiences. I felt so sorry for my new friend. She was not only terrified of something she didn't understand, but despite our telling her not to be, she was embarrassed. While I knew she was feeling awful, I also knew that it would allow her to assess the causes, let go of the fears, and begin to heal. Healing past lives had been highlighted during our orientation channeling.

We walked around the top of the rim area and took tons of pictures. The colors were beautiful. We saw several condors soaring above the Canyon. They were on the brink of extinction, but were recovering through the efforts of many groups. It was a treat to see them enjoying the ride on the thermals over this immense place.

As I looked out over a canyon that seemed to have no end to it, I felt a sense of timelessness. It was inconceivable to me that water and wind had created this over eons of time. It was another of Nature's awesome and powerful places.

After we filled our spirits with enough of the beauty of the Grand Canyon, we found a picnic area for lunch. Going back, Sandie drove while Gregory channeled information about the Canyon. The Grand Canyon and its immense space emanated and reflected masculine energy. That was exactly what I'd felt: strong, domineering energy, which was very different from the Seven Sacred Ponds. The Canyon had been *saying* to me, "Look at me. I'm here and have been for eons; I Am!" It was encouraging to hear validation of my feelings. My confidence was definitely on the rise.

On the drive back, we altered our route to find a place that advertised itself as home to a herd of Sacred White Buffalo. I'd learned the legend of White

Buffalo Calf Woman from Eagle Man, who held the first Sweat Lodge Ceremony I experienced. The legend is the basis of the beliefs of not only the Sioux Nation, but many American Indian Tribes.

In the 90s, a female white buffalo was born and aptly named Miracle. It was believed to be a prophesized sacred sign from Great Spirit/Creator – a warning call to respect all species and return balance and harmony to all on Mother Earth. I wasn't aware of any others being born, but I guessed we were about to see a bunch of them.

We found the place with its white buffalo. They weren't really white, but cream colored. Synnove was thrilled. I was only saddened by the conditions that they lived in. They were in dirt lots, albeit clean, but not very large. It broke my heart to see them. I think I picked up all of their sadness. I've certainly seen horses confined, but they've chosen to spend their lives tangled in the web of humans; while buffalo haven't. To me, buffalo represent the wild freedom of the natural world.

The owner told the story of her white buffalo herd. That they'd been DNA tested and were pure buffalo with no cattle blood mixed in. They'd been selectively breeding for white ones and had succeeded. Miracle was the name of their first white calf.

Their profiting from something considered a sacred Being sickened me. I worked hard to not be noticeably angry. But, I was angry and confused. I didn't understand why sacred white buffalo would come to a family who looked at them with dollar signs in their eyes. My heart broke for the animals, and I was furious with the people, which was nothing new for me.

As we drove on, I tried to understand what my heart was feeling. I couldn't explain why, but I knew how my heart *felt* and it wasn't filled with reverence and awe. I'd been enamored by the birth of Miracle years earlier. The fulfillment of this prophecy had been significant to me.

Being confronted with a herd of white buffalo, which people selectively bred, took all the mystery away. Miracle wasn't such a miracle when you're looking at seven of them. I couldn't ignore my feelings and discussed them with everyone, trying to understand.

Sandie googled White Buffalo Calf at the motel and found the truth behind my mysterious feelings. What we saw was not *the* white buffalo that had been born in the 90s, fulfilling the prophecy. The first female white buffalo, Miracle, was born in Wisconsin in 1994 and died there in 2004.

It had been prophesized that she'd change coat colors several times during her life, which she did. Miracle had been the first white buffalo born since 1933.

The people to whom she came were not American Indian, but they learned of her sacredness and honored the gift they'd been given. Their farm was open to visitors *free of charge* allowing all who wanted to honor her admittance. She was *not* a commodity. They still allow those who want to visit her grave free access to it.

My faith had been restored and my beliefs washed clean with Sandie's information. My heart had been telling me, through my emotions, that this woman was nothing more than a deceptive and dishonest person. This wasn't the original female white buffalo calf, Miracle, who was born to signal a warning to us that we needed to heed – a warning for renewed respect for all Beings, and to strive to re-establish peace and harmony amongst "all our relations."

While my conscious mind didn't know the facts at the time of our visit, some other part of me did and ignited my angry confusion. It handed me a valuable lesson in trusting my feelings. While my mind may not always know the truth, my heart *always* does. I felt vindicated with the knowledge that honorable people had been sent the gift of the White Buffalo Calf, who was to me a spirit messenger not to be capitalized upon. Sandie's discovery allowed me to rest easier that night.

Early the next morning, Gregory and I were off to ride in Sycamore Canyon. We did a half-day ride in order to be ready for Bearcloud's Sweat Lodge Ceremony later that evening. I'd been looking forward to this experience for months. Riding a horse in natural surroundings is *the* most spiritual thing I can do. Horse, woman, and Nature as one entity – for me there's nothing better.

The area we rode in was very beautiful and isolated and the horses were very adept at the rocky, rough trail. There was a nice breeze, which made the temperature quite bearable. I rode along taking in the beauty of the area and the wonderful energy of the horse.

All of a sudden we were informed that this was as far as the half-day rides went. I was shocked and very disappointed. It felt like we'd just started. My soul was just getting into the serenity of the experience. I knew from other such experiences that our ride back would go faster, since we'd be going down instead of climbing.

Our drive out to Sycamore Canyon had taken much longer than had been described back in March. For the longest time, we drove on a very rough dirt road, so we couldn't go very fast towing horses. We were back at our hotel at the time promised, but the drive time and riding times were reversed. We ended up trailering for three hours and riding for two, which was a very bad ratio. Gregory and I agreed the ride was great, but it was too much trailering.

My experience had a lesson in it for me. After researching outfitters in the area, I'd been attracted to a different one. When Synnove backed out and Gregory expressed an interest, I sent him the info on the company I liked best. He spoke with the group we used and decided their trip sounded more personalized and isolated.

Given the extra money we spent and the short time in the saddle, I should've stuck to my first instinct. My heart was showing me the best experience for me, but I didn't listen.

We had an enjoyable time, but it was diminished by the lengthy trailering. I've shipped horses all over in the past 40-plus years of showing jumpers and breeding mares. My purpose was to ride, not trailer.

I've learned from this experience, especially when it deals with horses, to listen to my little rider's voice inside. I didn't learn in pain or fear, but it was a lesson learned with an abbreviated amount of time in the saddle, which translated into abbreviated joy.

While I waited to go to Bearcloud's home for the Sweat Lodge Ceremony, also called Inipi Ceremony, I reflected on my first Inipi in 1993. It had been at the beginning of my journey along my spiritual path and was quite powerful and very sacred for me.

I thought about the 13 years between the two ceremonies, as well. I was grateful to Bearcloud for inviting our group. I was sure he wouldn't regret his decision, since we'd all come for very serious journeys of spiritual healing and growth.

We found Bearcloud's home nestled in the forest of Oak Creek Canyon. Synnove, who'd spent the day with him, told us he'd be ready in a bit. Each of us sat quietly preparing in our own personal way for the experience we were about to have. Gregory and Sandie had done many sweat lodge ceremonies with many different people. I'd done one at the Omega Institute with Eagle Man, who was a very sharing Lakota Sioux. I don't think the other gals had any previous Inipi experience.

Each ceremony reflects the person leading it and those who've taught him. Bearcloud welcomed us into his lodge. The temperature of the hot rocks and total darkness can be intimidating. The sweat created is meant to purify the attendees of any and all toxins held within the mind, body, and spirit. Bearcloud's Inipi lasted quite a while and was very hot. In between prayer rounds he opened the flap to get more hot rocks, allowing in fresh air which was greatly appreciated by us all.

Bearcloud had very humble, wonderful energy. He expressed his gratitude to us for coming into his lodge many times throughout his Inipi Ceremony. We were all so grateful to him to be invited.

Bearcloud was very sympathetic when a couple of our group had to leave due to the intensity of the heat, and the power of the purification ceremony itself. It is meant to illicit issues that need to be healed. He took extra time in between rounds helping those who were really stressed release what was necessary and reenter the lodge if they wished.

To me, Bearcloud displayed a great amount of patience, flexibility, and empathy towards non-native people, which endeared him to me. I was convinced that I was meant to have his painting in my home. Not only would it remind me of my transformation story, but also of the humble and gentle American Indian who had shared his lodge with us.

We were each allowed an opportunity to express ourselves. Some did, while others chose to do it silently. We ended smoking the peace pipe to close the ceremony. It had been another profound and powerful Inipi experience for me.

As I emerged from the lodge, which represents being reborn from the darkness of Mother Earth's womb, Bearcloud gave me a big, warm hug. I took in as much of his gentle energy as I could. I hoped he was enjoying the energy I gave back. The cool air hitting my over-heated body made me almost faint. I knew my normally low blood pressure was having a hard time adjusting.

I found a chair and sat for a very long time. I stared at the stars with Gregory in a chair next to me in the same state. We just couldn't move. I felt extraordinary. Eventually, Gregory went inside to get something to eat, but I just kept looking skyward.

Bearcloud came out and invited me to eat. I told him I didn't think I was all the way back yet, meaning in my body. He just smiled and said, "Oh, I know that feeling." It took me quite some time before I joined everyone inside. I just didn't want the feelings I'd found inside Bearcloud's lodge to end.

I felt whole once more and thanked Bearcloud from the bottom of my heart. I came in for water and did eat a little something, because I knew from a physiological standpoint I'd better. Spiritually, I was still soaring with Eagles.

I walked around the house looking at all of the original oils, which hung everywhere. They were simply fantastic, and each told its own story. Synnove told Bearcloud I was the person who'd bought his painting and he thanked me with great humility. Briefly, I told him the significance of it to me and that it would be living in the mountains of North Carolina.

Bearcloud asked where we were headed next. When he heard Mt. Shasta, he and his fiancé commented on the sacredness of our destination and looked really envious. We thanked them for a wonderful evening and the hospitality they'd shared with us.

I've been fortunate to spend time with several American Indians. They've all been very gentle in nature and probably the most humble people I've ever known. They have quite willingly shared their beliefs and culture with those of us not of Indian blood, but with a similar respect for the sacredness of Nature, our animal brothers and sisters, the Universe, Great Spirit, Creator, God, or whatever label you choose.

Their willingness to share their beliefs showed a great respect for all, which is a characteristic to which we should all aspire. I believe they act as a mirror to reflect the way to live peacefully with all that surrounds us: people, animals, plants, and Mother Earth herself. Through mutual respect, trust, and understanding, we might attain harmony for all of humanity, which will secure the future for those that follow.

The Indian way is to do nothing that will adversely affect the seven generations to follow – a wise way to live one's life. The gentle nature that I've felt within these people makes it all the more appalling that they were deceived and betrayed by the first white settlers. The fact that there are any American Indians willing to trust and share their culture with any white people serves as an example of their generous nature.

I will be forever grateful to those who work to reunite "all our relations." We were blessed with this time with Bearcloud and all the spirits who entered his Inipi. It was a busy day that ended with an amazing memory. It was the perfect end to our spiritual journey in Sedona.

Chapter 21

Mt. Shasta – An Old Friend

We drove back to Phoenix, caught a plane to Sacramento, and then drove four hours to Mt. Shasta. We were happy campers heading north to our destination. I was really anxious to see this mountain, which I'd heard so much about for the past ten years. Good things do come to those who wait.

As we got further from Sacramento and closer to Mt. Shasta, the terrain changed to that which I am most attracted to: lakes, mountains, and lots of trees, which meant green! We finally had Mt. Shasta in our sights as the sun was setting. It was gorgeous. I couldn't take my eyes from it – or as we dubbed it, "her." She was simply majestic!

I was thrilled that we were gifted with a perfect view of her summit, since she stands over 14,000 feet. Having been in the company of several high mountains, glimpses of the peak are real gifts and we got one the first time. Blessings… .

Our hotel was in a wonderful location just a few blocks down from the main street of town. The view of the mountain from the hotel was fabulous, as long as Mother Nature kept cooperating. We had all come so far to be here: physically, emotionally, and spiritually. I knew Nature wouldn't disappoint our reverent group of spiritual travelers. I could sense the anticipation in everyone,

240

but we couldn't wait to get into our rooms to recover from the travel day.

Before breakfast, I walked outside to see if I could catch a glimpse of the mountain. She was right where I'd left her with not a cloud in sight. She was resplendent in the early morning light. I just stared at her, getting reacquainted. My heart *knew* I'd been here in many other lifetimes. I was positive!

After breakfast, we headed up to the snowy mountain to get to know her better. When we walked out onto her, I couldn't believe my feelings. Being in her energy exploded my heart chakra wide open. I looked at Sandie, laughed, and said, "I think my heart just broke open!"

We experienced a fantastic channeling through Gregory as we stood in a circle among the trees. It proved to be very emotional for me. Several incredibly powerful Beings spoke to us and said we were encircled by Sages, the Ascended Masters, the Seven Archangels, and others of the angelic realms.

We were taught some amazing facts. Mt. Shasta is a vertical portal connecting many dimensions. The energies of three ancient civilizations gather together there. Mt. Shasta contains a library of all wisdom: past, present, and future, as well as a vast repository of Atlantean crystals deep within.

We were being showered by the healing energies and unconditional love of all that were present. While I could feel their power healing my being, their effect on our surroundings was just as remarkable. It had been uncomfortably cold and windy when Gregory began channeling. Incredibly, these remarkable energies began to warm us. At one point, I even felt hot.

Some of my passionate emotional response came from simply realizing that these immensely powerful Beings chose to share information, guidance, and healing with me! Other emotions arose from very old memories hidden deep within my being of having been to this place many times before.

I felt like I was home; the same sense of home I'd felt when I first stepped onto my mountain property in North Carolina – my soul's home. I was so grateful that I hadn't missed this experience and this memory, which was my soul's creation. The tears just flowed with all the sensations stirring within me. I was truly blessed.

After the channeling, we each went off to spend some time alone. I stood amid the trees staring at the summit of this resplendent mountain. The views of the surrounding area were spectacular, and the forests so welcoming. I felt one with her, which transformed me. It was simply extraordinary! I never anticipated the exchange I'd had that morning. If nothing else happened this was enough for me. I was purring inside with contentment – Mountain Lion Woman was home.

After lunch, we headed off to a local mineral springs that claimed the highest mineral content in the world. We were to soak in the mineral water, sit in the sauna, and end with a jump in the mountain creek outside, which was breathtakingly cold. The jump into the creek was a test of will for me each time. It never got any easier, but I did it.

After I finished with my sequence of cleansing, I sat on a bridge over the creek. For me, this was even more cleansing. The motion and sound of the rushing waters were cleansing my psyche and my soul. The bath, sauna, and creek jump sequences cleansed toxins from my body, but this time alone with the creek washed the toxins from deeper within.

When I left the creek to join the others, I felt calm, peaceful, serene, and whole! It had been quite a first day in Mt. Shasta. I was ready for whatever this area needed to teach me. I'd been waiting for a decade.

We woke up to some iffy weather with the wind blowing quite strongly. Clouds were covering the peak of the mountain. We ate and headed to Castle Crag Park. Along the way, my cell phone rang. It was my friend Barbara in Florida calling to tell me that Joe was gone. He died three days after we'd spoken. She sounded pretty good, but I knew the realization hadn't sunk in yet. She and Joe had known each other for more than 60 years. Talk about a void in one's existence – his would be enormous for Barbara.

I was relieved to hear Joe's fight was over, but saddened at the thought that he was gone. Nothing is permanent. I knew in my heart his spirit was free, healed, and soaring in the ethers, which wasn't a bad place to be. I thanked her for calling, told her I'd be home soon, and I'd check in with her then.

So, the roller coaster of my emotions was back: the thrill of the day before, the news of Joe's death, and the anticipation of the experiences planned for today. I reviewed in my mind and heart my memories of Barbara and Joe – times that had forged a friendship that survived years and miles in between and memories I was blessed to hold dear.

We arrived at Castle Crag in conditions that changed our plans for hiking. It was just too cold and windy. We walked up to a scenic lookout, which offered a magnificent view of the ridgeline. It looked nothing like Mt. Shasta. It had very rugged peaks, hence the name, and no snow.

Gregory channeled there, since we weren't hiking any further towards the Crags. I was disappointed that the weather interrupted our plans to hike. I really needed to get more up-close-and-personal with Mother Nature.

After a snack break, we headed off towards Burney Falls and whatever encounter awaited us there. Being Piscean, I love any place that has water and a waterfall is the ultimate. As we got closer to the falls, we saw another spectacular snow-covered mountain in the distance.

I looked at the map and decided it was Lassen Peak, which was in a park I'd been considering for my alone day. Well, seeing it sealed the deal. Lassen Park was a definite on my agenda. If I'd been missing the message from my inner voice, this glimpse of it assured that the message was received loud and clear.

When we got to Burney Falls, the place was packed with people, which always disappointed me. The chaos of lots of people always diminished my ability to commune with the natural energies of a place. Gregory wasn't sure what was going to happen, but we all marched down to the base of the falls in anticipation.

It was gorgeous, very high, and quite wide. The sound of the water was deafening. Gregory began to channel the spirit or deva of the waterfall. *She* confessed she'd never done this before, but responded to Gregory's request. She referred to herself as the Maid of The Falls. She told us about the healing power in the mist from her waters, so we should let ourselves be covered with it. She said, "Many people come, but they don't stay long enough to be healed."

Then, she started asking us all sorts of questions. She didn't understand what a man or woman was. She had no concept of time when we asked how long she'd been in this area. Based on her answer, it had been a very, very long time. She didn't know anything outside of the falls and the animals that shared it with her. It was fascinating. She was as curious about us as we her, but we were interrupted by other people and had to cut the channeling short.

There was a hiking trail around the falls, which a few of us took. Finally, I was at peace walking in this wonderful place. This was an extraordinary experience. I haven't shared specifics for most of the channelings due to their personal nature for our group and myself. I've shared only my feelings in order to elucidate their significance to my healing. I felt our communication with the Maiden of the Falls warranted details.

Echoing the owl's message to me, I want to illustrate the magic present all around us. Be aware, stay alert: don't miss the magic just because your mind doesn't think it exists. Let your heart illuminate it for you. It may be where you least expect it and when you least expect it. Be vigilant and don't miss it. It is mystical and magical! Two days down two to go in this most amazing place on Earth.

The next morning, I received a wonderful message that the Lab pups had been born. There were eight and the last-born was struggling. I couldn't help but compare my phone message the morning before announcing the loss of an old friend and this one heralding the arrival of two new ones. The circle of life in less than 24 hours – sadness transmuted into joy.

I knew there were two souls in the litter who had come to be my new teachers. I had a very strong feeling that one of my dearest soul friends resided in one of these puppies. Time would reveal if my intuition was true. I couldn't wait to meet them, but for now I was just pleased that their mother and most of them seemed well. For now, I put aside my fascination with the puppies, and we headed to Pluto Caves!

Personally, I'm not a big fan of being underground. I'm better than I used to be thanks to the SRT process. I'm a big fan of light, sky, sun, open spaces, etc. We had flashlights and rope to keep us in contact with one another. We got tied together and headed into the caves. There was definitely some tension in the air. We started down into the caves, when Gregory stopped! He just stood there miffed, while we all started to laugh uncontrollably, which broke the tension.

The cave we were standing in had a very high ceiling and didn't go anywhere. It was like a big room. Here we were with flashlights at the ready, tied together so as not to lose anyone in the bowels of Mother Earth, and standing in a room totally open to the light. It was too hysterical. We must have looked ridiculous.

After we finished laughing at ourselves, we heard Sandie calling. She'd found the entrance to the actual caves which still had high ceilings, but were very dark with rocky floors. This was more like what we'd expected. I for one was glad we weren't crawling into a very confined lava tube, but rather a spacious cave.

I think most of our anxieties regarding the caves centered on being trapped somewhere dark and tight. These were definitely dark, but not restrictive. This was one of those good unexpecteds. We still had our lights, but we had untied ourselves, throwing caution to the wind.

As we moved further into the caves, which seemed more like large mining tunnels, a rather large, light-colored bird flew out over our heads – an owl! How interesting, another owl in my sights. During our adventure in the caves, we disturbed no less than three owls. I felt bad, but it was difficult to walk over the rocky terrain in the dark without disturbing them. We had anticipated bats in the caves, which we didn't seem to disturb, thank goodness.

The high ceilings made it more pleasant to climb around the caves. We found what seemed like an appropriate spot for Gregory to channel. It was a remarkable session, which offered me a glimpse into my future work. It was otherworldly, yet familiar. The experience stirred a lot of deeply stored memories from times when I'd had similar experiences, yet I held no memory of them in my conscious mind. I seemed to attain a higher level of awareness from my time deep within the caves.

As the cave became more illuminated by the sun as we hiked back, something made me look down. I was about to step on a beautiful feather – a small colorful puffy under-feather of an owl. By the time we left the cave, I'd found three large beautiful wing feathers and several smaller ones. I have an affinity for feathers and have been gifted with many in my life, but not in quite a while.

I was remembering the owl's message, "Watch for the magic, it is everywhere." Sandie and Synnove couldn't believe I was finding these feathers. I gave them each one of the large feathers. I searched and searched for a few more for those that had gone ahead, but there were no more gifts. The appearance of these feathers was very significant to me. They marked my return to harmony and wholeness. I accepted each one with grateful thanks to the owls. I smiled inside and out and felt more connected than I had in a very long time.

As we made our way back out of the caves, I was struck with the resemblance to the metaphor of my Tunnel. While my Tunnel was mental/emotional/spiritual, I'd just emerged physically from something akin to a tunnel. I'd left the dark and entered the light. Symbolically, I was leaving my dark night of the soul and entering into *the* Light. I didn't recognize this in that moment, but it was revealed to me in this moment as I write.

The gifts of the feathers upon my exit from the caves/tunnel were physical symbols of the gifts that are ahead for me as I rejoin my spiritual path, which had been put aside so many years earlier. The wounded healer was bringing to a close a long detour from her life's purpose.

On the walk back, I sensed movement and noise simultaneously. I turned quickly to see a long, yellow and black striped snake slithering away from me. I don't care for snakes. The fact that he/she was heading away was a relief. There had been a snake crossing the road when we headed to Sycamore Canyon, too. Two snakes in five days couldn't be a coincidence. Neither could four owls in eight days. I had seen two owls and one snake in 27 years on my farm.

I equate snakes with shedding skin. Shedding, i.e., letting go, was something I'd been working at for a while now. Owl and snake medicine were screaming at me on this trip. Rest assured their messages and their lessons would be uncovered, if not in the present moment, definitely when I returned home. A destination in Gregory's itinerary that I hadn't really resonated with turned out to be so extraordinarily significant to me. "There is magic all around. Stay Alert. Be aware. Don't miss the hidden magic."

Leaving the caves, owls, and snake behind, we headed toward Castle Lake. We arrived at a frozen lake cluttered with lots of people and deep snow. The color below the ice hinted at the beauty of the water when thawed. This spot held no attraction for us. Its energy was non-existent. It didn't feel like a place that had anything to share with us.

After a number of locals asked if we'd visited Castle Lake, I began to ponder our experience with it. My guess was its quite beautiful and healing when not frozen. I was intrigued that the freezing of the water negated the energy of Castle Lake. My scientific left brain busied itself analyzing the situation. When water was solid it definitely affected the energy created by the area.

Looking for meaning, significance, and lessons in everything I experienced, I pondered the lesson being offered by Castle Lake. What came to me was a lesson in contrasts. Without contrasts we can't appreciate our experiences. Without sadness we can't appreciate happiness, which was a monumental lesson for me these past two years. Joy without sorrow, hot without cold, day without night – you get my drift.

Well, the neutral feeling of Castle Lake provided a perfect contrast to the overpowering energy of Mt. Shasta. The comparison between the frozen, unfeeling Castle Lake and the towering Burney Falls, whose Maiden spoke to us and shared her intensely healing energy, was as different as night and day. The contrast was astounding as evidenced by our reactions and responses to each. We didn't want to leave the falls. We couldn't wait to leave the lake!

Contrast is a necessary component in order for us to appreciate our experiences and our lives. Castle Lake was offering the lesson of contrast – at least, it was to me. I couldn't wait to come back when it was thawed and see if my musings were accurate. I'll bet they are.

We headed back to meet a friend of Gregory and Sandie's at a local store called The Crystal Room. The shop was fairly large with a very extensive collection of every type of stone and crystal you could imagine. There were about six rooms filled with stone people. While I have a great affinity for rocks and crystals as well as feathers, this shop was uncomfortable to be in. There were just too many and I was sensing very chaotic energy.

We met Gregory's friend, Lahaarija, who had begun channeling recently. Look out, here's another one of those coincidences. Don't worry owl friends, I'm on the alert. Lahaarija invited everyone for a channeling session at the shop later that evening, which I felt was very generous of her.

We headed to our rooms for a little down time. We'd been having such incredibly powerful experiences that we needed time to just *be*. No one seemed interested in joining Lahaarija for her channeling session. I was tired, but couldn't see passing up the experience. All I had to do was walk a short way to The Crystal Room. I felt compelled to go despite everyone else's disinterest.

I strolled to town with no expectations of what I might find. Lahaarija was in a room I hadn't seen earlier. Apparently, you have to ask to enter it. When I announced I was the only one of our group coming, the shocked look on Lahaarija's face made me glad I'd shown up. I knew she was disappointed.

I was overwhelmed by the energy of this room. Instantly I felt calm, serene, and just wonderful. It was as different a feeling as you could imagine when compared to the other rooms – my earlier lesson in contrasts was being reinforced this evening just in case I didn't get it. I got it!

As I looked around at many, many large quartz crystals, I thought to myself, "Okay, here's where the real crystals live." I'd never seen so many healing crystals in one place before. The healing energy within the room was phenomenal. My intuition told me that these were crystals used for information storage, communication, healing, etc. These weren't ornaments but rather tools with their own purpose(s). I smiled when I thought of my big crystal at home and how it had come to me.

Years earlier, a friend of a dear friend of mine knew a gal who mined crystals in Arkansas. Through this connection I was invited to a talk on quartz crystals, which I knew nothing about. We stopped by earlier in the day and were introduced to the crystals she'd brought with her for sale. One crystal in particular grabbed my attention. It was one of the smaller ones, but it just took over my thoughts.

For days I thought of nothing but that crystal. I even drove past the street the farm was on without turning, so focused was I on this crystal. When I asked how much it was, she told me it wasn't really for sale. Apparently, its job was to awaken memories in people about quartz crystals. Well, it was very good at its job.

I was obsessed with learning all I could about quartz crystals, which I did over the next few weeks. I was convinced that there was a crystal somewhere that would help me develop my newly found skills of animal communication and healing. Every day during my morning mediation routine, I asked if there was a crystal I needed that it come to me via this crystal miner.

After three months, I got a call from my friend's friend saying the crystal miner had a crystal that was mine if I were interested. You bet I was interested. The miner didn't know what I'd been doing, but this crystal was insistent that it was mine! The price wasn't cheap, but I never hesitated. I grabbed some cash and headed to meet this crystal that had answered my call.

When I got to the woman's house she had the crystal sitting in the middle of her living room on a pink cloth in dim light all alone. It is a scene I will never forget. As I approached the crystal I was drawn to it by some other-worldly power. I just stood there staring at this magnificent being and my tears flowed. I was overcome with emotions, which I didn't understand. It was as though I was being reunited with an old friend that had been missing for an extremely long time. I couldn't wait to bring my old friend home.

Thus began my relationship with quartz healing crystals. The arrival of this spectacular crystal was my first conscious experience with the power of manifestation that I possessed, and we all possess. For months I was blown away by the crystal and how it had found me. It was quite a teacher. I learned that this magnificent crystal is one of immense information storage amongst other purposes. My friend has been waiting ever since for the perfect time for us to unlock the treasures contained within it for me. That time is rapidly approaching almost a decade-and-a-half later.

I was grateful to be in the presence of all these powerful quartz crystals in Mt. Shasta, and the energy they were putting forth, but I had healing crystals already. One very odd-looking crystal sitting on a bottom shelf caught my eye. It was a long, thin, clear crystal attached to an opaque base, whose shape reminded me of a comet's tail. It looked like an antennae or a wand rising out of this very strange, uniquely shaped base. It was in total contrast to all of the others. It just captured my attention. I'm so glad I have my crystals.

Bev, the shop owner, announced that after the channeling session, she'd been instructed to do a 13-bowl healing session for us. The sounds would align our energies horizontally, vertically, and diagonally. Two gifts from the Universe and all I had to do was walk a few blocks.

Lahaarija channeled a very powerful Being whom Gregory had channeled several times in his home and here on Mt. Shasta. It became even more powerful for me personally when the Being, Lord Sananda, acknowledged me as the only one of my group who chose to be present. As Lahaarija spoke *his* words her head turned in my direction. I felt honored to have my presence recognized by this most sacred of Beings. It was a moment in time that I will *never* forget. It was truly humbling.

Lahaarija channeled for almost an hour. It was fascinating information, but several times during her session I turned to look at the odd crystal sitting behind me. I couldn't believe myself. What was directing my attention away from this amazing presence sitting directly across from me? What was with this crystal? I didn't want any more crystals. Leave me alone.

When Lahaarija was finished, she thanked us for coming. She was quite emotional about her experience. I got the feeling that this might have been a first for her in front of a group. I was glad, if for no other reason than her gratitude, that I'd made the effort to accept her invitation.

I'd experienced a crystal bowl healing meditation at Gregory's first gathering. The bowls vibrate at different frequencies affecting the varying energy centers in our bodies. Bev's alignment session lasted more than an hour and was exceptional.

Despite the tranquilizing affect of the singing bowls, I was still interrupted on several occasions by the crystal behind me. I sat on the floor through the channeling, but halfway through the bowl meditation I had to lie back because I felt like a marshmallow. Now my head was even closer to the crystal.

Several more times I opened my eyes and turned to look at it. There was no doubt this crystal was screaming at me. I didn't want another crystal. But, this distracting little being was telling me that I needed another crystal. I needed it!

When Bev stopped playing, I gave in to my newest partner and asked Bev to put the odd one aside for me. I would be back for it the next afternoon. I thanked Bev and Lahaarija for a fabulous evening. My choice to listen to my inner voice gifting myself with this wonderfully spiritual and healing evening strengthened my self-confidence and self-esteem. I was putting Self first and it was giving me terrific rewards. I was still puzzled about the mystical crystal encounter. "There is magic all around. Stay Alert. Be aware. Don't miss the hidden magic."

When I got back to the room, Synnove asked me about my evening. I relayed the events as briefly as possible since I still felt like marshmallow. I think she was surprised to hear how significant it had turned out to be for me. She'd met Gregory and another of our group, Lene, who hadn't been feeling well, in the hot tub for a healing. Gregory channeled healing and information that was significant to all of them. Everyone was in the appropriate place to get exactly what we each needed.

Everything is *always in perfection*, even when we don't recognize or acknowledge it. We all received the proper healings and I was introduced to a new colleague. I'd learn much more about the odd crystal from Bev when I purchased it. I'd started the day with the news that my highly anticipated new puppies had been born and ended it by meeting a completely unanticipated partner in my future healing work.

I felt sad that tomorrow would be our last day with Mt. Shasta, but I felt so full from all of our experiences that I would leave without feeling any regrets. We had one more visit to the mountain in the morning. We'd been blessed with incredible views of it throughout our stay. Clouds did surround the summit and added their own beauty to the peak, but they never stayed all day.

After breakfast, we headed to Mt. Shasta where Gregory channeled three different Beings. The first was the Guardian of Mt. Shasta. I was thrilled to be communicating directly with a place that had become so very significant to me. Once more as Gregory channeled, my tears flowed. The energy that spoke was masculine. *His* message was poignant, yet powerful. Two old friends, Archangel Michael and Quan Yin, followed. By the time all three were finished, my self esteem and my respect for Self had taken quantum leaps.

Given the essence of the Guardian of Mt. Shasta, I couldn't refer to the mountain as "her" any longer. I think most of us gals wanted the mountain to be feminine because we no longer trusted men. We needed to trust the mountain to facilitate the incorporation of its healing gifts into our bodies, minds, and souls – hence the desire for the mountain to be feminine.

Mt. Shasta was commanding, powerful, and definitely masculine. The experiences of the past ten days allowed me to accept its masculinity and its gifts without reservation. Without doubt, I trusted this sacred, mystical mountain. As much as we hated to leave, it was time.

I had a date with Bev and an odd little crystal at The Crystal Room. I found Synnove at the crystal store finding her own stone person. It wasn't quartz crystal, but a beautiful blue stone called kyanite. Synnove couldn't believe the crystal that was waiting for me.

A sales gal saw me showing it to Synnove and asked if I'd held the crystal. "Not yet, but I'd love to." I'd learned years ago not to touch quartz crystals without permission. It's a definite no-no. She asked if I knew that it was Atlantean. I knew, but not because anyone told me. My other two crystals were Atlantean and I *knew* this new friend was, too.

All my curiosity surrounding this crystal and its command of my attention reached a climax as she handed it to me. It calmed me instantly. It felt familiar like I'd held it before, which made no sense. I perceived that it was happy through our contact. The sales gal just smiled, and said, "Ah, it is yours." She said many, many people had looked at it since its arrival. It was unique and unusual. I thought to myself, that's me: odd, unique, and unusual. It had been waiting for me.

While the channeling and bowl meditation were things I needed to hear and feel, my little voice sent me to Lahaarija's session to meet this crystal. "Hidden treasure, hidden magic." Just what the owl alerted me to as I began this spiritual adventure ten days earlier.

Bev recognized me from the night before and gave me a big hug. She took my new crystal friend, looked it all over, and gathered information about it on crystal personalities, which are characteristics and functions that a crystal possesses. It was obvious Bev was much attuned to rocks and crystals. I am always humbled in the presence of someone who is so adept at his or her craft, and Bev was that.

While she worked with the crystal, I asked her where it had been mined. I was curious, since my two at home came from Arkansas. She said all of her inventory came from one woman in Brazil. Bev handed me a stack full of pages and said, "This is an amazing crystal!" I smiled and then told her about how it distracted me during Sananda's message and her bowl meditation, which had turned me into a marshmallow. It had been relentless, but now it was perfectly content and silent since I'd gotten its message.

It was a crystal with many different personalities, abilities, and purposes. Even Bev was surprised by the extent of them, which spoke volumes about this odd little crystal given the hundreds or maybe thousands that she'd come upon. I knew it would become an essential component of my healing practice. My mind didn't want a crystal. Thank goodness my heart knew I needed this crystal, and my soul created the scenario that brought it to me. Whatever would I do without my stubborn little soul?

I decided not to ship the crystal, because I just didn't want to let it out of my care. Not only would it teach me and work with me in whatever capacity it was supposed to, but it would always serve as a reminder of Mt. Shasta, my wonderful traveling companions, and our spiritual adventures along the way.

I was glad my two-year hiatus from work was coming to a close. I needed to start to earn a living. The crystal was a complete surprise and a perfect end to my stay in Mt. Shasta, much like Bearcloud's mystical painting and Inipi on our last day in Sedona. After I got everything packed, I *spoke* with Licorice and told him I'd been home in two days. He felt good and was pleased to hear I'd be home soon.

Chapter 22

Beyond My Wildest Dreams

*B*efore I went for an early breakfast, I walked out and up towards town to take my last pictures of my other special mountain, Mt. Shasta. It was clear and bathed in early morning light. I was sad to bid this sacred place farewell, but I would be back for another visit when there was less snow, so I could venture farther up on him. I was being dropped off in Redding for my experimental first day on vacation *alone*.

I said a fond good-bye to the two Danes. Synnove was going to Carolina to work further with Gregory, so I'd see her in a few days. Everyone in our group really had complemented one another. We'd had a harmonious, fun-filled, and at times quite serious spiritual adventure.

I found the highway to Lassen Volcanic State Park and headed for it. It looked to be less than an hour's drive. I wasn't too far along when the mountain came into view. It was beautiful. I'd never been here and didn't know the roads, but I felt no anxiety about being alone in a strange place in an unfamiliar car.

I was fixated on my destination – the glorious snow-covered mountain straight ahead. The road led right to the park entrance, making it hard to get lost or confused. My excitement diminished when I noticed that the road through the park was closed in ten miles. I didn't drive an hour to turn around without seeing Lassen Peak from as close as I could get, however it was a huge park, and without snow I could've driven for miles through it. For now, I'd make the best of what I had in this moment!

I drove till the snow stopped me, which was where the lava flow had come down from the peak in the early 1900s. There was a self-guided trail, which I walked. It was very different from the area around Mt. Shasta: more lessons in contrast. The view of Lassen Peak from the trail area was stunning. Mother Nature gifted me with spectacularly clear weather for my first day on my own.

After I walked the trail, I sat on one of the huge rocks that had been blown from the peak 90 years earlier. I spent half an hour just mesmerized by the mountain itself. It was striking, but less imposing than Shasta with less dynamic energy. With my confidence soaring from my time with Mt. Shasta, I decided to see if I could communicate with Lassen's Guardian. To my delight I did so with no trouble. Wow! I'd only ever talked with animals and the entities that helped me in my animal healing practice. Until Gregory's channelings, it hadn't even occurred to me to try to talk to mountains, waterfalls, etc. This was way cool.

The voice I heard was masculine like Mt. Shasta, and I wondered if all mountains were masculine. I sat by myself, but never felt alone or lonely. I never felt like someone was missing, a feeling that had plagued me in Maui 15 months earlier. I was a different person now: stronger, more confident, healed.

On my way into the park, I passed Manzanita Lake, which had a hiking trail around it. I was in need of a good hike. I also was in need of a snack and more water for my hike, so I stopped at the camper store. I mentioned I was going to walk the lake trail and the manager told me I'd get a gorgeous view of the peak.

The great thing about lake trails is you just turn right or left and keep going until you get back to where you began. Circles were the perfect form in Nature. There are so many hidden meanings within a circle.

I found the lake and did just that. I headed to the right and kept on. The weather was perfect for a nice walk. There was a gaggle of Canada Geese out on the lake. I'd shared my farm with them for almost thirty years and missed seeing them in the mountains. I was amazed that I hadn't a care in the world about walking alone in a place I'd never been before. Sounds like a John Denver song to me.

I was completely in the present moment with not a thought about anything other than what I was experiencing right Now. Everything was alive. I had a heightened sense of awareness. I noticed everything: ducks and geese on the lake, birds in the trees, the trees, the mountain, the rocks, everything.

I am a very slow hiker since I take time to soak in the energy of the place.

I stop and look at the tiniest of things. Most people hike at speed, making a competition out of it. I'm guaranteed to spend twice the normal time. I don't want to miss anything for "There is magic all around. Stay Alert. Be Aware. Don't miss the hidden magic." I did this long before the owl was sent to remind me.

I only passed three other people on the trail, all headed in the opposite direction. At least four times I turned around thinking someone was approaching from behind and might want to pass given my slow pace. There never was anyone in sight. After the fourth time, I realized that I was sensing energy, unseen beings and entities. I could *feel* someone or something behind me, but in four attempts I never saw anyone. No doubt these were my guides and helpers.

My complete immersion into the present moment sharpened my ability to sense energy. I was thrilled because I'd been waiting for this ability to materialize. I *knew* it meant I was well on my way to being fully healed. My self-esteem and confidence were at an all-time high. How could I feel alone or lonely with this crowd following me?

I left the trail following some sounds of water, but couldn't find its source. I sat on a rock, drank some water, and ate my snack. I noticed a small lizard scampering through the rocks, which stopped to stare at me.

I asked if it was okay if I shared his home with him and what a beautiful home it was. He was surprised that I could speak with him. "Why can't the others? No one ever stops long enough to visit. Why are they all in such a hurry?" Good questions, all.

We talked for a short while – he on his rock and I on mine. I thanked him for sharing his home, but I had to be on my way. The minute I finished that thought he scurried from the rock and I never saw him again.

A little further along the trail, I found the source of moving water. It was a small rocky area where the lake spilled out into a brook through the woods. There was a huge rock on one side, which I climbed up onto. Rushing water was something that fascinated me. It always calms and relaxes me and keeps my ego occupied with its activity.

After staring at the water for several minutes, I felt a presence in front of me dancing in the bubbles in the water. I sent the same request to share its home as I had to the lizard. I *heard* a giggle and a greeting of welcome. The voice I heard was as bubbly and full of energy as the water itself. I was told "she" was a water sprite. Her questions were identical to the lizard. "Why can you... What's their hurry?"

I tried to explain most people's fascination with time and preoccupation with past and future. She couldn't comprehend either concept. "All there is, is now, isn't there?" Well, I could have stayed for a month trying to explain that one. I thanked her for the healing nature of her water and bid her farewell.

Just around the bend I found *the* most magnificent view of Lassen Peak. It was a calendar shot. The water was like glass reflecting the mountain in it. It would serve as a reminder of my first vacation day alone – but not alone. I'd spent five hours in Lassen Park with the road closed ten miles into it. Imagine how long I'd be here next time I visited when I could drive further into the park.

Years earlier, I'd bought a wood sculpture at a Craft Expo in Asheville. I'd walked through a huge convention center without anything catching my attention and was just about to leave when I spied this beautiful piece of wood sitting on an artist's display shelf. It just *called* to me. The artist had incorporated pheasant feathers in his sculpture. He told me it was a Manzanita burl from out west. I've enjoyed its beauty for years.

On several of our hikes we walked through Manzanita groves, especially near Burney Falls. They are low bush-like trees with an unusual colored bark that gave my sculpture its unique beauty. I was fascinated to meet Manzanita up-close-and-personal. The gifts I received from Manzanita Lake and its inhabitants were invaluable. My sculpture waiting at home has a new significance, given my experiences with Manzanita in its natural state.

The coincidence of my Manzanita sculpture and my spiritual journey, so many years later, just proves my point that everything is significant – *everything*. I had no idea that this day on my own would serve to teach me that my healing journey was complete. I felt truly healed, out of my tunnel, released from my cocoon, and prepared to open my wings and soar into my future of new experiences, new goals, and new dreams.

I went back to the store for more water, and to tell the manager how much I'd enjoyed their park. When she told me where she lived, I asked if she knew of the Wild Horse Sanctuary. She gave me directions right to it. I'd wanted to join a two-day trail ride that left the next day, but Jodi couldn't stay with my family that long.

As long as I was this close I wanted to stop by. The sign said they closed in an hour. I found one of their wranglers by the barns. I told him I'd just stopped by to see their operation and hoped to ride with them sometime. He asked if I had time to go see some of the mustangs. Are you kidding? I've got nothing but time. I grabbed my camera and water and asked if I needed to be back by 4 p.m. He smiled and told me they'd come find me if I wasn't back by dark!

We walked toward a gate that opened to the 5,000 acres where the 250-

plus mustangs lived. He told me where I might find some, which was only about a seven-minute walk. "Just don't get too close to them." No problem. Well, off I went on a never-expected adventure.

Before long I heard some horses moving in the same direction I was. I followed them towards the basin. When the bushes opened up, I looked ahead to see horses in all directions. I was in heaven with wild horses right before my very eyes. I was taking pictures like crazy just in case they saw me and fled. None of them were too concerned about me. I was doing my best not to be intrusive. There was no one that respected horses more than I. I'd never been in the presence of totally wild horses. This was a dream come true – a dream I hadn't consciously anticipated.

There were many groups of horses. I gave them their space, while making my way all over so I could watch them. There were about six mares with foals of varying ages. One of the mares with about a month-old foal was in heat. I watched a beautiful buckskin stallion breed her numerous times. Her foal was a riot running all over the place like a fresh little kid.

Being able to watch horses in their natural state was fascinating. I was practically a horse myself after 45 years of living with them. Mine were domesticated, so their behavior was influenced by their closeness to humans. These were mustangs, whose behavior was pure, unadulterated horse. I took a ton of pictures, but mostly, I sat and watched. They really seemed indifferent to me and let me get closer than I would have ever thought. I never sensed any uneasiness in them.

The stallion was busy running all over keeping track of everyone. He kept his eye on me, but allowed me to approach him quite closely. None of them ever sent me any sign or feeling that I was intruding. I was content to just watch them interact.

A palomino colt about two years old started to watch me. He was fairly far away when I noticed him watching. He grazed his way closer and closer until he was right on top of me. I stayed still and began to talk with him, which really took him by surprise. We had a short exchange, after which he moved off towards a donkey licking a salt block.

Without warning, off in the distance I heard several horses calling. It felt mystical and magical. "There is magic all around. Stay Alert. Be Aware. Don't miss the hidden magic." Their calls and answers caused a stirring in my heart that I didn't understand. I became a little teary for some reason.

I was born with an undying love and respect for the horse. I've been taught by them, humbled by them, loved by them, brought to the heights of joy and the depths of sorrow by them, and healed by them. I credit the person I am to a life devoted to understanding, caring for, training, and loving horses. They've made me a better person for the lessons they've shared. Horse represents freedom and power to the American Indian. They have given me both the freedom and the power to be who I am meant to be.

As I watched these authentic horses, I sat in awe of the feeling of acceptance that they gave me. I felt a part of their herd. They moved around me nonchalantly. I was so touched. I credited my expertise with domestic horses and the ease which I felt around them with my success at being accepted by these wild mustangs. I knew they felt the love and respect I hold for their species.

It was incredible to feel a part of something so wild within Nature, not unlike my exchange with the pod of wild dolphins off Oahu. Once more, I felt a sense of balance and harmony within my soul. In that moment, I recognized that the mustangs' acceptance of me was a reflection of my complete acceptance of my soul and its creations. I was whole and complete.

I could have stayed with my new family for so much longer, but I wanted to find my motel before dark. I told the wrangler that I'd found at least 30-40 mustangs, and was in my glory just *being* with them. I thanked him and told him I'd be back when I could to ride with them. The thought of riding out and finding a couple hundred together was just too enticing. I wanted to sit, watch, and learn even more from the Wild Ones, so I would be back.

I found my motel very easily. After I showered, I reviewed my first alone day, which had been *perfect*. Not one thing went wrong. I felt a keen awareness for everything that surrounded me, both seen and unseen. I felt it was a bird's-eye view into what my future would be like. Everything just flowed.

I'd had a day spent in pure joy, which I hadn't had in forever. I felt this day was a reward created by my soul to say, "Congratulations for a job well done." I was exhausted mentally and physically from the adventures of the past 11 days, but exhilarated emotionally and spiritually by them as well. I felt happiness in my heart. I had survived. I was healed.

I woke the next morning ready to get back home and excited about my future. I called Jodi to tell her I was starting back. When I asked how Licorice was, she said the past two days he'd been acting really lively and barking at her. I smiled and told her I'd talked with him about starting my trip home.

Even after all these years of doing this, I still was amazed when I got unsolicited validation of its happening. You'd think I'd get used to it, but I don't.

LETTING GO

It's a wonderment every time. It's magic!

As I headed through security, the girl I was behind announced to the agent that she'd never flown before. I laughed, "Oh, great, and I'm flying with you." We sat together waiting to board. She was flying to Charlotte, too, and our seats were next to one another on the flight to San Francisco. Okay, whose idea was that?

I told her to stick with me and we'd make the connection just fine. We had to switch terminals in San Francisco and security was a little slower than in Redding. We got to the gate just as they began boarding. She was very grateful for my help in navigating the airport.

Since I know there are no coincidences, I spent some time reflecting on my chance meeting with this young gal. I felt a sense of satisfaction from helping her. Her inexperience was another example of contrast, which helped me acknowledge my own levels of expertise, not only in travel, but life itself.

I'd been getting hints about helping people as well as animals and I wasn't so convinced that was a good thing. My time assisting this girl changed that perspective. There it was again, my friend perspective which changes everything. I was grateful for everything up until two years ago when, on first appearance, my life imploded.

My inner journey of the past two years and the writing I'd been doing for the past nine months have taught me that my implosion was a necessary component of my spiritual growth. The old clichés – don't judge a book by its cover, beauty is only skin deep, etc. – all popped into my head.

When I heard those words, "I never wanted this house..." I thought my life was over and it was, at least my life as I'd known it. It ended in a heartbeat. For the past two years, I'd been looking at that moment as an end. Now, having emerged from my inner journey to awareness, and this outward spiritual journey I'd just completed, I look at that moment in my history as a beginning.

I liked the Who-I'd-Become. I was ready to get on with my life's purpose, to discover what my soul had in store for me, and to live a happy, joyful life. I was grateful for this glimpse into what helping people might feel like.

By the time I reached my motel in Charlotte, I was really tired. I applauded my decision to stay near the airport. I could never have driven the two hours home. I hoped I could get to sleep with the three-hour time change. Not to worry! I was asleep in a flash.

I had a quick breakfast and headed back to the mountains and Licorice. As I drove up the mountain, I couldn't help but contemplate the future I was heading towards. My resounding success in Lassen Park had me conjuring up all kinds of possibilities. I was feeling more positive and optimistic than I had in two years.

Licorice was so happy to see me. I was relieved that he'd handled my absence as well as he had. Jodi's presence in my life was a gift that appeared at my darkest time. I was so grateful that she'd been available to allow me to travel as much as I had: many trips back to Jersey, which were integral to my healing; my much needed trip to Maui where my healing began in Hana; and finally my phenomenal trip to Sedona and Mt. Shasta, where I emerged from my Cocoon and my Tunnel simultaneously.

All of these excursions were invaluable to my growth and return to sanity and Self. None of them would have been attainable without her willingness to care for my aging dogs and cats. When you least expect it, an angel appears. Jodi had been an angel for me in perfect timing!

Chapter 23

Free To Be

*M*y spirits were soaring as I arrived back in the mountains. I was almost as upbeat as when we left the farm headed to what I thought was our dream home on our spectacular mountain property. When I checked through my emails, there were more specifics about the litter in Virginia, which included four yellow males, two black females, and two black males.

Since there were three people ahead of me, I felt assured of getting my yellow male. Four was the perfect number. Isn't the Universe amazing? The sex of the black one didn't matter to me. I just wanted one of each color.

Kathy sent pictures almost every day, which really helped ease my impatience. I was so grateful that Licorice had stayed with me for so long, because I simply wouldn't have been able to cope with Shadow's loss without Licorice's companionship and teaching.

As anxious as I was for the new pups to arrive, I simply couldn't think about losing another dear soul from my life. Licorice seemed fine, but time would tell what he'd choose. I'd honor whatever decision he made.

The next morning the survey crew showed up, ending my four-month wait. Their arrival brought me back to reality. The generator still wasn't working properly six months post-installation. The progress I'd made in my learning and healing allowed me to accept these situations in a much less reactive manner.

The survey crew would have to come back because one of the corner markers was missing. I wanted this boundary issued resolved and the easement established before anyone changed his or her mind. I'd been waiting forever, so I could wait another week. What choice did I have?

Waiting seemed like a recurrent theme in my life of late. I wondered what lesson I'd been missing. Maybe the lesson is about control or the lack of control. What do we really have control over in this life?

From my recent trauma and drama, I'd learned that I only had control over myself, and at times I didn't even have that. I'd let my ego with its negative reactive emotions take control for a long time without even knowing it. I regained control of my life by focusing on the present moment, which disallowed any negativity from past or future to interfere.

My glorious day in Lassen Park was like my final exam. Residing in the Now allowed me to control all of my experiences. The present moment is the place of pure creation – a place unfiltered by fears of past or future or the negativity those fears elicit. I felt totally in control of my life, my Self, and my experiences that day.

My challenge was to bring that experience and those feelings back with me to be lived daily. My mission was to create a life in which those fantastic occurrences in Lassen became the norm. I was shown the pot of gold at the end of the rainbow that day and it was enticing. I couldn't wait to begin to live everyday from that perspective.

The log house was starting to feel like a home – a transitional home. I had to admit that I was feeling more comfortable living in the area with my good friends Sandie and Gregory. Their friendship contributed to my thought of remaining in the mountains once the Deltec sold.

I never realized the importance of people to me before my Ex's betrayal. I always considered myself an animal person that could live very easily without human contact. My need for people in my life was one of my first and most startling lessons.

Having been in Carolina for two years, I'd learned how truly difficult it is to meet people and establish new friendships. Based on my track record, I felt blessed to have Gregory and Sandie as friends, as well as the close proximity of our houses. Now I felt I had someone I could call in an emergency.

It's not something you even consider when you live with another person. I'd been blessed with a husband and parents on the same farm, so I was very rarely ever alone. I always knew I was fortunate, but not until recently did I realize how fortunate. Always the lessons.

I spent the first week back catching up with all my friends via phone and email and getting Stormy back into training, which was my favorite distraction from the woes of everyday life. The contrast between his resentfulness of last summer and his willingness of this summer was stunning. Since I knew he reflected my own willingness to listen to my soul's influence and control in my life, I was pleased for both of us. It was so gratifying to have such a cooperative partner. I knew my soul felt the same way.

Stormy's training was fun, which I hadn't had much of recently. I gave myself tons of credit for exerting patience and tolerance with him last summer, which was rewarding me with such a happy and willing partner this year. I was saying a silent thanks to my soul for doing nothing less with me. Apparently, my soul has more patience with people than I. Lucky me!

The surveyors came back and their preliminary map showed a very disturbing thing. The porch on the side of the house was actually in the setback from the property line between the two lots. Very powerful, expensive lessons were being confirmed: I would *never* purchase property without a survey and I would *never* take a builder or realtor's word about anything.

Instead of wallowing in the frustration of the news or launching into a reactive, fighting mentality, I simply acknowledged what was and set about trying to make the best out of a very bad situation. I had to eliminate all my judgment of the builder and the realtor and accept that it wasn't right or wrong, it just was. I'd begun to recognize and accept my soul's creations. If I hadn't been such a stubborn student, I wouldn't have had to be confronted with these problems. I had no one else to blame but myself.

My decision to spend my time in the present moment kept me from wasting energy on what might have been, what could have been, what should have been. The only thing that matters was what *is*. The only thing I had any influence over was what was happening right *now*. It was a hard lesson to learn, but I had some great teachers who didn't give up on me.

A week and a half after I got home, my dear friend Gary emailed that his mother, Selma, was on her deathbed. She'd been failing for months and her transition was close. He asked if there was anything I could do with my healing skills to assist her soul.

I did an SRT clearing for Selma that I'd done for numerous animals that we'd euthanized over the years. I had cleared Michelle's husband when I knew his transition was imminent. The clearing doesn't cause anyone to transition sooner; it simply facilitates their release from the physical body and eases the transition back to spirit.

I cleared Licorice again for his thunderstorm and fireworks fears and made more flower essences for him. Later that night we had thunderstorms, so his touch-up clearing work couldn't have been timelier. He got through the night quite well with several doses of essences.

The next day was gorgeous and I decided to give Stormy a break from the tedium of training with a walkabout around the farm. He was being so wonderful when a bird flew up in front of him. He spooked and flew sideways and I ended up on my butt in the grass. My biggest worry wasn't about myself, but would Stormy run off? He was free on a 33-acre farm and able to run wherever he wanted.

I wasn't angry since he'd simply had a natural behavioral response to the bird "attack." Horses are fright/flight creatures and their safety resides in their ability to run away. I walked towards him with very non-confrontational energy. I was telling him telepathically it was okay and not to worry. He just kept looking at me *asking*, "What are you doing down there?" It was pretty comical.

I mounted and finished our ride, so he didn't learn he could dump me and then go in. Both of us were completely relaxed as if nothing had happened. I certainly didn't want to fall, but I guess I needed to fall. The fall taught me that despite my advancing age, I still knew how to fall without getting hurt. It taught Stormy that he wouldn't get punished for doing something natural even though it resulted in my hitting the ground.

More thunderstorms were around that night, but Licorice coped well with a couple of doses of flower essences. Despite the fact that I'd been working with animal communication, the SRT modality, and vibrational remedies for 12 or more years, I was still amazed at the results. Licorice was a powerful teacher who was restoring my self-confidence in the work I was about to launch back into. I was sorry he had issues with thunder, but on another level I understood that it had a lot to do with helping me regain my self-respect and self-confidence and lose my self-doubt.

My friend Kit called me that night to tell me Gary's mother was still here and in and out of lucidity. At one point, she'd told her daughter Karen that she'd been in North Carolina. Karen didn't understand what her mother was talking about. Gary and Kit were stunned by the comment. No one was more bewildered than I.

My understanding of the SRT process is that my soul works with the person's soul, and we both work with elevated beings from another realm. Why she would sense North Carolina I had no idea. I knew there were no coincidences, so her comment was very significant to me. I thanked Kit for her call and pondered its meaning.

Kit called again early the next morning asking if I could clear Selma again. I could but I wasn't sure what else to clear. I'd never done this type of clearing twice. After my morning meditation, I decided to *ask* for some guidance. What I *heard* was, "Talk with her soul." Well, that stopped me in my spiritual tracks.

Talk with her soul? I've never talked with a person's soul. Obviously, I was capable of talking with animals, but people? Well, what did I have to lose? I had a wonderful chat with Selma. I won't go into the specifics, but it was profound for me. Selma showed me an ability I had no idea I possessed.

This startling revelation initiated a leap to an assumption that my capabilities in communication could perhaps be unlimited. Up until now, the limits had been created only by my lack of belief. Kit called to tell me that Selma had passed at 4 p.m. Gary's mother taught me a fantastic lesson about my talents, my future purpose, and myself. I was motivated to help her because of my love and friendship with Gary and Kit. I got back far more in value from the experience than any amount of money. Selma's lesson to me was, and always will be, priceless.

When the student is ready, the teacher appears. How many times had I heard this? Selma was another of those unexpected teachers for me. Our teachers are everywhere. We just have to be open to receiving their lessons. I wished I could've been in Jersey for Gary, but there was no way to do it. I knew he understood.

The listing on the mountain property was up shortly at the end of June. I knew my Ex wouldn't sign with Jack again, and I thought we needed fresh ideas, too. It was bad enough that my dream had been crushed two years ago, but then I'd been forced to handle all the issues with it. The dream was gone, yet the obligations remained. The continual responsibilities were like rubbing salt into a wound, which kept it raw and unable to heal.

I'd worked so hard trying to find the best realtor with such dismal results that I felt incompetent. The thought of starting the search for representation again was overwhelming. I was running on an empty tank, so to speak. I knew the importance of the job, but I just had no reserve left where realtors were concerned. It was uncharacteristic of me to procrastinate, but I just wasn't inspired to take any action.

Stormy's training was a pleasant balance to the frustrations of the two properties. He was really focusing and not letting outside distractions affect him, which was a definite sign of maturity.

One day his left fore tendon was swollen. I used some topical jelly to take the heat and swelling out. Of course, this meant no riding. It took three days for his leg to return to normal. I was continually amazed at my lack of reactive emotions when confronted with a possible health issue with Stormy.

My ability to calmly and correctly deal with the challenges that he presented showed that my confidence with horses had never been in doubt. My confidence in all other venues of life had been dragged through the mud. My soul's creations of issues with Stormy served to show me that I was that same capable, competent woman who'd left Jersey two years earlier. I just needed to acknowledge it.

I had a session scheduled with Gregory to review my trip experiences from Sedona and Mt. Shasta. My own intuitive knowing of having emerged from my cocoon in the Tunnel was confirmed. The chrysalis had matured into the butterfly and was ready to soar towards her future. She was *free*!

We discussed many of my experiences on the trip, most especially the day in Lassen Park, which had been so transforming. All of my experiences were reported to be valid experiences, not fabricated or imagined. They were the *real deal*. I'd known that in my heart, but the validation was reassuring. The day I don't need to be reassured is the day I am completely and unequivocally healed. For now, I still needed their assurance.

We discussed the arrival of the much-anticipated puppies. I was given some information that was in direct conflict with my own feelings regarding Licorice. I hadn't thought that Licorice would wait for the puppies to come, but I was told that he would. I was thrilled to hear this since it meant more time with this wonderful soul.

We focused on my successful navigation of the Abyss and the Tunnel, i.e., my dark night of the soul. All of that was behind me now. It seemed like I'd been traversing them for eons learning, growing, evolving, and emerging. In reality it was a mere two years. Everything is relative. Perspective, my old friend – I had new perspectives on so many things.

Having been informed of the amount of negativity I'd come into this lifetime to purge, it did seem inconceivable that I could accomplish such an enormous task in just two short years. I swelled with pride at the achievement of completing one of my soul's reasons for incarnating. I was ready to deal with anything that befell me.

My self-doubt was abolished, my self-confidence was restored, my self-esteem was soaring, but more importantly I was filled with self-respect, which reflected my big issue of respect. I could feel my soul deep within me smiling. I had arrived at that place of self-love that had been a long time in the making. It was 13 years since the first time I felt love for Self during one of Michael Road's guided meditations – 13 years and a myriad of lessons.

I enjoyed a morning walkabout with Stormy and Kim on a boarder's horse on the second anniversary of the infamous words that changed my life forever. Stormy was enabling me to let go of my frustrations. Things that had proved to be so challenging for him last summer just didn't bother him anymore.

Working through issues with youngsters, using patience and tolerance, reaps wonderful rewards. It was what I most treasured in starting young horses. The progress made through willing cooperation molded the partnership more deeply.

I'd survived the frustrations of the Stormy of last summer to be rewarded with a wonderfully agreeable Stormy right now. I laughed inwardly at the knowledge of my soul's pleasure working with the agreeable person that I'd become, always recognizing Stormy's attitude as a reflection of my own.

I was headed up to the mountain to spend a little time on my dream property on this auspicious day. I reflected back to how I felt a year ago on this day. There really was no comparison. I was a different woman then, one wounded, broken, and hurt. I'd given control to my ego and to my Ex, allowing them to dictate my emotional state.

Now, I felt quite empowered. I Am Woman – don't mess with me! I was a very different person from the one who almost fell to the floor two years ago when the world as I knew it came crashing to an end. As the ad says, "You've come a long way, baby," and it hadn't been an easy journey.

When I got home I found a very sad email from the U.S. sponsor for Michael Roads. I was stunned and in tears. Michael's dear wife, Treenie, had died suddenly on the first morning of their retreat, which I'd decided not to attend in order to go to Sedona and Mt. Shasta. My heart broke for Michael and his family. I had such mixed emotions over my choice to not join them.

First, I felt relieved that I wasn't present for such a sad event, but then I realized it meant that I'd never get to share any more time with Treenie in this lifetime. All I could focus on was *everything happens for a reason.* I knew my decision had given me incredible and necessary experiences to complete my healing. But more importantly, I knew that my soul understood that I just couldn't handle another loss.

Once again, listening to my heart had me in the most beneficial place for *my* growth and healing. I will forever miss Treenie's "My Say" columns in the newsletter that Carolyn organizes.

Being the highly advanced spiritual teacher that Michael is, I knew he'd deal with his loss better and faster than most. However, as I've stated before, loss is loss. It is devastating no matter what level of spiritual expertise you have. The person who was by your side for everything is no longer there, at least not in the physical sense. Been there, done that, and it isn't pleasant or easy.

At least for Michael's sake, he was with Treenie. I felt great sadness for their children who were so far away and unable to have that final good-bye. Obviously, there were lessons for everyone and I wished them well in learning them. I answered Carolyn right away. My response to Michael had to wait a little while since I needed some time to process the news. Michael's loss brought my loss two years earlier on this day into perspective. Any semblance of feeling sorry for my plight flew into never-neverland.

Since I was running out of time, I was finally motivated to leave a message for the prospective new realtor. I got an email informing me that my Ex was coming to the area. As much as I was uncomfortable knowing he was coming, his arrival would facilitate signing the new listing agreement.

I finally met with the prospective realtor, Kim, who I really liked. She gave me a very impressive run down of their marketing scheme. At the time, her partner was in negotiations with *The New York Times* about placing ads. We agreed to meet in two days at the property.

In the meantime, I did SRT clearings for several friends' and families' dogs with thunder issues and sent vibrational remedies for them. Licorice was having wonderful results. He only worried a bit and didn't tremble or salivate like before. I heard back from everyone that their dogs were much improved.

I'd gotten the message the Universe, my soul, or whoever was sending, "It's time to get back to your work." I understood, but wanted to bring my writing to a close before I resurrected my healing practice. My inability to devote the time and attention to it on the farm made me hesitant to start before I'd finished writing. I knew the time was approaching, but I had to feel ready in my heart.

It was the puppies' one-month birthday in Virginia. It was killing me not to be able to see them, which was another lesson in patience. I headed to the mountain to meet Kim to show her everything and sign the listing agreement. We spent almost three hours walking and talking about the property. I told her my Ex would be in town on Friday.

She loved the place, but then again who wouldn't? She was so enthusiastic. Her enthusiasm renewed my hopes of getting it sold soon. My hopes soared. Her partner had come to terms with *The New York Times*, so it would be advertised in the *Times*.

I almost couldn't believe what I'd just heard. My two-year-long struggle to get the mountain marketed in this newspaper was coming to an end. I was ecstatic! It took me four realtors to find one who would spend the money for the ad.

My lesson of focusing only on the present moment kept my ego from dragging me down a road of regrets for the past two wasted years of internet marketing. I wasn't going to let any choices from my Past, which I felt were the best choices at the time, negate the happiness I was feeling with the knowledge that I had persevered. I had succeeded. *Good things come to those who wait.*

I emailed my Ex with my impressions of the new realtor and her contact info. I was still doing whatever was necessary to make it easy for my Ex. I guess old habits die hard. It was another of those coincidences that he'd be in town on the exact day that the current listing was ending. I wanted to take full advantage of the synchronicity the Universe was providing.

I marveled at how a job too overwhelming to think about a few weeks earlier resolved itself with such positive results. I attributed the success to my heightened sense of connection to my ability to create, to my renewed self-esteem, and my diminishing self-doubt. I was finally getting out of my own way and allowing.

It was ironic that the mountain property was quite possibly the greatest example of my creative powers. I felt encouraged with my creation of this new realtor without great effort or struggle. I acknowledged that and gave myself credit for allowing the creation to progress. Finally, I was flowing again. It had been so long since I'd felt in the flow. I was filled with optimism for the sale of my beloved, but unrealized, dream property. Irony surrounded me.

The next morning, I headed to the barn. Stormy worked wonderfully with the farm workers digging in the creek that ran past the ring. Last year, I wouldn't have even tried to ride him with them working there. This year I gave it a try and was rewarded with a very satisfying experience. Stormy washed away all my frustrations. He was one of my grandest teachers and helpers.

I couldn't help but think about my Ex, his choice two years earlier, signing the new listing agreement, etc. His arrival in Carolina brought my focus right back to him. When he said he was only in town for an afternoon, I couldn't figure out why he bothered. There was a reason for sure, but I'd never know what it was.

I worked hard to let go of all the negative thoughts my ego was trying to get started again. I'd kept it at bay for longer and longer periods of time, but I *always* had to be wary of it. My time with Stormy was a very powerful deterrent.

Staying present in the Now, which was where Stormy required me to be, neutralized my ego. I was blessed with tremendous help all around me. I just needed to recognize and accept it. With Stormy it was very easy to do. He was, and is, one of my most powerful allies.

While waiting to hear the signing was done, I got a package from Linda in Hawaii. Well, I almost cried. It was a T-shirt with Black and Yellow Labs and the word *devotion* underneath them. Talk about irony – I was waiting to hear that the person I'd devoted more than half my life to had signed an agreement to sell what once was our dream retirement home. My sole support was none other than dear Licorice who had stayed with me since his brother's death almost five months earlier. Loyalty, devotion, and unconditional love had been their greatest gifts.

Linda's gift was a gentle reminder of her loyalty, devotion, and love, which offered me support from afar. Oh, the synchronicity of its arrival. You have to love it. I simply smiled inside and out. I loved it and Linda's continued presence in my life.

Kim called to report the agreement was signed. I let out a sigh of relief. She sent me a copy of the listing to review. I corrected a few things, but all in all it was the best one so far with the least corrections. I'd had more contact with her in the past couple of days than the three other realtors in two years. Of course, I had learned already realtors were very attentive in the beginning. Time would tell with Kim, but I was more optimistic since she was a woman. The mountain wouldn't be off the market for even a day.

The start of this listing marked the two-year anniversary of putting my dream up for sale. I remembered that horribly emotional day as if it were last week. Thanks to living in the moment, I wasn't confronted with the memory of it very often. I'd moved on. The fact that it wasn't relived didn't lessen the agony of the moment, which was rooted in my inability to let go of my dream. This listing I looked forward to with a deep hope that the mountain would finally find its new steward.

With the help of many friends, my own efforts, and time, I'd fully *let go* of this special spot although it was, and always would, remain dear to me. Its lessons were painful and powerful for me. It played an integral role in the dark night of my soul. I had released it in my heart and was anxious for it to attract its new people.

This wonderfully spiritual mountain's role in my "movie" was finished. My heart had accepted this fact; now, it was time for the property to accept it as well. In some respects this was the easiest change of realtors I'd accomplished. I embraced that as a good omen.

In among real estate issues, I kept in touch with Little Michelle. She loved what I'd written about Mike's funeral even though it elicited tears every time she read it, which was good, because she needed to let go of her grief and sadness.

She told me that her sons had read the chapter too, which I thought was great. She was surprised that Mikey had finished them, since he suffered from A.D.D. He'd read every word, which was more evidence of the significance of my writing for others.

The topper was a call from Michelle's older son, Cip, who wanted to speak with me about writing. I offered whatever help I could and told Michelle that it would be the best thing he could do to help him deal with his loss. If he could express his repressed emotions, he could start to heal. Time would tell if he followed through.

Writing has to come from your heart and on your own terms. It had proven a remarkable outlet for my own trauma and had facilitated tremendous healing. If my writing helped Cip find a way to begin to heal, there would be nothing more satisfying for me. Once more, I marveled at the power of my written words.

Michelle was having a hard time. It was so difficult to be supportive from 600 miles away, but just as she had done for me, I did the best I could. She was flying down in three weeks to visit and then we'd drive back to Jersey together. This gave us both something to look forward to, which was always a good thing.

It had been six months since Mike's death. I thought about where I was and how I'd felt six months after my own husband's sort of death. Our losses were different, yet very similar. We counted the days till Michelle's flight, maximizing the anticipation of her visit. We were two wounded friends who would've never thought we'd find ourselves divorced and widowed at our ages. Even though I'd been divorced for 17 months and she widowed for six, it was still surreal for both of us.

Now that I was out of my Cocoon and Tunnel I was anxious to find my home. I wanted to find *my* home. I've always been connected to where I lived except for the log house. I recognized that my disconnection from my Self and soul for the past two years was no doubt contributing to my lack of feeling for this acre. However, my recently renewed connection to Self hadn't changed my feelings. It was just not where I was meant to be.

I needed to find my home, but I couldn't buy until the mountain sold. My belief is the same as when I'd waited for years to move to the mountains. I have faith that the place I'm supposed to be won't be available until I'm ready. I just keep repeating it whenever I get frustrated and my patience is low. It worked in the past and it will work again. It seemed the more healing I achieved, the less patient I became.

The next morning, the Fourth of July, I had a great ride with Stormy. He was really starting to show the results of all his training. It was very gratifying. I was concerned about Licorice with possible fireworks later. It was last Fourth of July when he'd been frightened so badly and his thunder fears were triggered.

While I waited for the fireworks which never materialized, I noticed that the right side of Butch's head was swollen. I brought him in where the light was better. As I was examining it, an abscess burst open and spewed bloody, smelly pus everywhere. Good thing I'm not squeamish.

I put him over the sink and worked the area to get as much of the pus out as I could. I found two holes, which meant he had been bitten again. The entire time I was treating him, which had to be pretty uncomfortable, he just kept purring. I knew he needed oral antibiotics as well, so I called the vet office in the morning and got some.

Butchie and I had a chat about his fighting. I threatened him that his hospital allotment was all used up. He'd better stop fighting or else! The last time we had this same chat he was good for about eight months. Since I knew *everything happens for a reason*, I tried to figure out why Butch was having all of these health issues.

He'd had a few problems back on the farm, but nothing like this. He was thin, looking old, and doing things he normally didn't do. I knew something was up, but I just wasn't sure what. I couldn't send him back to spirit unless I was sure it was what he wanted and he wasn't telling me anything definite. I just kept flushing his wound twice a day, applying the topical antibiotics, and dosing him with the orals.

The power went out in the middle of a rainstorm while I was on the phone with Michelle. There wasn't any thunder or lightening, so the outage was really unexpected. Well, I'd finally get to use this very expensive generator. I heard

271

the generator start and smiled to myself feeling clever for having purchased the generator.

About two minutes later the generator quit, which shouldn't happen unless the main power had come back on. Nothing in the house turned on. Of course, my cordless phones were useless, so I had to run upstairs in the total darkness to answer Michelle's call back. She just couldn't believe it. We talked a bit longer, and then I told her I'd better make some calls.

I felt anger swelling from deep inside me. I got my flashlight and the oil lamps that my brother convinced me to get. So there I sat with my $5 oil lamp, infuriated that my $6000-plus generator worked for only two minutes. Licorice was a little unnerved, but I reassured him and he lay back down. Luckily, it was one of our cooler nights, so Licorice wouldn't be stressed by the heat.

I called Travis, but got no response. I sat in the dark trying to control the seething anger that was building within me. I couldn't believe that I'd spent all this money seven months ago and now sat in the dark. This was the first time I'd needed it and it failed me. I struggled with my beliefs of *everything happens for a reason, always in perfection*, etc. What lesson my soul had created with this experience totally eluded me.

Just sitting with Licorice in the dark, I could feel myself losing control. I decided to call the power company to report my outage. This event was challenging all of my recent progress.

The phone rang and I stumbled up to answer it, hoping it was Travis. Alas, it was the power company asking if my power had returned. No. They were sending a repairman since everyone else had power. I called Travis again and left more messages, not nearly as pleasant as my first ones.

The fact that everyone had power meant the generator was probably preventing mine from returning. I didn't know how they worked, but there ought to be a bypass. But then, what did I know? I only knew how to spend thousands of dollars for peace of mind and instead created more aggravation and stress for myself.

The repairman arrived and told me the outage had only lasted about 45 minutes. Thanks; I didn't need to know that since mine was approaching two and a half hours. He said the generator smelled like something had burned. Great; I'm lucky the house didn't catch on fire.

He'd installed generators, knew where the bypass switch was, and asked my permission to use it just in case something broke. I said, "It's already broken. Please go ahead." Once he did that, the power came on. I felt such a surge of relief and gratefulness that the power company solved my problem, even though it wasn't their fault.

As the repairman left, Travis called with apologies. I used all of my pent up anger to tell Travis to replace this generator with a completely different one. It hadn't worked properly since the day it arrived. I wanted it off my property immediately! He'd call me as soon as he'd spoken with the manufacturer.

I was completely drained from the experience, but gave myself credit for working through a very difficult experience as well as I had. I was thankful that the refrigerator was working. I recognized that this creation of my soul could have been worse. It was a cool night, so I didn't have to fret that Licorice would expire from the heat. The new screens let air in the house. The house hadn't caught on fire.

I remembered when I'd been paralyzed with fear and panic over being alone in the dark during shorter outages the first year. I hadn't experienced any of those emotions with this much longer siege. While I had gotten reactive, it wasn't intense enough to prevent me from responding and coping with the circumstances. I gave myself credit for acknowledging my progress, for allowing my emotions to be felt, and then for letting go of them. Licorice and I were ready for a good night's sleep.

I spent the next day writing to keep my mind off the aggravation of the failed generator. My curiosity about which two puppies would be coming home with me was getting to me. I asked Kathy if the three people ahead of me had picked theirs yet. Her answer baffled me, since now there were five people ahead of me. How'd that happen?

My ego took off, flooding me with fears that I wouldn't be able to get one of each color. She guessed she'd forgotten to count herself. Well, that was one person not two. She wouldn't make her pick until the pups were eight weeks old. All she knew was if the two females had good conformation they were spoken for. I'd be happy with brothers.

My friends were concerned. Each time I spoke with them, I reassured them that I had intended from the start to get one of each color, so that's what I'd created. In my heart, I felt very strongly that my soul created one of each color for me. I still had weeks to go before I would be able to know for sure. I truly believed that we'd find each other as always in perfection.

From the photos Kathy was sending, I was getting attracted to the yellow male in the green collar. I already knew that the two black females were spoken for, which left two males. My concern was that there wouldn't be a black pup available.

My strong feeling about the return of my dearest soul friend, Ben/Rainbow/Randy, included the belief that he would be in a yellow body, which was more intuition. My friends didn't have the same faith that I did about the situation. I just kept telling them the right pup would find the right person, which in my case were two pups.

Kathy gave me a tiny concern when she mentioned she'd never sold two puppies to one person before. It was just something she never did. She knew I had raised two great puppies before so she'd leave it up to me. I didn't understand her reasoning, but I wanted two. Everyone needs a friend.

Travis called and the company would replace the generator. I told him I wanted it done before I headed to Jersey in a few weeks. I didn't want Jodi to be left caring for my animals without the security of a functional generator. He said that should be no problem. I thought to myself: I've heard that before.

The next day was the five-month anniversary of Shadow's death. I was so thankful to still have his brother with me. Since his transition I'd spent my time training my wonderfully willing horse or writing. Both projects benefited me greatly. I'd been riding for 47 years, so the satisfaction I felt from my time in the saddle approached joy. Stormy's attitude made our time together downright fun. He filled me with a sense of purpose and fulfillment.

I'd been writing for ten months in comparison to those 47 years, but it had proven to be equally as important to my sense of well-being. My writing had brought me back from the depths of despair and returned the strong sense of Self that I used to have. Through it, I'd learned more about myself than I'd ever known before.

Without my riding and my writing I simply couldn't have dealt with all of the frustrations that continued to surround me, especially the fact that the mountain property was still without an acceptable offer. Trying to live in the Now, I didn't focus on the property that often.

The inability to find the mountain's next caretaker would've given my ego fuel to take back its control, but my renewed sense of Self wasn't going to allow that to happen. I still marveled that a place I'd expected to give me more freedom than the farm allowed had turned into an anchor that prevented me from moving on with my life. I felt trapped by my unrealized dream.

Chapter 24

The Swinging Pendulum

I'd been tree trimming on the gravel road since I was tired of my car being hit by branches, which meant Licorice had to stay alone. Licorice was more stressed than usual when I got back from the barn and trimming. He was having a harder time getting up, too. I tried not to leave him too long, because I was very worried about him. When I was home he didn't want me out of his sight. I wasn't quite sure what was going on, but he was different – and different with animals is always worrisome.

I'd planned an evening with Gregory's friends who did aura work. I'd always been intrigued with auras and wondered what mine looked like. I hated to leave Licorice, but I wanted to take advantage of these people's expertise. I was trying to practice my put-self-first lesson, which was always difficult for me. I gave in to my lesson and was rewarded with an interesting evening. When I got back I was horrified that Licorice was caught under one of the glass top tables. I didn't know how long he'd been trapped. I felt so guilty for having made the choice I had.

I had an appointment for an aura photo and reading the next afternoon. I brought Licorice and kept the car's air conditioner on. The photo was phenomenal as well as the explanation of it. The colors around me were amazing and their significance even more remarkable. I joked that if they'd come last year my aura probably would've been black. The timing of this photograph, after my two-year healing journey and my experiences in Sedona and Mt. Shasta, was nothing less than perfect. Happily, Licorice was content in the car.

The next day I was ordained into the Universal Brotherhood Movement by Sandie, Gregory, and George, who'd done the aura work. We performed the ceremony on the deck of the Deltec gazing at the million dollar view. There wasn't a more fitting spot to express my commitment to my future healing work. The mountain had been the catalyst behind the tremendous journey of trauma, learning, growth, and eventual healing that I'd recently emerged from.

Being ordained was a public dedication to the healing work that I'd failed to make a priority in my earlier life. I had no idea where my path would lead, but I was determined to follow it in joy and happiness. My heart knows where to take me. I'd let go of all the obstacles that had been placed in my path. I was prepared and anxious to follow my heart to my new life.

It was fitting that Gregory and Sandie perform the ceremony, because without them I wouldn't have been ready to make such a commitment. The lessons I'd been shown through Gregory's sessions, the experiences we shared on our trip together, but more importantly the friendship they had given me since we'd met were all major factors in my emergence from the Abyss, Cocoon, and Tunnel. I was blessed to have them in my life.

My greatest blessing was dear Licorice, who'd been with me for every minute of my two-year struggle from the depths of my trauma. He lay inside while outside Mother Nature provided a glorious day for this momentous occasion. After the ceremony we walked around and I shared my used-to-be dream with everyone. Licorice was happy on the mountain and usually seemed five years younger there, but not that day.

The puppies still weren't due home for a couple of weeks, which started me thinking that my intuitive thoughts about Licorice not waiting for them were coming true. My heart, which had been soaring with glee only a few hours earlier on the mountain, was heavy with the thought of another possible good-bye. Michelle would be arriving this week and I couldn't wait to see her.

My car needed rear brakes before the long drive to Jersey, so I had an appointment in the morning. I had no other option but to leave Licorice home alone. I *explained* to him where I was going and hoped that would quell some of his distress.

I kept asking the dealership how much longer. The service manager kept telling me the car would be ready soon. Sitting there, knowing how much

Licorice didn't want to be alone and how stressed he'd been lately, had me in an emotional turmoil. The more I stressed, the slower the time passed.

Two and a half hours later the car was done and I flew back to hear Licorice barking. His voice sounded hoarse and filled with anguish. I *felt* his pain. I rushed inside to find him caught under the chair next to the door. The seat was covered with spots of saliva, which told me he'd been like that for a long time. He was distraught but so happy to see me.

My heart broke with the meaning of his plea. I *knew* what he wanted. I was filled with guilt even though I'd done nothing wrong. I sat with Licorice and told him I understood what he wanted. I would let go, so he could go Home to find Shadow. I left a message at the vet's but knew I'd have to wait an hour for a response.

The tears just poured out of me. My heart knew it was Licorice's wish, but it also broke with the pain of another good-bye. It didn't matter how much healing I'd done and how much stronger I was, I was consumed with sadness, grief, and pain all over again.

From my years of communication consultations with animals about to transition, I knew they were happy, looked forward to the return to spirit, and considered it the beginning of a new cycle. Only we humans look at it as an end. I didn't want to cause Licorice anymore stress than he'd suffered through that morning.

I vowed to make our remaining hours together the best I could. I owed him nothing less. He'd been by my side for almost 15 years. Along with his brother, he supported me through the most horrific events of the past two-plus years. His devotion had been unwavering.

I remembered back to the night in the camper when my then-husband noted that Licorice never took his eyes off me. While Licorice had seemed more bonded to my husband, I knew he loved me as well. To my husband's surprised comment I responded, "We're buds." I think Licorice knew that I needed him more than Bob did and he was right.

Without Licorice and Shadow, I wouldn't have made it. Licorice knew that I was healed enough to survive his departure. It was as though my ordination signaled that he could leave now. He also knew from our discussion that I'd have new helpers soon.

Sometimes I hate having such accurate intuition. I just *knew* he wasn't going to wait for the puppies, which was his parting lesson: "Believe what's in your own heart regardless of where conflicting information comes from. You know best."

The vet office called with a time of 4:45 p.m., which gave us two and a half hours. Licorice seemed much better, which I knew was only because he understood that his waiting time was almost over. A few times I had brief thoughts that maybe he wasn't ready to leave, but knew from my years of consultations that once an animal knows that its wish to go Home has been realized, they become very upbeat, appear younger, and almost normal. I always warned clients not to misinterpret their friend's behavior. I spent the afternoon telling myself the same thing over and over.

The phone rang again and I thought it was a wrong number since the man was asking for Randy. When I said wrong number I heard, "Nancy," and recognized my brother's voice. He hit the wrong speed dial. I told him what I was waiting to do and my tears started. He said, "Guess what I did two days ago?" He'd put his old dog, CD, down. Now, we both were crying.

We all know there was no coincidence in his misdialed call. The synchronicity of the Universe was working overtime for me. Our family was dwindling. When I told him the puppies would be coming home in two weeks, he said he was taking a break from a dog for a little while. I told him about Michelle's visit, so I wouldn't be alone too long.

I devoted the rest of the time to Licorice. I struggled with my emotions as I remembered our years together. They were mostly happy times. We'd been blessed. He'd been the greatest teacher. I only hoped that I'd taught him what he'd come to me to learn. As we headed to our destiny, I used every ounce of self-control that I could muster.

I sat on the floor with Licorice's gray head in my lap stroking him and crying. I tried but failed to keep my tears in check. It was impossible. Licorice was so sedate so quickly that I felt his chest several times to see if he was still breathing. I thought maybe he left with just the sedative. His reaction to it was a stark contrast to Shadow's. I prayed that he wouldn't wail like his brother had. I could still hear that sound and always would.

The vet returned and injected the solution. His spirit was on its way Home before very much of it had been given. It was the easiest transition I'd ever seen, which was Licorice's final gift to me. He was so ready to go Home. I tried to feel his exuberance and exhilaration as he left his body, but my grief blocked my connection once again. I was relieved it was over, but consumed with sadness that I'd lost yet another of my family.

The deed was done, my promise kept, the last greatest gift given, and my heart broken one more time. The fact that I'd been anticipating his departure did nothing to lessen the pain of it. Now, they were both gone. I returned to the house and felt totally alone. The silent house felt dead, and that intensified my sorrow.

The stillness of the house was unsettling in my fragile emotional state. I just couldn't stop crying. Licorice's passing marked the end of a time in my life that had been rewarding and filled with purpose. I felt *so alone*!

As soon as I regained control, I sent an email to all my friends. I received calls and emails in return as each read my sad news. Everyone knew how devastating this loss was for me. I tried to focus on Michelle's arrival in a couple of days, which seemed like an eternity from now.

I was happy for Licorice that his spirit had left his aging body behind. I was grateful for the time he'd given me since Shadow had left, which was almost five and a half months. It was time I needed to recover from Shadow's death, complete my healing journey, and emerge from the dark night of my soul. His willingness to stay to allow me to achieve these things was a priceless gift.

I honored his choice to leave as best I could. I listened when he asked to go, I accepted it, and I *let go*. The fact that I was a stronger person, out of my Tunnel, and nearly healed didn't diminish the pain I experienced. As I lay in bed trying to get to sleep, all I could hear was *nothing*. It was excruciating.

I used to hear breathing next to me – now, nothing. I used to hear Shadow and then Licorice repositioning themselves in their beds right next to me – now, nothing. For more than two years, I had to clean up Licorice's poop accidents – now, nothing. For the last year, I'd had to let Shadow out to tinkle multiple times through the night – now, nothing. I would give anything to have to wake up to take care of those chores again – *anything*!

I woke the next morning exhausted. I wasn't sure how long I'd slept, but it hadn't been long enough. The silence was deafening. I headed directly to the barn to my four-legged angel who'd gotten me through so much pain these past two years. I needed him to force me into the moment and out of my pain. He did his job and did it beautifully. As long as I worked with him, I forgot my grief.

I dreaded heading back to the dead house, but it needed cleaning before Michelle's arrival. I talked with friends as they called to offer support. Gregory actually stopped over to pick up some wood I had for him. His visit brought the sound of breathing back into the house. I figured Gregory's decision to come for the wood wasn't a coincidence. I was so thankful to have him and Sandie in my life.

I found it intriguing how affected I was by silence. I used to look forward to quiet times. Pure silence was different from quiet, which was a lesson I was learning big time. I got through the evening on the phone with Pam and my in-laws, who were always available when I needed them.

LETTING GO

The next day Sandie and I met for lunch after I finished at the barn. Stormy had been so wonderful these past two days. I knew he could sense the sadness in my heart. Animals are so much more sensitive to our emotions than we are to theirs. My time on his back was starting to heal the hole in my heart left by my dear Licorice.

I was so appreciative of Sandie's compassion, friendship, and support. When I returned to the silence, I kept myself focused on Michelle's arrival the next morning. I kept reiterating to myself the advantages of Licorice's decision to leave. I knew it was positive for him. I was trying to make it positive for me, but I wasn't succeeding.

Mother Nature sent me a messenger that night in the form of *the* worst thunderstorm since moving to Carolina. For an hour-and-a-half I was subjected to continual loud thunder and lightning. This message was similar to the deepest snow storm of the winter just after Shadow's death. I lay there listening to the fury of the thunder thinking Licorice would've been terrified despite all his improvement with thunder issues. This storm had *me* trembling and salivating.

Finally, with all my heart I accepted the positive act that Licorice's passing was. I gave thanks for events always being in perfect timing. I gave thanks to Mother Nature for helping me to finally accept his choice and *let go* completely, which I hadn't until the storm's lesson was taught. Once more, Mother Nature came to my rescue. I slept well and awoke with a lighter heart.

I survived the two and a half days alone in the log house. I understood that my soul, who creates my experiences, and Licorice, knew I couldn't exist longer than that. I marveled at the universal perfection of the timing of my creations: a concert in Jersey scheduled months earlier dictated the timing of my trip to New Jersey, my desire to help Michelle deal with her tragic loss, which brought Michelle to Carolina so close to Licorice's departure, and the timing of the birth of the puppies allowing them to come home on my return from Jersey. The puppies' arrival home would mark two weeks from Licorice's transition.

The most significant timing was that Licorice's ashes would be back before we left, so I could spread both dogs' ashes in the big paddock where we used to play Frisbee every late afternoon. They had worked that farm by my side for most of their lives, so it was where they belonged. Shadow's ashes had been waiting on the fireplace for more than five months. They needed to go to the farm together and it was time.

As I reviewed all of these creations of perfection, I felt a tremendous amount of gratitude to my soul. My grief over the loss of Licorice was being balanced by the wonderfully positive events that I looked forward to: time with Michelle in North Carolina, meeting and picking out my new pups, returning Shadow and Licorice to their true home, seeing my dear friends in Jersey, taking in a concert, and returning with my new family.

While it looked like the pendulum was weighted more toward the positive, it wasn't, for the depth of my pain of losing Shadow and Licorice needed all of these positive circumstances to bring the pendulum back to the center point – the point of balance and harmony.

I was flooded with wonderment at these creations as I anticipated my drive to pick up one of my forever friends, my fellow wounded gal pal, my kindred spirit. The silence would disappear. My soul and Licorice had been very wise, because I wouldn't have lasted another day.

My cell phone rang just as I was getting to the airport. Michelle was waiting for me. We hugged each other trying to absorb one another's pain and sadness. Since we didn't have another passenger – one who couldn't handle the heat of Charlotte – we had total freedom to do whatever and go wherever. There were a few things I wanted to get that I couldn't find in the mountains. By the time we got to the mountains, it was time for ice cream at Kilwins. I'd told Michelle about Kilwins many times. Now, I was able to share it with her.

We didn't get back to the log house until 9 p.m. I'd done more on this first day of Michelle's visit than in the two years since I'd left New Jersey. I knew one thing for sure, I hadn't been this happy since I'd left. We talked until midnight. We had a session with Gregory in the morning, so we said good-night.

I was anxious to see who would come through Gregory for Michelle's introduction to trance channeling. I smiled when I recognized the booming laugh that heralded Archangel Michael. I thought to myself, "Wonderful, humor will break whatever apprehension Michelle might be having." He spent some time explaining a bit about the process for Michelle.

He then launched into a 20-minute dissertation on the personalities of the two puppies that were soon to join my family. He didn't say which character traits went with which puppy. I didn't bother to ask about the two colors or not, because I *knew* I'd created black and yellow. He confirmed my intuitive feeling that Ben was returning. Of course, he didn't tell me which puppy's body he was in; that was for me to recognize. I knew I'd have no trouble with that. We had a love bond that stretched across eternity.

A second Being arrived. She was an Angel named Cassandra who I hadn't worked with before. Her energy was in total contrast to Michael's. She was very gentle, quiet, and feminine. Her appearance had been created to help Michelle feel the difference between the two Beings. Cassandra shared with us some information about other lives that Michelle and I had spent together. We were old friends. None of this was really news to me. She took us on a guided mediation back to a time we'd spent together. I was very connected to the place and our experience there. It was magical!

I wondered how Michelle was doing with her first experience with such an exercise. I'd been on many journeys through the years so this was old-hat for me. I knew that my colleagues wouldn't do anything that Michelle wasn't ready to do. *When the student is ready, the teacher(s) appear.* We shared a mystical meditation, which I'll never forget. I knew Michelle wouldn't either.

I hoped our session had opened Michelle's awareness to a much larger picture of our selves and our souls. Our existence in the physical world is miniscule compared to the multi-dimensional Beings that we truly are. I created a peek into a new reality for Michelle that is an awareness of higher and more positive energy, which is a more healing frequency.

After our session, we followed Gregory's directions to a local waterfall on our way to see Stormy. Michelle had known Stormy as a baby. She was shocked at his size even though I'd sent her pictures. Michelle was blown away by the farm.

During lunch, I got a call that Licorice's ashes were back, which brought me back to reality. We'd been having such a great time that I hadn't had time to feel sad. We retrieved his ashes and placed them next to his brother's. I'd always been able to bury my animals, so this was another first. I'd been having too many firsts lately.

Gregory and Sandie came for dinner. I wanted Michelle to get to know the two friends I'd made. I hoped it'd make her feel better about my living here. I was so pleased to have three of the people who'd contributed so much to my recovery together. The house was anything but dead or silent.

I couldn't help looking over at my two departed friends in their boxes. My one consolation was that they were together again, and I firmly believed that. Michelle and I played show-and-tell until past midnight again. We were like two little kids on a sleep-over.

The next day, we headed to the mountain property. Michelle had been privy to everything about the house and property for the last five years. I was glad she could spend time on it to see just how special it was. Pictures don't do it justice; you have to walk around on the property to truly appreciate its amazing energy.

I took advantage of Michelle's help to move a small desk/dresser, which had been my parents'. I didn't need it or really have room for it, but I wanted it. My days of having help around were long gone.

After we had a little lunch, I took her to Mt. Jefferson State Park. The 360-degree views from the top are quite spectacular. The weather was cooperating, and I wanted to share the mountain beauty with my forever friend. We hiked an easy loop trail around the ridgeline. The more we walked and shared in the magnificence of Nature, the more I let go of the sadness about Licorice.

Once again I was amused that something I thought I was doing for another benefited me as well. I was reminded of the Universal Law of Attraction – like attracts like, what you send out comes back to you. This was a perfect example.

We sat on an area that I'd been sent to by Gregory a year ago. It was an area of immense healing energy that I wanted Michelle to be bathed in. It was Mike's birthday and Michelle's first without him. Oh, those dastardly firsts. I'd been through numerous ones in the past two years and they were agonizing. I thought it might be easier to get through in Carolina. I wanted the mountains to work their magic on her the way they had for me in my darkest of times. We ended back at the log house without retracing any of our steps.

We hauled my folks' little piece of furniture up to the guest room, laughing hysterically the entire time. Michelle was teasing me and moaning about moving furniture. I don't think either of us had laughed like that in a very long time. It was cleansing. We were having pure, unadulterated fun while healing our wounds together.

Our evening at the concert with Arlo Guthrie and his family was next on our agenda. Neither of us was sure what to expect, but we'd both loved, "Alice's Restaurant," Arlo's biggest hit. I thought it would be a nice way to end Mike's birthday. Well, we had a blast. Arlo, his son, daughter, and son-in-law sang for three hours. It was great to hear so many familiar old songs, which took us back to happier times in our lives.

Arlo had wonderful stories about the circumstances surrounding each song. His sense of humor, which is so evident in "Alice's Restaurant" hadn't diminished with age. They also played songs from the archives of Arlo's father, Woody. It was folk music at its best.

The auditorium was packed and everyone sang along. It was a perfect antidote for my grief. The music just melted it away. By the time we left the university, I was singing away remembering my life back when Arlo was at his peak. Little did I know when I asked Michelle if she wanted to go, how important the concert would be to my own sense of well-being and happiness.

LETTING GO

I was glad to have shared Mike's first birthday after his transition with Michelle. We stayed busy and in the moment, which allowed the sadness surrounding the day to be tempered by our positive activities. I knew the healing energy of our hike and the wonderful music contributed enormously to help Michelle navigate one of her most difficult firsts. Oh, these coincidences. Our souls were on a creating roll.

It was hard to believe, but we only had one day left so we headed toward Grandfather Mountain – the jewel that had lured me to the area. Michelle was snapping pictures right and left. I smiled because I still do that although I've been on the mountain many times. It's just that kind of beautiful. Each time the view is different depending on the clarity of the air. When you look out from the top of Grandfather there is no doubt how the Blue Ridge Mountains got their name. I was pleased to see how much Michelle was enjoying him.

The animal habitats are almost as rewarding as the views from Grandfather. They house bear, bald and golden eagles, deer, river otters, and the ultimate: mountain lions. I hoped I could find a cougar for Michelle to see. Mountain Lion Woman wanted to share her namesake with her friend. They are solitary and elusive creatures, not unlike me.

When we arrived at their enclosure, I searched all the spots I'd found them hiding in before. My attention was fully on finding the cougars. The people were insignificant to me. All of a sudden, the people came into my awareness and I realized why there were so many people there. I just laughed at myself, the animal communicator, when I found the cougars lying in full view below us. Michelle just gave me a look of disbelief and said, "I don't believe it." We'd been truly blessed.

We traveled back along the Blue Ridge Parkway to Moses Cone Park, which has a craft store in the original Cone Mansion. I wanted Michelle to see some of the beautiful crafts sold there. We purchased a few mementoes and continued on to Kilwins.

After our treat, we found a card store that had the funniest cards we'd ever seen. The two of us were hysterical reading them. Our laughter really was cathartic. Anyone who saw us would have never known the pain and trauma we were recovering from. Humor is powerful medicine.

I found a magnet that said, "Just when the caterpillar thought the world was over, it turned into a butterfly." Well, how could I leave that in the store? It illustrated exactly what I'd just experienced – my journey of healing, growth, and transformation. It resides on my fridge to remind of my accomplishment. I was thrilled that our time in North Carolina had kept Michelle in the Now and allowed her to laugh again. My mission had been accomplished. We headed back to the log house to pack and call Kathy to confirm our plans for the next day.

This was our first phone conversation regarding the pups. I hoped the people ahead of me had made their choices by now. They had and there was a black pup left – the red collared one. My heart smiled with her words. My faith hadn't let me down nor had my soul. I'd be getting what I wanted – black and yellow males. I had manifested my intention. I took this as a good omen for my future.

I then heard that the green collared one was available. "He's going to be a hellion," Kathy said. He sounded like he matched Archangel Michael's description. I told her I wouldn't really know until I felt his energy and met his soul, but I was attracted to him from her photos. I simply couldn't wait until tomorrow. I had repressed my enthusiasm about the puppies as a method of keeping myself from going crazy with the length of time I had to wait. Now, I unleashed it.

I had to admit that a few times I asked myself if I really wanted to be obligated to two more souls. The freedom Michelle and I had experienced over these past four days was something I hadn't felt since college. I'd been *the responsible one* for the dogs and horses for 30-plus years. I didn't entertain those thoughts for very long. The memory of the dead house washed away any hesitation I might have felt.

I knew I couldn't live without dogs in my life. It was my reality and my Truth. These were new puppies coming to join my new life. My put-self-first lesson would help balance my needs with theirs. I knew we had important things to teach one another.

After we finished packing, we talked for a long while. While I was ecstatic about meeting and picking out my new family, I wanted Michelle to be with me longer. We both needed the joy we'd experienced together. It had been very healing. We were immersed in the Now, preventing any of our painful past to interfere with our experiences.

We'd created a powerful four days for ourselves and went to bed satisfied that we'd made the most of our time. I think Michelle was as anxious as I was to meet the pups. I was thrilled to have her with me to pick them out. We were making a happy forever memory together, which are the only kind to create.

Chapter 25

Joys and Sorrows

*T*here was a buzz of anticipation in the house as we prepared to leave for Kathy's. When I checked my email I found a proof of *The New York Times* ad. Kim wanted my feedback. I thought it was great. I loved the view picture she'd chosen. I told her I'd be reachable on my cell for the next week.

While we drove, I had all sorts of thoughts flying around regarding the puppies. I'd given myself permission to focus on them now that my wait was almost over. In a few hours I could answer everyone's questions of which two. The color question had already been put to rest.

We found Kathy's and followed a long drive back to her house. Kathy ushered us to the whelping area where the puppies awaited. My eyes were wide with expectation. I'd been waiting for this moment for what seemed like an eternity.

All eight were leaning against the board that held them in. If I'd had my camera I could have gotten a treasure, but I didn't. I was focused on meeting puppies, feeling energies, recognizing old friends, etc.

We carried them all outside and let them loose. Each one was cuter than the next. They were in perpetual motion. The black pup was decided for me, so I just picked him up as he went running by and got my first black kiss.

Next, I focused on the yellow pups that were available, mostly the green collared one who was zooming all over the place. Every time he whizzed by, I tried to stop him to see if I recognized an old friend. He was totally focused on anything and everything but me. He was cute, but he just didn't connect with me or me with him. Interesting!

All of a sudden, I noticed one of the yellow pups sitting still staring at me, which was unique since no one was still. When our eyes locked, my heart melted. I'd found my old friend Ben/Rainbow/Randy. The smile spread across my face, into my heart, and to every cell of my being. There was no doubt. He'd found me again just like he did when he reincarnated into a cat's body at a client's farm. He sat by me now in the identical way he sat by me then. He wore a black collar and had a cowlick the length of his nose.

When I showed Michelle my pup she asked, "Did you see his nose?" I laughed. Her two-year-old Yellow Lab was the first dog I'd ever seen with a cowlick on its muzzle. I knew she was getting blown away by the coincidences the Universe was throwing at her this week. This one was the coolest so far.

Kathy was by the above-ground pool that she'd been letting the pups swim in. I said, "It's the black collared one." She smiled and said, "You're right!" I was in puppy heaven. We played with them for a while, but I didn't want to monopolize Kathy's afternoon and we still had several more hours to drive. Michelle took pictures of me holding my two new children. My smile was back and had reappeared within moments of meeting them. I hated to put them down, but we had to get going.

As we drove out, I pondered another private coincidence, which hadn't been lost on me. My new brothers wore red and black – the exact colors their predecessors had worn. I hadn't needed physical clues, because I recognized my old friend as soon as I looked into those eyes and *saw* his soul. I thought about the cherished ashes that I was bringing to the farm and the circle of life.

Our route took us right past a beautiful spot where Bob and I had met Kathy for lunch once. I wanted to show Michelle the Lodge at Peaks of Otter, which sits on the shoreline of a gorgeous lake. I was still reeling with the joy of picking out my new puppies, relieved that I'd found the souls who'd chosen me, and pleased that they were two colors. My jeans were covered with dirt from the puppies' feet, but I didn't care. I'd been waiting so long to lose myself in their joyful exhilaration.

Michelle found a few gifts for friends in their shops, but I didn't see anything that I needed. What I *needed* was back at Kathy's. I thought I was going to get out without a purchase when I spied a ceramic wind chime with trees and a buck deer on it. Its message convinced me that it had to come with me. "There is always music amongst the trees, but we must have a very quiet heart to hear it."

Well, I almost started to cry when I showed it to Michelle, since Mike had been a deer hunter. Not only were the words very meaningful to me, a woman who lived surrounded by trees, but it would remind me of this special time with Michelle, picking out my puppies. It hangs it in my bedroom near my dream catcher. I see it first thing in the morning and last thing before sleep.

And, just to keep Michelle scratching her head in awe, a doe deer wandered by as we drove out of the parking lot. She snapped a couple of photos of her on the fringe of the woods. It was as if she waited for us to get our pictures and then disappeared. I reminded Michelle of the message that comes to me whenever I see deer, "Be gentle with yourself."

As I drove, I called to leave a message for Gloria about which puppies were mine. I was so surprised and happy when she answered. I explained which my old friend was and immediately she asked, "Who's the other one?" I didn't know yet and was too tired to find out tonight. I'd ask in the morning and leave her a message.

Our trip to the motel was uneventful. We settled in and just collapsed. It had been a whirlwind five days. My emotions over Licorice's loss had finally caught up with me, but Gloria's curiosity was infectious. I couldn't wait till morning to find out who the black pup was. I quieted my mind and asked if I knew the soul in the black body? I heard, "You are old friends. You have been in many, many lifetimes together, but not yet in this one." Okay. That fit with my lack of familiarity with him.

I'd learned through my communication work that companion animals come to answer our soul's cries for help, so I knew these two dear souls had heard mine and came running. I'd never before been in such abject pain. I couldn't wait to get reacquainted with the soul in the black pup.

I didn't bother to ask about names, because I felt very deeply that the names that I'd been thinking about for months were appropriate: my two favorite places on Earth and the most healing places I'd ever experienced – Hana and Saba. Saba is a volcanic island, so I thought it apropos that the black pup be Saba. Officially, he was Simply Saba.

The yellow pup was Hana. Officially, he was Heavenly Hana. They'd come to help me heal so being named after spectacular places that emitted amazing healing energy seemed perfect. I did connect with the pups, told them what I'd like to name them, and asked if that was okay. They loved their names. I fell into a deep, contented sleep.

We were up early and on our way. I left a message for Gloria with the information I'd received. I couldn't help but think about the return of Ben/ Rainbow/Randy. Before we moved, a dog client of Bob's, who knew nothing about horses, offered to give Randy a home for life rather than put him down if we decided to euthanize him. At that point, I still had hopes that he might heal. Many people think dying is the end of being, but when you have a belief that dying is merely a change of form, it doesn't carry the same finality to it.

It was a kind offer from the client, but I told my husband no. If Randy wasn't meant to live a long, pain-free life, I knew his soul would come back to me in a new body. My belief in reincarnation was challenging for the born-again Christian, even though he'd commented on the similarities between Ben and Rainbow. I knew on some level he believed in reincarnation, whether he was willing to admit it or not.

Randy's euthanasia had been the single-most difficult thing I'd done in Carolina. It was, and still is, the event that I don't think I'll ever be able to forgive my Ex for allowing to happen. My belief that my soul creates my reality challenges me with this event to this day. Being reunited with the soul that was housed in that big, gorgeous, yet unsound equine body reassured me that Randy's euthanasia had been the right decision. I never doubted it despite the outside judgment of others. I felt vindicated.

My decision had cost me someone who I'd thought was a good friend. Her judgment of my decision taught me that she wasn't a friend, so what had I really lost? If she'd been a true friend, I shouldn't have had to justify my decision. I'm not saying she had to agree with me, simply not judge me. The return of Randy's soul was proof enough that I'd chosen wisely, which was all that mattered in the end. Yes, Archangel Michael, this does matter!

To have a soul return to share its life with you four times is extremely humbling. His return taught me even more about the purpose of Randy's short life, which made it easier to accept and allowed me to *let go* of the residual pain from Randy's death. If I hadn't made the choice to send Randy Home two years earlier, I wouldn't be looking forward to sharing, learning, and growing for the next 12 to 15 years with him as this handsome yellow fellow. *Everything happens for a reason and for our best and highest good.* Everything!

While yesterday had been a day focused in the Now and towards my life with my new family, today we had some chores that would take us back to our painful Pasts. I'd called ahead and asked the new farmhouse owner if it'd be alright to visit my folks' trees and stones. He said he and his girlfriend would be working in the house.

Our first stop was the farm, so my long awaited promise of returning the dogs to the only real home they'd known was about to be kept. As we drove in, I just cringed at more of the fencing that had fallen down. The white siding on the house I'd lived in for 23 years was green with mold. As we pulled further in my heart broke with what I saw. The shed in front of the barn, which kept untold numbers of horses protected from the inclement weather, had collapsed.

Whatever residual joy I'd been feeling from my puppy pummeling had just been converted to sorrow. I was so glad Michelle was with me. I don't think I could have borne this experience alone. My soul knew how affected I'd be and created support for me with my fellow wounded gal pal.

We drove towards my folk's house finding more fencing down, dead bushes, etc. We met with the new owners of the house. They were very pleasant and showed me through the house. I answered whatever questions I could for them and mentioned my dismay at the condition of the rest of the place. They said no one from the town was around much. I told them my plan to spread the dogs' ashes out in the big pasture.

What they asked me next almost knocked me to the ground. The owner's girlfriend asked if I wanted to take my parent's stones with me. No!!! I explained about the deed restriction, which was obviously missing from his deed. It had been a condition of the sale that the restriction would follow if they ever sold the farm.

Michelle and I headed out into the big pasture with my friends' ashes. I hoped putting their ashes in the place we'd spent so many hours playing would bring me some closure. It brought a sense of peace to my heart knowing they were *home*. As we sprinkled their ashes in the breeze, all my grief and pain erupted like a dormant volcano. My anger at the town's disrespect of the farm fueled my emotions. Michelle and I spread their ashes and cried. I cried for the life that had been stolen from me by my Ex's choice, and she for the part of her life that had been stolen by Mike's cancer.

After we finished our task, I showed Michelle a grave marker that my dad had made for our old mare, Larkswing, who died trying to foal. As I looked at the handmade marker that represented my father's love, I dropped to my knees and started uncovering it. Larkswing had died 22 years earlier and the grass had engulfed it.

I wasn't leaving this special stone to be disrespected. It was priceless to me. The madder I got the more furiously I tugged at the thick grass around the stone. My nails were filled with dirt as I clawed to loosen the earth's grip on my treasure. I sent Michelle to ask the new owner if he had a shovel. She returned with a metal bar that I used to pry the stone at the edges, which freed it.

As we drove out, I stopped the car with a gasp. I sat in horror and disbelief. My absolutely favorite tree had been cut down. I'd been so distracted by falling down fences, mold, and imploding sheds that I hadn't noticed the missing tree before – a spectacular weeping white pine that sat behind the farm sign, which had been a gift from my folks for our fifth wedding anniversary and was planted 23 years ago.

"He" was my friend and a very wise being who'd shared wondrous energy that contributed immensely to the beauty and serenity of the farm for many years. Now, he was nothing more than a stump cut off at ground level – another loss to add to my list. I couldn't wait to leave the farm before I noticed anyone else that was missing.

Our next stop was Mike's grave to see his headstone. Michelle had designed a very tasteful, simple tribute to Mike. It was a perfect spot for Mike as deer were prevalent in the woods, so he rested where he'd found great joy in life. A wonderful picture of Mike that Michelle put on the headstone made it even harder to comprehend that he was missing. He was just too young for us to be standing over his grave.

I was humbled to be sharing some time alone with Michelle at Mike's grave. I knew it was a very private place that she visited often. Our destinies had been cemented together by our traumatic losses. Who would have thought that our friendship, which grew out of my early morning visits to Perkins to escape the stress of my parents' cancers, would become so crucial for us five years later? Our synchronistic friendship had been a brilliant strategy of our souls' creations.

After a very peaceful visit to Mike's grave, I dropped Michelle off at home. I knew she was as emotionally exhausted as I was from our afternoon schedule. We'd been on a seesaw of emotions these past two days. Our afternoon embodied Gibran's words on joy and sorrow from *The Prophet*. We had just lived it – the pinnacle of happiness and joy with the puppies in Virginia, and the depths of grief and sorrow on the farm and at Mike's grave. The trick was to hang on to the joys and let go of the sorrows, which was something I'd been struggling with for the past two years, while Michelle had only just begun.

On my way to meet Master Michele, Marie, and Alice for brunch at Perkins I stopped by the farm to take pictures to document the conditions. I wanted to have proof in black and white. As I walked around the farm taking pictures, the tears started again. I felt so responsible, so guilty, for what had happened to this old friend of mine.

It had been my home for 27 years and provided us with a wonderful lifestyle and comfortable income. Its care had taken its toll on my body, but I still loved the farm and the life I'd lived there. So much of the movie of my life and so many of the important lessons I'd learned had happened on this farm. To see it now just broke my heart.

Disrespect was what I saw everywhere I looked and what I felt deep in my heart. As I cried, I apologized to my old friend. I apologized to my parents and made a commitment to secure their stones' places for the future.

The farm taught me a valuable lesson as I tried to let go of my disgust and agony over its plight. It showed me how integral my care, my energy, my respect, and my love had been in making the farm the wonderful place it'd been. The healing sense of peace that everyone felt when they came to the farm was gone, because I was gone. I'd been a huge ingredient in the energy of Fair Chance Farm, as well as the animals that lived there. Now, all of us were missing.

Trying to accept the demise of my fabulous weeping white pine, I came to realize that my friend was better off having been cut down rather than live with no one to love and care for him. My friend had emitted the energy of a wizened old man for so many years. This realization allowed me to let go of my sadness over his death.

As I drove out, I wondered if I'd ever return. Each trip back the farm looked worse and worse. This had been so painful to see and so emotionally draining that I didn't know if I could subject myself to it anymore. I'd kept my promise and brought my dear friends' ashes back where they belonged. They were home. Besides visiting my parent's stones, there really wasn't any other reason for me to return. Depending on my success or failure with the town, the stones might be among the missing the next time. Who knew?

The farm was *dead* and there wasn't a thing I could do about it. I'd done my best to ensure its continuation as a farm. My intentions had been honorable. I acknowledged my choice, accepted the farm's fate, and let go of the rest. The farm didn't hold me responsible, so I released all my guilt and headed to brunch.

Just as I drove into Perkins' parking lot, my cell phone rang. It was Sandie. Butch was beaten up again and his face was swollen. My heart, which had already taken a beating on the farm, sank even further. I listened to her description, which allowed me to make the decision I'd been struggling with for months. I hated to ask her to do such a thing, but could she take him to the vet to be put down? I'd call the vet and tell her what I needed them to do. I'd never euthanized an animal without being with him/her.

This was an excruciatingly difficult decision for me, but I didn't see any other choice. Butch's needs were my biggest consideration. After I talked with the vet's office, I communicated with Butch to tell him what was happening. He was ready. He would find Sandie.

I was teary when I walked in to Perkins. Little Michelle looked at me and asked what was wrong. When I told her what I'd just done, she couldn't believe it. When we were leaving the log house, Butchie had appeared to say good-bye. I scratched him, told him I was going away, and to behave himself. Then, I told him I was bringing back two new puppies. When I stood back up, I said to Michelle that he'd be the next one to leave me. I just *knew* it. I hadn't expected it to happen this soon, but I had expected it.

My cell rang again. Sandie had Butch and was headed to the vet's. I thanked her profusely. The tears flowed again. My soul and Butch knew I'd been through too much to withstand another euthanasia experience so soon. I hated not being with him, but it was out of my control. At least I wouldn't realize my greatest fear for Butchie, which had been coming home to find him torn to pieces by some bigger animal. He would be Home soon.

My powerful intuition, which had finally returned to me, was a gift that kept me from being totally devastated by sudden losses. I was so thankful Butch had come to say good-bye before we left. I had no idea it would be our final good-bye, but I was sure that Butchie knew.

When the doe deer crossed our path at the Peaks of Otter Lodge, bringing its message to be gentle with Self, I'd thought her message was more for Michelle, who was returning to the reality of life without her husband. Little did I know how important a reminder her message would be for me in preparation for the unexpecteds that lay ahead – the debacle on the farm and Butch's transition. Ah, the perfection of it all.

We enjoyed a great brunch, which kept me distracted from what was about to transpire in Carolina. My angels without wings were always available when I needed them most. I had to give my soul credit for some excellent creating.

At dinner with Kit and Gary, Kit informed me that Bob had stopped by their farm recently. Apparently, he was taking the latest wife's ashes to New York State. It touched me that she wanted me to know about his visit. I was grateful for her information because it shed some light on his half-day visit to

Carolina. Gary thanked me for the help with his mother. I told him she'd taught me a powerful lesson. I was the one to give thanks.

I left early for Staten Island to meet my in-laws for breakfast at the Perkins near Vince's home. My relationship with my in-laws was as valuable to me as any of my friends. They had been loving and supportive of me throughout these difficult two years. Their love never wavered and I was humbled by that.

Gloria was so excited about the puppies. Vince was thrilled too. He remarked that there was nothing like the love of a dog. He was right. It is unconditional and unwavering just like theirs had been to me. It was so good to see them both. Vince was obviously aging, but Gloria was a doting daughter. I wished I wasn't so far away, but... .

Gloria told me about her brother's visit. She hadn't told me when he'd been there, because she didn't want to add to my already overloaded stress level over Licorice's loss. I appreciated her concern for my emotions, but I was much stronger these days. Where or what he was doing really didn't matter to me unless he interfered with my life. I thought of Archangel Michael's reference question about the mountain property. "Does it really matter?"

Bob, the Ex, the *imposter*, no longer mattered, which gave me a tremendous sense of freedom. I was very proud of my accomplishment of letting go of the hold he had on my emotional well-being. I was free of him now. I couldn't wait to be free of the unrealized dream property. Its sale would bring closure to that segment of my life's movie.

After a nice long visit, I pointed the car towards Little Michelle's house. As we sat in her kitchen, I thought back to when it'd been filled with family and friends after Mike's funeral. It was heart-wrenchingly quiet now, exaggerating Mike's absence.

We had a wonderful dinner with Marie before our fantastic concert where we caught up with Pam and her friend Fran. I'd seen Linda Eder with the Boston Pops at Radio City Music Hall. She has a phenomenal voice with an incredible range – truly a gift.

Michael Feinstein, who I'd enjoyed for years, challenged me with some melancholy moments as I recalled taking my folks to see him on Broadway. My parents listened to favorite tunes from their era with teary eyes. That memory is priceless to me. I was making another precious memory with my dear friends now. It was a perfect end to my visit.

I had mixed emotions when I got ready to leave. Usually, I didn't look forward to my return to Carolina, but this time I had two new puppies to go back for. I always hated to leave my friends, which would never change. With my new perspective, or should I say reinstated opinion about life in Jersey, I wasn't convinced that I'd be moving back. Until this trip, I hadn't seen the down side of Jersey. I equated my ability to see the bad in Jersey with my own level of healing. The more I healed, the less attractive returning seemed.

Michelle and I just held on to each other with a big hug, which confirmed in the silence what a fabulous time we'd shared. Michelle thanked me for everything, but I'd received much more than I'd given.

As I left New Jersey, I thought about Licorice and Shadow and how bringing their ashes to the farm would grant me closure on our life together. It did, but I think the finality was what unleashed torrents of tears and sadness. I thought about Butch. I thought about my once beautiful Fair Chance Farm and its deplorable condition. All it needed was a *fair chance*. I thought about my once impressive weeping white pine tree. And, I worried about resolving my parent's stone situation.

My volcano of emotions that I thought I'd let go of just exploded on the way out of the state. Later, I realized the actual catalyst was the Truth in my heart that I wasn't moving back. My heart knew it as I drove towards my new family and away from my old life. I drove and cried and cried and drove. The finality of it all just crashed in on me. I was walking away from Who-I'd-Been and heading towards Who-I-Was-Becoming.

My ego was still trying to force me to feel the victim, but I wouldn't let it. Maybe I hadn't made the original decision that set the dominos in motion two years earlier, but I recognized and accepted my soul's role in its creation and that made the difference. I'd been enlightened by the introspection that my writing required. It was uncanny, but the minute I drove over the state line my tears ceased. I'd let go of a huge impediment to my future. I'd *let go* of New Jersey. Now, I'd be free to find my home.

The closer I got to my new puppies, the more my ego created anxiety about them. Two pups were a huge responsibility. Was I up to raising two puppies alone? Could I do this? As these thoughts kept running through my mind, I could feel my body tensing up, which was a physiological reaction to the negativity my ego evoked. My self-confidence was wavering slightly.

With all the work I'd done to keep my ego quiet, I was astonished at how quickly it reared its ugly head. Once I recognized what was happening, I kept my focus on those two little faces that I'd seen a week ago. I used my wonderful memories of life with Shadow and Licorice, and my horrific memory of the two days in the dead house to combat any reservations I might be having.

Of course, I could do this. Be gone, you nasty ego! It tried and failed. I hoped this would be its last attempt to gain control over my emotional well-being, but I doubted it. I'd learned the hard way about the power of the ego. It required constant surveillance. Constant!

At dinner, Kathy and I talked about Ben, Shadow, and Licorice, who she'd known back in New Jersey. I told her about the soul in each pup. I admitted my amazement years ago when I'd discovered that Shadow and Licorice had been related to Ben. She asked who Ben's sire was. She thought he was in Dini's pedigree.

I'd been wondering if there might be a chance since Kathy had lived in Jersey for most of her life, too. I just smiled at the possibility and the synchronicity of this litter's arrival in my life. All of my dearest companions related – it would be *perfection*. Can I do this? Be gone, Ego!

I didn't feel the aloneness as much in the room that night. I thought a lot about Licorice and couldn't believe he'd left only two weeks ago. It'd been a whirlwind since then, so it seemed like much longer. I thought about Butch and the orchestration of his departure. I put the past behind me and turned my focus to the next morning. Are you sure? Give it up! No turning back now. My new teachers were ready, willing, and waiting, and so was I.

Chapter 26

Sick But All Smiles

*T*he excitement of taking charge of my new family had me up early. My ego was devising fears regarding my ability to handle anymore loss in my life. "Do you really want to assume the risk of possible injuries to these pups?" I couldn't take any more loss for sure. My ego tried to fuel my self-doubt and attack my self-confidence with its preoccupation about threats to the puppies' well-being. By staying present, I silenced the negativity.

I headed towards Kathy's knowing that these two dear souls were coming to help me complete my healing process, not create a need for more. Their presence in my life was going to plug up the holes in my heart and allow me to love without condition and without fear of being hurt. The puppies would fill my life with joy and erase the pain that remained in my heart. Sorry Ego, nice try, but you lose!

As I approached Kathy's, I had to admit to some trepidation over the enormous responsibility I was about to undertake. Being *the responsible one*, I always put pressure on myself. I vowed to give these puppies the best possible lives and to keep them healthy, happy, and safe. All I needed back from them were manners and love.

Kathy had everything ready: paperwork, a blanket, familiar toys, marrow bones for the trip, and collars and leashes for them. What else but red and black! Dini's pedigree contained Ben's sire. It gave me such a sense of continuity and perfection. The five Labs that chose to be with me were all related. My heart was so full. It was as though Ben, Shadow, and Licorice were still with me. Obviously, Ben's soul was, but genetics linked Shadow and Licorice as well. It was like icing on the cake.

Every cell in my body vibrated in pure joy and happiness. I couldn't stop smiling. I marveled at how well Kathy bid them farewell. She was a unique gal, who I'd be forever grateful to for my new family. My next stop was to introduce the pups to my niece.

For the next hour and a half, I was battered with continual yelling from Hana. He wasn't crying as if he missed his mother and siblings. He was having a temper tantrum. Saba was being a perfect gentleman. I called Perkins to tell Michelle because Michael had forewarned about a screamer. I wanted to make Michelle aware of the veracity of his information. She had no trouble hearing Hana!

A few minutes before I got to Krissie's Hardees, Hana stopped. I wanted to keep going and not risk the screaming again, but Krissie was expecting me. We had a brief visit before I showed her the puppies. Hana started up as I left. Knowing I had another two-plus hours to go, I just cringed with the thought of listening to his canine expletives for the rest of the trip. About a half hour later he stopped. He must have been exhausted. I knew I was. And poor silent Saba, I wondered what he thought.

We arrived home a little worn from the two hours of constant yelling. As we got to know each other that afternoon, I realized that just two weeks earlier I'd sent dear Sweet Licorice Home. I glanced at the fireplace from time to time to where the two boxes had waited. All that was left were the David Dalton photos of them.

The house was no longer silent or calm. It had been 15 years since I'd raised pups and I hoped I was up to it. Anytime I had any question in my mind, I looked into those adorable faces, my heart melted, and I knew we'd be fine.

My schedule had the flexibility to handle the intense supervision they required. I expected, especially based on Archangel Michael's warning, to be subjected to whining the first few nights. It was typical with new pups leaving their family behind.

I put the pups together in a crate in front of the fireplace. I just felt the living room was the best place for them at this stage. It would allow some space between us at night. Space is good. As expected, the whining started up right away. This time it was a plaintive whine. I assumed it was Hana.

I quietly peered into the living room and to my surprise it was little black Saba. He sounded so pitiful, but I knew better than to rush to him. I didn't want them to learn that they could whine to get what they wanted. Luckily, he gave it up after about ten minutes. He was much less determined than Hana had been.

I let them out several times through the night, which I'd anticipated. It was no different from the early morning needs of my elderly pair. With pups, I could look forward to the age when they could last until morning. It wouldn't be that long and I was *in love*. Welcome to the first night of the rest of your life, animal lover!

All in all we were off to a good start. After a morning of puppy fun, I loaded them in the car and made a run to the food store. Hana was right back at his yelling. This time he only complained for a short time while Saba remained silent. At their young age, they were eating four times a day, which didn't allow much time in between meals for errands. Their needs preempted everything else in my life. As they aged I'd begin to assert my needs into the mix. For now, it was all about them. They were my priority.

Puppies are intense – full-out play or sound asleep. While the experts felt two puppies were only for the rare person, I wouldn't have had it any other way. I didn't consider myself rare. I considered myself twice blessed with the unconditional love of two dogs. I had an insatiable need to be loved and looked at with adoring eyes.

We had an appointment at the vet's for a simple physical. I knew they were healthy, but I wanted to create a happy visit to set the tone for future visits. Once again Hana complained as we drove off. I wondered how long he'd keep up his whining since it wasn't netting him any results.

As expected, the pups passed with flying colors. Everyone came in to see them. Already they were working their wonders on their circle of influence. They endeared themselves to everyone and everyone to them with unending liver treats. The best way into a Lab's heart is food. Hana weighed 11 pounds and Saba 15 pounds, which were the sizes of my cats.

Our next stop was the farm, so Kim could meet my new family. I'd been bringing her pictures of them for weeks. They showered Kim with their unbridled joy of meeting people. Labradors are people dogs, plain and simple. I've always found it amazing that dogs bred for hunting are so enamored with people. They seemed to love Stormy's home as much as their predecessors. They didn't know it, but this would become their second home in the mountains.

LETTING GO

They'd had a very big morning, and I didn't want to overdo it with my babies. I also had a tight feeding schedule to adhere to. My life had been dictated by the needs of the dogs and horses for most of my life, so this was nothing new for me. I was a responsible surrogate mother for the puppies. My lesson of putting Self first would have to take a back seat for a while. I knew my soul understood that.

While they slept, I talked with Travis. Apparently, the generator was functional. The company had reversed the wiring, which he hadn't noticed. I was impressed by his honesty. He was being accountable. I was so obsessed with people not being accountable that it was hard for me to be angry with someone that was.

I wondered if Travis would've been so forthcoming if I hadn't finally become accountable for my soul's creations. Would he have admitted his error if I still needed to learn the lesson of accountability and responsibility? I think not. I'm so glad I've embraced that one.

Most of my time was involved keeping an eagle eye on the pups for signs of needing to go out. I knew the usual times to be sure they were outside. Housebreaking is the biggest chore in the beginning. The intense attention is exhausting, but necessary. Accidents happen – it comes with the territory, but having hardwood floors made clean-up much easier. The pups were smart as whips, learning their names in one day. Not biased or anything, am I?

I took advantage of their naptime to call the township administrator about my folks' stone issue. His secretary would have to get back to me. I headed to the mountain to let the puppies experience another new place. They were so good there on their leashes. I didn't walk them too far due to their young age. I couldn't help but reflect on the five months Shadow, Licorice, and I had spent on the mountain. Their presence kept me from turning the gas on several times. Now, I was introducing the next generation to the mountain property.

While my old friends had left me so I might find my new life, the property still hadn't. It would serve as a great place for allowing the puppies some freedom from their leashes when it felt right. They were way too small yet. I was afraid they'd fall off the slope in their enthusiasm for following those Labrador noses everywhere. As always, I stopped on my way out to see Eunice and introduced her to the pups.

When we got home, Sandie and Margo stopped by to visit. It was Margo's birthday. We sat out on the porch watching the boys fly around in pure joy. Their *joie de vivre* was infectious. It was nice to have a couple of friends to

300

share them with. Many of my friends had been calling to check on how we were getting along. Fabulously!

The next morning I woke up feeling like I was trying to get sick. I hoped I wasn't getting Gary's illness. He'd been so sick at dinner. I really didn't have time for sick with two new puppies to chase after. I started my usual herbs to boost my immune system and stave off any illness.

We made another visit to the farm and Kim fussed over them. They adored their new Auntie. They also saw a horse for the first time up-close-and-personal. They were fearless. I was astonished by their self-confidence. It reflected what a great start Kathy had given them. They'd have to learn to respect the horses in time. For now, horses were strictly off limits.

The next morning I felt really punk, so I doubled my herbs and stayed at home on puppy patrol. When they slept I napped on the loveseat, which was very unlike me. While I didn't feel pain in my chest, I started to cough at night. Luckily, I had some cough syrup. I felt slightly better in the morning and was encouraged that my increased herbs were doing their thing.

I had to go to town because the property's ad was in the Sunday *New York Times Magazine*. After a two-year wait, I wasn't going to let any illness interfere with seeing it. I took a quick peek at the ad and closed the paper in denial and avoidance. The gorgeous view picture that the realtor had chosen didn't reproduce at all. It was a blur even for someone who knew what it should look like.

Based on my extensive experience of looking at listings, I knew the ad was a total waste. My heart sank with the realization. I'd waited so long for the property to be advertised in *The New York Times*, and it was a complete failure. I emailed the realtor, thanked her for placing the ad, and gently acknowledged my disappointment at its quality. I felt so defeated and emotionally exhausted, which, combined with my burgeoning sickness, left me without any reserve.

I woke up the next morning feeling awful. I spent the day resting whenever the puppies rested. Lying on the loveseat, grateful that they slept a lot, I acknowledged the wisdom behind the timing of Licorice's transition. While the pups had been good for their age, they were way too busy for Licorice. They were way too busy for a sick dog lover, too. I silently thanked Licorice for choosing to go when he did. I was having enough trouble caring for the puppies as sick as I was. It was another of those perfect occurrences that was revealed at the proper time.

I was having trouble sleeping due to the incessant cough. I couldn't understand why my soul created this scenario. As far as I was concerned, it sucked. In addition to my physical illness, I was emotionally sick as well. I was very blue. I felt lonely, which I found strange given the addition of the puppies to my life. My illness had progressed enough for me to know I had bronchitis. I just kept taking my herbs, drinking fluids, and resting. I had virtually no appetite, which was good since I didn't have the strength to fix anything to eat.

Being alone and sick is about as bad as it gets. When I was awake, I pondered my depression. I was so upbeat and happy when I'd returned from my spiritual adventures. Here I was with two wonderful new souls and I was depressed. What was wrong with me? I realized I was very sick, but why should I be so sick emotionally?

The constant supervision was taking its toll, along with my lack of sleep due to *the* most violent cough I'd ever experienced. I wasn't getting any better; in fact, possibly worse. I didn't have any chest pain, so I didn't feel the need to try to find a doctor. All I did was rest and observe the puppies.

Gregory called to see how I was feeling. When I explained my symptoms he brought me some catnip tea, which he'd been given for bronchitis by a naturopath. I was so grateful for his concern and friendship. It helped alleviate some of my loneliness. The catnip tea was to be brewed and then inhaled. It was a powerful bronchodilator and created a productive cough.

The next day was August 10, which was the sixth anniversary of my father's death. I'd been thinking a lot about him before Gregory arrived. I shared with Gregory that I'd lost a dozen family members, which included horses, cats, and dogs. I think Gregory was amazed at the extent of my loss.

I told Gregory about my blue mood and almost depression. He admitted to being in a funk also. We decided the planets must be in some disastrous alignment again. Just knowing that I wasn't alone in my bad mood was a help. Gregory's visit made me feel less alone, less isolated, less helpless, and more cared about.

I kept fixating on the number of losses I'd experienced since my dad had died. No wonder I was consumed with letting go. I'd been having to let go even when I didn't know I was. Later, I realized an extremely momentous thing. I'd forgotten to include someone in my list – my Ex.

To have forgotten him showed how far I'd come in my healing. Two years ago his virtual death was *the* most traumatic event in my life. Today, I'd forgotten to count him. I marveled at that and gave my Self and my soul credit for a job well done. So, I'd actually lost 13 family members in six years, which was unfathomable.

Sick But All Smiles

Michelle called to tell me her sons bought a Lab puppy. They'd been teasing her about getting one when I was up there. Now when Michelle and I spoke, we were both watching little butts going about their business. Lily was 16 days younger than my boys. Neither Michelle nor I thought she needed the added work of a puppy, but we figured the boys had gotten Lily to make Michelle smile.

Two things puppies are great at are being happy and making people smile. They are perpetual motion, unbridled joy, and exhilaration. They add to your energy rather than take away from it, which was something Michelle and I both needed.

While I struggled to get well, Mother Nature brought us some real rain, which didn't make my forays outside any easier. Hana was very good about going right out and doing what he needed to. Saba, the dog that loved leaping around in the water, didn't want to be out in the rain. The last thing I needed with my illness was to be walking around in the rain. Each time I'd have to don my rain gear and umbrella and accompany him. He'd sit by my feet under the umbrella. Of course, the trick was to outwait him. Well that's fine if your patience level is high, but mine was almost non-existent.

After having stood out in the rain for too long, I picked him up and yelled at him as I walked to the house. Instantly, I felt tremendous remorse. He looked at me with those adoring eyes questioning my outburst. I was filled with shame. There was no excuse, as far as I was concerned, for losing my temper with him. He didn't understand at such a young age. I not only felt physically awful, but I felt worse emotionally. Guilt overwhelmed me. I wouldn't accept the excuse of being terribly ill.

About an hour later, after admonishing my Self thoroughly, sweet Simply Saba came over and lay down on my foot. My tears flowed. All of my self-loathing disappeared. His lesson of forgiveness was so powerful. My heart just melted with his teaching – this tiny little creature that forgave my indiscretion so quickly. If only we people had that same degree of forgiveness, the world would be at peace.

His gesture allowed me to let go of most of my guilt and move out of the shroud of negativity that had engulfed me. The rain finally stopped, and with what little strength I had, I walked the pups around my driveways twice. They were wonderful on the leashes and had a blast sniffing everything in their path. I felt better knowing I'd allowed them an enjoyable, yet short walk.

I had to make a trip to town for more cough syrup, so I headed to the farm afterwards. I was still harboring some guilt and I felt an adventure to the farm would make up for my unconscionable outburst. Being creatures of the moment, Saba had let go of my reprimanding long before. Animals are masters of living in the Now. Saba's instant forgiveness was perfect proof.

Kim was thrilled to see the puppies. The farm owners and a couple of the boarders were chatting in front of the barn. The owners' miniature schnauzer, Sampson, was there also. The pups were really happy to meet him, but were being very pushy. I knew him very well and wasn't worried when he started a low growl. They deserved it because of their enthusiastic curiosity and lack of respect for him. What I didn't anticipate was getting two puppies in my lap as they flew into my arms for protection. I just laughed at my big brave puppies that wanted to run up to a 1000-pound horse, but this little 15-pound dog sent them flying in the opposite direction.

After I stopped laughing, I sat with the pups in my lap with their eyes on Sam. They got much less pushy and almost quiet, which allowed Sam to come closer. I just let them work it out. Eventually, the pups lost their fear of Sam and slowly approached him with respect. It was a wonderful and necessary lesson Sam taught them. I was so grateful to him.

They needed to learn to have respect for other dogs, otherwise they might get hurt. It was a perfect experience for them. The pups weren't the only ones that needed to be socialized. I'd been living the life of a hermit in my log house in the woods. I needed to become more social.

Linda called later in the afternoon and we discussed everything from the joy of the puppies to the substandard *New York Times* ad. The distance between us never seemed to alter our deep friendship. She was, and is, my soul sister. While we don't talk as often as I'd like, we know each is there for the other 24/7 and that knowledge is priceless.

My time with Linda and the people at the barn had me feeling somewhat better. I wasn't near as blue. I'd been concerned that I might have slipped back into my Tunnel, but I'd just had a little hiccup in my mood, which was perfectly acceptable. Whew!

I could hear the pups playing in the crate at night. Kathy had advised that I'd need to separate them eventually. When I put them in separate crates I expected to hear complaints even though they were right next to one another. Happily, my expectations proved to be wrong. They accepted the two crates, which made for a quiet night for us all.

My inability to do anything other than oversee the puppies kept me from dealing with the poor quality of the *Times* ad. I'd emailed my realtor and left a phone message with no response. I finally got a brief email back from her saying there had been no response so far. Her email sent my already weakened mood plummeting to the edge of the Tunnel.

Two years of work to get the ad placed and it was worthless. I tried to bolster myself with my *everything happens for a reason* belief. I told myself that it really didn't matter, because whoever was meant to buy it wasn't a reader of the *Times*. Sounds good, doesn't it?

I'd lost the first two weeks of August to my debilitating sickness. As I began to feel somewhat better, I started to focus on all the issues that needed my direction: my parents' stone issue, an additional floodlight for the dog yard, and of prime importance, the marketing of the mountain property. I'd do a few chores and then collapse on the loveseat while the pups rested.

I couldn't find little Hana in the yard, because he'd found the one place in the fencing that was suspect. Saba's eyes were on him, so I knew where he was. I rushed to him before he decided to venture elsewhere. He was worried about being outside his yard and separated from his brother. By the time I finished my repair job, I was down for the count. Hana showed me that my efforts were totally necessary since he went right to that spot again – little devil!

While I was feeling better each day, just a few errands would sap my strength. My mood was better, but not what I had expected it to be post Mt. Shasta. My most satisfying activities, riding and writing, had been put on hold. Luckily, Kim was keeping Stormy in work for me, but no one could write for me. I was trying to be smart and not over exert myself. I'd become a little more comfortable with not *doing* over the past two years. As my strength returned, I realized just how sick I'd been.

It was time for another trip to the vet. The puppies were 12 weeks old and needing more vaccinations. They had everyone smiling and laughing. The painful memories of my last two visits with Shadow and Licorice were washed into never-neverland by the puppies' unadulterated joy. They had doubled in weight since their last visit.

Sandie and I had arranged to meet for lunch after the vet. While we were eating, my cell rang. It was the long-lost township administrator, so I took the call since it had taken forever to get him to call back. We discussed the deed restriction for my parents' stones. He was trying to handle me, so I just let him think he was. I let him know in no uncertain terms how upset and angry I was at the condition of my old farm. I'd held my anger in check and hadn't alienated the person I needed to get this mess straightened out for me.

I took the puppies to the mountain property the next morning and let them off their leashes. Manned with a pocketful of treats, I walked around the roads with them. They were so fast. I remembered my walks with Shadow and Licorice with Butch and Lucky following us. It had been a little train of critters. They each had been such a large part of my life. Thank goodness for my pictures and my memories. Now, I was starting new memories with my new family. I secured the puppies in their crate and did some weed whacking. I only got a bit done around the house before I was completely drained of energy.

I went back to the mountain to finish weed whacking the next day, which would've been Shadow and Licorice's 15th birthday. It was a bittersweet day. My missing brothers had lived longer than any of my other dogs. It was hard to be unhappy about such an achievement, but I wished they were still with me. I needed the distraction of the property maintenance to prevent any sadness from creeping in. I needed the jubilance of the puppies running free on that same property to show me that life goes on.

While we were walking around, I took some pictures of the wildflowers on the property. Despite the heartache I had experienced from the unrealized dream, the mountain still contained the same beauty that had attracted me to it in the first place. All of my pain had hidden that beauty from me for so long. Once again, it was brought into my view.

On the way back to the log house some deer crossed the road in front of me. I just smiled and agreed to be gentle with myself. My messengers were always around when I need them. Whatever regrets I had over my recent losses vanished with the appearance of the deer.

I found it astounding that I still wasn't fully recovered in three weeks. I started to wonder if I might have something else going on. I'd been in touch with Gary about some issues with his dogs and he said it had taken him a month to get better.

I talked with Little Michelle while I rested. She was having a bad day. My heart just broke for what she was going through. She had her challenges trying to learn to live without her husband.

Chapter 27

Multi-Levels of Healing

I'd had lots of time to think while I was sick and started feeling guilty about not writing. It had taken me a terribly long time to get used to not working every minute of every day. It was all I'd known up until we left the farm. I'd been so uncomfortable doing nothing, or what I perceived as nothing, because it wasn't physical activity. It was *being*. I suffered through lots of guilt way back then. I was experiencing some twinges of that as I lay around trying to recover from my illness.

In actuality, I had been working the past two years when I felt I'd been doing nothing. I'd been working at the hardest job of my life while I was simply being. I'd been healing, but I was completely oblivious to what I'd been doing until I began to write. This has proven to be the most important work of my life – healing. Learning to *be* unearthed my lessons and in turn initiated my healing. What I eventually realized was the step-wise process that deep healing required. There was no quick fix. It takes honest commitment and discipline. Healing is an ongoing process and my rocky return from New Jersey taught me that much.

After a visit to the barn and another swim for the puppies, I sat at the computer to get to work on my writing. I worked for more than an hour on a couple of pages. Somehow I lost the copy. I was tired and frustrated. I didn't really understand how it vaporized, but I understood why. I was working at writing. I was writing mechanically from my mind instead of creatively from my heart. It didn't contain any emotion, insights, or meaningful words.

The Universe taught me a very powerful lesson, which only cost me an hour or so of my time. I can't force my writing. If I'm not ready to write from my heart, then don't write. I can't write from a *place* of negativity, which is where guilt resides. I can certainly write *about* negativity, just not from a place of negativity, which is a big difference. I'd been writing out of a sense of guilt.

I spent the next day on writing that didn't evaporate. My heart was fully engaged. I was back in the flow, but my strength still wasn't where it needed to be for my favorite passion of riding. With young horses, it's important to always work through any difficulties and finish on a good note. I knew I didn't have enough energy to do that. I wouldn't risk a problem with Stormy just to satisfy myself. He was too important a friend for that. I was just pleased I could focus enough to write – one step at a time.

Just before dinner, my sweet little Saba stuck his nose where it didn't belong and got stung. I knew immediately what had happened. I applied an ammonia-soaked paper towel to neutralize the venom. Saba was very unhappy with my stinky treatment. Knowing his acute sense of smell, I understood his protest.

Of course, it was past office hours at the vet's. I knew what he needed, just not how much. I called Gary, my vet angel, and got the appropriate dose of benedryl for Saba's size. I sat with him in my lap with a bag of ice on his nose and flowed healing energy into him.

Believe it or not, within an hour the swelling was lessening, and he wanted to play. Saba looked absolutely normal by morning, but I gave him one more dose of benedryl just to be safe. Saba's crisis was handled without any feelings of panic, merely sympathy for his plight.

The absence of fear allowed me to make quick, accurate judgments. I responded the way I used to respond to medical challenges. I hadn't felt this secure in a long time. While I hated for Saba to have any pain, his lesson about respecting bees provided a lesson of my own. He taught me that I'd returned to the capable woman who left her farm two years earlier.

Four and a half weeks after I'd gotten home, I was finally feeling almost normal. I felt well enough to do some animal healing work for Gary's and Little Michelle's dogs with thunder and loud noise issues. I'd felt awful about making my dearest of friends wait so long, but I've always held to my steadfast rule of not doing any healing work unless I feel 100 percent. My friends were very patient and understanding, which was more than I was with my Self. I was, and always will be, my harshest critic.

Working for another always necessitates clearing myself first. The healing I received would ensure my continued recovery. I did SRT clearings and made up vibrational remedies for any threats. Once I finished my healing work, I felt a huge weight removed from my shoulders.

The more I wrote, the more I assimilated the events since Licorice had died. My practice of staying in the present moment kept me away from the emotional reality of what I'd experienced during my Jersey trip. It wasn't until I began recounting it that I realized the multilevel nature of the emotions I was dealing with.

While I'd thought I'd let go of my pain and grief, in reality I'd only released the surface pain, which is the quickest and easiest to dismiss. As I left New Jersey, my uncontrollable tears should have alerted me to the extreme depth of my pain.

As I began to relive those events through my writing, my heart showed me the extent of the hurt I was letting go of. I understood better why I got so sick and stayed sick for so long. My health had been compromised by the release of my deep rooted grief and pain.

Initially, I'd attributed my compromised immune system to my loss of Licorice. I assumed I was simply physically sick, since I believed that I'd already let go of 95 percent of my grief and pain. I felt almost healed after my return from Sedona and Mt. Shasta and my emergence from my Cocoon and Tunnel. Based on what I was experiencing, I'd been deluding myself with my estimation of being 95 percent healed.

The severity of my illness, along with the length of time it took me to recover, was an indicator of the amount of pain and grief I'd been hiding from myself. I'd uncovered the same type of insight when I wrote about moving into the log house. I'd blamed my stomach illness back then on bad food.

Upon closer evaluation, I'd acknowledged the fact that my physical symptoms had been a direct expression of my deep-seated fear of living alone with such an uncertain future. My writing provided a clarity that was missing when I experienced each of my soul's creations.

Once it dawned on me about the true cause of my prolonged illness and my very melancholy blue mood, I began to uncover the lessons before me. I'd been hard at work for the past two years experiencing *my* creations and writing my movie. While I knew that my soul was multi-dimensional and immense beyond what I could even imagine, I *finally* comprehended the true complexity of my soul.

My repressed pain and its effects on my body and my psyche offered me a tremendous lesson about the incredible power of our emotions and the far-reaching effects of them, both positive and negative. Of course, I'd spent the past year of my honest self-analysis attempting to move out from under the constraints of my negative emotions and return to the flow of more positive emotions. While I knew I'd come a long way, I was only now recognizing the extent of work that still lay ahead for me. My *everything happens for a reason* belief was being reflected in my recent discovery.

As I struggled with the care of my new puppies, I began to comprehend the significance of my illness, the importance of the painful emotions of my visit to the farm, and the pain of the finality of returning Shadow and Licorice to their home. Although I never anticipated the intensity of what I experienced, my writing put it all in perspective for me. I had let go of an enormous amount of my grief, pain, anger, and resentment, but what was left was the deeply buried, resistant part.

The difficulty my body experienced trying to rid the discharge from my bronchial tree with the most intense deep cough I'd ever felt reflected just what my psyche was doing on an emotional level. I was trying to rid my Self of the last vestiges of my grief, anger, resentment, and pain. As my body let go, so my heart *let go*. My job would be easier now that I better understood the vast complexity of my emotions.

Almost a year after writing about what I intuited was the underlying cause of the deepest and most violent cough I'd ever had, I received confirmation in another of Michael Roads' newsletters. When Michael started his first world tour after the loss of his dear wife, Treenie, he struggled with severe respiratory symptoms. In his newsletter, he shared that a natural health therapist told him that "deep grief usually goes to the lungs."

As I read this, I felt the wonder and power of intuition and of truly having all the information we need somewhere deep within us just waiting to be called upon. My interpretation of my violent and persistent cough came from within me as I wrote. Michael's newsletter simply reinforced its veracity and fueled my self-confidence. Both of our illnesses were in perfect timing for our release of deep and powerful grief. My revelation regarding the significance of my illness hastened my recovery. I regained my strength in direct proportion to my self-realization.

Multi-Levels of Healing

I was physically strong enough to start back with Stormy. I was so fortunate that Kim was able to keep him worked for me. He felt wonderful the first time I rode him. My heart was full with gratitude for my beautiful horse, and my two new puppies. Sometimes, as I was bringing in Stormy to ride, I'd look at the gorgeous farm that surrounded me and think how truly fortunate I was despite the circumstances of the past two years.

Often I felt guilty that I wasn't working in my sense of the term, but I'd remember the pendulum concept. I'd worked so much for most of my life without being able to ride that I needed this time on the farm from Heaven to bring my pendulum back to its center point – the point of balance and harmony. I told myself that I'd earned this time and I deserved it, which was a huge step for *the responsible one.*

I gave myself credit for learning my lesson of not settling and of putting Self first. It was a lesson that had been at the root of much of the trauma in my life. I was living my lesson and reinforcing it with my time with Stormy. His wonderful willingness encouraged me that I'd let go of much of my stubborn resentment, anger, and pain. Had I not, Stormy would have reflected that to me with his behavior.

After about a week and a half on his back, I felt it was time to introduce him to some small jumps. I couldn't remember the last time I'd jumped, but he was ready. I just hoped I was too. I didn't ask him to do much. His acceptance of this step-up in his training was so encouraging.

His cooperative attitude confirmed that I'd made the right decisions for him with my method of training. Each horse is an individual, no different than we humans, so each requires specific modes of training. I'd been challenged by him last year during a time when I was fighting for my own survival. It was gratifying to know I'd made the right choices.

As I drove home after his first jumping experience, I realized it had taken eight years to achieve what I'd just experienced. I'd bred his mother, dear Squiggles, for the first time eight years ago. Through disasters with his two brothers, Dash and Randy, I'd suffered so much pain and disappointment, but eventually learned the lessons they were teaching. The fun and joy Stormy offered me after just a few jumps began to wash away the memories of the losses of his brothers. He's one of my four-legged angels, who is helping me move into the flow of positive experiences. Did I say *joy*? I did.

The healthier I got the more I began to enjoy my new puppies and learn their powerful lessons. While the chore of teaching new puppies the acceptable way to live with humans can be challenging, I needed them. From the first time I'd met them I felt the smile return not only to my face, but deep within my heart and soul.

Their presence in my life was in perfect timing to help me to let go of whatever residual negativity I was clinging to. It is impossible to be unhappy around them. They look at life from one perspective only, which is play. The simplest thing becomes a toy. Their happiness, joyful exuberance, and life-loving, blissful nature provided powerful lessons for the woman who'd misplaced those childlike traits. The obligations and responsibilities of life had buried them along with so much else.

I knew these two special souls could help me regain my happiness, my joy, and my passion for life. All of these had been missing for too long. I had three powerful four-legged allies committed to helping me find that part of myself again. I couldn't have asked for better teachers. Once again, my soul created wonderful partners in life for me just when I needed them the most.

September marked the second anniversary of my move into the log house. When I reflected back, I saw the enormous amount of change I'd gone through since then. The transition was truly stunning from the broken woman who'd made herself physically ill with her repressed fears, to the woman who'd emerged from her self-imposed Abyss, Cocoon, and Tunnel in Sedona and Mt. Shasta. The transformation into the butterfly, which occurred in Lassen Park, was gratifying and humbling.

Stormy continued to amaze me with his calm approach to something completely new for him – jumping. He taught me how I needed to approach something completely new for me. As my writing was coming to its conclusion and my healing approached completion, I anticipated starting my animal healing practice back up and from there following wherever my soul led me. I had another of those nagging intuitive notions that my devilish little soul would take me in a completely unexpected direction. I felt some trepidation towards rejoining the workforce, but Stormy was showing me how. I know you've heard this before, but I just recognized his lesson in this moment of writing.

Stormy enjoyed jumping, which was a necessary component for me. I can't enjoy something if my partner doesn't. Now, there's a lesson for the ages. So, I was thrilled that *we* were enjoying his new job. I hadn't had this much fun in ages. With all the pain and heartbreak surrounding the losses of his brothers, I looked forward to lots of joy with Stormy in order to get to that point of balance and harmony. Stormy helps me look towards my future with enthusiasm and happiness. I can never repay him for his contribution to my new outlook on life. He is such an important contributor to my happiness and healing.

As my health improved through September, the challenges presented by my very busy little pups were met with increasing patience and tolerance. Heavenly Hana was definitely the mischievous one. Simply Saba had a very calming personality. They were a perfect combination. Little Saba needed contact while Hana was content to lie apart from us, but with his eyes riveted on us. These traits reminded me of their predecessors. Shadow had been the contact fellow and Licorice more to himself. Despite their young age, they were already teaching me valuable lessons about living life to the fullest, which was something I really needed to master.

There were many times they'd do something that brought me to tears. The similarities to my missing brothers caused the release of emotions that I'd thought I'd let go of already. They helped me reach deep into my being and cleanse myself of the last of my sadness over the loss of Shadow and Licorice. They helped me rid myself of the remnants of pain over all of my 13 deep losses.

The healing they gifted me in the short time that we'd been together was truly astonishing. They looked at me with adoring eyes, which melted my wounded heart. When either of them put their head on top of my foot, I was filled with a warm, loving sensation. My self-esteem soared. My love in return was so intense that it almost hurt.

While I had occasional concerns about something bad happening to either of them, my overwhelming love washed away the fears my ego was trying to create. My mind would only contain thoughts for a long and healthy life for all of us, because we had so much to teach one another. They were teaching me that I was still worthy of being loved and that I was still capable of loving.

Loving animals had never been an issue for me. They'd never betrayed or deceived me. I'd never lost my trust in them. The amount of loss I'd experienced over the past six years had caused me to wonder if I'd feel free to give my love to the same extent as I had before, or if I would hold back to protect myself from future pain. Had I reconstructed the fortress around my heart? Would I allow my traumatic Past to influence my Future?

These two dear souls taught me straightaway that I was capable of "loving like you've never been hurt before" just like the plaque over my French door counsels. When they looked at me with their soulful loving glances, they pierced any semblance of negativity that might be trying to reconstruct itself around my heart. The love expressed in their eyes was like a powerful laser straight into my heart. They brought joy into my life.

I took pictures of them every day and sent them to everyone via the Internet. Since I didn't want to intrude on peoples' computers, I slowed down sending the pictures. Well, I got all kinds of complaints as to the missing puppy pictures. Everyone, absolutely everyone, wanted pictures. These little souls were creating a tremendous amount of joy just by *being*, which is a powerful lesson for us all. Their images brought a smile to everyone's heart.

Many of our lives are so difficult and filled with pain that we're desperate to find joy and happiness wherever they're hiding, which includes puppy pictures from the woods of North Carolina. Whether the pictures were of them sleeping on top of one another, swimming in the river, running free on the mountain property, or playing in their yard, their sense of bliss was apparent and infectious. We all want and *need* what they offer. I am blessed to have them in my life and feel obliged to share their healing gifts.

While I'm teaching them to sit, stay, down, and not pee in the house, they're teaching me profound lessons about my Self: how to trust again, how to love again without condition, how to stay in the present moment and make the most of each one, how to live in joy, how to take life less seriously, and my most challenging – how to forgive and *let go*.

Who is the more intelligent species? My soul cried out and the best teachers I could ever want came running. I've caught their infectious enthusiasm for life already. Look out Future, we're coming and coming fast – Hana, Saba, and Me!

My brother stopped by for a visit and to meet the pups after his summer fair schedule was over. I took Ejay to see Stormy and his gorgeous home and from there to Grandfather Mountain. The gal at the entrance gate mentioned the fudge sold in the little restaurant. I just chuckled to myself. Ejay had just finished his seasonal fudge business, which we'd just been discussing. The entrance gal was regaling the quality of the fudge that her best friend Anita made.

We went to the top to enjoy the views before any clouds rolled in. Our next stop was for lunch and to taste the fudge. I noticed a gal fixing a plate of samples and her name tag said Anita. I knew Little Michelle would have been shaking her head at the synchronicity of it all. I pointed her out to Ejay and we struck up a conversation about fudge. She was very helpful and open with him and he was thrilled with the information. Our way home included a stop at Kilwins for ice cream. I had to agree with the gal at the gate that the fudge from Grandfather was as good as Kilwins.

The pups were all over Ejay and I knew he was loving it. He was headed back to his home in Florida that no longer had a dog in it. Ejay, the pups, and I enjoyed his two-day visit. I hoped there would be more in our future. Once the pups were older and more trustworthy, I might even bring them to Florida to visit his home on Long Key. I knew my folks were smiling down seeing that we'd spent some time together.

Kim's grandmother was approaching her transition in Pennsylvania. Kim enlisted my aid on the farm, so she and her brother could make one last visit. I was more than happy to do anything Kim needed. She'd taken such great care of Stormy when I was sick.

One of the boarder's horses had a foot infection that required daily treatment. I fell right back into the groove. I'd treated this type of condition many times before. I felt every bit as strong and competent as I had back on my beautiful Fair Chance Farm for all those years. It was almost like déjà vu. However, I was a very different woman than I was back then. I'd grown immensely from my own personal traumas.

I'd been so uncomfortable missing my busy schedule two years earlier. Now, I was safely entrenched in the new lifestyle my soul had created for me. My days on barn patrol taught me how fortunate I was to be free from the daily grind of caring for horses. I didn't want that lifestyle any longer. I'd let go of my need to be so physically active. Good thing, since my body was deteriorating from all the heavy horse related work.

This was fascinating to me since my future work in the healing realms contained only a small physical component. My skills are mental, emotional, and spiritual elements originating from within my right brain. Ah, there is a method to the madness. My current physical life was rooted in the training of Stormy, Hana, and Saba. They offered me all the physical activity I needed, and then some.

The puppies were growing like weeds, and once I'd recovered fully, they became a delight to have. I'm not saying they weren't a challenge, but it was a challenge I embraced in pure joy and good health!

Chapter 28

The End Is Where You Start From

*U*pon returning from my spiritually transforming trip four months earlier, I believed the traumas and dramas of my life were over. Naïve, wasn't I? In reality, the only thing that had changed was my ability to respond with control rather than react from unmanageable emotions. The absence of reactive emotions allowed me to function in a much healthier way.

I accepted the lack of accountability in others, which used to infuriate me. I didn't like it, but I'd let go of my intense reaction to it. I knew the root cause for my tolerance grew from my own acceptance of my soul's creations. I didn't need the dramas of others' lack of accountability to reflect my own back to me.

My lesson had been embraced, which allowed me to let go of the need to create further frustrating experiences surrounding lack of accountability for myself. Life, post-Mt. Shasta, was still loaded with frustrations, nuisances, and annoyances, but I was better prepared to cope with them. I had all of my teachers, both seen and unseen, around me for whenever I might slip backwards towards the Tunnel, or heaven forbid, the dreaded Abyss.

My third fall in the mountains was the charm, as the saying goes. The colors of the leaves were simply breathtaking and balanced the challenges facing me from all directions. The puppies and I allowed ourselves several outings to take in Nature's splendor. During one, we went to Grandfather Mountain and took our first hike. It was a short nature trail near the lower picnic area.

The pups were inundated with smells along the trail. They were quite good despite their almost out-of-control curiosity and enthusiasm. I couldn't wait to be able to hike on longer trails free from the constraints of their leashes, which was out of the question at this stage of their young lives. Their innocence and passion for everything was so refreshing.

I wondered if I could ever recover either of those long-lost traits. I'd been experiencing a seesaw of emotions since I'd brought the puppies home. I was anxious to finish releasing the last of my remaining negativity. I realized that until I let go of the bulk of it, I'd continue to have ups and downs.

It seemed like each fall had been more attractive than the previous one. I wasn't sure how much of that was due to the shroud of negativity that had encased me up until recently. I knew it had to be a factor, but I'd also heard others marveling at the colors this season. I had to live where there were four seasons. I needed to experience the cycles of Nature, for each season held its own unique essence.

Fall colors were perhaps the most beautiful of Nature's bounty to me. The richness of the colors and my memories of their radiance helped to contrast the starkness of winter. It seemed apropos that the most colorful season be followed by the least. The starkness of winter white restored the balance.

The changing of the seasons of Nature is quite possibly the only type of change that people find acceptable and even look forward to. I find great solace in the changing seasons. They provide a sense of continuity and an assurance that life goes on. Fall gives way to winter; spring erupts and transforms into summer; summer ushers in fall and the cycle comes full circle. Balance and harmony are guaranteed by the cycles of Mother Nature.

A single woman marries; then she's divorced or widowed and becomes single once more. Not so unlike the seasons of Nature are the seasons of a Woman, especially this woman. I found encouragement for my own continuation from the changing of Nature's seasons and the changing cycles of *me*.

Winter was approaching along with its potentially harsh conditions. In the Native American tradition, winter is a time for introspection. I'd been actively focused on introspection for more than a year – my commitment to self-discovery and healing. While I'd made incredible strides releasing the destructive negativity that consumed me when my dream was annihilated by my Ex, I admitted that I wasn't completely free from its grasp.

LETTING GO

When I began writing, I had very little knowledge about the act of letting go. From the experiences of my movie, which my writing reflected back to me, I felt qualified to be *the* poster gal for letting go. I learned that releasing repressed negativity is much more complicated than I'd ever imagined. In order to release it you must first be aware of it. I'd learned how effective I was at hiding things from myself, which had seemed to be an act of self-preservation.

In Deepak Chopra's, *The Book of Secrets*, he teaches, "Sadly, most of us keep shutting out thousands of experiences that could make transformation a reality. If it weren't for the enormous effort we put into denial, repression, and doubt, each life would be a constant revelation." I had practiced each of these in my life in New Jersey. Chopra says, "Ultimately you have to believe that your life is worth investigating with total passion and commitment." I'd made that pledge when I began my writing.

The circumstances that surrounded my reading of Chopra's book are an excellent example of things being *always in perfection*. I'd lost this book somewhere in my travels. Eventually, I bought another copy and put it in my pile of books waiting to be read. I've never lost a book before. At the time, I interpreted it as a lesson in not being attached to material things.

One day as I headed to get my car serviced, I grabbed it off my pile. Within the first few pages, Chopra was espousing many of the concepts I'd recently begun to embrace. It was as though a need for reinforcement directed my hand to just the perfect book. Ya think?

I'm sharing these circumstances to show how the Web of the Universe flows through the simplest of our decisions and choices like something as simple as which book to pass the time with at the car dealer. I let my intuition guide me and I received an immediate benefit. Everything is significant and contains lessons.

Personally, I learned that I let go of unwanted negative energy in the same manner that one peels an onion. It was only when I'd eliminated the bulk of my anger, hurt, and pain that I even realized that there'd actually been layers, upon layers, upon layers of anger, hurt, and pain; layers formed over lifetimes that I'd been holding onto for eons of time.

The process was initiated by the acknowledgment of the pain I'd so effectively hidden from myself. Abject honesty was vital to allow me the awareness of what was being offered within my experiences, which were my soul's creations, i.e., the lessons being presented. There were lessons virtually everywhere. The recognition of them didn't need to be concurrent with the experience. In fact, most of them were recognized at a much later and much less emotional time.

Letting go, the current theme of my life, had been hidden from me by none other than *me*. It hadn't just begun when my Ex betrayed me, but long before with the deaths of my parents. The seeds of my trauma were sown while I was trying to live up to all the obligations on the farm.

I knew in my heart I was meant to be a spiritual healer and was destined to establish a spiritual healing practice of my own. By not letting go of some of my responsibilities on the farm and allowing my soul's purpose to flourish, I set myself up for disaster by denying my destiny. In order to force me to follow my destiny, my soul had to get creative. My inability to learn to let go in New Jersey led me to the most traumatic lesson in *letting go* that I hope I ever experience.

I disregarded the message within my heart telling me that my purpose involved the healing skills being revealed to me and chose not to make them a priority. *The responsible one* felt obligated to her previous commitments. I didn't know how to let go of any of them. Had I let go, I wouldn't have lived up to my over-zealous sense of responsibility, which I felt was an admirable trait. Since my spiritual healing skills were the last to be unveiled to me, they were last on my list of priorities. I chose not to investigate any of the infinite possibilities, which could have allowed my healing practice to move to the top of that list.

My choice ignited my soul's need to create a scenario that would eliminate the distractions from my movie and allow me to focus on my purpose. Our lives are dictated by the choices we make – our choices, no one else's. I clung to my sense of responsibility for the care of my husband, the farm, the animals, the vet office, and my dying parents, which were all noble causes indeed, but not in line with my soul's purpose.

As luck would have it, my soul is a very crafty and innovative creator. It understood the conditions that would be necessary to force me to focus on me. So, my soul created what I needed by moving me 600 miles from all my friends and obligations in Jersey, which were distracting me. Just to be sure I wouldn't fail, my soul eliminated my biggest distraction – my husband. Totally alone and isolated, what other choice did I have? Well, I had an infinite number of choices, actually.

My enormous sense of responsibility together with my tunnel vision necessitated extreme measures to move my focus from everyone else's needs to my own. Harsh and extreme were the experiences my soul created to accomplish this task. In hindsight – always 20:20 – I had to admit I had no one else to blame but myself. Of course, in the moment I felt blameless and victimized.

Once the intricacies of my soul's plan were revealed through the process of self-discovery that my writing necessitated, I accepted responsibility. The more I let go of the layers upon layers of negative emotions, the clearer I could see the true reality. As I released the mantle of gloom and doom that blanketed me, the window opened to the lessons that had been hidden by my pain, guilt, anger, rage, resentment, and ultimately, by the apparent absence of love.

As each layer peeled away, my vision became clearer and more acute. I'm not speaking about vision through my eyes, but my inner vision that functions through my heart. The return of my inner vision was proportional to the degree with which I was letting go of my veil of negativity. I saw events from a new perspective, which led to experiences with entirely new and different significances. As the lessons were exposed, my growth and eventual healing commenced.

The unveiling of the lessons hidden beneath my cloak of pain and fear were critical for my successful navigation out of the Abyss, the Tunnel, and my Cocoon. Metaphorically, my pain and fear was my Cocoon. Michael Roads, who'd lost his dear wife five months earlier, explained in his latest newsletter just what I'd been experiencing. "Our deep despairs are also our unrealized triumphs, for it is then that the fabric of our potential wings strengthens beneath the cocoon of our self-deception. From our despair, Truth emerges."

Though we lived a world apart physically, we were neighbors metaphysically. Truth is Truth, regardless. As I've stated before, everything is significant. Every experience contains lessons. It's imperative that we don't hide them from ourselves. Once I'd let go of all my destructive emotions through my journey of self-examination, my Cocoon dissolved and the chrysalis transformed into a brilliant butterfly, ready to fly into its next stage of life.

The act of writing, which allowed me an honest analysis of my movie, was the catalyst behind my healing. For me, they are a package deal. One without the other just wouldn't have accomplished my goal. Without the writing, I wouldn't have recognized my lessons as readily and quickly. Of course, these are my lessons created by my soul. I don't consider myself exceptional, so I'm sure there are components of my lessons that would form your lessons.

It's only human nature that we tend to learn much more from pain than joy; more from the hard times than the easy. When everything is flowing and we're happy, content, and satisfied, we don't search for lessons. When we lose that happiness and saturate our being with negative emotions, we stumble and become confused and disoriented. Our pain gives us reasons to seek answers.

My pain, grief, hurt, and sense of abandonment were the impetus behind my journey of self-awareness. My pain and fear and the depression they gave birth to were horrible at the time. However, they were necessary ingredients of my process of learning, growing, healing, and evolving. While the extreme negative emotions were painful and difficult to embrace, the opportunities for growth that they contained were priceless. The trick is to recognize the lessons hidden within the negativity as quickly as possible, embrace them, thank your teacher(s), and bid them farewell by *letting go.*

Without my trauma, I wouldn't have learned or grown as much as I have in the past couple of years. My pain and fear forced me to look inward and honestly take stock of my life. I owe a debt of gratitude to my negative emotions for bringing me to the Abyss. From its depths, I struggled to understand and learn, and then heal and grow.

I'm forever in debt to my anger and fear. While they were necessary components of my learning path, they don't need to be. Now that I've acknowledged their contribution, I pledge to learn in their absence. I don't need negativity to teach me any longer.

The lessons they offered I've received, allowing me to let go of the last remnants of them completely. The trick is to let go of what no longer serves you. If you're angry and you haven't figured out why, letting go is impossible. I shed my layers of negativity only after the lessons contained within those emotions were acknowledged.

What you decide to do with the teaching is crucial. Will you choose to embrace what you've been shown or choose to ignore the lesson altogether? Based on my experience, you'd better learn it or your soul will continue to create experiences to teach the lesson. For me, the drama intensified the longer the lesson stayed buried.

Once my lessons were revealed in their perfect timing, my naturally analytical mind needed to review my movie to ascertain just how long I'd been missing the teaching. Some of my lessons were familiar, while others were brand new. I'd been dancing around the familiar ones for awhile. The new ones appeared as I was learning, growing and evolving. *When the student is ready... .*

What have I unearthed from my journey of self-actualization? I've reawakened within me the Woman-That-I-Truly-Am. What have I learned that allowed this rebirth to occur?
- To love Self.
- My consciousness, my Self, my soul is immense beyond my

imagining and cannot be defined merely by the five senses.
- Everything does happen for a reason and for our highest good.
- There are no coincidences.
- Everything is always in perfection.
- There are no mistakes – only opportunities for learning.
- To follow my heart.
- To put my Self first and not settle.
- To trust and respect my Self and soul and not to ignore its/my creations.
- To be accountable for all of my thoughts, which inevitably create my reality.
- To live in the present moment because the Now is the only place that truly matters, for how we experience the present determines our future.
- To keep my ego under control.
- To live free from judgment – nothing is good, bad, right, or wrong. My experiences just are.
- To embrace negativity, learn what it teaches, and release it.
- To hold tightly to all that is positive and nurturing, especially memories.
- To *let go* of what no longer serves me.
- To love unconditionally.
- *Being* is enough.
- To trust that I am my own best authority, bar none.
- I will survive and be provided everything I need.

These are my top-20 hit tunes, so to speak. They are not the only lessons, just the most noteworthy.

One of the most significant things I've gleaned from the recent traumas I created for myself is that I can only be responsible for my actions. I don't have control over anyone else. It isn't my job to teach others to be responsible and accountable. It is their soul's job. This was one of the hardest things to acknowledge and embrace, which caused me all kinds of stress and anxiety.

While my life's been consumed with letting go, it's also been bathed in change. I've become much less rigid and more accepting of change. Change doesn't frighten me in the same way it did two years ago. When Gloria lost her job, I sent some scrumptious toffee to cheer her with the message, "Change is inevitable, but seldom fatal." I was the living proof behind my statement.

Change happens to everyone all the time. From my perspective, nothing stays the same except change.

Michael Roads' recent newsletter contained a highly meaningful quote from his book, *The Oracle*, on Change. "To resist change invokes delay; to delay change invokes reaction; to react to change invokes suffering; to suffer change invokes pain... You can change painfully, or you can embrace change and do it gracefully. However, change cannot be denied."

Well, my life of the past two-plus years was a perfect expression of Michael's teaching about change and its effects. I welcomed the change caused by my choice to move from the farm. I was terrified of the change that resulted from my husband's betrayal, which wasn't my choice. I suffered immensely until I began the layer upon layer release of fear and anger. My ability to embrace the changes before me was proportional to my ability to let go.

As my layers of stored negative emotions melted away, my fear of change and my uncertain Future diminished concurrently. Michael is accurate in saying change is undeniable. Change happens, whether wanted or not. I've experienced change both ways – painfully and gracefully. I'm choosing graceful from now on.

The five months since that fantastic day in Lassen Park have taught me some incredibly important lessons for my future. Life happens. Even though I'm a stronger and less wounded woman, the trials of my life will continue. My ability to cope with those trials will be the barometer of my healing and growth.

I've been on a roller coaster of emotions; from my elated sense of connectedness in Lassen Park to my blue moods of August and September. I've learned to accept the highs and lows as part of the process. Each time I open my refrigerator and read my magnet, "Just when the caterpillar thought the world was over, it became a butterfly," I'm reminded of the fantastic journey of transformation I've been on these past few years. Even the memories of my dark depression following the annihilation of my dream are fading. My little magnet signifies to me the difficult circumstances I survived in order to emerge as a healed woman.

The unrealized-dream property is the only facet of my Past that hasn't been resolved. While I once mourned its loss as powerfully as any of my others, I've *let go* of it. Now, it has become a hindrance, a weight upon my shoulders, a burden. The mountain hasn't changed, merely my perspective about it. It no longer serves me, so it needs to find its new caretaker. I neither want it nor need it any longer. I've learned all it had to teach me, which was considerable.

While I want to live somewhere other than this log house, I don't need to.

I look to my core beliefs to strengthen my faith that the mountain will sell at the perfect time and in my best interest. Deep in my heart, I truly believe that to be Truth. I just get a little impatient. I look forward to the days after closing when I can marvel at the perfect orchestration of the sale of the mountain. For now, I keep sending out positive thoughts. Since I embrace the belief that *everything happens for a reason*, there must be a reason it hasn't moved on yet. I hope I discover it soon, allowing its sale to bring closure to the most traumatic, yet enlightening, time of my life.

My conflicting emotions of the past few months left me confused and in need of a session with Gregory. I felt like I'd lost all the momentum I'd garnered in May. I was so pleased when I heard the soft voice and felt the gentle energy of Quan Yin. The wisdom she imparted to me was crucial to my progress at this specific moment in time.

We started with my new puppies. She wanted to know what they'd taught me so far. After enumerating all of their lessons, she told me their purpose had been to allow me to be able to love again. Mission accomplished. She praised me for the remarkable amount of healing I'd achieved and instructed me to appreciate my growth. She helped me understand about my recent state of confusion and lack of inspiration. The specifics are personal.

She discussed what my life would've been if my dream had been realized. From her perspective, it would have become a nightmare based in my ever-expanding spirituality and Bob's penchant for religious doctrine and dogma – again, neither right nor wrong, merely fact. I continued to be amazed at the power of a change in perspective. Maybe I was better off.

Quan Yin helped me to appreciate a broader concept of dreams. Her insights involving dreams are universal, so I'll share her wisdom for those of you who've had dreams shattered. She counseled me that a dream is merely an expectation. It's not reality. She called it a fabrication.

My fabrication, my expectation, my dream imploded with my Ex's admission that it wasn't his dream or expectation. As soon as he uttered his words, the reality of the gorgeous mountain house and property was doomed. It was never to be.

She encouraged me to begin to create a new fabrication. She even offered some possibilities that were totally foreign to me. I realized that I'd fixated on one, and only one, possibility for how my future might unfold. I didn't allow my vision to include more creative ways to fabricate my future. All that I envisioned was a future based on experiences from my Past. I gave no thought or energy to any other scenario. I was locked into one expectation. Since my thoughts create my reality, this left me with a *very* limited future.

Quan Yin pierced that illusion with one interpretation of a possible future for me, which opened my eyes to the infinite choices I truly had. Her view was quite stunning and one that I would've never considered. It was outside my realm of possibilities.

In *The Book of Secrets*, while discussing the power of creation, Chopra teaches that the same power is available to all. It is one power. The difference in its effectiveness is that those who are aware "believe in limitations that are self-imposed... You acquire full power only by realizing that you have been using that power all along to thwart yourself. You are potentially the prisoner, the jailer, and the hero who opens the prison, all rolled into one."

Once Quan Yin shed light on my limited view and my constrained use of the power to create, I transformed into the heroine who opened my prison of limitations. I chose to believe in the infinite possibilities that were available to me.

The timing of reading Chopra's book was in perfection. His insights reinforced the teachings I was receiving from the unseen realms. To me, there was no better proof of the connectedness that we all share, or what I like to call the Web of the Universe – similar to the World Wide Web of our computers, but infinite and powerful. Just like the Internet, it's available to everyone. The service provider is your *belief*. So, as the saying goes – the sky's the limit.

The only limiting factor was my own lack of vision, which Quan Yin eradicated with the verbal scene she painted for me. My future was in my hands and only my hands. My thoughts would manifest my new dream. While my trampled dream of the mountain property left me paranoid about having expectations, I'd learned through my suffering that an essential ingredient of expectation is flexibility.

Quan Yin's peek into a different view of my future threw open the door of infinite possibilities for me. I felt back on track with an unlimited potential for my future. Quan Yin handed me the key to my prison door, but I made the choice to unlock it.

While I've shied away from sharing specifics from my sessions, this particular session contained quite possibly *the* most significant lesson for me. It provided the missing piece to the puzzle and answered why the mountain still hadn't sold. It was complex, yet simple, but ever so hard to grasp. It centered on the theory of living in the Now, which I thought I'd gotten quite good at.

LETTING GO

As Quan Yin spoke, I realized that my focus had switched to my Future after Lassen Park, which caused my focus on the present moment to dissipate. I was scattered between the Now and what the future for the newly healed me might hold. It was a future I looked forward to rather than feared. But, it was the future nonetheless and not the best thing to be focused on, as Quan Yin pointed out so eloquently.

Quan Yin's wisdom really brought the teaching of Eckhart Tolle home. It was like a graduate course in *The Power of Now*. While I'd thought I had embraced Tolle's teaching, I'd only done so partially. This session was essential to my process, my education, my growth, and my healing. Quan Yin categorized this as one of my primary lessons.

Knowing that forgiveness is a key element in healing, I admitted to Quan Yin that I wasn't quite ready to forgive my Ex yet. I understood his part in my movie, but until I knew how my Future played out I wouldn't be able to fully let go of my resentment towards him. I confessed, "If I only knew my Future, then I could ascertain if all these challenges and difficulties were worthwhile. Once the mountain is sold and I'm able to find my new home, I'll be better able to know if it's all been worth it. Once I know that I'm happy in my Future, then I'll be able to forgive my Ex for his betrayal."

Well, this was just what she'd been waiting to hear. She challenged me to change my view, my perspective. "Perhaps, see it as in your best interest, as worthwhile Now, and then the future would be clear." Perhaps... I just love the way the wisdom comes – always as a gentle suggestion, never rigid dogma or doctrine. The Truth she shared was that only this moment, the here and now, is critical. "If you appreciate the here and now, the future doesn't matter." I'd heard that before from Archangel Michael with his "does it matter" question.

Quan Yin expanded Michael's earlier teaching. Speaking for me, she said, "In this process, I decide (choose) to be happy, to enjoy relationships I have Now, to enjoy them with great love, peace, and happiness. In doing so, I allow myself to create space for a future that's filled with happiness. I deserve happiness Now – not predicated on, dependent upon, or determined by my Future (i.e. sale of the property), but rather it is here *Now*." She taught that if my present moment happiness was tied to some future circumstance, my present moment happiness was impossible.

I emerged from my confusion with a clear picture of what she was teaching. It seemed so simple, yet it had eluded me for so long. "Happiness is here already. It is a state of mind." Quan Yin confided to me that as soon as I

326

fully embraced this lesson, the mountain property would leave. Once I learned this lesson, I no longer needed the mountain to teach me. Okay, embracing, embracing, embracing... .

So, there was something I hadn't received from the mountain yet. Without the help of my unseen friends, I might never have understood the lesson thoroughly enough to embrace it. How can something so simple be so hard to comprehend? It's my hope that the little light bulb in your head might shine some illumination on a similar experience you've been struggling with. Oh, so simple.

The more I pondered this powerful tweak of my understanding of the concept of living in the here and now, I couldn't help but recognize another thing that I'd completely missed before. My new perspective gave me new eyes to see with. With my new eyes, I saw the roles of two very significant players in the past two and a half years – my Ex and my beloved mountain property.

I was startled with the similarities that my altered perception revealed. Although the time spent with each was radically different, the parts they played were so alike. Each one started out as very positive influences in my life. Events changed each into very negative influences in my life. While the hurt my Ex caused was more traumatic, the inability to sell the mountain created its own type of pain and anxiety.

Out of the trauma of my husband's betrayal and the drama of the failed marketing of my unrealized dream, the most profound learning and spiritual growth was born. My husband played the role of the initiator – the catalyst of my healing – while my spectacular mountain accompanied me through my healing. Both were major contributors to my accelerated growth.

Once I've let go of the last of my anger and resentment towards my Ex, I'll be able to appreciate the gift he gave me with his choice to live a different dream. I thank the mountain wholeheartedly and release it to its next student. My Ex will have to wait a little while longer.

Quan Yin described my spiritual growth as remarkable. I liken myself to the mythical Phoenix who rises from the ashes of its death to be reborn. The legend teaches that the Phoenix sets itself ablaze in order to shed the old Self that it no longer needs. It arises embracing the new stronger Self. My acceptance of my soul's creation of my traumas meant that I'd metaphorically set myself ablaze, just like the Phoenix.

Through Quan Yin's generous teaching, I received the sense of renewal of Self espoused by the legend of the Phoenix. I've been reborn with a new perspective, an infinite number of choices for my future, and renewed enthusiasm to begin my newest fabrication.

Quan Yin opened my eyes to such a fresh way to perceive my Past, my Present, and my Future. My consciousness was reeling with the enormous number of possibilities before me. I had a myriad of choices I could make. Taking her advice, I began by appreciating my present moment – my life as it is, not as it was, or might be. In all honesty, I was happy and I had so much to be thankful for:

- A soul that didn't give up on a stubborn student.
- Tremendously supportive family and friends.
- My two newest family members, Hana and Saba, who'd already shown me that I could love again and that I was worthy of being loved.
- My beautiful horse, Stormy (Follow Your Heart), who was my salvation in the darkest period of my life.
- The spectacular farm Stormy lived on and the joy it gifted me.
- My two remaining barn cats, Bandit Hope and Crystal, who'd chosen to stay a while longer in spite of the high-energy canines that had joined our family.
- A very nice house.
- A reliable car.
- Family money, which allowed me the time to focus on my project of healing the wounded healer.
- Last, but most important, my good health.

I was, and am, blessed. Quan Yin's insights allowed me to let go of my dependence on future events to determine my happiness today. Her evaluation of my accelerated spiritual growth reminded me of the enormous changes that had come from the trauma I'd suffered. Without all the pain, sadness, anger, resentment, and on and on, my growth would have been negligible.

Reflecting on my achievement of clearing a superhuman amount of negativity from my Self and my soul, the question of being worthwhile was answered. Regardless of anything else that occurs, I decided that all the challenges and difficulties I encountered were most assuredly worthwhile and of great value to me.

As I embraced the worthiness of my trauma, I felt a massive release, a freeing, a letting go at a very deep core level. My session with Quan Yin was just the impetus I needed to help me find my direction and focus. *Always in perfection... .*

"Sometimes on the way to a dream, you get lost, and find a better one." I'd been reading this ever since the little plate had come to me almost two years ago. After the guidance Quan Yin gave me, I finally felt like it was time to begin my new fabrication. Until now, I'd steered away from any thoughts about my better dream, always blaming the mountain property. Quan Yin had shown me my mistake, i.e. opportunity for learning.

If my thoughts truly create my reality as I believe, I need to become co-creator of my movie again. The huge, lovely but unfinished house sitting on the shoulder of my spectacular mountain property was all the proof I needed of my ability to manifest.

My mission, should I choose to accept it, is to send out intentions concerning my future desires. I'd learned the hard way not to have any expectations. I learned the hard way to let go of the details of how my fabrication would manifest itself. With my renewed sense of Self and core beliefs, I handed over the how of its manifestation to universal orchestration. My co-creator possessed the capacity to send all that I needed to me.

What I needed to do was define my wants, needs, desires, and intentions with my thoughts. I was reminded of Archangel Michael's teaching, "You may not get what you want, but you *always* get what you need. Once you get what you need, then you get what you want." I was hoping that I'd gotten all that I'd needed and I was now aligned with getting my wants. Time would tell as my fabrication became reality. For now, I needed to formulate my intention and initiate the creative process.

My better dream consists of a house that feels like home sitting on land that I'm connected to. It doesn't need to be a large amount of land, but enough to give me privacy. It must have good winter access and be safe for my animal family. It will fill me with feelings of peace, harmony, and belonging.

It'll be conducive to an animal healing practice, allowing people and their animal families to feel safe to express themselves freely in order to better understand their roles in each others lives. It will be the perfect setting for me to again be a spiritual liaison for animals and their people.

The section of the house devoted to my healing work will be functional while incorporating the essence of Nature. My spectacular Atlantean quartz healing crystals will generate a sense of calm and serenity while enhancing the healing potential of the space. The sound of falling water from a rock garden fountain will put everyone at ease. There will be members of the Plant Nation present for the same warmth they brought into the log house.

Mother Nature's gifts – my stones and feathers – will contribute to the healing energy of the space. Their presence will align their gifts and my memories of each acquisition, thereby enhancing my connection, since we are all related. Within this protected and soothing environment, all will feel free to communicate honestly and engage in all levels of healing.

My arrival in the Blue Ridge Mountains was no coincidence, since we know there are none. What attracted me originally, the beauty and powerful healing energy of these mountains, remains. It was hidden beneath my cocoon of pain, but has begun to reveal itself again. The water, the air, and the mountains contain very high vibrational energy, which elicits the power to heal.

There is no place better than here to reestablish my healing practice and develop additional hidden talents. My own ability to heal is proof enough of the potential that resides here. Ironically, I became my own first patient. I'm anxious to tap into the phenomenal healing gifts of this area and allow them to enhance my own innate abilities. It's a match made in Heaven – no pun intended. Quan Yin's vision has broadened my awareness to the extent that I recognize that anything is possible. The more attention I focus on my *better dream* the stronger my intent is. The stronger my intent, the quicker things will manifest.

The fact that I'm writing this final portion of my healing saga as the leaves fall from the trees, restoring my ability to see far into the distance, I find synchronistic. With the completion of my journey from the Abyss through the Tunnel and from the Cocoon to the *butterfly*, I've arrived at a place where I can see farther than I ever have before. The *leaves* that obscured my view of Who-I-Truly-Am have fallen and blown away.

I can see lights in neighboring houses at night, which help me feel less alone, less isolated, and more a part of humanity. I'm able to see the full moon, which fills me with such a sense of power, awe, and belonging each time it comes to call. I can see the stars, which call to a place deep inside my soul to come Home, but I ignore their call because of the need I feel within my heart to stay and help others heal their wounds. My heart tells me to stay to help bridge the rift that has developed between people and animals.

My life has been, and always will be, integrated with Nature. My desire to devote my life to better understanding and communication between animals and people dictates an intimate role within Nature. It's no surprise that I *see* and *feel* more than most in the Web of Nature. I'm not better than anyone else. I'm not rare, but I am unique. Each of us is unique and perfect with our own lessons to learn, challenges to manage, tunnels to navigate. It's been my experience that when you're focused on your purpose in this life, things are facilitated.

I began this writing 14 months ago with the sole purpose of trying to understand how I got to the place I found myself in – abandoned on the side of a mountain 600 miles from everyone I knew, totally alone. That was my physical reality. What I was totally unaware of was the utter complexity of the mental, emotional, and spiritual components of my life that had brought me to that moment in time.

Mind, body, and soul make up our Beingness and all must be addressed or healing cannot occur. My honest self-examination revealed facets of myself that I never knew existed. What I've experienced has been both frightening and freeing. The Universal Truths that shaped my experiences are the same Truths that shape all experiences, including yours.

I've taken back my power as co-creator of my movie. I no longer feel the powerlessness that I felt in the camper with only my support staff of dearest Shadow and Licorice by my side. I look forward to what lies ahead with curiosity laced with trepidation. Have I embraced my lessons completely, so I won't have to learn in pain anymore? I believe so.

The ending of my life as I knew it has transformed itself into the beginning of the rest of my life and one that I look forward to rather than fear. When this first happened, I used to walk around the mountain saying, "Today is the first day of the rest of my life," hoping to convince myself of it. I no longer need to convince myself. It is *my* Truth.

My wonderful new puppies and teachers, Hana and Saba, will keep me focused in the Now, filled with happiness and joy, and in touch with that essence of the child that was buried for too long. Stormy will continue to reflect lessons I need to embrace. Bandit and Crystal will continue to teach that simply *being* is enough.

Centered in joy and happiness, I am ready for whatever my soul has in store. Years ago someone sent me a quote that I felt was worth saving for some reason. It's become profound and prophetic for me. Never forget, everything is significant.

When we come to the edge of the light we know,
And are about to step off into the darkness of the unknown,
Of this we can be sure,
Either God will provide something solid to stand on,
Or we will be taught to fly!
–unknown author

LETTING GO

With the help of many, I have truly been taught to fly as Stephen Schwartz's lyrics suggest in *Wicked* –

Something has changed within me
Something is not the same
I'm through with playing by
The rules of someone else's game
Too late for second-guessing
Too late to go back to sleep
It's time to trust my instincts
Close my eyes
And leap...
I'm through accepting limits
'Cuz someone says they're so
Some things I cannot change
But till I try, I'll never know!

Never forget:
You are never alone!
You are truly loved!
You are unlimited and designed to fly!
Search out your lessons, embrace them, then *let go* and get ready to *soar*!

THE END
(is where you start from...)

Epilogue

Epilogue

I'm writing this mesmerized by the magnificent water outside my perfect timeshare unit on Maui. It is a little over three years since my last visit, which was my first as a divorcée. Three years of immense change and growth are evidenced by the experiences that I've created this time on Maui.

This morning I awoke to the soothing sounds of the sea with a whale or two visible from the lanai. I hadn't expected any whales to be here, but I guess they felt I needed the thrill that comes from seeing their "blow!"

The "clouds" of my unhappiness are gone. The spectacular beauty of Nature has been available to me and my three forever friends who have joined me on this adventure.

Little Michelle is with me for the entire time. Marie joined us for the first half of the trip and my dear friend Alice met us here a few days before Marie headed off to Kauai.

I haven't been challenged by any troubling thoughts from the Past. I've been fully present in the Now reveling in the gift of friendship and the gorgeous offerings from Mother Nature. Everything has been accessible to see and experience, which is a stark contrast from my previous visit.

My beloved Hana blessed Michelle and me with a spiritual hike through giant bamboo forests to the majestic 400-foot high Waimoku Falls. I know Hana's healing energy will help continue to cleanse Michelle of the grief over her husband's passing two years ago.

Early the morning after our hike, while strolling along Hana Bay, we were treated to two double rainbows while we became one with the water once more. To be able to share this special spot with someone who has been so instrumental to my own recovery was truly rewarding.

I was thrilled to share the one-of-a-kind beauty of Haleakala Crater with Alice and Michelle. Their amazement at its stunning colors and landscape filled me with feelings of joy. Haleakala's clouds were thin and wispy and allowed us a wonderful view. I shared my two adventures riding across it with Bob with no negativity attached. My memories are no longer tainted!

My previously ill-fated circumnavigation snorkel adventure around Lanai was experienced in the perfect moment proving, once again, that everything does happen for a reason. Michelle, Alice and I were blessed with glorious weather, a fabulous boat company, spectacular snorkel spots and stunning up-close-and-personal views of the rugged Lanai coastline all the way around. To end the perfect day, a small pod of bottlenose dolphins graced our path as we headed back to Maui.

The pesky Iao Valley of 2005 was cloudless and brilliant for Alice, Michelle and me yesterday. It rewarded us with a spectacular short hike to view the multitude of small waterfalls, and the showpiece of the park, the Iao Needle. We learned that *Iao* means "cloud supreme." Iao was even clearer than Haleakala further reinforcing the knowledge that my unhappiness is completely gone.

I felt compelled to share the differences between by two trips three years apart. The pendulum has definitely swung towards the positive for me. The butterfly is free to create unencumbered by the pain of her past.

I only wish I could include a color photo of the sea that I sit looking at to prove to everyone that there is a wonderful future lying buried beneath the pain of whatever trauma challenges you. The key is to confront your demons, ask what your painful creations have come to teach, learn and embrace their lessons, and then *let go... .*

Feel free to ask questions, offer comments, and/or share stories concerning *Letting Go*. Nancy can be contacted at nancy@nancykaiser.com.

To find out more about Nancy and her services, please visit www.nancykaiseranimalcommunicator.com.

Learn how Nancy moves forward with her life and work in her second book *Tales of an Animal Communicator ~ Master Teachers*. Personalized, autographed copies are available on her website.

LETTING GO
An Ordinary Woman's Extraordinary Journey of
Healing and Transformation

ORDER FORM

Phone Orders: (828) 265-4220 Have your credit card information ready.

Web Orders: www.nancykaiseranimalcommunicator.com

Postal Orders: Nancy A. Kaiser, P.O. Box 51, Todd, NC 28684

No. of Copies _____

Payment options:

_____Money Order _____MC or VISA _____Paypal

Name on Card: _____

Billing Address: _____

Email: _____ Phone: _____

Account Number: _____ Exp. _____

Security Code _____

Signature: _____

*Shipping & Handling $5.95   Priority Mail with Delivery confirmation
(add $2 for each additional book)
*subject to postal rate changes

Name: _____

Mailing Address: _____

_____

Thank you for your order!

www.ingramcontent.com/pod-product-compliance
Lightning Source LLC
Chambersburg PA
CBHW022004080426
42733CB00007B/464